The Play Called Corpus Christi

In this critical study of the Corpus Christi drama, the chief interest is in genre, form, and meaning, in what can be discovered about the artistic intention and achievement of these enormously ambitious plays. Though some fifteen hours were required to play out a common story dealing with the whole of human history, from Creation through Doomsday, the audiences of these plays came to watch them again and again. The Corpus Christi drama held the stage for more than two hundred years, testifying to a remarkable vitality in the form and its detail. This book seeks to make that vitality understandable.

It investigates the medieval idea of theater as *play* and *game*, and examines anew the relationship between the establishment of Corpus Christi feast and the growth of drama cycles, suggesting connections more intimate and important than have been noted before. The essential structure of the Corpus Christi play is isolated, and principles-of-selection are deduced which can account for the shape the cycles took and which explain their formal meaning. An analysis of the place of laughter within medieval religious contexts serves as background to a close critical reading of the plays of Noah's Flood and the Shepherds' Adoration. The form of the Passion-Resurrection sequence is described in new and suggestive ways, and attention is paid to the drama's modes of characterizing fallen man.

Each of the four extant Corpus Christi plays—the York, Chester, Towneley, and *Ludus Coventriae* cycles—has its own life and character, and a study of their common features necessarily involves some consideration of their differences. But the focus of this book is on the Corpus Christi drama as a whole, on the elements essential to the tradition.

contemporary with the Corpus Christi drama and concerned with the same central Christian story. The quotations from these sources on their own furnish an anthology of interpretive comment, richer than any currently available, that can serve as an introduction to a fuller, more sophisticated reading or staging of these plays.

V. A. Kolve

The Play Called Corpus Christi

1966
Stanford University Press
Stanford, California

For My Mother and Father

Acknowledgments

I have incurred many debts in the preparation of this book and it is a pleasure to acknowledge them here. Miss K. M. Lea supervised its research and writing in an earlier form, and her warm support made those early years of my study very happy ones. My former tutor, Mr. R. E. Alton, taught me much of what I know about reading literature, and to him and his wife, Janine, I am indebted not only for a close and critical discussion of many of these ideas when they were first taking shape, but for valued friendship over many years. Professors Glynne Wickham, Nevill Coghill, Robert Ackerman, and Eleanor Prosser, along with Mr. Peter Bailey, the Reverend Graham Midgley, Mr. Jesse Allen, and Mr. Robert Cornfield, have all read this manuscript (or parts of it) at some stage in its writing and made it the better for their help. Miss Beryl Smalley, Mrs. Prue Fuller, Canon J. N. D. Kelly, and Professors Herbert Meritt, Martin Evans, Peter Hughes, Thomas Cole, and Ronald Rebholz have all given help or advice on specific matters. I am grateful to Mrs. Shirley Taylor for editing the manuscript, and to Miss Helen Jaskoski for making the Index. Much of the research for this book was carried on during my tenure as Research Fellow of St. Edmund Hall, Oxford; to the Principal and Fellows of the Hall I owe much gratitude, for their generous support and for the pleasure of their company over a period of four years. The first year of my research was supported by the Rhodes Trustees, and to them also I owe thanks. My last-named debt is really my first, to my good friends, Major Peter and Hilary Bell, of Thirsk, Yorkshire, who long ago took me to see the York plays. None of us knew then what that would lead to.

I am grateful to the Early English Text Society for permission to quote extensively from its publications, and to the Huntington Library for permission to reproduce some lines from the Towneley manuscript as part of the jacket design of this book.

V. A. K.

Stanford University
December 1965

Contents

A Note on Medieval Orthography

Two letters now obsolete occur with some frequency in these medieval texts; they are simple to learn, and since this book addresses itself to students of the drama as well as to students of medieval literature, some brief information concerning them may be useful.

þ: called "thorn." A runic letter that stands for the voiced and voiceless sounds now represented by *th* in *this* or *thin*. Examples (and their modern equivalents): þe, *the*; þan, *than*; þridde, *third*; wheþer, *whether*; þynkeþ, *thinketh*.

ʒ: called "yogh." This derives from the Old English script form of the letter *g* and represents a group of spirant sounds:

  1. In initial position, it is sounded like our *y* in *yoke* or *year*, even where that sound has changed to *g* in modern English. Examples: ʒow, *you*; ʒelde, *yield*; ʒeue, *give*; ʒonge, *young*; ʒate, *gate*; forʒetful, *forgetful*.

  2. In medial or final position, it represents the guttural or palatal spirant, lost in modern English pronunciation but still spelled in words like *night, high, through*. The modern silent *gh* in such words was written ʒ and pronounced like the German *ch* in *ich* or *ach*. Examples: myʒt, *might*; bouʒte, *bought*; tauʒte, *taught*; ryʒt, *right*.

  Sometimes in medial position but chiefly at the end of words, and distinct from the above in origin and sound although identical in script form, ʒ can be equivalent to modern *z* or *s*. Examples: clyffeʒ, *cliffs*; Goddeʒ, *God's*; spekeʒ, *speaks*; ʒateʒ, *gates*; profeʒies, *prophecies*.

The Play Called Corpus Christi

Chapter One

Introduction: The Medieval Dramatic Image and Its Audience

The Corpus Christi drama is remarkable in many ways—in size, comprehensiveness, tone, and popularity. It was "homemade"—largely written by local clergy, supported by local guilds, and acted mostly by townspeople—yet it was rich and elaborate to a degree we would associate only with professional theater. It staged the largest action ever attempted by any drama in the West, an action that included the comic and the pathetic, the grotesque and the transcendental, all in one complex dramatic design; and though some fifteen hours were required to play the story out, its audiences came to watch it again and again. It held the stage for more than two hundred years, the most truly popular drama England has ever known.

These are all, in the history of theater, remarkable facts, and they will have due attention paid them in the chapters that follow. Many of the questions I raise are here being considered for the first time. Others are not new, but the customary answers have seemed to me unsatisfactory. My interest has been in genre, form, and meaning—in what can be discovered about the artistic intention and achievement of these great cycles that begin with the Creation of the World and stage its history through Doomsday.[1]

There are extant four Corpus Christi plays, known as the York, Chester, Towneley, and *Ludus Coventriae* cycles.[2] Each of them, of course, has a life and character of its own, and to study their common features we shall have to take frequent note of their differences. But the focus of this book is on the Corpus Christi *kind,* on the elements essential to the tradition.

My goal has been to understand the plays in their own time, to find from corroborating sources what a medieval dramatist might have put into his text, and what a medieval audience might have understood in seeing it staged. I hope at best to be working with a dramatist's meaning, with what he specifically meant us to understand; at the very least I hope always to be discussing ways in which a member of the medieval audience might legitimately have understood the play before him. Because a lowest-common-denominator approach to the medieval audience has characterized too much of the scholarly attention this drama has received, I have taken great care not to underestimate the scope of the dramatist's address, the size and comprehensiveness of the audience he wanted to reach. I have sought to join that section of the medieval audience equipped to respond to the plays most fully—intelligent and attentive laymen, whether lettered or not, as well as priests and clerks—by reading extensively in those works of religious meditation and instruction that they and the dramatists might have known, or whose traditional materials would have been in some form familiar to them. I have concentrated on works in the vernacular because they are most closely related to the actual dramatic texts, because they were available to those who knew little or no Latin, and because such a choice could impose some reasonable limit to my study. Such material, better than any other, can bring to modern readers of these texts some of the ideas and attitudes held by their original audiences.[3] It can illustrate the range of choices open to the dramatists in dealing with their central story and can allow us to consider the effect upon expressive meaning of the choices made. Not least, it can furnish an anthology of relevant commentary contemporary with the plays, more rich and comprehensive than any presently available.

The relationship I postulate between the drama and these vernacular religious works is one not of parentage but of cousinship: I draw no conclusions regarding the influence of specific works on specific drama texts. One of the distinguishing marks of a source is its similarity to a later text, but in traditional religious material—the common inheritance of a whole civilization—similarity does not necessarily involve an immediate source relationship: only documentary evidence can actually establish that, and there is little such evidence available.[4] Instead of comparing two or three works to suggest possible textual relationships, I use well over a hundred volumes of popular religious literature contemporary with the drama as a *general* source, as members of the same family. About this background material I make only two assumptions: that it represents ways in which the events staged by the drama were commonly told, visualized, or explained, and that this material (or material like it) would have been familiar to clergy and/or laymen in England during the fourteenth and fifteenth centuries. To enter into the habits of thought and feeling of another age, we must use whatever evidence has survived as fully as possible. A disciplined reading of the analogues and sources is our only substitute for the direct interrogation and experience denied us by the intervening centuries. Such study can reveal things about meaning and method that are perhaps of greater interest and importance than the narrow hunt for verbal parallels.

A more generous conception of the medieval audience, its needs, capacities, and heterogeneity, is crucial, and as a prolegomena to all that follows, I wish briefly to defend it here. To do so, I must make some general statement as well concerning the medieval dramatic image and its uses.

In the Middle Ages, sacraments existed which could bring man to heaven—that was confidently believed—but their efficacy for any man depended in part upon his understanding something of their meaning, which is to say, their authorization by Christ, their necessity, and their future consequence. God had made man a rational creature that he might "know" Him and share in that way the bliss of heaven. Before the Fall, such knowing had been immediate and without obstruction; with the Fall, that perfection of knowledge, that intimacy and likeness, was lost.[5] Instruction became necessary, and in this enterprise the medieval Church relied on confessional teaching, sermons, wall paintings, stained glass, and, in certain parts of England, a drama that showed the history of the world. The vastness of that subject should not surprise us. Christianity as a religious system has traditionally made its ultimate claims not in terms of philosophical truth but in terms of history: its authentication resides in what has happened or will happen. At its center is a story superior to all the theological refinements erected upon it in its power to save men's souls. Unlike the morality plays, which chiefly focus on human ethical choices, the Corpus Christi drama was most significantly concerned with the ways God has allowed Himself to be known *in time*. And it is clear, as a means of rehearsing this essential story, that the cycles addressed themselves above all to the unlettered and the un-Latined.

But medieval dramatists (like the preachers and the writers of religious poems) were not content to address a simple audience merely. Expositions of theological subtlety are included within the very action of the play: characters with names like *Expositor, Poeta, Profeta, Prologue,* and *Doctor* exist chiefly to facilitate a more advanced understanding, and what is more, they work at several levels, speaking to a heterogeneous assembly. Occasionally the attention of the learned is directed toward something included especially for them. In the Chester *Last Judgment,* when the demons fear that Christ's mercy may empty hell, one of them quotes *in Latin* the biblical text that says the saved will be separated from the damned, and prefaces it thus:

> which wordes to Clarks here present
> I will rehearce, by the roode![6]

On a larger scale, we might look at the way a *doctor* in the *Ludus Coventriae* defines his function:

> To þe pepyl not lernyd · I stonde as A techer
> Of þis processyon · to ʒeve informacion
> And to them þat be lernyd · As A gostly precher
> that in my rehersayl · they may haue delectacion.[7]

Even in intellectual terms these plays addressed their total audience, and their near-monopoly as theater greatly increased the effectiveness of their voice. The Corpus Christi cycle was repeated at frequent intervals, and a citizen of Chester or York could easily have seen the plays performed ten times in his lifetime; all his life long, in church and at market cross, he would have heard sermons that drew doctrine and *moralitas* out of those events so vividly familiar from the cycle-plays.[8]

But beyond all this, and superior to it, drama in the later Middle Ages sought to increase the emotional richness and depth of man's existence as a creature under God. Franciscan devotional modes had revolutionized the spiritual life of the fourteenth and fifteenth centuries. Men were taught that by feeling—by the experience of pity, grief, and love for Mary and Christ in their human roles—they could best come to an understanding of the Godhead, to a true awareness of the price of their salvation, and to an adequate sorrow for their own sin. They were invited above all to contemplate the human tragedy

of the Passion, and through that contemplation to share in its transcendental victory. Every detail had to be registered and responded to;
sermons were preached, images painted, poems written and recited,
all to this end, that these events might be felt as well as understood.
In this function most especially we must forgo thinking of the drama
as addressed only to simple, unlettered men. Its true use was to all
Christians, whatever their theological learning.

John Mirk, in a fifteenth-century sermon, wrote an eloquent defense of images, which deserves a careful reading:

And þerfor roodes and oþyr ymages ben necessary in holy chirch, whateuer
þes Lollardes sayn....For, as Ion Bellet tellet, ymages and payntours ben
lewde menys bokys, and I say bo[l]dyly þ þer ben mony þousaund of pepul
þat couþ not ymagen in her hert how Crist was don on þe rood, but as þai
lerne hit be syȝt of ymages and payntours.[9]

This defines a central contribution of the artist, as a man gifted with
a lively visual sense and schooled in the traditions of religious iconography. He helps men to imagine; he gives substantial form to that
which is past, or to come, or invisible, in images designed to alter a
man's life in relation to those things. In this function, images—of
whatever kind—must be understood as useful to priests and clerks,
lords and ladies, quite as much as they were to the common people.

The Corpus Christi drama furnishes images too, but of a superior
sort; the plays are "quike bookis," living books that speak, move, and
can imitate whole sequences of events and interactions. They image
more vividly and more unforgettably than any other art form of their
time, but they too seek to serve in these ways. When a tormentor in
the Cornish *Passion Play* speaks the following words while crucifying
Christ, he is guiding audience feeling toward a devotional end:

> I beat him hard without pity,
> That all may have shuddering,
>   Looking at his body,
> As I strike him behind,
> That his hair may be bloody,
>   And all his body, before leaving off.[10]

The dramatist thus seeks to lead the spectators, detail by detail, into
a more deeply felt response. In the York and Towneley cycles, Christ
speaks from the cross in the same manner, addressing the audience

directly and guiding their meditation. The Towneley version is very beautiful, and a small part of it may be quoted here:

> I pray you pepyll that passe me by,
> That lede youre lyfe so lykandly,
>   heyfe vp youre hartys on hight!
> Behold if euer ye sagh body
> Buffet & bett thus blody,
>   Or yit thus dulfully dight;
> In warld was neuer no wight
>   That suffred half so sare.
> My mayn, my mode, my myght,
> Is noght bot sorow to sight,
>   And comforth none, bot care.[11]

This complaint from the cross is the subject of innumerable lyric poems from the fourteenth and fifteenth centuries. But even the finest is no match for either drama version, because the context of this speech in the drama is action imaged by human beings. The violence, noise, and savagery of the Crucifixion play subside for a few moments to allow this solemn address by Christ, and then the horror begins again. The lesson is less to the mind than to the heart, but it, too, is part of the medieval "knowing" of God.

The author of *Diues et Pauper* justifies the use of images on three grounds, and his discussion can put into final order the premises upon which this book has been written:

They serue for thre · thynges / For they be ordeined to stere mannys mynde to thynke on cristes incarnacion / and on his passion & on his lyuynge / & on other seintes lyuynge Also they ben ordeined to styre mannys affection · and his herte to deuocion For ofte man is more steryt by sight than be herynge or redynge / Also they be ordeyned to be a token & a boke to the leude peple / that they may rede in ymagery & painture / that clerkes rede in the boke ...[12]

Only the last of these uses pertains exclusively to the unlearned. The other two relate to all Christians, whatever their learning and station: images serve as objects to stir the mind to contemplation and the heart to love. And so it was with the Corpus Christi plays. Their audience included clergy, aristocracy, burgesses, and peasants, all together. The Coventry cycle was seen by Henry V (as prince), by Queen Margaret in 1457, by Richard III in 1485, and twice by Henry VII; the great cycle-plays at Skinners Well in London are recorded in 1411 as having played before "the moste parte of the lordes and gentylles of Ynglond."[13] The medieval popular audience was as large as William Langland's "felde ful of folke"; it was as diverse as the later audience at the Globe. And like the Elizabethan drama, the Corpus Christi cycles owe much of their power, delightfulness, and variety, as well as the astonishing range of human experience they present, to this need to address a widely varied assembly. If we would get inside these plays, we must renounce certain oversimple conceptions of their audience and their purpose. The plays were neither written by the unlearned[14] nor staged exclusively for them. The medieval drama was catholic and comprehensive.

The plays furnish images then, but of a special kind. They are scores for speech and action whose final artistic life is only suggested on the manuscript page, and I have tried never to forget that. It has been my good fortune to see several productions of these cycles: the York plays produced at York in 1957; an Oxford production of the life of Christ, using an eclectic text, in 1960; and productions of the Towneley cycle at the Mermaid Theatre in London in 1961, and at Grace Cathedral in San Francisco in 1962. Because these texts were designed for the stage and not for the study, our first major inquiry must be into the medieval conception of theater, into the dramatist's sense of his medium and its relation to reality. These cycles grew in terms of that conception, and only in its terms will they yield their greatest force and beauty.

Chapter Two

The Corpus Christi Drama as Play and Game

Medieval drama owes nothing to the tragedy and comedy of either Greece or Rome; it was a fresh beginning, unrooted in any formal tradition of theater. The notion was common among learned men that Roman dramatic performances consisted of a poet or reciter reading from a pulpit while others mimed in silence the action he described.[1] A few scholars, among them John the Scot, Peter Abelard, and Gilbert de la Porrée, seem to have realized that the persons who recited were also the persons who mimed, that actors represented in speech as well as by gesture the substances of other individuals. The contribution of Boëthius to the Trinitarian controversy of the early sixth century, *De Duabus naturis et una persona Jesu Christi, contra Eutychen et Nestorium,* which used a conception of personae and masks drawn from the classical stage, may have helped spread such a realization, for it was a work of theological importance.[2] Yet this was, in sum, a small legacy. Despite fragmentary survivals of the entertainer's craft after the fall of Rome, and despite the nun Hrothswitha's literary imitations of Terence, there was no continuing tradition of the dramatist's art. Indeed, it is precisely because the Middle Ages were not inhibited by any real knowledge of earlier theater that they were free to invent their mimetic modes in direct response to the Christian story that had once again called formal drama into being. The story existed *before* the genre was reconceived and reformulated, and we may be sure the exigencies of that story were of the first importance in redefining the nature of the medium. The story turns on supernatural and miraculous actions; it involves a sequence of events spread out across all historical time; and it employs a very diverse and complex group of characters. Certain characters, in fact, posed problems so great that they might have prevented the development of a religious drama altogether.

If the Corpus Christi plays had been concerned merely with human beings—Adam and Eve, knights and Jews, midwives and thieves—the range of dramatis personae would have presented no real difficulty. But medieval men believed that human history could not be explained in purely human terms, and therefore in their drama, a mimesis and interpretation of that history, they could not restrict themselves to the representation of human characters. God the Father must appear, God the Son in his human form; there must be angels and devils, there must be the Mother of God. Here a crucial difficulty arises, which Etienne Gilson, in another context, has stated concisely: "Images so obviously participate in the nature of their objects that to religious images, for instance, is often attributed a sort of inherent sacredness that really belongs to that which they represent, that is, to their meaning."[3] Thus a player for the Waterleaders' Guild in Chester could take the role of Noah without jeopardy: since Noah was a man and is to be acted by a man, the image and its referent are of the same nature. But a player for the Drapers' Guild chosen to enact God ran a certain risk, as when he opens the play of *The Creation* with these words:

> I God, most in maiestye,
> in whom beginning none may be,
> endles alsoe, most of postye,
> I am and haue bene ever.[4]

Here the image and its referent are so different in kind that blasphemy or sacrilege may be involved. The actor's human nature risks defiling the most awesome of Christian images; man is not God, and God will not be mocked. Lucifer, they believed, fell because he imitated God. By sitting on God's throne and demanding the forms of adoration due to God alone, he sinned in pride and was condemned to hell. (The Chester cycle stages this very action.)[5] Might it not be analogous to the Corpus Christi dramatic endeavor?

Authors writing in genres less imitative than the drama were certainly conscious of the risk involved. For instance, though the *Cursor Mundi* poet cannot resist describing what the historical Christ looked like, he prepares the way with an elaborate apology:

Of his visage þat es sa bright
Me for to mele it es vn-right,
For angels es na sun sa light,
þair mast ioi es on his sight,
To se him þar he sittes nu,
In heuen als we aght to tru,
Bot of his licknes þat he bar
Quils he went prechand here and þare.[6]

Plays as decorous and reverent as The Creation and those of the ministry of Christ pose this problem acutely enough, but the mature Corpus Christi drama went much further. Its central subject is the Passion of Christ, which entails not merely the representation by a human actor of God the Son, but also the playing of His humiliation, torture, and death. It involves the mimetic maltreatment of a sacred figure. The question was put: if men taunt and scorn and put on a cross him who plays Christ, are they not guilty of the very crimes they represent? There were those who thought so. Gerhoh of Reichersberg (1093–1169), writing about monastic performances, said that those who represent Antichrist or the rage of Herod are guilty of the very vices they portray.[7] A Wycliffite preacher, whose attack on the vernacular drama is our most important contemporary notice of it, believed all social assemblies to be occasions of sin, and when he says that he would prefer the playing of "pure vaniteis" and "rebaudye," he is not advocating a secular drama.[8] He means only that this would be less sinful than a sacred drama, the playing of the miracles and Passion of Christ, the history of Antichrist, the Doom.[9]

The problem was not new; there is evidence of occasional uneasiness throughout the medieval drama, even in the Latin drama of the Church. It may lie behind the fact that the Rouen *Pastores,* probably dating from the eleventh century, uses men and a boy to impersonate the shepherds, the midwives, and the angel who makes the Announcement, while at the center of the action, the Virgin Mary is represented by a constructed image.[10] Much Latin drama was equally cautious, though not all; but always it relied on its liturgical setting, the use of sung dialogue, and an extreme liturgical decorum to grant it safety.

The mature vernacular drama could not limit itself in these ways. The cycles had more complex ends in view, and they resolved these problems instead in terms of a specific conception of the dramatic genre. For neither a single author nor a group of authors could produce a dramatic cycle of such length without some coherent notion of what they were attempting, what means were available to them, and what advantages and difficulties these means entailed. In response to new problems, a new idea of theater was born. Fundamental to any idea of theater is a notion of precisely how the theater is to relate to reality. To reconstruct that conception—to investigate the generic "self-awareness" of the Corpus Christi drama—is the purpose of this chapter. Hardin Craig—and here he speaks for many others—can provide us with both a caution and a challenge:

Indeed, the religious drama had no dramatic technique or dramatic purpose, and no artistic self-consciousness. Its life-blood was religion, and its success depended on its awakening and releasing a pent-up body of religious knowledge and religious feeling. Therefore to carry to the study of the medieval religious drama a body of criteria derived from Aristotle, Horace and their Renaissance followers, or of specialists in the technique of the modern drama or of drama in general is to bring the wrong equipment.... Few studies of the techniques of playwrights and actors of the medieval religious drama have been made, except by persons who have not understood this aspect of the task, and perhaps for lack of definite materials none can be made.

This drama had no theory and aimed consciously at no dramatic effects, and, when it succeeded, its success came from the import of its message or from the moving quality of some particular story it had to tell.[11]

I think this underestimates the evidence available, and, perhaps as a result, underestimates the importance of the question as well.

I shall begin by asking a very simple question: What words were used to describe theater? For a time, the answers I get may seem as simple as the question, but this semantic evidence will make it possible to harmonize facts about the drama text, the personae, and contemporary production techniques, deducing from them a conception of theater at once coherent, sophisticated, and significantly different from those other ideas of theater that in time succeed it.

The Latin liturgical drama of the Church was almost entirely sung or chanted, and the performers themselves (the priests and the choir) were often the only audience of the piece. The first episode to be dramatized by the Church was the visit of the Marys to the tomb on Easter morning; of the four hundred-odd texts extant of this dramatic episode, that of the *Concordia regularis,* a tenth-century manual directing Winchester usage, has particular interest: *Aguntur enim haec ad imitationem angeli sedentis in monumento atque mulierum cum aromatibus venientium ut ungerent corpus Ihesu.**[12] Even at this early date, the Church conceived of dramatic action as something performed *ad imitationem,* although most of the generically descriptive words that came to be used did little more than emphasize the formal, liturgical element: titles such as *ordo* or *officium,* and plays designated only by their subject, such as *De Peregrino,* are common and have no specifically dramatic connotation. More suggestive of genre are *similitudo, exemplum, miraculum,* and most common of all, *repraesentatio.* (The records can be studied in Karl Young's *Drama of the Medieval Church.*)[13] Though these plays continued to be performed until the Reformation, the most elaborate texts had all been composed by the end of the thirteenth century;[14] and it is a striking fact that the vernacular cycle-drama, which came into existence in the last quarter of the fourteenth century, in naming itself rarely used an English translation of any of these words. Instead, it employed English equivalents of a much rarer term, *ludus,* which seems to have been used only in late Latin plays—in the *Ludus breviter de Passione,* the piece entitled *Incipit ludus, immo exemplum, Dominicae Resurrectionis* (both from the *Carmina Burana* manuscript of the thirteenth century), the superb Beauvais play of Daniel (*Incipit Danielis ludus*), and a play of the twelfth century by Hilarius, the *Ludus super iconia Sancti Nicolai.*[15] As a generic term, its lack of precision has tried the patience of distinguished scholars. Thus Chambers has written that *ludus* is "a generic term for 'amusement,' and the special sense of dramatic play is only a secondary one,"[16] and Young has called it "a designation rendered generally ambiguous through its common association with popular revelling."[17] Yet this very ambiguity may prove an entrance into the medieval idea of theater, for it is this word *ludus,* in its English equivalents "play" and "game," that becomes the ubiquitous generic term for the vernacular drama.†

Certain vernacular words not deriving from *ludus* are used on oc-

---

* These things are done in imitation of the angel seated in the tomb and the women coming with spices to anoint the body of Jesus.

† Similarly, the vernacular drama in France called itself *jeu,* and in Germany, *spiel.*

casion. "Processe" and "processyon" occur in the (non-cycle) Digby Plays, implying in the first instance little more than a formal arrangement of speech and action, and in the second, the act of playing the *Conversion of St. Paul* at three different stations with the audience following it to each, in procession.[18] A more common word is "pagent," used to describe both the wagons on which some cycles were played and the episodes staged on them. Manuscripts of the Chester cycle preface each new play with the Latin form, *pagina*; its English equivalent is sometimes used in the Digby plays and it occurs frequently in the Proclamation to the *Ludus Coventriae*.[19] It had a secondary sense of trick, deceit, or merry game.[20] The word "shewe" was also in use, both as substantive and as verb, and involved conceptions such as revealing, displaying, demonstrating.[21] The term "miracles," very common in contemporary notices of the drama, clearly should indicate subject rather than medium, but it was applied so loosely that the protesting Wycliffite preacher uses miracles as a blanket term for plays of the Passion, the Antichrist, and the Doom, as well as for plays of miracles performed by Christ and the saints.[22] Each of these terms is important, but none rivals the Englished *ludus* in frequency or suggestiveness.[23] The Corpus Christi drama was spoken of as "play" or "game."*

The gathering of evidence that the English Middle Ages used the word "play" for a dramatic performance might seem tedious and unprofitable. Yet evidence of medieval usage does have value, for the word has gone dead; its specialized dramatic sense is now largely divorced from its root. Some of its original force can be restored by quoting several contexts in which it is used (it is the commonest generic term of all) and I shall then bring forward "game" usages to confirm the richer meaning of "play" evident in passages such as these. From the Chester Banns:

> you bakers, see that the same wordes you utter,
> as Christ hym selfe spake them, to be A memoriall
> of that death and passion which in play ensue after shall.[24]

---

* "Game" as a substantive could also mean simply "pleasure." "Play" and "game" were both used to mean amorous sport, and heaven and hell could both be described (with differing connotations) as places of "play" or "game." The only usages of interest here are those that are demonstrably generic in force.

And from the Chester *Prophets*:

> Moe prophetis, lordinges, we might play,
> but yt wold tary much the daye;
> therfore six, sothe to say,
> are played in this place.[25]

From York, when Herod lays a trap for the three Kings, and is content to await their return thus:

> Go we nowe, till þei come agayne,
> To playe vs in som othir place.[26]

From the Proclamation to the *Ludus Coventriae*:

> In þe xxiij[ti] pagent palme sunday
> in pley we purpose ffor to shewe.[27]

And from the same Proclamation:

> the mawnde of god þer xal they play.[28]

Of Mary, from a prologue by *Doctor* later in that cycle:

> how sche was assumpte · here men schul be pleyand.[29]

And as a final example, stage directions from that cycle's *Passion* play:

here enteryth Satan in to þe place in þe most orryble wyse · and qwyl þat he pleyth þei xal don on jhesus clothis · and ouerest A whyte clothe and ledyn hym A-bowth þe place and þan to pylat be þe tyme þat hese wyf hath pleyd.[30]

Many other instances could be cited, but these few will serve to alert us to a slight resonance of meaning no longer present in modern speech. The frequent description of action as being performed "in play" is suggestive, and it is important, too, that the verb is always "to play," where we might use "to act," "to produce," "to perform." This was so because drama was conceived *as a game,* and was frequently identified by that word as well. In England in the Middle Ages, one could say "We will play a game of the Passion" and mean what we mean when we say "We will stage the Passion." The transition from one to the other is more than a semantic change; it is a change in the history of theater.

"Game" usages are crucial to an understanding of the medieval conception of drama. Because even the twelve-volume *Oxford English Dictionary* takes no clear notice of this usage, evidence for it must be presented in some detail.[31] From the Proclamation to the *Ludus Coventriae* comes this description of the play of *The Fall*:

> and þan almythy god ffor þat gret dyspite
> Assygned hem grevous peyn · as ȝe xal se in game
> In dede.[32]

In a concluding passage, the whole cycle is designated so:

> whan þat ȝe come þer xal ȝe sene
> this game wel pleyd in good a-ray
> Of holy wrytte þis game xal bene
> and of no fablys be no way.[33]

The word is twice used to describe the earliest extant morality play, *The Pride of Life,* as here by the play's prolocutor:

> Nou beit in pes & beit hende,
> & distourbit noȝt oure place
> ffor þis oure game schal gin & ende
> Throgh Jhesu Cristis swete grace.[34]

And the long and beautiful morality play called *The Castell of Perseverance* concludes with this speech by God:

> all men example here-at may take,
> to mayntein þe goode, & mendyn here mys:
>   þus endyth oure gamys![35]

There survives a short play from the early sixteenth century entitled a "Cristemasse game, made by Maister Benet Howe. God Almyghty scyde to his apostelys, and echon off them were baptiste, and none knewe of othir."[36] Similarly, John Skelton's morality play, *Magnyfycence,* probably to be dated 1516, closes with an address to "ye that haue harde this dysporte and game."[37] Sixteenth-century records from Bungay, Suffolk, dealing with the Corpus Christi drama in that town, speak of the "game gear," the "game booke," the "game pleyers,"[38] and of "ye game on corp's xxi day."[39] In Harling, Norfolk, payments were recorded in 1457 for the "Lopham game" and the "Garblesham game," in 1463 for the "Kenningale game," and in 1467 (clearly a variation on the same) for the "Kenyngale players" (Lop-

ham, Garboldisham, and Kenninghall all being towns near Harling).[40] In 1493, the churchwardens of St. Nicholas' Church, Great
Yarmouth, were paid for a "game" played on Christmas Day.[41] Bishop
Bonner in 1542 enjoined that no "common plays, games, or interludes"
be permitted in holy places.[42] And as late as 1605, in Ben Jonson's
Volpone, Nano the dwarf announces an entertainment to be performed by himself, the eunuch, and the hermaphrodite, with the
words, "Now, room for fresh gamesters" (I, ii). Finally, to establish
the currency of the term throughout the centuries that saw the birth
and the full maturity of the vernacular religious cycles, there are two
drama fragments, the first of them dated by Robbins as not later than
1300 and possibly written twenty-five years earlier. It is a prologue,
and includes these lines:

> nu sittet stille and herknit alle
> zat hur no mis ting ev bifalle
> and sittet firme and wel a-twe
> zat men moyt among ev go
> þey zat beut igadert fale
> ne maknet nayt to lude tale
> hit uer ev bot muchel scame
> for to lette hure game.[43]

The second, from the sixteenth century, is an epilogue that concludes
with an appeal for money:

> Souereyns alle in same ȝe that arn come to sen oure game
> . . . .
> Vnto holy chirche to ben in-cressement
> alle that excedith þe costes of oure play.[44]

"Play" and "game" are here used interchangeably, in exact apposi-
tion, just as in these lines from *Magnyfycence*:

> For though we shewe you this in game and play,
> Yet it proueth eyrnest, ye may se, euery day.[45]

It is clear that the "play" usages cited earlier also carry with them this
reinforcing sense of "game."

Some of the formulas in which these words customarily occurred,
and some of the ideas associated with them, provide further and

especially important clues to the medieval idea of theater. Then, as now, play or game could describe children's pastimes, adult sports, and elaborate jokes alike: elements of pleasure, diversion, or gratuitous action are always involved. Both words were used as antonyms of "serious," as in the *Cursor Mundi* description of Lot's terrible warnings to the citizens of Sodom:

> Bot al þat loth to þaim can sai
> þam thoght it was not bot in plai.[46]

Another example is the *Gawain* poet's description of his hero as he rides out to keep his promise in a Christmas "game" which may cost him his life:

> Now rideȝ þis renk þurȝ þe ryalme of Logres,
> Sir Gauan, on Godeȝ halue, þaȝ hym no gomen þoȝt.[47]

Lydgate wrote, in his *Troy Book,* "It is an ernest and no game," and in the *Assembly of Gods* he used the phrase, "Chaunge from ernest in to mery play."[48] Two kinds of human action and motive, fundamentally different, were distinguished by these words, and from a conception of drama as play and game—as something therefore not "in ernest"—a drama involving sacred personages and miraculous events could be born.

In *Magnyfycence* we can find the antithesis used in both its general and its generic senses. Counterfet Countenance explains his duplicity in these terms:

> Counterfet eyrnest by way of playes.
> Thus am I occupyed at all assayes.

And later the dramatic world is itself offered as a game and play analogue to a world in which actions *are* "eyrnest," that is, to the world of everyday reality:

> Beholde howe Fortune on hym hath frounde.
> For though we shewe you this in game and play,
> Yet it proueth eyrnest, ye may se, euery day.

We are thus shown truth "vnder pretence of play."[49] This polarity, "play" and "ernest," also explains the Wycliffite preacher's antagonism toward the drama. His attitude is somber: "al holynesse is in ful ernest men," and play, by nature not in earnest, is therefore both foolish and false, and can offer nothing to men who wish to be holy. He mentions a defense that men make for the drama: "And sythen as ther ben men that only by ernestful doynge wylen be convertid to God, so ther been othere men that wylen be convertid to God but by gamen and pley … now it is tyme and skilful to assayen to convertyn the puple by pley and gamen."[50] But he denies it out of hand: only things done in earnest are relevant to truth and Christian life. We shall examine his other arguments later; here it is enough to note that he defines the nature of the drama just as the banns, proclamations, and drama texts themselves do, as "play" and "game," opposed to "ernest." He sees, too, its kinship with the game amusements of children and men; the drama is only one kind among others:

Dere frend, beholdith how kynde tellith that the more eldere a man waxith the more it is aȝen kynde hym for to pleyn, and therfore seith the booc, *"Cursid be the childe of han hundred ȝeer!"* And certis the world, as seith the apostil, is now at his endyng, as in his laste age; therfore, for the grete neȝyng of the day of dome, alle creaturis of God nowe weryen and wrathen of mennus pleying, namely of myraclis pleyinge.[51]

Cursed be any man who has not put away childish things. The only scholar ever to pay close attention to this Wycliffite sermon was the late George Raleigh Coffman; he noted that in the course of it the preacher uses six specific examples of play: Sara's abstention from play and the company of players; Ishmael's playing with Isaac, which caused him to be driven into the desert; the playing of the followers of Abner and Joab, in which they destroy one another; the playing of the children of Israel before the Golden Calf; the playful mocking of Elisha by the children of Bethel, who were torn to pieces by bears in punishment; and David's playing before the ark of the Lord. That this variety of event was all designated by the same word seemed to Coffman incomprehensible, and he considered it an adequate reason for disregarding the whole treatise: "A man who shows such a confused state of mind with regard to the use of important terms can certainly not be expected to give us a logical idea of what the dramatic type, Miracle Play, includes."[52] But he is fighting the facts. The Latin drama of the Church had avoided the Crucifixion and had little connection with game. The church and the liturgy were its natural milieu.

It was simple, dignified, ritualistic, limited in its means; it was called *ordo, processio, repraesentatio.* When the drama moved into the streets and the market place, into a milieu already the home of men's playing and games, it was redefined *as* game and allowed to exploit fully its nonearnest, gratuitous nature at the same time as its range of subject and its cast of sacred personae grew. It was a special kind of game, of course, its unique character clearly defined in a Latin-German dictionary, the *Variloquus* of Johannes Melber (*c.* 1479), where play itself is given as one of the meanings of *scena*: "Etiam pro ludo capitur in huiusmodi loco facto ubi rusticus efficitur rex vel miles, et ludo peracto quolibet est sicut prius rusticus fuit."[53] It is the kind of game in which a peasant is made a king or knight, and after it is over becomes once again a peasant.

My preliminary exposition is at an end. I have put forward evidence that the English Middle Ages described their religious drama as play and game; that this conception of genre involves the common medieval antithesis, "game" and "ernest"; that there was little fundamental distinction made between drama and other forms of men's playing. And I have argued that this conception of theater developed in response to difficulties intrinsic to the Corpus Christi story.

To go deeper into this matter, we must leave philology. The nature of drama conceived as a game needs also to be explored within a larger and more theoretical framework, and Johan Huizinga's admirable analysis of the nature of play, in *Homo ludens,* can serve us as a new point of departure. Once its implications have been examined, it will be possible to attempt a full-scale generic description of the Corpus Christi drama, to relate what we know about medieval staging to the dramatic theory I have been seeking to reconstruct in these pages. Huizinga wrote:

Summing up the formal characteristics of play we might call it a free activity standing quite consciously outside "ordinary" life as being "not serious," but at the same time absorbing the player intensely and utterly. It is an activity connected with no material interest, and no profit can be gained by it. It proceeds within its own proper boundaries of time and space according to fixed rules and in an orderly manner. It promotes the formation of social groupings which tend to surround themselves with secrecy and to stress their difference from the common world by disguise or other means.

It is ... a stepping out of "real" life into a temporary sphere of activity with a disposition all of its own. Every child knows perfectly well that he is "only pretending," or that it was "only for fun."... The consciousness of play being "only a pretend" does not by any means prevent it from proceeding with the utmost seriousness.... The inferiority of play is continually being offset by the corresponding superiority of its seriousness.[54]

These generalizations deserve to be read carefully. They are broad enough to cover all forms of drama, as well as children's games, athletic contests, dance marathons, or what you will. But the seriousness of "ye game on corp's xxi day," as the Bungay records term it, goes beyond the absorption intrinsic to any form of play. In ways we have already examined, it "imaged" sacred personae of the highest importance to man, and it sought to instruct in matters central to the salvation of souls: it was considered profitable game. Formal and repetitive in nature, it played year after year within a specifically limited time and place. Within those limits special conventions applied, creating a temporary world within the world of real life, and dedicating this created world to the performance of an act in some sense gratuitous to urgent daily concerns. Once this conventional world had been established, it was easily recreated until it became traditional. Like all play, this drama depended on formal order, without which progress within a game and pleasure from a game are alike impossible: anyone who breaks the rules spoils the game, makes it a poor and foolish thing. The formal order of the Corpus Christi game, its sequence of action, was determined by the playbook; failure to observe this order, an arbitrary limitation on the possibilities of action, was considered an offense punishable by civic authority. Records exist of fines paid by guilds and individuals for playing badly or incorrectly, to the shame and displeasure of the community.[55] The particular order that this game sought to create was not only aesthetic, but historically true: it sought to pattern human experience, to give to the history of men an order that would reveal its meaning.

Play and game thus creates a world within the real world, and the dramatist's art relates the two worlds meaningfully to each other. But the two need never be mistaken or confused. When the *Ludus Coventriae* promises us "the mawnde of god þer xal they play," we may be sure that this is to be serious, all-engrossing play, but play nevertheless, which is to say of an order of seriousness different from the historical Maundy Thursday which is its referent. Similarly, when the

Chester Banns alert the city at Whitsuntide that the days from Monday through Wednesday are to be devoted to the playing of the cycle, and when the location of stations has been determined, a formal world has been delimited within which the dramatic game can be played. One may see how important was this sense of a world apart by juxtaposing two late anecdotes concerning the devil. The fourth tale of *A Hundred Mery Talys,* published in 1526, is entitled "Of hym that playd the deuyll and came thorow the waren & mayd theym that stale the connys to ronne away," and concerns a player from a pageant who wears his devil's costume while going home, frightening everyone grievously.[56] A very different reaction can be found in the reminiscences of Mrs. Tattle in Ben Jonson's play, *The Staple of News*: "My husband Timothy Tattle, God rest his poor soul! was wont to say there was no play without a fool and a devil in't; he was for the devil still, God bless him! The devil for his money would he say, I would fain see the devil."[57] Although Timothy Tattle enjoys seeing a devil within the carefully circumscribed world of play, the villagers are terrified when a refugee from that world suddenly enters the world of real life.

Though the Wycliffite preacher shares with the dramatists an exact sense of the drama as play, he understands differently how this play world relates to the world of actual experience. He is unable to see the dramatic artifact as something analogous, but in a root-sense "unrelated," to real life: "And therfore many men wenen that ther is no helle of everlastynge peyne, but that God doth not but thretith us and is not to do it in dede, as ben pleyinge of miraclis in sygne and not in dede." He believes the drama teaches men that hell is only a *locus* on a pageant stage, and that the wrath of God is merely a dramatic attitude, for it is obvious to any spectator that the damned souls are not really punished in any Judgment Day pageant. This view grows out of his belief that only real action should occupy men, and that all else is falsehood, feigning, and a work of the devil (three terms constantly equated in his mind): "Not he that pleyith the wille of God worschipith hym, but onely he that doith his wille in deede worschipith hym."[58] Here his argument is intrinsically more convincing, but it remains irrelevant. The duration of play is a momentary interval in, and abstention from, the real concerns of life; when the audience disperses they resume these concerns, the most significant of which for the Christian Middle Ages was the doing of the will of God.

For a religious drama to have existed with the full approval of the Church, such a consciousness of the dramatic medium was necessary. The Wycliffite critic is interesting, not so much because he opposed the drama—a hyperzealous, Lollard fear of images and idolatry could lead to that very naturally, and the practical consequences of his opposition probably amounted to little—but because he often summarizes the arguments of those who valued the plays, and because his own objections furnish an explicit contemporary statement of some of the difficulties that seem from the very beginning to have shaped the medieval conception of theater. His final answers are confused, because he thought action that was unreal was therefore untrue, clinging rigidly to two polarities: real and unreal, true and false. Whatever was false he considered to be an abomination to God and a peril to men's souls. In this he may have been right, but his categories are muddled: the world of play (and its mode of meaningfulness) lies outside the antithesis, truth or falsehood. This fact is common to children's games, knightly tournaments, champion wrestling, and all drama that has ever been.

Although any drama can be reduced to a game analysis, the medieval cycles furnish for the English theater the first major example of that genre, influencing in ways that have not yet been fully understood the great drama of the Elizabethan and Jacobean periods. And what is more, they furnish the purest, most explicit, and most comprehensively detailed example of a theater of game that has existed until our own time. After the Restoration, theater in England and elsewhere took a very different turn, reaching its climax in the heavily naturalistic theater of the early years of this century. Dryden, as early as 1672, had signaled this new direction, in claiming deception as the dramatist's aim; in his *Of Heroic Plays, An Essay,* he argued that trumpets, drums, cannons and sound effects offstage are essential "to raise the imagination of the audience, and to persuade them, for the time, that what they behold in the theatre is really performed. The poet is then to endeavour an absolute dominion over the minds of the spectators; for though our fancy will contribute to its own deceit, yet a writer ought to help its operation."[59] Until recently, we were heirs chiefly of this "theater of illusion"—a very different kind of dramatic game. Though we never actually confuse dramatic action with real life, we are asked to grant it our maximum credence within the structure of the theatrical experience. Everything about the texts, the acting, and the staging is carefully contrived to make the fact of "theater" as unobtrusive as possible. The medieval drama required different habits of its spectators, and gave them a different kind of artistic experience in return. Today, playwrights like Brecht, Ionesco, and Beckett have gone back to this older idea of theater or have worked in terms consonant with it. But the cycles can give us the thing itself in its first flowering, and if we would read them, stage them, and understand them properly, we must learn first of all to respond to the game nature of their action. In the pages that follow, I shall examine the relationship between this theory and the procedures and practices of the medieval stage.

The Corpus Christi drama took place in broad daylight, in the streets and open places of the town. The audience surrounded the playing area, as clearly visible to one another as the players were to them; occasional exits, entrances, and even dramatic action took place on street level in their midst. Richard Southern's researches into the meaning of "place" and *platea* in medieval dramaturgy have led him to an important conclusion: the "place" was simply the area in front of the stage or scaffold, to which the actors might descend if necessary. It was never geographically localized, and there was no pretense that what went on there went on in an imagined locality relevant to the action. Action itself told the story, and it happened *there* in England, in front of and amid the spectators. In Southern's words, "It was not until the Italian Renaissance that the place of a performance could become attired in costume like an actor and take a part in the drama— and scenery was born."[60] The pageant wagon or scaffold would indicate the *locus* or *loci* of the action, but in terms of the "place" itself these reference points were only conventions in a game: when Mary and Joseph traveled from Bethlehem into Egypt, the meaning of the action was clear, though the actual distance between the *loci* may have been only several yards.

Furthermore, this drama used actors from the community who were known to the audience in real life. From Coventry records we learn of "Ryngold's man Thomas thatt playtt Pylatts wyff"; of wages "payd to Robert Cro for pleayng God iij s iiij d"; and of fines levied by the Weavers' Guild in 1450 against Hary Bowater, who played Simeon's clerk, Crystover Dale who played Jesus, and Hew Heyns who played Anne.[61] A few records in York suggest that occasional performances were graced by actors imported from outside: the visits of three players from Donnington, one from Wakefield, and four from London are noted in the mid-fifteenth century.[62] But this was the exception, not the rule; local, familiar faces in biblical roles would have made any fully developed kind of theatrical illusion impossible. Moreover, because each pageant wagon had its own complete cast to play its episode at each assigned station on the route, no single actor (except perhaps in the *Ludus Coventriae* Passion plays) performed the entire role of any major character. The York cycle, for example, employed in any given year no fewer than twenty-four different Christs in the adult episodes alone; the Chester and Towneley cycles both used eleven. This does not necessarily imply incoherent characterization, for there were undoubtedly traditional approaches to the major roles; but it did serve as a powerful check against illusion.[63] These townsmen would have been astonished by Stanislavsky. They were ordinary men engaged in a certain kind of game, distinguished from their fellows only by a more generous mimetic gift. To take an extreme case, those who played God would not have sought (even for the duration of the pageant) to *be* God, nor to get inside His personality: such a notion would have seemed to them blasphemous and absurd. They presented not the character of God but certain of His actions. This approach encouraged a formal stylization in both writing and acting wholly foreign to the chaotic world of real life.

Such a conception of theater also made possible the presentation of large, complex actions in swift and simple terms. In every cycle Noah builds the ark in front of the audience, either using prefabricated parts or wheeling a finished model onto the pageant stage; but always he claims it is taking him a hundred years, and the audience enjoys the speed with which the ark is actually readied as a kind of merry joke unique to the drama. The Chester stage direction makes the game nature of the action clear: "Then noy with all his familie shall make a signe as though they wrought vpon the shipe with diuers instrumentis."[64] When the ark is ready to be filled, painted boards representing the birds and the beasts are brought on; there are instructions that the verses and pictures should strictly accord in sequence.[65] The escape of Moses and the Israelites from Pharaoh and his forces was played with the same game literalness. In the *Exodus* I saw produced on a pageant wagon in front of York Minster in 1957, the Red Sea was a long linen cloth, painted with waves, and held facing the audience while Moses and the Israelites walked behind it; when Pharaoh and his men came in pursuit, it was thrown up and over them, and they lay "drowned" beneath. The Israelites rejoiced in song as the wagon was pulled away. The action, strong, clear, and delightful, probably represented something very close to medieval practice; records from Coventry specify, with no sense of incongruity, "it. p'd for halfe a yard of rede sea vj d."[66]

There was need for a kind of theater that could stage mythic actions as well, which could make phenomena never experienced in the normal course of things visible and dramatically "real." Because these plays were intended as "quike bookis" for the unlearned,[67] they sought to make the whole of doctrinal meaning tangible in this way. Greban's *Le Mystère de la Passion,* written before 1452, begins by staging the creation of the world, a difficult but unavoidable subject, with a Prologue to explain that so far as possible it will be shown literally—shown, that is, in a way the spectators can apprehend through their *senses*:

> Mes la creacion du monde
> est ung mistere en quoy se fonde
> tout ce qui deppend en apprès :
> si la monstrons par mos exprès;
> car *la maniere du produyre*
> *ne se peust monstrer* ne deduire
> par effect, *si non seulement*
> *grossement et figuraulment;*
> *et selonc qu'il nous est possible,*
> *en verrez la chose sensible.*[68]
>   [my italics]

Just as the halo around a saint's head in a picture imparts abstract meaning and gives the saint a kind of appearance familiar only in pictures,[69] so the medieval drama stages actions which, though unlike anything we encounter in ordinary human life, are nevertheless as "real" as anything else in the play world. Thus the whole drama becomes charged with a mythic quality, where inner meaning is made as external as any other kind of outward appearance. Mary rides on an ass into Egypt, and she is physically "assumpt" into heaven: in this drama, both actions *happen,* and they happen in equally literal ways. God was played by a man, but He was distinguished from the order of men by a gilt face.[70] And, as in the visual arts, the profound mystery of the Trinity was established very simply: in the Chester play of the *Pentecost* the actors playing God the Father and Christ sit together to hear the prayer of the disciples that they be sent some comforter, and when God the Father speaks He refers to *His* incarnation, even though the incarnation was performed by the Son at his side. It is *Deus Pater* who says:

> But while I was in that degree,
> in earth abyding as man should be,
> chosen I haue a good menye,
> on which I must haue mynd.[71]

When His long speech of recapitulation is finished, the stage direction reads, "Tunc Deus emittit Spiritum sanctum in spetie ignis."[72] The doctrine of the Trinity has been made visible as three-in-one, the most mysterious of its membership—the Holy Ghost—being shown as fire, probably in the form of a hank of burning hemp lowered from above.

In all the cycle plays there is much mechanical to-and-fro-ing between earth and heaven. When the York Jesus is about to ascend into heaven he says, "Sende doune a clowde, fadir" and a cloud comes down; He gets into it and is hoisted aloft out of sight.[73] The action was not designed to resemble reality, but rather to translate it into a game mode, a play equivalent. It is possible that the guilds staged the seven days of the Creation with movable charts, decoratively painted, as we might illustrate a lecture,[74] for part of the compact implicit between the medieval audience and dramatist was the acceptance of such devices as signifying reality. Even music in these plays was symbolic, and was never used simply for atmosphere or emotive effect. In the words of its best student:

It is there, like God's beard of gold, or the horned animal heads of the devils, because it signifies something. It is easy to be misled by the directions which require music to be played, or sung, at some of the great dramatic moments. The point was not to increase dramatic tension or to "soften up" the audience, but *representation*. "Heaven is music," so at the crises in the drama when heaven actively intervenes, music too intervenes.[75]

The need to instruct in doctrinal truth, to clarify and make visual certain important meanings that were spiritual and mysterious in nature, undoubtedly played its part in shaping the medieval conception of theater: it had to be a medium in which these things could "happen." This necessity liberated it, and greatly increased its expressive potential.

Never was a suspension of disbelief invited; instead, the game episodes were played in their turn, and in the Chester cycle and the *Ludus Coventriae,* characters like *Nuntius, Expositor, Contemplacio,* and *Poeta* served to direct them, introducing new actions and making doctrinal comments. Their function is to enclose the action, whether natural or mythic, in a frame of commentary which puts the playing unmistakably at a distance from reality. The Chester *Expositor,* for example, really does control the game—hurrying here, moralizing there, now briefly narrating a story that cannot, because of time, be played, and occasionally stepping forth to address the audience directly on what they have been watching together. The French medieval drama often used a *meneur* (or *maître*) *du jeu,* and we know from a miniature by Jean Fouquet that he could be in the very middle of the action, holding the playbook in one hand and a baton in the other, conducting the game.[76] We know also that the *meneur du jeu* often spoke the moralizations and sermons of the play.[77] It is possible that the Chester *Expositor* or the *Poeta* of *Ludus Coventriae* moved among the actors in this same fashion, although no evidence exists one way or the other. What matters is that a similar conception of genre is involved, one far removed from that later kind of theater in which the happenings on stage, once under way, have the air of being autonomous, inevitable, and independent of author or director.

Classical conceptions of the "three voices" of poetry were available to the Middle Ages, one tradition deriving from Suetonius through Isidore of Seville, the other more important one deriving from the fourth-century grammarian Diomedes, through Rabanus Maurus; though they were not greatly different, the Diomedes version was more widespread and its definitions more extensive. To distinguish the dramatic from the lyric and the epic voices, Diomedes had offered this definition: "Dramaticon est vel activum in quo personae agunt solae sine ullius poetae interlocutione, ut se habent tragicae et comicae fabulae."*[78] But such a distinction, *sine ullius poetae interlocutione,* is superbly ignored by the Chester and *Ludus Coventriae* cycles, where the *Expositor* figure (by whatever name) exists solely in order to speak for the dramatist—responsible for the design of the episode—and for God—responsible for the total historical and ethical design that the cycle imitates. (In York and Towneley it is not uncommon for a character actually involved in the story to address the audience to the same end.) This convention fundamentally affects the kind of drama we see; characters conceived in this way demonstrate biblical history, but no attempt is made to sustain an illusion of being men caught up in that history. The technique may be fairly represented in this speech by the Chester *Expositor,* which bridges the plays of the *Temptation* and the *Woman Taken in Adultery*:

> Thus overcome Christe in this case
> the Devill, as played was in this place,
> with those three synnes that Adam was
> of wayle into woe wayued.[79]

He has not himself "acted" in the play of the *Temptation,* but he is there to underline a doctrinal meaning (the Second Adam has withstood the temptations by which the first Adam fell), to acknowledge genre ("as played was in this place"), and to introduce the episode that follows. He creates in his own person a drama of play and game, an experience, as it were, in quotation marks. As Alan Nelson has noted, a spectator "cannot think of himself both as Noah and as the object of Noah's exhortation."[80]

The Passion episodes, of course, created the greatest difficulties and provided the greatest challenge for the Corpus Christi drama. I shall take up the artistic challenge and achievement in a later chapter, but the solution to those problems that were generic—that concern the propriety of playing God the Son and His torture and death—may properly bring this present inquiry to a close. The Wycliffite preacher argued "by figure" from the Old Testament to prove that men should

---

* The "dramatic" or the "acted" is that in which characters perform alone without any interruption from the poet speaking in his own person, as is the case with tragedy and comedy.

play neither Old Testament patriarchs and prophets, nor most especially the Passion of Christ. The terms of his argument should now have a special resonance for us:

Frend, peraventure ȝee seyen that no man schal make ȝou to byleven but that it is good to pleyen the passion of Crist, and othere dedis of hym. But here aȝenus herith, how, whanne Helyse steȝede up into Bethel, chyldre pleyingly comyng aȝenus hym, seiden, *"Steȝe up, ballard, steȝe up, ballard;"* and therfore hee cursid hem, and two bores of the wylde wode al totoren of hem two and fourty childre; and as alle seyntis seyen the ballednesse of Helisee betokeneth the passion of Crist, thanne sythen by his storye is opynly schewid that men schulden not bourden with the figure of the passion of Crist, ne with an holy prophete of Crist.... Men shulden not pleyn the passion of Crist, upon peyne myche grettere than was the venjaunce of the childre that scornyden Helisee. For siker pleyinge of the passion of Crist is but verre scornyng of Crist.[81]

Whereas the Latin drama of the Church had rarely played the Passion, and then only in a grave and stylized way, the vernacular plays emphasized the scorn, the jesting, and the violence, and thus the problem was correspondingly acute. An anonymous poet who satirized the friars and the plays they presented offers an interesting description:

> First þai gabben on god þat all men may se,
> When þai hangen him on hegh on a grene tre,
> With leues & with blossemes þat bright are of ble,
> Þat was neuer goddes son by my leute.
>
> . . . .
>
> Þai haue done him on a croys fer vp in þe skye,
> And festned in hym wyenges, as he shuld flie.
> Þis fals feyned byleue shal þai soure bye,
> On þat louelych lord, so forto lye.[82]

He attacks what seems to him the ludicrous unconvincingness of this drama: characters who are so clearly "only" friars playing, stage conventions that are unrealistic, "mythic" costumes and properties.

But the poem is primarily an attack on the friars themselves; their plays are only a secondary target. It is, throughout, an expression of hatred and contempt, and had we seen the performance, it is possible we might have judged it differently. We may enjoy the poem's sardonic description of a friar,

> Þer comes one out of þe skye in a grey goun,
> As it were an hog-hyerd hyand to toun,[83]

yet if we would estimate accurately the mood and look of the medieval drama on stage, we might well set against this description that moment in the York *Resurrection* when the first Mary says to the others as they make their way to the tomb:

> Sisteris! a ȝonge child as we goo
>   Makand mornyng,
> I see it sitte wher we wende to,
>   In white clothyng.[84]

This derives from Mark 16:5, "And, entering into the sepulchre, they saw a young man [*iuuenem*] sitting on the right side," but its translation is affected by dramatic tradition: the angel is being played by a child in white clothing. It is unlikely that the audience would join in the scorn of the anti-friar poet, because they know that the actors are engaged in a mimetic game, and that the purpose of the game is to reveal, not to deceive (even temporarily or in part) through illusion. As we have seen, it was important to the medieval Church that men should be able to imagine in their hearts and minds the Fall, the Passion, and the Judgment; and though *all* images are inadequate, yet they have their use and suitability. In a remarkable passage from *Diues et Pauper,* an early fifteenth-century work now too little known, Diues asks, "Why ben aungelles peynted in liknes of yong men sith they be spirites & haf no bodies," and Pauper replies:

Ther may noo peyntoure peynte a spirit in his kynde And therfore to the bettre representacion they be peyntyd · in the lyknesse of a man / Which in soule is mooste accordyng to aungellys kynde And thoughe the aungel be nat suche bodily · as he is peynted · he is nathelesse suche gostly / & hath suche doing & beyng spirituel.[85]

Men and angels and God are different in kind, and the image that unites them is to that degree discordant, yet men are next to angels in the order of creation and are made in the likeness of God. No more suitable *material* for the image may be found.

A post-Reformation copy of the Banns to the Chester plays, included in Roger's Breviary of 1609, advertises a performance very different from those of the Middle Ages. God will not be acted, it says; only a voice will be heard speaking His lines, for no man can "proportion" to the Godhead.[86] The medieval vernacular drama was more confident of its modes. To conceive of theater as a special game world furnishes a generally satisfactory solution, and other devices were employed as well. In the twelfth-century Anglo-Norman *Mystère d'Adam,* God is named (in the Latin stage directions) first as *Salvator,* and immediately afterwards as *Figura*; all His speeches in the text bear the latter designation.[87] It is not God, but a "figure" of God who plays. More characteristic of later medieval drama is a sudden abandonment of the dramatic role within the play itself. In the Chester cycle, when Christ has shown Himself resurrected to several apostles, including Thomas, He concludes the play with this speech:

> Who so to this will consent,
> that I am god omnipotent,
> as well as they that be present,
> my Darlinges shalbe aye.
>
> . . . .
>
> Whosoeuer of my father hath any mynd,
> or of my mother in any kynde,
> in heaven Bliss they shall it fynd,
> with out any woe.
>
> Christ geue you grace to take the way
> vnto that ioy that lasteth aye!
> for thers no night but ever day;
> for all you thither shall goe.[88]

Until the last quatrain the actor speaks as Christ. To sustain this role, he need only have blessed the spectators in the words Christ might have used, "I geue you grace to take the way." But instead, he steps out of character and invokes *Christ's* blessing upon them. The *Ludus Coventriae* episode of the *Woman Taken in Adultery* likewise ends with a speech technically outside Christ's role:

> Now god þat dyed ffor all mankende
> saue all þese pepyl both nyght and day
> and of oure synnys he us vnbynde
> hyȝe lorde of hevyn þat best may.[89]

The conclusion of the Towneley *Crucifixion* is of the same sort; Joseph and Nichodemus are taking Christ's body away for burial, but Nichodemus' final speech is not focused on the actor's body in their arms:

> It shall be so with outten nay.
> he that dyed on gud fryday
>   And crownyd was with thorne,
> Saue you all that now here be!
> That lord that thus wold dee
>   And rose on pasche morne.[90]

The Castell of Perseverance closes with the character of God leading the singing of *Te Deum laudamus*; the actor playing the resurrected Christ in the French *Passion de Semur* does the same thing.[91] Such moments are not frequent, but they should not be regarded as indications of naïve simplicity or careless writing; a sophisticated game conception of theater leads to them quite naturally.

On the strength of this evidence, I think we must dissent from the judgment of Hardin Craig that this drama had no "theory," no self-awareness as genre. The aim of the Corpus Christi drama was to celebrate and elucidate, never, not even temporarily, to deceive. It played action in "game"—not in "ernest"—within a world set apart, established by convention and obeying rules of its own. A lie designed to tell the truth about reality, the drama was understood as significant play.

We, for the most part, have to reconstruct this idea of theater as a historical phenomenon. It was the only kind of theater the Middle Ages knew.

Chapter Three

Corpus Christi Feast and the Impulse
toward Cycle Form

No aspect of the Corpus Christi cycles has received less attention than their formal artistic structure, yet it is precisely their size, their comprehensiveness, and their cyclical form that make them unique in the history of the English stage. They were not, as we know now, an unprecedented development in the drama of Europe: a group of plays, in Latin, staging actions from the Passion through Doomsday, was presented by clerics at Cividale in Italy on Whitsun in 1298; and in 1303 a similar cycle, somewhat amplified and including a play of the creation of Adam and Eve, was performed in the same place.[1] But that was in another country, a local phenomenon with no historical consequences that can be ascertained. Certainly those Englishmen present at the first performance of the York cycle in 1376 (if our earliest recorded performance was in fact the first) must have been astonished at the novelty and scope of the undertaking. Lacunae in the records will prevent us from ever writing a proper history of the early growth of these cycles. Using a different kind of evidence, I wish to discuss instead the genesis of an art form. In the course of my argument, I shall propose a new classification of the *kinds* of scriptural drama extant in England during the medieval period. Through a study of their essential differences, I shall attempt a new account of the impulses that led to the creation of a cycle-drama, paying particular attention to the influence of the Corpus Christi feast day which gave these cycles their name.

To attempt a useful classification of the kinds or categories of medieval drama in England is a hazardous undertaking, for the records, though numerous, are often fragmentary and unclear. The first distinction to be made when confronting this drama is the single distinction all scholars have made: some of it is in Latin and associated with the offices of the Church; some of it is in the vernacular. Within the latter category, it is customary to distinguish scriptural plays, morality plays, and dramatized lives of the Saints. The distinction is obvious but it does not go deep; it has led to the suppression of certain questions that need to be asked. Since Latin drama preceded drama in the vernacular, it is usually assumed that the one engendered the other, and that the Corpus Christi cycles, which are one kind of vernacular drama, must be traceable to the Latin drama of the Church. This is, I think, largely untrue; but before I can present an alternate account of the growth of cycle form, the reader must be provided with a new set of categories, at once simpler and more accurately descriptive of the range of scriptural drama. Categories are like spectacles: their quality determines how much you will see. I wish to offer a new pair.

The decisive change in the history of religious drama was probably not the change from Latin to the vernacular: that was inevitable and comparatively easy. It makes no difference to dramatic kind: even in English translation, Racine's *Phèdre* is a neoclassical tragedy. Nor need we associate the purely linguistic transition from Latin to the vernacular with the movement of the drama from church to marketplace. Vernacular sermons had been preached inside the church for centuries, and France and Germany both furnish a number of Latin dramatic texts with vernacular passages that were meant for performance inside the church.[2]

In England, the Shrewsbury Fragments, as they are called, exhibit a similar mixture of languages. Although part of a manuscript of Latin anthems intended for use inside the church, they are proper drama, a partbook of speeches for the Third Shepherd, the Third Mary, and one of the pilgrims to Emmaus. (The manuscript dates from the fifteenth century, but the dramatic fragments are certainly of an earlier date.)[3] In the comparatively minor detail of language they look forward to the later drama—they are mostly in English— but nothing about them looks forward to a drama cycle's completeness. They remain liturgical drama, and they have their mature vernacular descendants. The two-part play known as *Christ's Burial and Resurrection* is a good example. A rubric at its foot reads thus: "This is a play to be playede, on part on gud-friday after-none, & þe other part opon Ester-day after the resurrectione, In the morowe."[4] Here, though the performance was to be outside the church, the two parts are still attached to the liturgy cycle, and their mimesis of historical time is exact—three days intervene between the playing of the Entombment and the playing of the Resurrection. Their length (1,631 lines in all) marks a change from the earlier form of the Latin liturgical drama, but their artistic decorum and their lyric quality of lament and recollection display a deep kinship with it. Throughout England, villages and cities that did not possess cycles have left behind numerous records of "occasional" drama of this kind.[5] It is to such plays that the Latin drama of the Church led, not to the plays called Corpus Christi.

I would therefore suggest that we call the first of the two major kinds of scriptural drama in England "liturgical," but that we recognize that this kind was written in English as well as in Latin, for performance outside the church as well as within. Such plays, at their most elaborate, might include a series of episodes—for instance, an Annunciation, a Salutation, and a Nativity. But these are best called sequences, not cycles, for they are firmly anchored to their proper liturgical season: the final action of each is the action proper to the anniversary day on which it is performed. We can define it by its occasion: both the play and the church service would commemorate the same subject.[6] To play the *Magi* on Twelfth Night, in Latin or in English, in church or in civic hall, is perfectly straightforward: the Epiphany audience is the Epiphany congregation; twelve days earlier it celebrated the Nativity and twenty-eight days later it will celebrate the Purification. To play the *Magi* in, say, mid-June is another matter: to play it then, alone, would be to play it out of its proper time and season. Secular drama—*Volpone, The Sea Gull, Annie Get Your Gun* —can be suitably played at any time, but it is different with religious drama. The Christian story, alone among the histories and myths important to our culture, has imposed its rhythms upon the Western year, and we cannot play fragments of that story without respecting their place in the year's anniversary sequence. When I speak of liturgical drama I mean drama of this strict anniversary sort.

There is, of course, another kind of liturgical occasion, much rarer, which stands intentionally outside this sequence of anniversary moments: Trinity Sunday and Corpus Christi day are two notable examples, both of them outside the ritual "remembering" of the major events in Christ's life, from the Nativity through the Passion, Resurrection, Ascension, and Pentecost. Only after this anniversary sequence has run its course are these other feasts observed. One of them is particularly important to this study, for the second major kind of Scriptural drama in England was a comprehensive cycle-drama, of which the most widespread and important form was the Corpus Christi play. Plays by this name existed at Newcastle-upon-Tyne, Kendal, Preston, York, Beverley, Wakefield, Chester, Lincoln, Louth, Norwich, Ipswich, Worcester, and Coventry.[7] Besides these, there were two other cycles of a rather special character, and we may briefly note them here. One, from Cornwall, written in the old Cornish tongue, is a variant on the Corpus Christi form: it neglects the Nativity plays, and concludes with the Ascension. The other, the Skinners Well plays of London, seems genuinely to represent a different tradition and development.

It is difficult to discuss the genesis of the Cornish cycle because, although we have the actual playing text, we have no contemporary records of its performance. We do not know when it began, or on what days of the year it played, or who was responsible for the production. Lacking such facts, it is difficult to reconstruct the impulses that may have generated and shaped the cycle as we have it. For the great London cycles, reconstruction is impossible. There exist but a few records of performance, with only the briefest description of subject matter, and no texts whatever. We do know that the cycles were very long, lasting five days in 1384, four days in 1391, five days in 1409, seven days in 1411, and that they attracted large and distinguished audiences. We also know that their subject matter ranged from the Creation to the Day of Judgment, presenting "the history of the Old and New Testaments," and that they played on days having no great importance in the Church calendar: in 1384 they began on August 29, and in 1391 on July 18. In the surviving records, they are never called Corpus Christi plays. It seems likely that they included all the material we know to be part of the Corpus Christi cycles, plus a good deal more. We might expect them to have played additional Old Testament episodes, perhaps some of the legendary Childhood of Jesus, and a fully developed group of Ministry plays, in order to fill their playing time. They seem to have grown up independent of any specific liturgical occasion, and for that reason to have been formally influenced by none. William Fitzstephen wrote a famous description of London in the late twelfth century, in which he noted the number of plays—probably in Latin—available there. "Lundonia pro spectaculis theatralibus, pro ludis scenicis, ludos habet sanctiores, representationes miraculorum quae sancti confessores operati sunt, seu representationes passionum quibus claruit constantia martyrum."* But not until 1384 is there notice of the great cycle-play at Skinners Well,[8] and it is idle to guess at what was happening in the two centuries between. The London cycles undoubtedly have a history all their own, but it is one that cannot be written.

In contrast to the cycles of London and Cornwall, it is possible to discuss the genesis of the Corpus Christi play: we have extensive records, we have four cycle texts still extant, and we have information about the feast occasion it honored. These facts, put together, allow certain deductions and conclusions which are my real interest here. The distinction between the liturgical piece or sequence and the Corpus Christi cycle is of considerable importance,[9] but before it can be discussed further, we must first consider the relationship between these two during that long century from which few documents survive to tell us what the drama anywhere was doing. We must examine the fourteenth-century silence, and then the theories scholars have used to break it.

The period 1318–76 concerns us particularly because during those years the Corpus Christi drama was born and grew to maturity. The Feast of Corpus Christi was effectively established in 1311, and in 1318 a contemporary chronicler records: "Nota de festivitate Corporis Christi. Anno Domini Millesimo trecentesimo decimo octavo incepit festivitas de Corpore Christi generaliter celebrari per totam ecclesiam anglicanam."†[10] Our other terminus is established by a record of Corpus Christi plays in York in 1376, the first known mention of such drama;[11] in 1394 the pageant stations there are spoken of as *antiquitus assignatis*. The situation in Beverley (Yorkshire) was

---

* In place of theatrical spectacles and dramatic performances London has a more holy type of performance: representations of the miracles which the holy saints performed or of the sufferings by which the steadfastness of the martyrs became renowned.

† Note concerning the feast of Corpus Christi. In the year of Our Lord thirteen hundred and eighteen the feast of Corpus Christi began to be generally celebrated through the whole English church.

closely akin: its cycle is first recorded in 1377, and is mentioned again in 1390 as *antiqua consuetudo*.[12] We cannot know exactly when the cycles first began to take shape; we only know when our earliest records appear. But it is just possible to place in those intervening years a few relevant facts.

The *Holkham Bible Picture Book* seems to have been influenced by drama traditions, and if so, it suggests that full cycle form may have been achieved much earlier. It is not an illustrated Bible, but rather a sequence of pictures to which the Anglo-Norman text is in a sense merely decoration; it was probably made in London (a city whose plays we know little about). Divided intentionally into three parts (blank folios are left between each section), it shows in numerous small scenes these sequences: (1) the Creation, through Noah's exit from the ark; (2) the life of Christ; (3) the Last Things—the Fifteen Signs before Doomsday, the Second Coming, and the Last Judgment. In certain formal respects it resembles the mature English cycles: its poles are the same, it has the same center. Its probable date (*c.* 1326–31) is surprising, being much earlier than our first records of the Corpus Christi cycles.[13] Perhaps better than any other illuminated manuscript, this work can show us how the medieval drama, with its costumes, settings, and devices, might have looked in performance.

But the drama records themselves are meager and obscure: to know of a versified speech for Caiaphas on Palm Sunday (*c.* 1300) that may have involved impersonation in its reciting,[14] or of a Cambridge record (*c.* 1350) that speaks of expenses *in ludo filiorum Israelis* portioned out among members of the Corpus Christi Guild,[15] or of six lines of verse (in a sermon manuscript from about the same time) that might belong to a vernacular play of the Fall of Man,[16] is not to gain enough light to see far. It is clear that the rise of a prosperous middle class, the growth of towns, the development of city fairs, and the formation of religious and trade guilds were all circumstances favorable to the beginnings of an elaborate vernacular drama, just as there are good general reasons why it was slow in developing: the Black Death, the social unrest that led eventually to the Peasants' Revolt, and the fact that papal edict had in no way enjoined (or even suggested) the expression of the Corpus Christi feast in dramatic form, all help to explain the length of the interval.[17] Reasons can be given to explain the "documentary" silence as well, for until the plays became affairs of municipal importance, they were not noted in the records of towns and cities.[18] But the documentary silence remains.

With so few facts to work with, our only recourse is to theory. Scholars have traditionally held that in this period the Latin liturgical drama was being translated into the vernacular, and that its constituent plays were being combined into groups and cycles.[19] I want to examine this view very closely.

Behind this theory lies an assumption common to almost every study of the medieval drama ever written—the assumption that the Latin drama of the Church was both richly developed and widespread. This assumption has had long life because either of these epithets can be justified singly: if one is speaking of the total corpus of this drama, one can say it is rich and varied; if one is speaking of its total provenance, of the number of communities in Europe that had some Latin drama among the traditions of their church, one can say it was widespread. But not the two together. What seems never to be noticed (at least not at the moment when theories are made) is that this provenance pattern is almost entirely without density. Not only did most churches having Latin drama have only one or two short plays, but most often they had the *same* plays (that is, plays devoted to the same subjects); the repertoire of plays available in any given city was generally small. The most extensive collection of Latin drama that has come down to us, an Orléans manuscript known as the Fleury Playbook, contains ten plays, only five of which deal with subjects that ultimately appear in the great French Passion cycles or the English Corpus Christi plays. These five are the *Visitatio Sepulchri, Officium Stellae, Ordo Rachelis, Peregrinus,* and a *Resuscitatio Lazari.*[20] There is nothing like the beginnings of a cycle in this list, nor any visible impulse toward cyclic form. Yet it is unusually comprehensive. Most communities had merely a simple Christmas or Easter play (most commonly, the *Pastores* or *Visitatio Sepulchri*); some few, such as Bayeux, might add a *Peregrini.* Laon was nearly as rich as the home of the Fleury manuscript, having an *Ordo Joseph,* a *Prophetae,* and a Christmas play that combined an *Ordo Stelle* with an *Ordo Rachelis.*[21] As on the Continent, so too in England. The statutes of York Minster, which date from about 1255, provide for the *Pastores* and the *Stella* only.[22] The Shrewsbury Fragments give evidence of the drama available in another English city—Lichfield may be their true home—in providing for three plays, the *Pastores,* the *Quem quaeritis,* and the *Peregrini*. Lincoln Cathedral account books furnish our most complete English records of Latin drama, and they show continuous but limited dramatic activity. An Easter play of St. Thomas of India and a Christmas play of the Three Kings were performed through most of the fourteenth century; these later were replaced by a Salutation (at Christmas), and in the fifteenth century, long after the beginning of Corpus Christi cycles, an Assumption and Coronation of the Virgin was added.[23] Clearly the Latin liturgical drama, though spread widely over England and the Continent, was nevertheless scanty in any given community. This situation never radically altered simply because the house of God has its continuing concern with sacramental worship, not with dramatic mimesis. Though it nurtured certain plays under its roof, they were severely limited in length and expressive potential. They crowned the liturgical feast day with a brief representation by clerics of the historical events of that day, but they were never substitutes for the liturgical observance itself. This environmental control upon the growth of the Latin drama had important consequences.

For although the zeal of the Reformation destroyed many of the manuscripts in England that were likely to contain Latin plays, this religious upheaval affected only a small part of the Continent, and the records there may be taken as a fair guide. Thirteenth-century records at York specify only that a play of the Shepherds (for Christmas) and a play of the Magi (for Epiphany) were presented at York Minster, and it seems probable, in the light of the Continental records, that this repertoire continued unexpanded into the next century. Thus it is difficult to ascribe far-reaching implications to Mary Marshall's conclusion: "The tradition of the liturgical drama established certain basic modes of dramatizing the materials of sacred history which persisted through the course of mediaeval religious drama."[24] And Hardin Craig's account of the period builds upon the same insubstantial evidence: the drama, he has maintained, "passed from Latin to English by a method of repeating and amplifying the Latin texts in the vernacular.... What seems to have been done was to transfer to Corpus Christi day and to arrange, in the extensive cyclic form, plays [developed from Latin originals] already of considerable development....

The same cycle was not borrowed, but other places constructed out of their own local plays similar cycles."[25] It will not do to argue as though the total range of Latin liturgical drama in Europe was at the disposal of any local versifier asked to produce an episode for a cycle:[26] texts of sufficient variety and adequate distribution were not available as models. Since we lack a satisfactory set of possible dramatic parents, it is of little use to develop theories of blood-descent.[27]

There is still another argument against postulating the development of vernacular cycles from Latin liturgical plays: the theory neglects the real availability of other adequate sources. The drama of the Church was local and uneven, but the liturgy of the Church was available everywhere, and what is more, available in its total richness. That the Latin drama grew out of the liturgy has never been in doubt; a learned and little-known study by Edward M. Clark has established a similar connection between the liturgy and the vernacular cycles.[28] Common sense would seem to point to an explanation along lines such as these: just as dozens of simple versions of the *Quem quaeritis* scene at the sepulchre could evolve in Latin all over Europe, without any deeper interrelationship than their independent origin from the same source, so could vernacular plays concerning these same events be written independent of Latin dramatic traditions. If, for example, Chester Cathedral had a *Pastores* in Latin, then this text (or simply the experience of having often seen it played) might have exerted some influence upon the original author of the *Shepherds' Play* in the civic cycle. Lacking an actual text, we cannot tell. But we may reasonably reject theories that try to prove this *Shepherds' Play* developed from a version extant only in a manuscript from Rouen. Similarly, if Chester had no version of the Purification of Mary in its Latin repertoire, that fact would not at all prevent the development of such a play in the civic cycle. The lay dramatists could turn to the liturgy of the actual feast; they knew the basic Vulgate story and its amplification in legend; and they shared with the Church in general certain received theological understandings of that story. Whatever can be "invented" once can be invented again and again. The influence of the liturgy on the cycle-drama was direct—akin to that of the Vulgate and the vernacular religious poems—but it is unlikely that the Latin drama of the Church was often midwife at its birth. Liturgical plays in Latin probably had some few direct descendants in English, but they were not the Corpus Christi cycles. Generation is within kind. A new account of what was happening in these decades is needed.[29]

I think it extremely probable that the thirteenth and early fourteenth centuries were a period of rest in the development of the drama; the Latin liturgical plays had reached their full development, and some were perhaps already being played in English in the churches. These plays would continue to be performed at the proper time in the Church year, as they were in Lincoln until 1561.[30] They were adequate to their purpose, they were capable of great ceremonial beauty, and they could rely on the emotion of the liturgical occasion to deepen the congregation's experience of their meaning. There was no external cause for dynamic change. A form had found its fullness, its fruition. There is no "restlessness" about these plays, no impulse toward a comprehensive cycle form. In the *Carmina Burana* manuscript from Benediktbeuern, a Christmas play and a Passion play have each linked together several short related scenes, a technique that might in time have spread further; but it was used only to allow a larger narrative line, to tell a central Christian story in more detail. These combinations I have called *sequences*; they differ from the object of this study, which is, rather, the origin of a cycle that tells the Christian story of the world from its beginning to the end of time.

Our first inquiry must be into the reasons underlying the stability of this liturgical drama, its lack of an impulse toward cyclic growth. The answer, quite simply, depends upon the nature of the Church year. It has its own completeness, celebrating on the proper calendar days all the major events of Christ's life. These feasts provide the first-level context for the Latin plays we have been discussing: it is possible to play the *Pastores* as the only play of the year, without feeling it to be incomplete as a unit of meaning, for the Church year itself is the play's total unit of meaning. The Feast of the Innocents will be celebrated on its day, whether an *Ordo Rachelis* is played or not. Each year there will be Good Friday, Easter Sunday, the day of the Ascension. Christ's life is the center of Christian ritual, and no important event in it lacks liturgical notice.

But even Christ's life is a unit of meaning incomplete in itself: a second-level context is needed to relate Him to what has gone before (the Old Testament beginnings) and to what is to come after (the Last Things and the Judgment). For the Incarnation was made necessary by the Fall; it was necessary in order that the outcome of historical time might be altered, that the Last Day might be not simply a reiteration of the justice which underlay the curse pronounced on Adam. Here, too, the liturgy provides. The seventy days preceding Easter establish the Old Testament beginnings; during that time, the historical necessity of Christ's sacrifice is narrated. Caxton's version of the *Golden Legend* is (among other things) a convenient handbook to the liturgical year, recounting in their proper time the stories central to the liturgy. The year's reading for the Church is set out in this sequence:

The Sunday of Septuagesima beginneth the story of the Bible, in which is read the legend and story of Adam which followeth.

Here beginneth the History of Noah. The first Sunday in Sexagesima.

The Sunday called Quinquagesima is read in the church the history of the holy patriarch Abraham which was the son of Terah.

Here beginneth the life of Isaac, with the history of Esau and of Jacob, which is read in the Church the Second Sunday of Lent.

Here beginneth the history of Joseph and his brethren, which is read the third Sunday in Lent.

Here next followeth the history of Moses, which is read in the Church on Mid-lent Sunday.[31]

And a short paragraph sums up the rest:

The histories of the kings, which is read in holy church from the first Sunday after Trinity Sunday, unto the first Sunday of August. And in the month of August is read the Book of Sapience, and in the month of September be read the histories of Job, of Tobit, and of Judith, and in October the history of the Maccabees, and in November the book of Ezechiel and his visions. And in December the history of Advent, and the book of Isaiah unto Christmas and after the feast of Epiphany unto Septuagesima be read the Epistles of Paul. And this is the rule of the temporal through the year.[32]

During Holy Week itself, from Palm Sunday to the Great Sabbath, the Responsories would recite in sequence the last events before the

Resurrection. From Easter to Pentecost the readings are concerned with Christ's appearances after the Resurrection, with the Ascension, and with the sending of the Holy Ghost. The other great portion of the Christian story occupies the four weeks of Advent, when the readings are concerned with the Last Things: the *Sponsus* parable, the fifteen days before Doomsday, and the Last Judgment are all incorporated into responses, antiphons, and versicles. Sources for the *lectiones* included two sermons on the end of the world, the *Sermo beati Maximi episcopi* and the *Omelia beati Gregorii papae*,[33] and the Sundays of Advent draw stern lessons from Isaiah.[34] In the last week of Advent, the mood of the liturgy changes to joy as the Nativity approaches; the history of Christ's birth is read in the weeks that follow.

The progress of this Church year is in the hands of the clergy, who sustain it on behalf of the people. The actual *lectiones* under discussion are read at Matins in the three lessons of that office; they are read in Latin, and are not specifically addressed to the laity. Yet their influence pervades the offices of the rest of the day and often furnishes the theme for the day's sermon, a vernacular homily directed to the congregation.[35] The Latin drama was set into this liturgical cycle in a way that was purely ornamental—the liturgy was complete without it, and to dramatize an event was merely to reiterate a statement and celebration already made in purely liturgical terms. Thus, the Latin drama of the Church relied upon the Church for its contextual completeness. Its rhythms were leisurely, and annually stated in full. While the drama remained attached to its proper days in the Church calendar, it had no need to seek completion in itself. The drama was at rest.

The Corpus Christi cycle differs chiefly in supplying this contextual completeness in purely dramatic terms, for reasons that seem to be closely connected with the nature of the Corpus Christi feast. The history of the feast begins with the publication of the bull *Transiturus* by Pope Urban IV in 1264, but his death shortly thereafter prevented its implementation. Not until Clement V again ordered the adoption of the feast at the Council of Vienne in 1311 (incorporating Urban's bull into his decree) did it become effective.[36] Historians of the drama are not unfamiliar with these facts, but no one has provided any full account of the underlying reasons for the establishment of the feast. The reasons, as stated by Urban IV, turn out to be important:

In die namque Cene Domini, quo die ipse Christus hoc instituit sacramentum, universalis ecclesia pro penitentium reconciliatione, sacri confectione
crismatis, adimpletione mandati circa lotionem pedum et aliis plurimum
occupata plene vacare non potest celebritati huius maximi sacramenti.*[37]

It was not that the institution of the Holy Sacrament went unobserved
during the rest of the liturgical year—it is commemorated on Maundy
Thursday, the day of the Last Supper, with full solemnity. But Urban
instituted a feast date that was not an anniversary so that this maximum gift could be celebrated separately (Maundy Thursday is over-
crowded with significant events) and, more important, so that this
gift from God of Himself might be a source of rejoicing. During the
Passion week, Christians properly meditate on the terror of the Sacrifice and the sorrow and shame of human sin that requires such ex-
piation. The bull of Urban IV stresses, instead, the joy that the new
feast is to occasion:

Hec est commemoratio gloriosa, que fidelium animos replet gaudio salutari
et cum infusione letitie devotionis lacrimas subministrat. Exultamus nimi-
rum nostram rememorando liberationem et recolendo passionem domini-
cam, per quam liberati sumus, vix lacrimas continemus. . . . quia in ea et
gaudemus pie lacrimantes et lacrimamus devote gaudentes, letas habendo
lacrimas et letitiam lacrimantem.

In ipsa quinta feria devote turbe fidelium propter hoc ad ecclesias affectuose
concurrant, ut tunc cleri et populi pariter congaudentes in cantica laudis
surgant, tunc omnium corda et vota, ora et labia ymnos personent letitie
salutaris.†[38]

---

* For on the day of the Supper of Our Lord—the day on which Christ himself instituted this sacrament—the entire church, fully occupied as she is with the reconcilia-
tion of penitents, the ritual administration of the holy oil, the fulfilling of the commandment concerning the washing of feet, and other matters, does not have adequate
time for the celebration of this greatest sacrament.
† This is the glorious act of remembrance, which fills the minds of the faithful with
joy at their salvation and brings them tears mingled with a flood of reverent joy. For
surely we exult as we recall our deliverance and scarce contain our tears as we commemorate the passion of Our Lord through which we were freed. . . . because on this
occasion we both rejoice amid pious weeping and weep amid reverent rejoicing, joyful
in our lamentation and woeful in our jubilation.
    It is for this reason that on the same Thursday the devout crowds of the faithful
should flock eagerly to the churches—in order that clergy and congregation, joining
one another in equal rejoicing, may rise in a song of praise, and then, from the hearts
and desires, from the mouths and lips of all, there may sound forth hymns of joy at
man's salvation.

The office that St. Thomas Aquinas composed for the Mass of Corpus Christi also commands this joy, as in the following hymn:

> Sit laus plena, sit sonora,
>   sit jocunda, sit decora
>   mentis jubilatio;
> Dies enim solemnis agitur,
>   in qua mensae prima recolitur
>   hujus institutio.*[39]

The *Golden Legend* devotes a chapter to the feast, and in it discusses the meaning of the day as revealed in the reasons for which Christ instituted the Sacrament: "To the end that they that were sorrowfull and heavy for his absence, should thereby have some solace singular." This singular solace can only be celebrated outside the regular liturgical sequence, for within it a mood of rejoicing is impossible: "The surplus of the service of the same day apperteineth to the passion of our Lord." Therefore Corpus Christi day is set aside, the Thursday after Trinity Sunday, so that it "may be hallowed more solemnly."[40] This last phrase looks stranger than it is: "solemnly" then meant something close to "highly" or "worthily" and does not imply our later sense of "grave" or "somber," the mood of its Maundy Thursday occasion.

The date set aside for the feast can vary from May 23 to June 24. It is weather for an outdoor festival, and someone somewhere (later, many persons in many places, perhaps in emulation), had the idea to stage a play on that day. The history of this decision cannot be written, for no records exist. But it is possible to draw certain inferences concerning the range of dramatic possibilities open to them. After Easter, Ascension day, and Pentecost have passed and the narrative sequence of Christ's life as celebrated in the liturgy has been concluded, there follows a sort of limbo in the Church year, between Pentecost and Advent, in which the readings draw on the lesser books of the Old Testament and saints' days furnish the only anniversary occasions. The feast of Corpus Christi was fixed within this period, and it seems clear that only two kinds of dramatic subject were possible on that day.

The first of these is interesting, not because it was very common, but

---

* Let our praise be full and resounding, let our soul's jubilation be joyful and seemly; for a solemn day is being observed upon which the first institution of this table is commemorated.

because making the other choice involved rejecting this alternative. We may learn more about the Corpus Christi cycles by noting that it was open to Church or civic authority to celebrate the feast dramatically in another way: by playing Miracles of the Host.

The dogma of Transubstantiation had been promulgated in 1215, and it was undoubtedly a force behind the issuance of the Corpus Christi decrees of 1264 and 1311. A large number of legendary tales had grown up to prove that Christ—in His Real Presence—is in the consecrated bread and wine. In these stories, Christ is often miraculously seen in the Eucharistic wafer, as man or as little child, and sometimes His fresh blood is seen to run from it. Usually the miracle takes place before the eyes of a doubter—often a Jew—who is thereupon converted to true faith. Sermons on Corpus Christi day tended to use such stories as *exempla,* for this day, above all others, seemed their suitable occasion. The sermon for Corpus Christi day in Mirk's *Festial* closes with five narrations designed to establish faith in the miraculous power of the Eucharist; a metrical sermon for Corpus Christi day (appearing in the Vernon MS and elsewhere) uses two such stories; *Handlyng Synne* relates seven miracles of the Mass; and Nicholas Love, in concluding his translation of the pseudo-Bonaventura *Mirrour of the Blessed Lyf of Jesu Christ,* appends a "schort tretys" on Corpus Christi that chiefly recounts such miracles.[41] It was a ready theme for preachers and writers discussing the feast, and it may have found dramatic expression as well.

Two records in particular invite such a belief. There is first of all the record (dated 1389) of an *interludium* that was the duty of the guild of Corpus Christi at Bury St. Edmunds, though the record gives no clues either to its subject or to the manner of performance.[42] Second, there is evidence that at Chester, until the Reformation, the Corpus Christi cycle (which was eventually transferred to Whitsun) existed side by side with a procession and a new play on Corpus Christi day itself:

> Appon the day of corpus (ch)r(ist)i
> The blessed Sacrament caried shalbe
> And A play sett forth by the clergye
> In honor of the fest.[43]

Neither this notice nor that of the Bury St. Edmunds *interludium* implies a performance of great length: the subject of both may well have been miracles of the Host.[44] The single extant drama text that concerns such a miracle, the Croxton *Play of the Sacrament,* shows what such a play might have been like, although this particular example, apparently meant for a group of traveling players, is not addressed to a Corpus Christi occasion.[45] We may note too that this kind of subject must have become more important after Wycliffe began his attacks on the dogma of Transubstantiation in 1381; certainly the short treatise on Corpus Christi penned by Nicholas Love bristles with anti-Lollard indignation.[46]

Nevertheless it is clear that the primary dramatic response to the Corpus Christi occasion was of a quite different sort. To English ears "the plaie called Corpus Christi" meant a play of the history of the world, from Creation to Judgment.

This was a very different way of "celebrating" this maximum gift of God: instead of concentrating on the Sacrament's temporal power to work miracles, to convince and convert, it looked instead on its eternal power to alter the destiny of the human race. The Eucharist serves to recall both the Last Supper and the flesh and blood of Christ offered on the cross—events about which it is possible to rejoice only when they are related to man's fall, Christ's Resurrection, and the Last Judgment. Except for this sacrifice and gift, even the good would have been damned, guilty of Adam's sin. To play the whole story, then, is in the deepest sense to *celebrate* the Corpus Christi sacrament, to explain its necessity and power, and to show how that power will be made manifest at the end of the world. The homily, *Septem miracula de corpore cristi,* included in both *Handlyng Synne* and the Vernon MS, precedes its stories with a preamble that can explain why the Middle Ages characteristically played cycles rather than "miracle" plays on this day:

> Þis schulde leeue vche cristen mon
> And lerne þe treuþe of on þat con:
> Þat þe bred þat sacrefyed is
> On þe Auter, is godus flesch,
> fflesch and blod, þer hit is leid,
> Þorwh þe wordus þe prest haþ seid;
> Þat lihte wiþ-Inne þe virgine Marie
> And on þe Rode for vs wolde dye
> And from deþ to lyue a-Ros,
> God and Mon, in Miht and loos.

ffor hose troweþ not þis cler
In þe sacrament of þe Auter,
He schal neuere þe blisse a-byde,
ffor no þing þat him may be-tyde.[47]

The power of the Sacrament must be understood as well as believed in, and this requisite understanding is centered on a narrative. Because the Corpus Christi feast is fixed to a date outside regular liturgical "anniversary" time, and because it enjoins a *celebration* of the Eucharistic gift, the English Middle Ages played the whole story, from man's fall to the salvation of the blessed at the Judgment, to reveal the central episode—the Passion—as joyful in meaning. Of the two subjects possible on that day, the medieval guilds almost uniformly chose the one that was greater in importance as well as in dramatic potential. I do not argue that cycles could only have been born in response to the Corpus Christi occasion—the Cividale records make such a view untenable—but rather that in England the decision to honor the Corpus Christi feast with religious plays determined in its turn the choice of dramatic subject and form.

These facts are perhaps ultimately more important than those records which were never made or have not survived, that might have documented the history of the Corpus Christi plays between 1318 and 1376. Somehow the cycles took form, and the form they took was determined by the facts we have been examining.[48] They are the facts behind the facts.

Once these cycles had achieved formal maturity, they could be played whenever the community wished. Lincoln in time seems to have played its cycle on St. Anne's day (July 26). Chester eventually moved its cycle to Whitsun.[49] Both communities continued to call them Corpus Christi plays. The *Ludus Coventriae* Proclamation says, quite simply, that the cycle will be played on "sunday next," although Corpus Christi day is always a Thursday. By the middle of the fifteenth century we are dealing with a specific kind of drama, not merely with a play presented on a specific date. It was Corpus Christi feast that caused them to be written, and influenced their subject and form, but when fully grown they were free of their birthday. The plays of the Last Supper make no specific reference to the Corpus Christi feast, nor does the play of *Pentecost* at Chester mention its Whitsun occasion. The cycles, because of their completeness, had wholly freed themselves from ritual time.

This account of the genesis of a medieval art form controls in its turn the way we describe the dramatic life articulated within it. The old literary-history account of how this drama began in Latin inside the church and then moved out through the porch and churchyard to its final home in the marketplace, meanwhile undergoing translation into the vernacular and displaying an increasing "secularization" of matter and manner, will no longer stand. Other scholars in recent years have attacked one part or another of this traditional view, the best of them basing their arguments on a closer and truer reading of the texts or on a study of the sympathetic involvement of Church authorities with this drama right up to its demise, nearly two hundred years after it was first recorded. I have here presented reasons for defining even the impulses behind cycle form in religious terms. What we find in this drama is not in fact an opposition of interests—the religious and the secular, the devotional and the profane—but rather a single coherent dramatic intent. To the general uses of the medieval dramatic image already discussed in Chapter 1, we must now add another, unique to the Corpus Christi kind—the capacity of the cycle-drama to celebrate in its fullest significance what the Middle Ages took to be the supreme gift of God, His body for man's sin.

This largest use of the drama was made possible only by the cycles' remarkable length and inclusiveness. Yet they were not totally comprehensive: choices were made, and a formally coherent sequence of actions was established. One sequence is common to all the surviving English cycle texts, and, along with their parent feast occasion it is a most important link between them. I shall offer new ways of describing their formal coherence in the following chapter; but I must first set down what the Corpus Christi form, in its essentials, seems to be.

Four full cycle texts have come down to us—from Chester, York, Wakefield (Towneley), and N-town (the problematic home of the *Ludus Coventriae*). We also have a complete list of the plays of the Beverley cycle from about 1520; although that cycle has not survived, it was recorded as early as 1377, and again in 1390.* Working with these five cycles, we may usefully seek to isolate a kind of *proto* Corpus

* The 1390 record lists thirty-eight crafts as having plays but does not name the plays; the 1520 record lists thirty-six plays but does not name the responsible crafts (see Chambers, *Mediaeval Stage,* II, 339–41). Thus in 1520 there were two plays less than in 1390, but we cannot tell which plays were lost or incorporated into other plays.

Christi play, the generic thing-in-itself, the irreducible core. For while each cycle has a distinct individuality, they are the same kind of drama, and to understand the kind we must search for those component parts that are essential, that declare identity. This protocycle—offered not as a mysterious "parent cycle" but simply as the essential structure gradually achieved by the various cycles in probably various ways— consists at the very least of these episodes:

> The Fall of Lucifer
> The Creation and Fall of Man
> Cain and Abel
> Noah and the Flood
> Abraham and Isaac
> The Nativity (Annunciation to Jesus and the Doctors)
> The Raising of Lazarus (the only Ministry play staged by
>   all cycles)
> The Passion (Conspiracy to Harrowing of Hell)
> The Resurrection (Setting of the Watch to the Ascension)
> Doomsday

This outline has a fivefold authority; each subject in it appears in the four extant cycles and the Beverley list.[50] In my discussion of principles of selection, I shall call these episodes plays of the first priority. It will be clear that this skeleton cycle already satisfies the inner demands of its central story, the life of Christ, by referring it to the beginning and end of historical time; the satisfaction of this need is the crucial difference between the cycles and drama that is liturgical in kind.

Because the records are occasionally incomplete or obscure, we must take this analysis one stage further and determine which plays can be regarded as second in priority—plays that occur in at least four of the five cycles named above. These are:

Moses (Exodus, or Laws, or both) . .	Beverley excepted
The Prophets	Beverley excepted
The Baptism	Chester excepted
The Temptation	Towneley excepted
The Assumption and Coronation	
of the Virgin	Towneley excepted[51]

We can be certain only of a fourfold authority for these plays, but it is probable that some of them were in fact part of that one cycle that seems to lack them. Twelve leaves are missing from the Towneley manuscript, between the end (or near-end) of the *Ascension* play and the play of the *Judgment*.[52] Two full-length plays could easily have been contained in twelve leaves, and one of them was almost certainly the Assumption and Coronation of the Virgin. The loss of the Virgin play from this manuscript was probably due to the same Reformation zeal that caused its suppression in Chester.[53] As for the Beverley record, since it is no more than a brief list, it is of value mainly for what it takes the trouble to state, not for what it leaves out. The fact that the Moses play and the Prophets play do not appear on the list is not necessarily proof they were not once in the cycle—in 1390 there were two more plays than there were in 1520, but we do not know what was lost. Alternately, Moses and the Prophets may have been played as incidents in episodes called by other names. Individual plays were often subdivided and often consolidated, according to city fortunes and the capabilities of the crafts. The York records, for example, do not list a separate Prophets play; but having the cycle text, we know that an abridged version has been attached to the *Annunciation* by way of a prologue.[54] The same may have been true of the later Beverley cycle. Similarly, if we lacked the Chester text, we might not guess that it includes Moses as part of a play in which Balaam and Balaack furnish the central episode, and which is followed in turn by the Prophets. This second-priority group of plays, in short, is organized around certain omissions that may not in fact be meaningful; at the very least, since the evidence allows no more confident conclusion, these plays bear a fourfold authority. The two groups together are sufficiently important to be termed a protocycle, and to be made the object of a generic study.

This essential Corpus Christi form is not incompatible with the far more fragmentary records of other communities that staged such plays. The Coventry cycle, the most famous of its time, was made up of ten plays, of which only two are extant, though the contents of four others are known. The information we have can be shown in this way:

> Shearmen and Taylors: Annunciation, Nativity, Innocents
>   (play extant)
> Weavers: Purification and Doctors (play extant)
> Smiths: Trials of Jesus and Crucifixion
> Cappers: Harrowing of Hell, Resurrection, Appearances to
>   Disciples

Mercers: Death and Assumption of Mary, Mary's appearance
    to Thomas
Drapers: Doomsday

The subjects of the other four plays in the cycle are unknown. Since
the Coventry plays were extremely large in scale (each is really a
sequence), and since the obligatory New Testament material is already substantially covered in the above list, it is quite likely that two
of the four unknown plays dealt with Old Testament subjects. Such
a likelihood has been admitted by the editor of the extant plays in his
latest edition.[55]

The cycle at Newcastle-upon-Tyne, from which the *Noah* play
alone survives, is also recorded only in part. It included the following:

Creation of Adam
Noah's Ark
Offering of Isaac
Israel in Egypt
Kings of Cologne
Flight into Egypt
Baptism
Last Supper
Bearing of the Cross
Burial of Christ
Descent into Hell
Burial of Our Lady.

But we know there were at least ten other plays, possibly fifteen,
making a cycle of between twenty-two and twenty-seven plays.[56] As
with the Coventry cycle, we can only guess at their contents. I would
offer a guess based upon a strange formal disparity between the two.
The Coventry list is complete at one end, with an *Assumption of
Mary* and a *Doomsday* play; the Newcastle list is substantially complete at the other, indicating a richly developed Old Testament beginning, but no eschatological end. With both we have a great deal of
unspecified material to charge against guilds we know to have been
involved. In view of this, we may assert the strong probability that
each cycle presented the triad we have found elsewhere: first things,
last things, and the life of Christ between.

The records from Norwich are curious. A list of 1527 gives only
the following plays:

Creation of the World
Hell Cart (presumably the Fall of Lucifer)
Paradise
Cain and Abel
Noah's Ship
Abraham and Isaac
Moses and Aaron with the Children of Israel and Pharaoh with
    His Knights
Conflict of David and Goliath
The Birth of Christ with Shepherds and Three Kings of Cologne
The Baptism of Christ
The Resurrection
The Holy Ghost[57]

The list is, of course, a late one; it is included in a request from the members of St. Luke's Guild that the cycle be made the responsibility of all the crafts of the town, for it had brought them close to bankruptcy. Assignments to the other crafts were made in this list. The financial difficulties of St. Luke's Guild seem to have meant artistic difficulties for the cycle, if this list is a true indication of its state either before or after 1527. Only two plays are notably missing—the Passion and the Doomsday—but they are important enough to cast doubt on the whole. The Passion is certainly necessary to a play that calls itself Corpus Christi, and since the selection from the rest of Christ's life (Nativity, Baptism, Resurrection, Pentecost) so clearly demands it, it seems unlikely that the cycle was originally conceived without it. Moreover, since the sequence of Old Testament plays is otherwise complete (Chapter 4 will make clear the basis of this judgment), it would appear that this was once a perfectly articulated cycle, in 1527 retaining its true formal design only in its early sequence. We cannot know for certain; but if we must limit ourselves to this list, we had best recognize it as the record of a civic authority that never rose to the Corpus Christi occasion with the sustained intelligence characteristic of the six or seven other English towns whose records survive in greater detail.

In summary, then, the formally significant material of the Corpus Christi cycles can be arranged so:

FIRST PRIORITY	SECOND PRIORITY
The Fall of Lucifer	
The Creation and Fall of Man	
Cain and Abel	
Noah and the Flood	
Abraham and Isaac	
	Moses and the Exodus, and/or Moses and the Laws
	The Prophets
Nativity plays	
	The Baptism
	The Temptation
The Raising of Lazarus	
Passion plays	
Resurrection plays	
	The Assumption and Coronation of the Virgin
Doomsday	

This protocycle will be the object of our attention in the following chapter. Because it forms the common structure of the four English cycles that are the subject of this book, we may put to it our most searching questions about how the Corpus Christi play is constructed, why its essential episodes are essential, and in what manner form in this drama governs and expresses meaning. My most immediate search will be to discover the principles of selection that underlie this series of episodes—the reasons why some stories are included and others excluded. I shall write only about those that seem genuinely to need explanation; there is no present need to discuss the Nativity, Passion, and Resurrection groups as such, for the importance of their subject matter is obvious, and all the cycles develop them generously. There are, it is true, several interesting variations—Chester neglects the Baptism, Towneley neglects the Temptation. But such omissions do not imply value judgments on the importance of that material in the same way as does the choice of Old Testament story, simply because the cycles stage so much larger a share of Christ's life. Nor do we need to consider here the inclusion of plays concerning the death, assumption, and coronation of the Virgin. The Middle Ages loved Mary, next to the Son, and in staging His life, they allowed her story an independent dignity within it.[58] Rather it is the Old Testament plays that chiefly require scrutiny. The Christian story begins with the Fall of Man and ends with Doomsday, termini perfectly adequate in themselves to make sense of the Nativity-Passion-Resurrection story. There is no need for filling. Yet these cycles play more than the skeletal beginning and end: indeed, they play substantially the same additional episodes. (The French *Passion de Semur* stages Adam and Eve, the Flood, the Sacrifice of Isaac, Moses and the Prophets,[59] in exactly the protocycle sequence, and the Cornish cycle includes all these as well, except that plays concerning David take the place of the Prophets.) The reason for these similarities probably has little to do with cycle interborrowings, or with literary accident, much less with a paucity of material from which to choose. The Old Testament is full of splendid stories, many of them equal or superior in color, action, and character interest to those dramatized; yet these others are largely passed over without apology or explanation. The following pages will seek to establish a series of principles of selection that can explain the form in which the cycles have come down to us.

Chapter Four

Corpus Christi Form: Principles of Selection

In the Accademia at Venice there is a large painting by Marco Basaiti (*c.* 1470–1530) called *L'Orazione nell'orto*. It is not one of the great treasures of that distinguished gallery, but its image will be worth keeping in mind in the pages that follow. Through a formal arch, we see in the middle distance the garden of Gethsemane with Christ praying and the three chosen disciples sleeping; in the foreground, standing on either side of the arch, are two friars, a bishop, and a saint; one friar reverently holds a holy book while the other studies in the pages of a similar volume. One way of reading this picture is as a statement about received Christianity: scriptural history is seen through an arch of scholasticism, commentary frames the event. The arch determines our field of vision, our angle of sight; it includes, and excludes, and it was the common inheritance of the Middle Ages.

The authors of the great Corpus Christi cycles did not themselves select the incidents to be dramatized. They were builders, not architects. Other men before them had determined a hierarchy of significant event in Scripture, and their choice decisively influenced all art forms for several centuries. It is for this reason that one can speak of the formal intentions of the medieval drama, even though we do not know the names, the numbers, or the sequence of the contributors. All these anonymous writers were engaged in translating into drama a story whose shape and meaning had already been definitively formulated by the Doctors of the Church. By a judicious use of popular religious commentary, and by occasional direct reference to the Fathers, we have access to a body of critical thought that was, in fact, instrumental in the making of this drama. The basic source was, of course, the Bible, but patristic commentary determined the form the matter would take. We must not think of these dramatists as searching the pages of the Bible, toying now with the idea of dramatizing

Lot's exit from the cities of the plain, now with Ruth among the alien corn, though the first would have provided great spectacle, the second moving sentiment, both greatly prized by medieval audiences. The scale of their drama was large, but it was barely large enough for all the things that were essential. The Chester *Expositor* apologizes:

> This storye all if we shold fong,
> to playe this moneth it were to longe;
> wherfore most frutefull there amonge
> we taken, as shall be sene.[1]

The selection of the "most frutefull" matter had been made long before the feast of Corpus Christi was first celebrated.

The authors of the Corpus Christi plays were for the most part clerics, and this body of common doctrine was the subject of much of their formal education. The audience, mostly lay, mostly illiterate, acquired their knowledge of it at second hand, but in several forms. It was the subject of the sermons they heard, and it exercised upon the visual arts—the stained glass, the altarpieces, the wall paintings, and the sculpture of the church—exactly the same "selective" authority. The dramatists simply took over certain significant patterns that had long been observed and studied in the Bible narrative, and by simplifying, abridging, or neglecting entirely the mass of incident and detail that surrounds them, they produced a cycle sequence charged with theological meaning—strong, simple, and formally coherent.

I have already suggested that the nature of the Corpus Christi liturgical occasion made necessary a cycle form sufficiently comprehensive to present the Sacrament of the Altar, and the Passion it commemorates, as a source of joy. We could say as well that a story seeks to complete itself, to continue until all its problems, conflicts, and histories are resolved; without the dramatists' needing to know Aristotle, something like Aristotle's "beginning, middle, and end" may be claimed for these cycles. But it is possible to be theologically more explicit about the cycle's skeleton story, for it staged the Three Advents of God as we find them set out in a medieval sermon:

Frendes, for a processe ȝe shull vndirstond þat I fynde in holy writt iij commynges of oure Lord; the first was qwen þat he com to make man; the secound was qwhen he com to bie man; and þe iij shall be qwen he shall com to deme man.[2]

In an age of religious faith, it is not surprising that the moments judged to be most important in human history are those in which God openly and decisively intervenes. The central Advent is never celebrated without reference both ways in time, to the first coming and the last. The *Golden Legend* describes one of the seven anthems of Advent thus: "We cry: O Rex gentium, veni et salva hominem quem de limo formasti, O thou King of peoples come and save the man that thou has formed of the slime of the earth."[3] The Church prepares to celebrate the birth of Christ by recalling His earlier Advent as the creating Logos—He who *made* man now comes *as* Man—but the address is also to the future: "Then let us pray that we may in this holy time so receive him, that at the day of judgment we may be received into his everlasting bliss."[4] God deals with man as Creator, Saviour, and Judge. Seeing these Advents on the Corpus Christi stage, we would notice particularly their differences from one another: the God of Creation comes in majesty and grandeur, God as Redeemer comes to be born among the poor and the lowly, and God as Judge comes as the Son, still clothed in flesh and wounds but with an altered aspect, described metaphorically in the *Golden Legend*: "The Son of Justice, Jesu Christ, shall be then so dark that no man shall dare know him."[5] The staging of the three Advents of God is central both to the structure and to the meaning of our protocycle.

An essential part of the first Advent is, of course, the Fall of Man. That man was created perfect matters little to his history or destiny, for he disobeyed the command of God almost at once; by eating of the fruit of the Tree of Knowledge he changed his own nature. The Fall became a kind of datum, a given fact, from which everything else follows: it made necessary the Incarnation, and this created a direct relationship between Adam and Christ which in turn shaped the understanding of the Redemption and the manner of its working out. St. Paul (Rom. 5:15; I Cor. 15:21–22, 45) had spoken of Christ as Second Adam, and the Church Fathers pondered the further significance of this relationship. St. Irenaeus termed it a *recapitulation*: Christ was tempted by Satan but did not fall, and He was obedient to the will of God, even unto His death.[6] Urban IV made reference to this doctrine in his bull instituting the feast of Corpus Christi: "De illo siquidem gustu dicitur: *Quocumque die comederis, morte morieris*; de isto autem legitur: *Si quis manducaverit ex hoc pane, vivet in aeternum.**⁷ The fruit eaten by Adam brought death; to eat of Christ's body brings everlasting life. The necessity of the second Advent of God is the result of man's sin at the beginning of the world. That sin must therefore be enacted in the Corpus Christi cycle, and that episode will influence other episodes in turn.

In the Towneley Cycle, for instance, God begins the *Annunciation* play with this speech:

> I wyll that my son manhede take,
> ffor reson wyll that ther be thre,
> A man, a madyn, and a tre:
> Man for man, tre for tre,
> Madyn for madyn; thus shal it be.⁸

The great middle section of the cycle is about to begin, and it is defined in terms of the first section's beginning—the one recapitulates the other. In the Chester *Temptation of Christ,* the *Expositor* is brought forward to moralize on the action in similar terms:

> Loe! lordinges, Gods righteousnes,
> as St. Gregorie makes mynde expresse,
> since our forefather ouercomen was
> by three thinges to doe evill:
>
> Gluttony, vayne glorye there be twooe,
> Covetuousnes of highnes alsoe,
> by these three thinges, without moe,
> Christ hath overcome the Devill.⁹

He goes on to work out the detailed correspondences: Christ has been tempted because Adam was; moreover, He has been subjected to the same three temptations, though before they were all united in the apple. Only within an exact repetition of the pattern can progress from it be made. This doctrine also furnishes one reason all cycles stage the Harrowing of Hell. To show Christ's victory over death it is only necessary to stage the burial and the Resurrection. But these cycles show more: they stage a play in which Christ breaks hell's gates and leads the patriarchs from limbo into paradise, there to await the

---

* Inasmuch as it is said of the one repast, "In the day that thou eatest thereof thou shalt surely die"; but of the other it is read, "If a man shall have eaten of this bread, he shall have eternal life."

end of the world. He brings them forth out of Hell Mouth, leading Adam and Eve by the hand, and the others follow. The theological relationship, Adam-Christ, reaches its fulfillment in this moment.

There is another episode associated with the first Advent that must be discussed, for it is also part of our protocycle: the Fall of Lucifer, which disrupts the progress of Creation and precedes the Fall of Man. Its dramatization is essential, and for interesting reasons. In Genesis, the serpent is merely the subtlest beast of the field. The connection between the Fall and the Redemption is made for the first time in the writings of St. Paul, who saw the Fall as leading not only to disease, labor, and death (the Jewish understanding) but more important, to the condition of sinfulness—and to this condition he referred the necessity of God's dying a human death. The problem of dramatic significance in the cycles is precisely parallel to the problem faced by early Christianity: unless the Serpent is more than serpent (i.e., unless he is the devil, or something like the devil) the issues of the Fall are not sufficiently weighty to bear the burden of human history, nor to justify the Incarnation. The Fall of Man must be preceded by a greater Fall, a more cosmic disaster. Augustine adopted the doctrine of serpent-as-fallen-Lucifer in *The City of God* xi. 33 and xiv. 11, and thereafter it became Christian orthodoxy.[10] In the *Golden Legend* one reads: "Then the serpent which was hotter than any beast of the earth and naturally deceivable, for he was full of the devil Lucifer, which was deject and cast out of heaven, had great envy to man that was bodily in Paradise."[11] In this same way, it was necessary for the Corpus Christi cycle to stage that event before the Fall of Man. It furnishes the serpent with a history, a temperamental malevolence, and a motive to deceive. The patterns of action are significantly similar— two rebellions against proper degree, two paradises lost, two exiles. The Chester Demon states the correspondence concisely:

> Ghostelie paradice I was In,
> but thence I fell through my sinne;
> of earthelie paradice now, as I myn,
> a man is geven mastrye.

> By Belzabub! shall I never blyn
> tyll I make him by some synne
> from that place for to twyn,
> and trespace as did I.

. . . .
they shall fare bothe, as did I,
be banished bouth of that vallye
and their offspring for aye.[12]

Both Fall plays are best understood as incremental to the first Advent of God.

Thus the Three Advents of God are of supreme importance to the Corpus Christi cycle: the first (the creation of man) leads to the second (the redemption of man) which leads to a last coming. Before Christ's Incarnation, all men had already been judged: the good and the bad were alike in bondage to Satan. The Redemption made it possible that some—those who believed in and followed Christ—should be saved, and therefore a Last Coming was necessary to separate the blessed from the damned and to judge once more, but this time forever.

In turning to the Old Testament episodes that follow the Fall of Man, we come to the central problem of this chapter: how to explain the selection of Old Testament plays. Out of the vast fund of stories available, these cycles stage only a few—almost exactly the *same* few— stories. The coincidence is too exact to be written off as mere accident, and the cycles are too many and too widespread to make it likely that they all derive from one common original or from one another. We stand a better chance of finding an explanation by examining the ways in which these stories were understood in the Middle Ages. Our search must be for principles of selection that can explain the choice of episodes in the Corpus Christi cycle.

The *Speculum Sacerdotale* distinguishes between two kinds of octave (called "vtas") in the liturgical year:

And there ben some only for soverayne worship, as is the vtas of this feste of the Natiuite and of Paske and of Witsonday. And ther ben vtas of signyficacion, as is the vtas of the Innocentis, whiche is takyn for a rememorynge and a tokenynge, for therby is signyfied the resurreccion of vs alle.[13]

The importance of the Old Testament episodes that come after the Fall is largely of this second kind: it lies in their "signyficacion." They stand for events greater than themselves. Reginald Pecock's *Reule of Crysten Religioun* tells its readers that God revealed His Advent in the flesh in three ways: by direct announcements to the Fathers, as when He told Abraham that the Messiah would be born of his seed; by announcements through the prophets to the chosen people at large; and by

figuris and tokenes afore rennyng, booþ afore þe lawe ȝouun to moyses and in the lawe ȝouun to moyses, and þat bi alle þe sacrificis and oþere obser- vauncis ȝouun in þe lawe of jewis, a[s] witnessiþ poul j- corinthies x° capitulo.[14]

It is chiefly this third form of announcement that is selected by the dramatists from the Old Testament material. The basic stuff of drama is action rather than words; the Corpus Christi cycles played an- nouncements made in "figures."

The term "figure" has become obscure, as will be apparent from this series of translations of the Pauline text cited by Pecock (I Cor. 10:11):

Greek: ταῦτα δὲ τυπικῶς συνέβαινεν ἐκείνοις.

Vulgate: *Haec autem omnia in figura contingebant illis.*

Douay: *Now, all these things happened to them in figure.*

Authorized Version (1611): *Now all these things happened unto them for ensamples.*

New English Bible: *All these things that happened to them were symbolic.*

The theological sense of "figure" has disappeared from the language of ordinary Christians, as has the Greek alternative, "type," but we shall do best to retain these older words. "Ensample" was a weak translation even in 1611, and "symbolic" is too often and too loosely used these days to mean anything very precise. By defining the older words exactly we can bring clarity to our discourse and at the same time supply ourselves with another critical term that was important to this drama and was used by the dramatists themselves.

What then is a figure? To cite a modern student: "*Figura* is some- thing real and historical which announces something else that is also real and historical. The relation between the two events is revealed by an accord or similarity."[15] With this brief and lucid statement to guide us, we may also explore the richer formulation made by St. Basil in the fourth century: "The type is a manifestation (δήλωσις) of things to come through an imitation (μίμησις) allowing us to see in advance the things of the future in such wise that they can be un- derstood."[16] Originally, this interest in the concordance of events arose from the need to prove the unity of the Old and New Testaments. The technique was used in the defeat of the Gnostic heresy, which held that Christ superseded the *demiurge* of the Jewish Old Testament, just as it was used against the Jews to prove that Christ was indeed their promised Messiah. It offered simultaneously an explication of the Bible as a dual revelation, and a demonstration of the Bible's truth.[17] It produced later works like the *Speculum humanae salvationis,* which tells the story of the Incarnation but pauses at each major incident in the story to narrate three Old Testament figures. The proem explains why (I quote from a fifteenth-century English translation):

> Take hede in ilka Chapitle / the certein guyse es this
> That of the new law forthemast / a sothe reherced is
> To whilk sothe suwyngly / out of the testament olde
> Thre stories ilk after other / appliables shall be tolde
> ffor to make seling prove / of the forsaid sothfastnes
> Be god schewed of olde tyme / be figuratif lyknesse.[18]

The drama, too, occasionally uses such a technique to prove the truth of another event, though its customary use of figures is simply formal and celebratory. For instance, in the Towneley *Thomas of India* an apostle seeks to allay Thomas' doubt by reminding him of a traditional figure—Jonah three days in the belly of the whale and then cast up—to prove that Christ has really risen from death. After three days in the grave, He also is set free. The speech goes as follows:

> *Tercius apostolus.* Thou wote, thomas / and sothe it was,
>   and oft has thou hard say,
> how a fysh swalod ionas / thre dayes therein he lay;
> yit gaf god hym myght to pas / whyk man to wyn away;
> Myght not god that sich myght has / rase his son apon the
>   thryd day?[19]

This is a particularly useful example, for it can tell us about the origins of the technique. The reference to Jonah and the whale as a figure of Christ's resurrection does not derive from some oversubtle medieval Doctor. Christ Himself used it in His teaching (Matt. 12:40), just as elsewhere (John 3:14) He taught that as Moses lifted up the serpent in the desert, so must the Son of Man be lifted up. He was the first to interpret events as figures, and the Gospels reflect this; one of the reasons the textual concordance is real is that it was deliberately made so.[20] But a fertile field was left for later cultivation, and when the Church Fathers began to seek more strenuously for correspondences between events, a formal mode of "figurative" exegesis was begun. Even after the technique ceased to be important in polemical controversy, it continued as a fruitful method of understanding, and was set against the allegorical exegesis that took its direction from Philo. Tertullian was an early champion of figural interpretation, and gave it a full theoretical statement. In contrast to the allegorists, he insisted on the historical validity of Old Testament events: for him the *spiritual* sense lay in perceiving the relationship between two apparently disconnected historical happenings. In his terminology the fulfillment (or second event) is spoken of as *veritas* and the figure that announces it as *umbra* or *imago*. Historicity is crucial, for him and for Augustine after him:

Ante omnia, fratres, hoc in nomine Domini et admonemus, et praecipimus, ut quando auditis exponi sacramentum scripturae narrantis quae gesta sunt, prius illud quod lectum est credatis sic gestum, quomodo lectum est; ne substrato fundamento rei gestae, quasi in aere quaeratis aedificare.*[21]

Augustine elsewhere suggested a three-stage sequence in which certain second events can simultaneously fulfill an earlier figure and become themselves figures of an eschatological completion.[22] Jonah can foreshadow Christ's resurrection, which can in turn foreshadow the resurrection of all men.

But our present concern is not with *figura* as such,[23] nor with the whole range of received "figural" understanding, nor with the history and development of any one figure in total detail. Rather, it is with a few specific central *figures* and their relationship to episodes of the Corpus Christi cycle. My object is twofold: to account for the obligatory presence of certain Old Testament plays, for their formal meaning and their hierarchic importance prior to the local dramatic meanings developed *within* the plays themselves; and to furnish the reader

---

* Before all things, brethren, we admonish and command you in the name of the Lord, that when you hear an exposition of the mystery of the Scriptures telling what things took place, you believe what is read to have actually taken place as the reading narrates; lest, undermining the foundation of actuality, you seek as it were to build in the air.

or spectator with knowledge that can deepen his response to certain patterns of language and action in these plays.

The play of Cain and Abel, since it involves the first-born sons of Adam and Eve and shows the first murder, has obvious importance as story. But it possesses, too, a deeper resonance that finally ensures its place in all cycles. The way in which the medieval Englishman would have heard this story from the pulpit may be fairly represented by three documents. The first, from the *Speculum Sacerdotale,* discusses Abel as a figure of Christ, and Cain as a figure of Christians who cheat the Church of its firstfruits or tithes:

> Abel offered a lombe and Caym handfulles of fruytes. And the tone of hem seruyd þe grace of God after that his offeryng was done with a riʒtwys mynde. Abel, innocent in figure of Crist, was the first marter, but the toþer for he ʒaue noʒt ryʒtwisly prymycies in yevyng that that was of no valowe to teþe, he displesid God and be-come kyller of his brother.[24]

Abel's offering is important, but it is finally less important than his death, for his death figures Christ's passion directly. Sometimes this fact alters the nature of his offering as well, as when in the *Ludus Coventriae* Abel dedicates the sacrificial lamb to Christ with these words:

> ... þi grace grawnt þou me
> throwh þi gret mercy
> which in a lombys lyknes
> þou xalt for mannys wyckydnes
> Onys ben offeryd in peynfulnes
> and deyn ful dolfoly.[25]

This offering is recalled daily by the Mass in a prayer just after the Consecration, and it is here made directly figural. But Abel's place in the drama depends above all on his murder. *The Miroure of Mans Saluacionne* (a translation of the *Speculum humanae salvationis*) also identifies Abel with Christ, but gives Cain an historical fulfillment as well. The poet, in speaking of the Betrayal, compares Cain to the Jews who killed Christ:

> Also ʒᵉ Jewes ere like / vnto the Enevyous kaym
> Wilk slewe his innocent brothere / yᵗ neure trespast til hym.[26]

The first murder is important because of a second greater murder, that of the Son of God.

As we shall see several times in the following pages, these writers of "clerge" were conscious that a fulfillment is more than just a repetition of its foregoing figure. Progress is possible—the differences between figure and fulfillment are as important as the similarities, once the similarity has been established. The poet of the *Meditations on the Life and Passion of Christ* muses upon the meaning of the Crucifixion:

> Also, forsoþe, it nys non other
> But Caym haþ slayn Abel, his brother.
> But þe ferste Abeles blod
> Cryeþ wreche as it be wod;
> Crystes blod doþ al an oþer:
> It cryeþ mercy for his brother.[27]

This is no invention of the poet; it goes back to Hebrews 12:24, where Christ's blood and Abel's blood are contrasted for the first time. The time of vengeance has passed, the time of mercy has been inaugurated, and both begin with a murder that violates ties of blood. By repetition of a figure, progress from the meaning of that figure is possible: its consequences are transcended. The medieval simplicity of stage setting and the confined space in which the action was played suggest that in many performances Abel fell dead in the very place that had previously served as an altar, thus becoming himself the sacrifice. (It was staged this way in the Mermaid Theatre production of the Towneley cycle, and the theological meaning was simply and powerfully established.)

The next episode common to all cycles is a play of Noah and the Flood. Here again the figural possibilities are too rich to be confined to a single interpretation. One meaning was given by Christ Himself in His teachings about the end of the world:

"Heaven and earth shall pass, but my words shall not pass.... And as in the days of Noe, so shall also the coming of the Son of man be. For as in the days before the flood, they were eating and drinking, marrying and giving in marriage, even till that day in which Noe entered into the ark; And they knew not till the flood came, and took them all away; so also shall the coming of the Son of man be." (Matt. 24: 35-39)

The second Epistle of Peter (3:3-7) compares the flood to the fire that will destroy the world next time. The cycle-drama often states such a relationship, as in this conversation from the York play:

> 2 *fil*. Than may we wytte þis worldis empire
> Shall euermore laste, is noȝt to layne.
> *Noe*. Nay, sonne, þat sall we nouȝt desire,
> For and we do we wirke in wane,
> For it sall ones be waste with fyre,
> And never worþe to worlde agayne.[28]

Within the historical moment there is figural awareness. But the real York achievement is larger in scale. The *Flood* action begins with a long speech in which God repents the creation of man:

> ... synne is nowe reynand so ryffe,
> Þat me repentys and rewys for-þi
> Þat euer I made outhir man or wiffe.
> . . . .
>   Al newe I will þis worlde be wroght,
> And waste away þat wonnys þer-in,
> A flowyd a-boue þame shall be broght,
> To stroye medilerthe, both more and myn.
> Bot Noe alon lefe shal it noght.[29]

Much later, when the *Judgment Day* begins and the cycle nears its end, a long speech by God again gets the action under way, and this speech deliberately echoes ideas and phrases from the earlier *Flood* Episode. Once again God repents the Creation:

> And man to greue me gaffe he noght,
> Þerfore me rewis þat I þe worlde began.
>
> I haue tholed mankynde many a ȝere,
> In luste and likyng for to lende,
> And vnethis fynde I ferre or nere
> A man þat will his misse amende.
> In erthe I see butte synnes seere.[30]

Before, He found Noah; now there is no one. Although the *Judgment* play makes no explicit mention of the Flood, it is nonetheless recalled with subtlety and power. The dramatist has exploited theological tradition to enrich both art and meaning. Even in cycles that do not develop the correspondence so carefully, that relationship—which existed long before the drama was ever thought of—is one of the reasons they all play the Flood.[31]

The other major figural importance of the Flood story derives from I Peter 3:20–21, in which Noah's ark, which brought some few souls to safety through the water, is compared to the waters of baptism, by which many are saved. Augustine generalized the correspondence into a formula, *Noe significat Christum, archa Ecclesiam*;*[32] as Noah gathered his family into the ark and together they survived the first "ending" of the world, so in the final destruction, only the family of Christ, housed in the sacramental structure of the Church, will safely journey into eternal blessedness. The *Meditations on the Life and Passion of Christ* emphasizes this detail:

> Crois, þou art shyp of Noe
> Þat sauest oure kynde wiþ þi tre.[33]

The tree, initially the instrument of our woe, becomes twice an instrument of salvation, as Noah's ark (by way of figure) and as Christ's cross (by way of fulfillment). The *Glossa ordinaria* comments on Genesis 6:9–12 thus, uniting the two interpretations: " 'Noe vir justus.' Hic per actus suos significat Christum.... Noe per aquam et lignum liberatur, et familia ejus; sic familia Christi per baptismum et crucem."†[34]

The *Holkham Bible Picture Book* of the early fourteenth-century includes a beautiful drawing of the Flood which makes just this point in visual terms: Noah is shown leaning out of the ark, releasing the raven and the dove; the seas are still high, and beneath them the animal and human drowned are clearly seen. In making Noah release both birds at the same time, the illuminator is not simply saving space by ignoring sequence. He shows Noah with arms widespread in the posture of Christ on the cross: in his left hand he holds the raven (a type of the thief who would not be saved, as well as of the damned at the Last Judgment) and in his right the dove (a type of the thief brought to Paradise, and of the eternally blessed). Thus Noah's posture, and its symbolic accouterments, serve to demonstrate Noah's

---

* Noah signifies Christ, and the Ark signifies the Church.
† "Noah, a just man." Noah, by virtue of his deeds, stands for Christ. Noah is saved by water and wood, and his family as well; just so is the family of Christ saved by baptism and the cross.

ecclesiastical importance as a figure of Christ.[35] The Cornish cycle stages the offerings made to God after the waters have retreated, and by specifying exactly the place of that offering, the action is made to figure God's offering of His Son to come. Japhet praises the site in this way:

> A fairer altar in any place
>   A man could not see,
> Than as is with us, without doubt,
>   Over Mount Calvary.[36]

This meaning is developed further by the action as indicated in a stage direction: "[hic paratur altare et deus pater stet iuxta]."[37] Calvary will later serve as the place of the Crucifixion, and though God the Son is not yet on the cross, God the Father stands on Mount Calvary beside Noah's sacrifice in token that it pleases Him, and to signify that He (in the person of the Son) will be Himself the sacrifice *in this place* when the figure is fulfilled. The emphasis is here shifting to the difference between the two, to the progress that is made in historical time. Just as we were shown how Christ's blood differed from Abel's blood, in crying for mercy rather than for vengeance, so too the difference between the Baptism and the Flood is commented on by the author of the *Meditations on the Life and Passion of Christ*:

> þou dreiedest þe flod of Noe,
> þou waschest water and water not þe;
> ffor whan þou were cristened þer-inne,
> þou ʒeue it myght to clense of synne.[38]

Once again justice is transcended, and the means of mercy are at hand.

The Flood is followed by the story of Abraham and Isaac, a subject of such importance that three of its themes are included in the Corpus Christi drama. The first of these, God's command that the Jews be circumcized, relates to another principle of selection which I shall discuss later on. The second, Abraham's meeting with Melchisedech, is dramatized only in the Chester cycle and therefore has no place in our protocycle as such. Brief comment upon it, however, will set in bolder relief the reasons for the obligatory staging of the third action, the sacrifice of Isaac; it will offer, too, further evidence that "figuration" as a concept was a part of the medieval dramatist's understanding of his material. The episode is one in which Abraham is offered bread and wine by Melchisedech, King of Salem (Genesis 14), and it bears an importance which the *Miroure of Mans Saluacionne* makes clear:

> In liknes of brede and wyne / gaf crist his blode and flesshe
> Melchisedek both king and preest / prefiguring this expresse.[39]

Because the offering is related to the Eucharist, the commemorative sacrament, rather than to the Passion itself, Melchisedech is a figure of the Christian priest at the altar. The Expositor in the Chester play explains to the audience the significance of the incident:

> Lordingis, what maye this signifie,
> I will expound apertlie,
> that lewed, standing hereby,
> may knowe what this may be.
>
> This offring, I saie verament,
> signifieth the new Testament,
> . . . .
> In the old lawe, without leasing,
> when these two good men were lyving,
> of beastes was all their offring
> and eck their sacramente.
>
> but sith Christ dyed on the roode tree,
> with bread and wyne him worship we,
> and on Sherthursday in his maundye
> was his Comaundment.
>
> But for this thinge vsed shold be
> afterward as now done wee,
> in signification, as leve you me,
> Melchisedech did soe;
> . . . .
> By Abraham vnderstand I may
> the father of heaven in good faye,
> Melchisadech a preist to his paye
> to minister that sacrament.[40]

The reason all cycles play the Sacrifice of Isaac, and only one the meeting of Abraham and Melchisedech, involves the relative impor-

tance of the things these incidents prefigure.[41] In the same way that
the Passion has greater theological importance than the Last Supper,
so Isaac matters more than the first Old Testament priest. He has a
place in the Corpus Christi protocycle, just as he has in the office composed by St. Thomas Aquinas for the feast of Corpus Christi itself:

> In figuris praesignatur,
> 　cum Isaac immolatur,
> 　agnus Paschae deputatur,
> 　　datur manna patribus.*[42]

In the daily Canon of the Mass, the priest consecrates the bread and
wine with these words:

Supra quae propitio ac sereno vultu respicere digneris, et accepta habere
sicut accepta habere dignatus es munera pueri tui justi Abel, et sacrificium
patriarchae nostri Abrahae, et quod tibi obtulit summus sacerdos tuus Melchisedech, sanctum sacrificium, immaculatam hostiam.†[43]

The offering of Abraham here referred to is that same sacrifice of
Isaac mentioned in the Corpus Christi hymn: it is a figure of a father
sacrificing a son innocent of any crime. The figure is significantly different from its fulfillment, for the tragedy of the former is averted—
God provides another offering in the place of Isaac—but the Son must
die when His time comes. This last-minute reprieve from death into
life was likewise related to the Resurrection as a figure of Christ's
triumph over death. Tertullian in *Adversus Marcionem* iii, 18, argued
that since the sacrifice is not actually accomplished, it was necessarily
done in type, its whole function is as figure.[44]

　The drama texts show this influence in subtle ways. An alert ear may
hear echoes of it in the Brome version, which allows Isaac to pray just
before Abraham raises the sword:

> A! Fader of Heuyn, to The I crye,
> Lord, reseyve me into Thy hand.[45]

---

* It is foreshadowed in figures, when Isaac is offered for sacrifice, when a lamb is set
aside for the passover, when manna is given to the fathers.
† Over these things deign to look with countenance propitious and serene, and to hold
them acceptable just as you deigned to hold acceptable the gifts of your just son Abel
and the sacrifice of our patriarch Abraham, and that holy sacrifice of an unspotted
offering which your high priest Melchisedech offered to you.

His cry is deliberately based upon the last words of Christ on the cross (Luke 23:46): "Father, into thy hands I commend my spirit." Similarly in the York cycle, when Isaac says:

> And I sall noght grouche þer agayne,
> To wirke his wille I am wele payed,[46]

his words recall those that Christ will speak in the Garden (Matt. 26:39): "Nevertheless not as I will, but as thou wilt." Abraham in the Towneley version speaks of Isaac in words very like those that Pilate will later use of Christ: "Bot no defawt I faund hym in."[47] And Chester allows its Abraham this moving prayer just before the stroke is to be made:

> Ihesu, on me thou have pittie
> that I haue most in mynde![48]

The anachronism is fully intended, for though Jesus is not yet born, He is mysteriously the explanation of this action; we are so reminded by the speech of *Expositor* that concludes the play:

> This deed you se done in this place,
> In example of Ihesu done yt was,
> that for to wyn mankinde grace
> was sacrifised on the rode.[49]

Even where the relationship is not stated directly, knowledge of its existence could be assumed in a large portion of its audience. Mirk's *Festial,* a popular collection of sermons for busy parish priests, includes Quinquagesima teaching of this sort:

Then by Abraham ȝe schull vndyrstonde þe Fadyr of Heuen, and by Isaac his sonne Ihesu Crist. Þe whech he sparyd not for no loue þat he had to hym; but suffered þe Iewes to lay þe wode apon hym, þat was þe crosse apon hys schuldres, and ladden hym to þe mount of Caluary, and þer dydyn hym on þe autre of wode, þat was þe crosse.... Þen as þus was fygur of Crystys passyon longe or he wer borne, ryght so Crist hymselfe þys day yn þe gospell tolde to his dyscypuls how he schuld be scornyd, and betyn wyth scorgys, and don to deth on þe crosse, and ryse þe þryd day aȝeyne to lyue.[50]

Quinquagesima Sunday itself juxtaposes the two patterns in its liturgical readings. Some of the details above derive from Tertullian, who had worked out an elaborate typology in which Isaac carrying wood for the sacrifice is a type of Christ carrying the cross, and in which the ram caught by its horns in the bush (the alternative offering provided) figures Christ decked with a crown of thorns.[51]

Although no cycle except Chester makes the figural connection explicit, we may be certain that the reason for the episode's inclusion in other cycles is the same. Towneley, for example, uses a variant form of this tradition. It begins with Abraham musing on those who have gone before him, on Adam, Cain, Noah, and on his own death; he thinks of their career in sin, and their sad fate:

> *Abraham.* Yit adam is to hell gone,
>   And ther has ligen many a day,
> And all oure elders euerychon,
>   Thay ar gone the same way,
> Vnto god will here thare mone;
>   Now help, lord, adonay!
> ffor, certis, I can no better wone,
>   And ther is none that better may.
> *Deus.* I will help adam and his kynde,
> Might I luf and lewte fynd.[52]

Abraham says none can release them from hell but God, and prays for that deliverance. God in turn takes pity, but it is *conditional* pity, and this is what gives such urgency to the testing of Abraham in this play. The sacrifice of Isaac can do nothing for those alive or dead—only the sacrifice of the Son can do that—but unless Abraham is willing to sacrifice his son, God will not sacrifice His. The fulfillment *depends* upon the figure. This reflects an idea found in Irenaeus (and probably elsewhere):

Since indeed Abraham, according to his faith, having followed the commandment of God's Word, did with a ready mind give up his only begotten and beloved son, for a sacrifice unto God: that God again might be well pleased to offer unto Abraham's whole seed his only begotten and dearly beloved Son to be a sacrifice for our redemption.[53]

Christ Himself implied this interpretation of the Abraham story when, in John 8:56, He said: "Abraham, your father, rejoiced that he might see my day, he saw it and was glad." He suggests that Abraham was allowed somehow to understand, outside time, the meaning of the figure he enacted, and in that understanding found joy. The story is essential to our protocycle, not because it is a good story (though it is) nor simply because it is in the Bible (so are many others never dramatized) but because, like Abel and like Noah, Isaac is in important ways a figure of Christ.[54]

The history of Moses was a particularly fertile source of figures. The thirteenth-century sequence of Old Testament stories carved on the spandrels in the chapter house of Salisbury Cathedral concludes with five scenes from Moses' life, and they can supply us with a preliminary selection of incident. The scenes depicted are Moses on Sinai, the miracle of the Red Sea, the destruction of the Egyptians, Moses striking the Rock, and the Law declared.[55] Other figures contribute to Moses' traditional importance as well, and we may briefly summarize them here. We have already mentioned Christ's teaching in which the Son of Man is likened to the serpent raised up by Moses in the desert (John 3:15). The Paschal Lamb, too, is first sacrificed under Moses' direction (Christ in time is also cast in that role). As Moses distributed manna in the desert, so Jesus gave bread to the multitude. The Temptation of Christ in Matthew 4 is partly based on Deuteronomy: just as the Jews spent forty years in the wilderness, Christ spends forty days, and His answers to Satan are drawn from these texts. (Deut. 8:3, for example, first instructed, "Not in bread alone doth man live, but in every word that proceedeth from the mouth of God," and Christ's final words, "For it is written, *The Lord Thy God shalt thou adore, and him only shalt thou serve*," in Matt. 4:10, are based upon the Decalogue.) And Moses striking the rock, which then gushes forth water, was held to figure the water and blood that flow from Christ's side on the cross. These bare statements will serve to show something of the richness of the Moses figure in Christian thought, as well as to suggest its early appearance within New Testament writings.[56] But Moses' greatest importance relates to the two episodes that the cycle-drama actually stages—the Exodus from Egypt and the Giving of the Laws. The dramatic incidence is rather complicated, but it may be shown thus:

The Exodus: Towneley (The Towneley version is borrowed from, and remains nearly identical to, the York version.)
   York
   Cornish

The Law: Towneley (Moses in Prophets play; recapitulated by Christ in
   Doctors play.)
   Chester (Dramatized and abbreviated as first part of Balaam-Balaack-
      Prophets play, and recapitulated briefly in Doctors scene which
      ends Purification play.)
   Cornish (Dramatizes episode fully.)
   Ludus Coventriae (Dramatizes episode fully.)

The Law occurs more frequently than does the Exodus, but both deserve attention. The superior claims of the Law, as episode, depend
upon a different principle of selection, soon to be considered. For the
moment, we may concern ourselves with figural significance only.

   The great sacramental importance of the Exodus was established
by St. Paul (I Cor. 10:2) when he wrote "And all in Moses were bap-
tized, in the cloud, and in the sea." The Red Sea becomes a figure for
the waters of baptism, and Christ the leader of the new Exodus which
frees men from the bondage of the devil. Tertullian in his treatise
On Baptism discusses it as the first of a series of figures establishing
the sanctity of water:

First, indeed, when the people, set unconditionally free, escaped the violence
of the Egyptian king by crossing over *through water,* it was *water* that ex-
tinguished the king himself, and his entire forces. What figure more mani-
festly fulfilled in the sacrament of baptism? The nations are set free from
the world by means of *water,* to wit: and the devil, their old tyrant, they
leave quite behind, overwhelmed in the *water.*[57]

   Baptism began as a rite of initiation as well as of purification, and
its metaphors are violent: the soul is released from old captivity by
victory over its former captor. Again, the early Church saw in it an
important progress from its earlier figure; St. Ambrose writes of it
thus:

What is more important than the fact that the People of the Jews passed
through the sea? Yet the Jews who passed through all died in the wilderness. But he who passes through the font, that is from earthly to heavenly
things—for this is the *transitus,* that is the Passover, a passing from sin to
life, from guilt to grace ... he who passes through this font does not die,
but rises again.[58]

Mirk's *Festial* can indicate the way in which ordinary Christians heard
this correspondence developed from the medieval pulpit:

Thus was Moyses a fygur and a token of Cryst.... For ryght as Moyses fatte þe pepull out of Egypte þrogh þe see to þe hull of Synay, ryght soo Cryst, when he com, he, by prechyng and myracles doyng, fat þe pepull out of þe darknes of synne and euell lyuyng þrogh þe watyr of folowyng to þe hull of vertu....

þe font, þat is now þe Red See to all cristen pepull þat ben folowed in font. For þe watyr yn þe fonte betokenyþ þe red blod and watyr þat ran down of þe wondys of Cristis syde in þe wheche þe power of Pharo, þat is, þe veray fend, ys drowned, and all hys myȝt lorne, and all cristen pepull sauet.[59]

The *Biblia pauperum* sets the Crossing of the Red Sea by the side of Christ's baptism, for the Red Sea is a figure of it and of all baptism that follows.[60] The relation of the Exodus to the first Christian sacrament is one formal reason for the inclusion of this play in three surviving drama cycles.

The Exodus had yet another figural significance, fully as interesting as the last. In the *Speculum humanae salvationis,* Moses leading the Israelites out of Egyptian captivity is seen as a figure of Christ leading the patriarchs out of hell after He has conquered Satan.[61] The English translation made in the fifteenth century is worth citing:

> The Sonday tofore the mornyng / fro derh rysyn the mydnyght
> The ffadres out of the lymbe / ledde crist thorgh his grete myght
> This Captivitee be the feende / tofore here remenbrid
> In the Egipcien thraldome / some tyme was prefigured
> Thare ware the childere of Israel / be pharao thralde hoegely
> And for delyveraunce to godde / cryed thay longe doelfully
> Oure lord till moyses at the last / appiered in a busshe brynnyng
>
> . . . .
>
> Pharao and alle his folk / godde smote and out ledyng
> The Childere of Israel to the londe / with mylke & hony flowyng
> So crist woundid the feende / and his foulle assembling
> And ledde seints out of helle / til eternale feding.[62]

Only when we know of this can we fully understand the substance of a shepherd's speech in the York cycle, in which he discusses prophecies of the Messiah's birth with his fellows:

> I haue herde say, by þat same light
> The childre of Israell shulde be made free,
> The force of the feende to felle in sighte,
> And all his pouer excluded shulde be.[63]

He is not using religious language loosely; two specific historical events are alluded to, and related in terms of theological tradition. The Towneley cycle expresses this in another way, by verbal parallels. God commands Moses in the *Exodus* play:

> Thou speke to hym Wyth wordis heynde,
>   so that he let my people pas.[64]

And in the *Deliverance of Souls,* Christ commands Satan:

> This stede shall stand no longer stokyn;
>   open vp, and let my pepill pas.[65]

The cycle stages first one Exodus and then another: from Egypt and from Hell Mouth, God's people are set free.

The importance of the play of the Laws is only in part figural. In the later plays at the Temple, Christ will astonish the doctors with His knowledge of the Law by reciting the Ten Commandments—though this is not really so impressive a feat for a boy of twelve—in order that we should see behind him the figure of Moses reciting that same Decalogue.* The further formal significance of this episode, along with that of the *Prophets,* will soon be considered. But for now we must leave the Old Testament plays temporarily in order to examine the figural importance of certain other episodes.

The first of these, included in the protocycle under the heading Nativity plays, is the play of the Slaughter of the Innocents. It reveals its figural resonance even in its early Latin liturgical forms, as in the beginning episode of the *Ordo Stelle* from Laon:

> Interim Pueri, agnum portantes, intrant cantantes:
> *Ecce Agnus Dei, ecce qui tollit peccata mundi, alleluia.*†[66]

The levels of figural meaning are in this instance very complex. The innocents bring with them the lamb, a figure of the Paschal meal as well as a traditional symbol of innocence; they bring it because they

---

* The exact typological fulfillment of the Moses-on-Sinai figure is the Sermon on the Mount; the mounts are seen to be related, and Christ as New Lawgiver refers back to His predecessor (Matt. 5:21–22, 27–28). The cycles do not dramatize the actual Sermon itself, but this understanding of Moses and the Laws is part of Moses' traditional importance.

† Meanwhile let the young boys, bearing the lamb, enter singing: Behold the Lamb of God, behold Him who takes away the sins of the world, alleluia.

figure Christ, who in turn had been figured by the Paschal Lamb. To make the connection clear, they speak the words of the Baptist not actually spoken until many years after their death. And though they carry the sacrificial lamb, *their* image stands between it and its ultimate fulfillment in Christ. They are its gratuitous fulfillment, and the pathos of their death is like that which attends His. In the York *Flight into Egypt,* Mary, distressed at the possible death of her infant son, speaks verses clearly modeled on the *Planctus Mariae* she will later speak at the foot of the cross.[67] And the Bodley *Burial of Christ* makes the connection backwards in time, when the third Mary laments over the dead body of the Lord:

> O pepull most cruell & furiose,
> Thus to slo an Innocent![68]

That last word is more than an adjectival noun—it is history remembered. The one who escaped the wrath of Herod has finally died the death prefigured by those innocents who did not escape. The true Coventry plays also make reference to this figure. While the knights skewer the children with swords, the mothers make strange and ironic lament, as in this plea:

> Thatt babe thatt ys borne in Bedlem, so meke,
> He saue my chyld and me from velany![69]

There is irony because the villainy they are about to suffer is *for* His sake, *because* of Him; He has come to save them, but in a different time and way from what they now suppose. To the Fathers of the Church it seemed no mere coincidence that Cain and Abel, Abraham and Isaac, and the Slaughter of the Innocents were all stories of murder and sacrifice; since they were all understood to prefigure the death of Christ, neither is it coincidence that all five cycle lists should feature them. The figures of sacrifice are of the first priority.

The Nativity, Passion, and Resurrection groups as such have no need of explanation; they are the core of the drama, as they are the center of the religion it served. The Ministry of Christ, however, does pose certain problems. Most cycles include an episode or two from it, but they vary widely in their selection. The Woman Taken in Adultery or the Healing of the Blind, for instance, could both be staged, and each is to be found in one cycle or another. But the Raising of

Lazarus alone has a final figural resonance that makes its presence obligatory: it foreshadows Christ's own resurrection. This importance is most clearly stated in the Digby play of *Mary Magdalene,* where Jesus bids His disciples accompany Him to the house of Lazarus, brother of the Magdalene, to save him from "grevos slepe," and explicitly declares His larger intention: "Therfor of my deth shew yow I wyll."[70] Lazarus is dead in order that they should believe in Christ's own triumph over death, a triumph yet to come. This saint's play (all its incidents are chosen for their importance in the life of Mary Magdalene) uses the figural identification as a major structural spar, joining its two halves together by finishing Part I with the resurrection of Lazarus and beginning Part II with the resurrection of Christ. The two figures are set side by side, and intervening matter (the Passion of Christ) is ignored in order to make this meaning the more clear.[71] Christ Himself uses it to argue the truth of His resurrection in the *Ludus Coventriae.* While his true identity is still unknown to the travellers to Emmaus, He says:

> Why be ȝe so hard of truste
> dede not Cryst reyse thorwe his owyn myght
> lazare þat deed lay vndyr þe duste
> And stynkyd ryght foule as I ȝow plyght
> To lyff Cryst reysid hym a-ȝen ful ryght
> out of his graue þis is serteyn
> why may nat Cryste hym self þus qwyght
> and ryse from deth to lyve Ageyn.[72]

If Christ could "achieve" the figure, He can surely achieve the fulfillment: it is both prophecy and prior demonstration. There is beyond this yet another figural resonance, arising from associated verses (John 11:23–25) in which Martha significantly mistakes Christ's meaning. The Chester version runs thus:

> *Iesus:* Martha, thy Brother shall ryse, I say.
> *Martha:* That leeve I, lord, in good fay,
>   that he shall ryse the last day,
>   then hope I him to see.[73]

The Digby *Mary Magdalene* makes the same point, and Christ in the York *Ascension* explains his post-Resurrection appearances to his disciples as a "figure clere" of their own resurrection after death.[74] A figure (Lazarus) is fulfilled (by the Resurrection of Christ) and this becomes itself a figure (for the general resurrection before Dooms-day).

Figures do not cease with the Ascension of Christ, but those that remain or appear thereafter are "figures" in a different way: they are *preceded* by their fulfillment, rather than serving to imitate its future event. The saints and martyrs who come after are spoken of as figures of Christ, though they are obviously less than their model, and the Eucharist itself is termed a figure of Christ's passion, left behind for our solace and remembering. In the *Ludus Coventriae,* Christ explains the meaning of the Last Supper to His disciples thus:

> þis fygure xal sesse A-nothyr xal folwe þer-by
> Weche xal be of my body þat am ȝour hed
> weche xal be shewyd to ȝow be A mystery
> Of my fflesch and blood in forme of bred.[75]

The Paschal Lamb is the figure that must cease; the Host is the figure that will follow. Between the two must fall the shadow of the Cruci-fixion. Thus the Host becomes the most important "post-Christian" figure, as the "Treatise of the Manner and Mede of the Mass" from the Vernon MS would remind us:

> Eueri day · þou maiȝt se
> þe same bodi · þat diȝed for þe,
>   Tent · ȝif þou wolt take,
> In figure · and in fourme of Bred,
> þat Iesus dalte · er he weore ded,
>   For his disciples · sake.[76]

Except for the sainted martyrs and the Eucharist, the life of Christ was understood to be the end—the summation—of figures. Even a play such as the Bodley *Burial and Resurrection,* essentially liturgical in kind, begins the *Resurrection* with the Magdalene recalling the figures that preceded this fulfillment:

> Cursid kayn was verrey Cruell,
> And slew his awn brothere Abell
> Of a maliciose mynd;
>
> · · · · · · · · · · · ·
>
> The sonnes of Iacob, gret envy had
> Agayns þer brother Ioseph · ȝonge, wise & sad,
> Os scriptur doth record;
> Thay intendit to slo hym malishosly,
>
> · · · · · · · · · · · ·

> Few ʒeres past, herod the kinge
> Put to deth many ʒonglinge,
> & many moders child
> Here in the land off Israell;
> But of such Cruelte harde ye neuer tell
> Ose done was one Fridaye.[77]

The Bodley play has staged none of these. (The Joseph figure is common in the Middle Ages, though for reasons shortly to be considered it was never part of the English drama.) But, it is fitting that they be mentioned. They compose the historical resonance, the complements and antecedents of the Passion. The Chester Christ tells his disciples that it is time to eat the Passover meal:

> ffor know you now, the tyme is come
> that signes and shadows be all done;
> therfore make hast, that we may soone
> all figurs cleane reiect.
>
> ffor now a new law I will beginn,
> to help mankynd out of his synne,
> so that he may heaven wynn,
> the which for synne he lost.
>
> and here, in presence of you all,
> an other sacrifice beginne I shall
> . . . .
> with great desyre desyred haue I
> this passover to eate with you, truly,
> before my passion.[78]

This beautiful passage is very revealing. Here concisely stated is the understanding inherited by the drama of the relationship between the history of Christ and the history of the Jewish people; here is the emphasis on sacrifice that makes certain figures more important than others, and for that reason essential to the protocycle. The local dramatic life of these episodes will vary, with other concerns and interests occasionally being substituted for this figural connection with Christ's life; nevertheless it is this connection that gives them their independent importance and accounts for their presence in the cycle, and it is this connection that is recalled when Christ's life reaches its climax in the sequence of the Passion. The scene here imitated by the drama gave birth to the Mass and, long after, to the feast of Corpus Christi.

We can trace the influence in a clear line. In the office composed by St. Thomas Aquinas for that feast, the Fourth Lesson of Matins makes this important point:

Hoc sacramentum instituit, tanquam passionis suae memoriale perenne, figurarum veterum impletivum, miraculorum ab ipso factorum maximum, et de sua contristatis absentia solatium singulare.[79]

The passage is translated without acknowledgment in the *Golden Legend* chapter on the feast, and it is important enough to bear quotation in Caxton's English as well:

He instituted this holy sacrament like a memory perdurable of his passion, as the accomplishment of ancient figures, and of the miracles that were done by him, and also to the end that they that were sorrowful and heavy for his absence, should thereby have some solace singular.[80]

The feast of Corpus Christi commemorates not only the gift but also the ancient figures which were endured in imitative expectation of that gift. So strongly were the feast and the idea of figures interconnected that when Lydgate came to write an ordinance for "a precessyoun of þe feste of corpus cristi," he devoted it entirely to such an Old Testament sequence. He states his intention thus:

> Þis hye feste nowe for to magnefye,
>
> . . . .
>
> In youre presence fette out of fygure,
> 　Schal beo declared by many vnkouþe signe
> Gracyous misteryes grounded in scripture.[81]

The series that follows is quite different from the drama (Abraham and the Three Angels, Jacob's ladder, Moses and the manna, Aaron, and so on), but it, too, exists to honor its fulfillment in the feast of Corpus Christi. Though the figures are but shadows, they make the true light more glorious, as the *Golden Legend* emphasizes elsewhere in its pages on the feast:

All those things there were done in figure, for to give knowledge of things more great and more notable. It is much greater thing of the light than of the shadow; semblably of verity than it is of figure.[82]

Lydgate, in another poem, celebrates the same difference:

> Oold shadwes wer torneyd to bryghtnesse,
>   Dyrkyd fygurys Recuryd haue ther lyght,
> *Moyses* lawe, veyled with dirknesse,
>   Haue drawe ther curtyn, shewyd a sonne bright.[83]

Where there had been only a liturgical tradition of Latin and vernacular drama, the new feast of Corpus Christi brought into being cycles that could establish around the central fact of Christ's passion a dramatic context so complete as to liberate them from liturgical occasion. The importance of figures to the offices of the feast was not without effect on the offspring. They had come to be a traditional part of its celebration, and the child resembles its parent. Where theology had sought out these figural patterns with an ingeniousness and exhaustiveness that finally came near to defeating itself, the drama took from theology only the central, unequivocal figures, and played them one after another, creating thereby a dramatic structure of considerable economy and narrative tightness. The diagram (Fig. 1) will make that structure more clear.

A great encyclopedic poem such as the *Cursor Mundi* has a plan fully as comprehensive as this. It, too, spans all human time, narrating not only all the figures in the protocycle but many more. The drama is necessarily more selective in its choice of material, not merely because its playing time is limited but because it takes longer to act out an event (such as the Crucifixion) than to describe it. These limitations were ultimately to its advantage as art: because its episodes are fewer and more fully developed, the patterns implicit in the material emerge much more strongly. They are nearer one another in audience time, and their structural potential becomes real. Thus in the Corpus Christi drama, the Old Testament plays invite us constantly to perceive in their far distance the Son of God; when they end, the Son and His cross are brought slowly forward. Though the figures recede they are never wholly lost from sight. Every moment is charged with memories of the past and expectations of the future; thereby we discover order and unity in a drama that tells several stories, each separate and apparently discontinuous, which span all human time. Like recurring chords in music, the figures and their fulfillment discover singleness in diversity. Form and meaning become one.

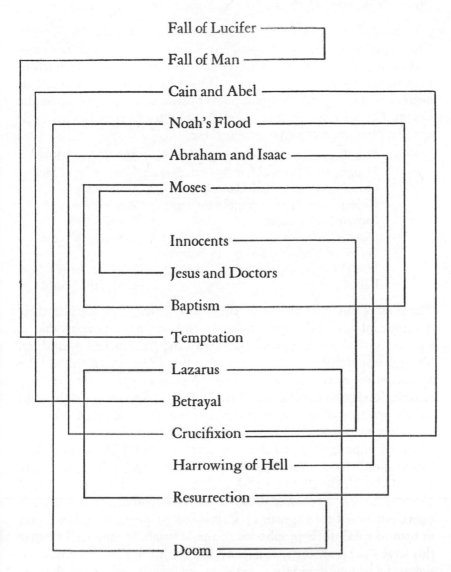

FIG. 1 Each bracket, whether [or], connects two episodes that are related as figure and fulfillment. The diagram serves to show the complex formal organization of the Corpus Christi cycle, as well as to recapitulate in schematic form some of the major theological relationships discussed so far.

Our search for principles of selection that can explain the Corpus Christi protocycle is not yet complete, however, for though the typological importance of these Old Testament episodes can do much to explain their *presence,* it cannot tell us why other stories, equal or nearly equal in figural resonance, never make their appearance on the Corpus Christi stage. It cannot tell us why no Corpus Christi cycle opens with a series of plays such as these:

Drunkenness of Noah *as prefiguring* . .	Mocking of Christ
Departure of Lot and family from Sodom	Harrowing of Hell
Carrying the grapes of Canaan	Crucifixion
Gideon receiving the Angel's message . .	Annunciation
Samson and Delilah	The Betrayal
Death of Absalom	Hanging of Judas
Queen of Sheba's offerings to Solomon .	The Magi
Daniel killing the dragon of Babylon . .	Temptation of Christ
Fall of Jericho	End of the World

These represent only a few of the possibilities.[84] Yet, despite their dramatic interest and figural richness, they are quite unthinkable as a prologue to that life which begins with the Annunciation to Mary. Though important enough to be used in the *Biblia pauperum* and the *Speculum humanae salvationis,* they compose a sequence bizarre and eclectic, foreign to the Corpus Christi drama. To account for the obligatory presence of certain episodes and for the absence of others, a secondary principle of selection is needed.

It used to be maintained that the vernacular Old Testament plays "budded-off" from the Latin *Ordo Prophetarum,* a liturgical play associated with the Nativity and itself based upon a homily entitled *Contra Judaeos, paganos, et Arianos sermo de symbolo.* In this sermon (once attributed to Augustine) a series of prophets are called upon in turn to speak their prophecies of the Messiah. It may well be that this *sermo* either directly, as a *lectio* for Matins in the Christmas season, or by way of the Latin drama of the Church, influenced the vernacular Prophets play, but it cannot explain the sequence of Old Testament plays in the Corpus Christi drama. Moses and David appear, it is true, but Adam, Abel, Noah, and Abraham are missing. Similarly this source cannot explain why most of its members are neglected: Isaiah, Jeremiah, Daniel, Virgil, Nebuchadnezzar never develop into separate plays in Corpus Christi cycles.[85]

E. M. Clark, in his distinguished study of the liturgical background to the Towneley cycle, briefly raises the question, and suggests an answer that is not implausible. Wondering why Hagar and Ishmael, Jacob and Laban, Gideon, Samson, etc., do not occur in the cycle he studies, he concludes: "All such subjects, obviously, were outside the ordered grouping of liturgical themes which controlled the matter of the cycle."[86] He suggests that the readings of the liturgical year determine which Old Testament episodes are staged and which are not. In the preceding chapter I described in some detail the order and range of these *lectiones*; a comparison of the Corpus Christi protocycle with them (as they are set out in the Sarum *Breviary* or as summarized in Caxton's *Golden Legend*) will reveal that Clark's solution is only approximate—close, but not close enough.

In the Church year certain stories that never occur in the drama are given great importance. The most singular of these is the story of Joseph and his brothers, which occupies the third week in Quadragesima but seems never to have been played on the Corpus Christi stage. The *lectiones* also deal at length with Jacob and Esau, characters neglected by all the cycles except Towneley. On the other hand, they almost completely ignore Cain's murder of Abel, though some few *responsoria* are drawn from it;[87] and the readings in Quinquagesima that tell of Abraham do not describe the sacrifice of Isaac. These inconsistencies in themselves suggest a certain looseness in Clark's theory, but the absence of Joseph, whose history was full of *figures,* may be regarded as decisive. If the content of the drama was significantly controlled by liturgical subjects, he could scarcely be omitted. We may note as well that although the time of Advent is filled with prophecies of the end of the world, the liturgy does not concern itself with the Doom as such. Clark himself admits that the play of the Judgment shows neither liturgical ancestry nor stimulus.[88]

There is yet another important difference. The liturgical year is complete in its narrative reference, but it is curiously arranged: Days before Doom, Nativity, Old Testament past, Passion of Christ, and Old Testament past. This is not the order of the Corpus Christi drama, and we may therefore be certain that a kind of mimesis of the liturgical year is not its intention. The order is worth stressing, because the time scheme of the drama differentiates it from a second possible way of presenting the life of Christ by means of figural antecedents. The

Miroure of Mans Saluacionne also extends from the Creation to the Doom, but within these poles the arrangement of figure and fulfillment is totally different. Chapter 1 tells of Adam and Eve in paradise, and their fall; Chapter 2 meditates upon the fallen Adam incarnate in all men; Chapter 3 begins with the Conception of Mary, and thus the life of Christ. The poem then employs a sequence based upon Christ's life, in which every major constituent action is briefly narrated, followed immediately by three Old Testament figures of that action narrated in turn. A jerky, disruptive rhythm results, the consequence of an interest in the Old Testament past which is exclusively typological. It is wholly unlike the Corpus Christi drama, though it is perhaps less the quantity of figures that makes the difference than their arrangement.[89] The drama plays them in a deliberate chronological sequence, as an ordered prelude to the life of Christ. This order, not shared by the arrangement of the liturgical year nor by the great typological treatises, can direct us to a secondary principle of selection adequate to explain the texts as we have them and the protocycle that embodies their generic identity.

I think this principle may be found in one of the theological traditions that divides all human time into seven ages. A drama that extends from the first day to the last may be said to offer all time in a dramatic image—so much is obvious—but a closer scrutiny will reveal an interest closely akin to that which found Ranulf Higden the title for his great historical opus: "And for þis cronicle conteyneþ berynges and dedes of meny tyme, þerfore I clepe it *Pollicronicon,* þat is þe cronicle of meny tymes [Trevisa]."[90] His *Polychronicon* gives these "meny tymes" as seven, and in his division he follows a tradition first stated in full by Augustine in the last pages of *The City of God*:

Then shall we know this thing perfectly, and we shall perfectly rest and shall perfectly see that He is God. If therefore that number of ages be accounted as of days according to the distinctions of times, which seem to be expressed in the sacred scriptures, that sabbath day shall appear more evidently, because it is found to be the seventh. The first age, as it were the first day, is from Adam unto the flood, and the second from thence unto Abraham, not by equality of times, but by number of generations. For they are found to have the number ten. From hence now, as Matthew the evangelist doth conclude, three ages do follow even unto the coming of Christ, every one of which is expressed by fourteen generations. From Abraham unto David is one, from thence even unto the transmigration into Babylon is another, the third from thence unto the incarnate nativity of Christ. So all of them are made five. Now this age is the sixth, to be measured by no number, because of that which is spoken. . . . After this age God shall rest as on the seventh day. . . . But this seventh shall be our sabbath, whose end shall not be the evening, but the Lord's day, as the eighth eternal day, which is sanctified and made holy by the resurrection of Christ, prefiguring not only the eternal rest of the spirit, but also of the body.[91]

There are several things to be noted here. We see that history is made to reflect the same pattern as the six days of creation and the sabbath rest that followed. Augustine's seventh age is in fact the age of the dead, the sabbath of the blessed souls, and it is contemporaneous with the other six, dating from the death of Abel to the death of the last martyr; the eighth age, in these terms, inaugurates eternity. These divisions are biblical in origin (Gen. 5:1, 6:9, and Matt. 1:1–17), and may be indicated more clearly thus:

Adam . . . . *inaugurates*	The first age
Noah's Flood	The second age
Abraham	The third age
David	The fourth age
The Transmigration	The fifth age
Christ	The sixth age
Doomsday	The seventh age

(For "seventh" read "eighth," if the seventh is regarded as
contemporary with all the others.)

Only the fifth age lacks a father, but Matthew 1:11 can supply him: Josias begot Jechonias in the transmigration into Babylon. This "Jechonias" is an alternate form for Jehoiachin, the son of Jehoiakim, carried away captive to Babylon in the eighth year of his reign (4 Kings 24). He takes his proper place in the scheme as presented in stained glass by a demiroundel of the twelfth century in Canterbury Cathedral. It flanks a center piece showing the miracle at the wedding in Cana, with six pots set prominently in the foreground. On one side of the center are shown the six ages of man; on the other, the six ages of the world. These latter are represented by six men, side by side, who may be thus identified:

Adam	(with hoe)
Noah	(with ark)
Abraham	(with fire in a bowl, and a knife)
David	(with a crown and harp)
Jechonias	(with a crown and sceptre)
Christ	(with an open book of the Gospels) [92]

The history of this schematization has been little studied, and though it would not appear to throw much light on the drama, since Jechonias never appears in these cycles nor is the transmigration of Babylon ever staged, it is nonetheless relevant. For there are variant traditions, almost the equal of this in importance, one of which can account for our protocycle's choice of major episodes. Before I explore these variants, I want to catalogue briefly some other occurrences of the scheme outlined above, for part of my argument turns on the importance of the "seven ages" idea in medieval times, and it has had no full-scale study elsewhere.

The Venerable Bede gave the scheme wide currency in his studies of biblical chronology. He first introduces it in his *Liber de temporibus,* written in 703, in which he briefly sets out the *sex aetatibus mundi,* as above.[93] In his much fuller study, *De temporum ratione,* written in 725, he adds a seventh and eighth age.[94] Most of the popular medieval histories include this division, among them the *Chronica majora* of Matthew Paris, which extends from the Creation to the year 1259,[95] the *Flores historiarum* extending to 1326,[96] and not least, Higden's *Polychronicon,* representing, as he tells us: "þe oþere sixe bokes, by þe noumbre of vi. ages, þat conteyneþ berynge and dedes from þe bygynnynge of þe world vnto oure tyme [Trevisa]."[97] The Augustinian division was taken over, without substantial change, by Eugippus, Isidore of Seville, Taio, Alcuin, Claudius Taurinensis, Rabanus Maurus, Honoré d'Autun, St. Julian of Toledo, Abelard, and Hugo of St. Victor.[98] Both the *Polychronicon* and the *Stanzaic Life of Christ,* which also includes an exposition of this eight-age structure,[99] were written in Chester, the home of a great drama cycle.

The importance of this notion of the world as having seven ages does not, however, finally depend upon a single method of determining those ages. The one we have been discussing bears pride of place through its close relation to scriptural text and the frequency of its occurrence; but alternative traditions and anomalies arose, chiefly, I should guess, as a result of the inadequacy of Jechonias to bear company with men so much more important than himself. He was merely a young king taken captive and never heard of again; that action, which begins the Babylonian captivity, is his sole historical importance. The Transmigration matters greatly to the history of the Jews, but he as king does not. It is possible to find the Transmigration given figural importance—Augustine[100] related it to the passing of Christ and the Gospel from the Jews into the hands of the Gentiles—but this historical fulfillment is seldom included in the narrative poems and is never staged by the medieval drama. The other five ages are each dominated by a single great figure, but Jechonias was never widely known. In some systems, therefore, he disappears; though the seven ages pattern is retained, it is differently constituted. The *Cursor Mundi* arranges its 30,000 lines upon this same structure, but it divides Christ's life into *two* ages: the fifth age begins with prophecies and the genealogy of Mary, and proceeds through the childhood of Jesus; the sixth age begins with the Baptism.[101] Jechonias and the Transmigration are noted in a few spare lines[102] among the events that bring the fourth age to its close. This intrinsic inadequacy of Jechonias may also explain the arrangement made by John Capgrave in his *Chronicle of England,* where classical history is absorbed into the pattern by making the reign of Xerxes inaugurate the world's fifth age.[103]

The traditional division drawn from the summary genealogies of the Bible had another shortcoming: in focusing its highly selective attention upon Jechonias, it neglected Moses, whose importance in time was rightly felt to be epochal. As the teacher of the Law, he instituted a new relationship between Jehovah and men; later, Christ defined His mission largely in terms of Mosaic law. Bede himself assigns this importance to Moses in another of his versions of human history, when he bases his division upon the five hours in which the laborers in the vineyard were hired. This gives him a five-period history of the world, divided thus: Creation, Noah, Abraham, Moses, Christ. Unhampered by biblical text, he can select the most significant figures: Moses is included, Jechonias is not. Ethelwerd based his system of ages upon this other version but brought the number to six by inserting Solomon between Moses and Christ.[104] The result is an alternative tradition much better suited to the visual arts—the iconography of Moses is distinctive, that of Jechonias common to any king—and to religious forms designed for a popular audience, for Jechonias and the Transmigration would not have been among the stories most familiar to a parish congregation. (As Bede's two systems show, even a sophisticated clerk, once free of the parent biblical texts, would think Moses more suited to the honor.)

This alternative tradition may be represented from the Anglo-Saxon period, in a short prose setting forth the ages of the world (MS Caligula A. 15, fol. 139b):

Her on ginð embe þises middan eardes yldo. Seo forme yld is fram Adame oð nôe. . . .
.ii. Ðonne is seo oþer yld fram nôe oð abrahâm. . . .
.iii. Ðonne is seo þridda yld fram abrahame · oð moisên. . . .
.iiii. Ðonne is seo feorðe yld fram moysên oð dauid. . . .
.v. Ðonne is seo fifte yld fram dauid oð cristes to kyme. . . .
.vi. Ðonne is seo sixte yld fram cristes akennednysse oð þissere woruld ende.[105]

It is precisely this version of the ages that is incorporated into the *Golden Legend,* an immensely influential work, in its discussion of the Circumcision. That event took place on the eighth day after Christ's birth:

And thus these eight days shall be understood by the eight ages. The first is from Adam to Noah; the second from Noah to Abraham; the third from Abraham to Moses; the fourth from Moses unto David; the fifth from David to Jesu Christ. The sixth from Jesu Christ unto the end of the world. The seventh of the dying on earth. And the eighth of the general resurrection to heaven.[106]

This follows Augustine in providing for eight ages, of which the seventh is contemporaneous with all the rest. But its understanding of the six figures who inaugurate the first six ages is different—Moses has replaced Jechonias—and thus it is linked directly to the structure of the Corpus Christi drama. The 1527 list of Corpus Christi plays at Norwich, otherwise so imperfect and corrupt, preserves a perfect six ages structure at its beginning, the ages represented thus:

Creation of the World	(First age)
Paradise	
Hell Cart	
Cain and Abel	
Noah's Ship	(Second age)
Abraham and Isaac	(Third age)
Moses and Aaron, with the Children of Israel and Pharaoh with his Knights	(Fourth age)
Conflict of David and Goliath	(Fifth age)
The Birth of Christ[107]	(Sixth age)

The cycle then tails off badly, staging only the Baptism, the Resurrection, and the Holy Ghost: the vicissitudes of time and craft-fortunes have clearly blurred the rest of the original design, and at this date no play of the Judgment remains to show the seventh age. But the sequence of Old Testament plays accords so closely in its choice of leading characters with this alternative seven ages tradition, and with the Corpus Christi protocycle, as to make still more convincing the attribution of this design to the Corpus Christi dramatists. Records of Corpus Christi pageants in Dublin are very closely allied. Though it is impossible to determine whether the Dublin records concern a dumb-show procession or an actual cycle-play, this much is certain: it was associated with Corpus Christi, and it mounted only these Old Testament subjects: Adam and Eve, Cain and Abel, Noah and his ship, Abraham and Isaac, Pharaoh and his host, the Prophets. It concludes with various events in the life of Christ.[108]

In a poem called "Þe Deuelis Perlament," written *c.* 1430, Christ breaks the gates of hell, and the Fathers in limbo salute his coming. Like the drama, this poem makes no specific reference to the seven ages idea, but its sequence of patriarchs is almost certainly determined by it:

> "A, ha!" seide *Adam,* "my god y se;
> He þat made me wiþ his hond!"
> "I se," seide *noe,* "where comeþ hee
> Þat sauede me boþe on watir & londe!"
> Quod *abraham,* "ye se my god so free
> Þat sauede my sone fro bittir bande!"
> Þo seide *moyses,* "þese tablis he bitook me
> His lawe to preche and vndirstande!"

Quod *Dauid,* "we spoken of oon so grym
Þat schulde breke þe brasen ʒatis."
Quod *Zacharie,* "& his folk out nym,
And leue þere stille þo þat he hatis."
Quod *symeon,* "he liʒtneþ his folk in dym,
Lo where derknes schendiþ her statis.
Þo seide *iohne,* "þis lomb, y spak of him,
Þat al þe worldis synne a-batys."

Oure lord them took bi þe hond,
And brouʒt þem to þe place of blis.[109]

Christ leads from limbo precisely the characters He would find if He
and they were characters in the Corpus Christi drama: they are the
central figures in the Old Testament plays. This concept of time survived even into the drama of the Reformation, becoming the act divisions of John Bale's *Tragedy or Interlude manifestyng the chief
promises of God unto man by all ages in the old law, from the fall of
Adam to the incarnation of the Lord Jesus Christ,* written in 1538. The
first six acts of this play portray the promises made by God to Adam,
Noah, Abraham, Moses, David, and Isaiah; the final act is a recapitulation and a statement that Christ (with the Baptist before Him) will
now come. Because Christ could not be *played* in post-Reformation
England, the scheme was modified slightly: David properly begins
the fifth age, Isaiah (not so properly) the sixth.[110] To this might be
compared a fifteenth-century window in Great Malvern priory church
showing the Coronation of the Virgin: she is flanked by figures of
Adam, Noah, Abraham, Moses, David, and a sixth which is now
lost.[111] The sequence is the same as that of the Canterbury demiroundel noted earlier, except that here we have a Moses tradition of
the world's six ages substituted for the earlier Jechonias tradition.

One major discrepancy between the drama protocycle and this
version of the seven ages tradition remains to be commented on: in the
former, we have to account for a play of the Prophets, and in the latter
for David alone as inaugurator of the fifth age. The curious cycle at
Norwich staged David's battle with Goliath, and the Cornish cycle
played episodes from his life, so they fit the pattern easily enough. But
there is a difference between the Cornish cycle and the proto Corpus
Christi drama: Cornwall played full actions for Adam and Eve, Noah,

Abraham and Isaac, Moses, and David, but it lacked a Prophets play. The English cycles give David no separate action; instead he represents the fifth age in a play that serves the larger purpose of reciting a multiplicity of prophecies concerning the coming of Christ. In it, he appears simply as Prophet, or sometimes more particularly as Prophet King. The Middle Ages understood this to be his chief significance. John Capgrave's *Chronicle of England* briefly records his reign, but it emphasizes his real importance in these terms:

Evyr he dred God. Cristis nativite, His baptem, His passion, resurreccion, ascension, His comyng to the dome, ful openly in his Psalmes he teld.[112]

He is discussed in a similar fashion in Caxton's *Golden Legend*:

This David was an holy man and made the holy psalter, which is an holy book and is contained therein the old law and the new law. He was a great prophet, for he prophesied the coming of Christ, his nativity, his passion, and resurection, and also his ascension, and was great with God, yet God would not suffer him to build a temple for him, for he had shed man's blood.[113]

The emphasis is apparent in the visual arts as well. A recent student of the images to be found in English churches says of David: "Although single figures of the King playing upon the harp occur fairly often, scenes from his life are rare."[114]

It is worth noting that in the "Deuelis Perlament" quoted above, when each of the patriarchs mentions the action that gives him his importance, Adam speaks of the Creation, Noah of the Flood, Abraham of the command to sacrifice Isaac, Moses of the Tables of the Law, but David and Zachariah speak simply of their prophecies. As Augustine observed, the chief importance of the age in which they lived was that it was an age of prophets:

All the time, therefore, between Samuel's first prophecy and the return of Israel from seventy years' captivity in Babylon ... is called "the time of the prophets." For although the patriarch Noah, in whose time the universal deluge befell, and divers others living before there were kings in Israel, for some holy and heavenly predictions of theirs may not underservedly be called prophets (especially as we see Abraham and Moses chiefly called by those names, and more expressly than the rest), yet the days wherein Samuel began to prophesy, were called peculiarly "the times of the prophets." Samuel anointed Saul first, and afterwards (he being rejected) he anointed David for king, by God's express command; and from David's loins was all the blood-royal to descend during that kingdom's continuance.[115]

The dual identity of David as prophet and king is important, and it is shared by many who come after. The *Prophets Play* of the *Ludus Coventriae* offers a somewhat special case: a full-scale prophets sequence (thirteen prophets, not counting David) has had added to it a full root-of-Jesse genealogy (thirteen kings, not counting Jesse), with the prophets and kings alternating in strict sequence. The root-of-Jesse motif is unique to the *Ludus Coventriae,* and part of the material that gives the cycle its distinguishing Marian emphasis. The play begins with the words "I am þe prophete callyd Isaye" (Isa. 11:1 is the source of the root-of-Jesse prophecy); it follows Isaiah with Jesse; and then David, king, prophet, and son of Jesse, comes forward to begin the king-prophet alternation.[116] David, unlike the others, has a multiple claim to place, and one of those claims, perhaps even in this cycle, is that he represents the beginning of the fifth age of the world.[117]

The seven age structure is largely buried in dramatic detail; it is sometimes masked by the playing of odd additional episodes; and it does not in any direct way determine cycle proportions, since the events inaugurating the sixth age are dramatized in vastly greater detail than any of the others. (Such a disproportion is, of course, even more marked in the medieval histories that employ a seven ages organization.) Nonetheless it has exercised its influence upon all the extant cycles, and its usefulness to a drama that sets out to imitate all human time is considerable. Only rarely does the drama make a specific comment upon it, as when Noah in the *Ludus Coventriae* declaims:

> In me Noe þe secunde age
> in dede be-gynnyth as I ȝow say
> afftyr Adam with-outyn langage
> þe secunde fadyr am I in fay.[118]

But in the other cycles, the point was perhaps not lost, even though it was given no statement more explicit than the choice and arrangement of dramatic episodes.

The relationship of these two organizing ideas—the figures of Christ and the seven ages—can best be seen when the action that begins an age is passed over in order to play an alternative action involving the father of that age but richer in figural importance. (The ages most often *begin* in terms of new sacraments or laws.) The priorities governing choice of episode are therefore quite clear. The figural principle of selection takes precedence over that seeking to chronicle the seven ages, but both are given satisfaction. We can see this, for example, in the Abraham plays, where the third age is properly inaugurated by God's command that all males be circumcized. No cycle, of course, goes so far as to stage the accomplishment of this order, though others might have done as Chester did, showing God issuing the command to Abraham, with the *Expositor* at hand to explain the temporary importance of the sacrament.[119] Or like York, they might have allowed Abraham this brief recollection:

> And als þe sternes wer strewed wyde,
> So saide he þat my seede shuld be;
> And bad I shulde be circumcicyd,
> To fulfille þe lawe; þus lernynde he me.[120]

But instead the rest are silent, choosing to play (together with Chester and York, once their preliminaries are over) an action that figures the sacrifice of Christ, though it does not directly matter to an ages-of-the-world structure. The age is nevertheless represented, and the central story of Christ is given a dual prelude: the third age is part of a sequence leading to the sixth; Isaac as innocent offered in sacrifice foreshadows the Crucifixion.

So too with the Moses episodes. In the Middle Ages there existed as well a threefold division of human time that could be superimposed upon a scheme such as the seven ages of the world; and Moses occupies one of its three transitional points. The *Polychronicon* defines it as the "distinccion of tymes": "Oon to fore lawe i-write, þe secounde vndir þe lawe i-write, and þe þridde vnder grace and mercy [Trevisa]."[121] This concept is used by the *Speculum Sacerdotale* to explain why three masses are sung on the Nativity:

Vnderstondeþ wel we dyuyde alle the tyme of this world by thre tymes. The firste tyme is that [that] was of natural lawe fro Adam vnto Moyses. The secounde tyme is of writen lawe that was fro Moyses vnto the aduent of oure lord. The thridde tyme is tyme of grace þat is fro the aduent vnto the ende of the world.[122]

It was Moses' importance in this scheme, as the one who received the written Law, that caused him to replace Jechonias in the drama tradition of the seven ages.[123] There is no sense of anticlimax when the lengthy cycle of Old Testament scenes carved in stone (*c.* 1270–80) in the chapter house of Salisbury Cathedral ends with the Declaration of the Law,[124] for a truly decisive change has been made. But the York cycle will illustrate again those priorities of interest that make Moses essential but do not limit him to the action that gives him his position among the seven. The Moses play from York deals with the burning bush, the ten plagues, and the crossing of the Red Sea (all episodes rich in figural meaning). It does not play the Giving of the Law, choosing rather to stage these actions as standing for his moment of history, and to reserve for the play of *Christ with the Doctors* a recital of the Ten Commandments. The subject is too important to be neglected, but it can be dislocated for typological reasons. The other extant cycles, Towneley, Chester, *Ludus Coventriae,* and Cornwall, require Moses to speak all, or part of, the Decalogue, but three of them play the Exodus in addition.

The drama did not attempt a mimesis of eternity; only Doomsday, which inaugurates the seventh age, is played. Without Doomsday, the drama, as in the Cornish cycle, presents a mimesis of human history —that is to say, the historical past as understood in six ages. With Doomsday, the thing imitated is all human time, the future as well as the past, the metaphysical conception in its totality. This completion is essential to Corpus Christi form, and together with a certain selection of Old Testament episodes constitutes the hallmark of the genre. We must, of course, recognize that since the history of dramatic performances is something different from the history of drama, the total design was not always achieved. Here in extract from the Coventry Leet Book of 1457 is one instance:

On Corpus Xpisti yeven at nyght then next suyng came the quene [Margaret] from Kelyngworth to Coventre; at which tyme she wold not be met, but came prively to se the play there on the morowe; and she sygh then alle the pagentes pleyde save domes-day, which myght not be pleyde for lak of day.[125]

It is idle to guess how common an occurrence this may have been. The York cycle was also played in one day, and since it is very long, it may occasionally have lacked its conclusion;[126] the Chester cycle was played on three consecutive days and would not have been affected. But incomplete performance must have been rare, for no guild would long stand the expense of time and money involved in preparing a pageant seldom performed. Since my inquiry is into the artistic potential of these cycles, into the intention behind the design, I merely note in passing the possibility of occasional local incompleteness. What is important is that to the ideal design, the seventh age (as begun by Doomsday) was essential.

Figures and their fulfillment, the mimesis of total human time—these are the core of the Corpus Christi cycle and the source of its formal shape. In this chapter and the one preceding it, I have sought to demonstrate that there is an obligatory content and form implied in the generic description "Corpus Christi play" as used by the medieval Englishman. I have attempted to disperse a fog of imprecision about what this drama is, an imprecision that has found its way into the introduction of even so distinguished a work as A. C. Cawley's recent edition of the Wakefield pageants, where he concludes his description of the Corpus Christi play with a phrase borrowed from E. O. James: the Corpus Christi play, Cawley writes, "took the form of an elaborate dramatic presentation of 'every phase of the Christian story as a commentary on the daily ritual of the Mass.' "[127] Hardin Craig offers a similar generality: "It is the same great and familiar story of the fall and redemption of man as that which we have in epics, sermons, commentaries, and histories all through the Middle Ages. The Corpus Christi play tells this story in its completest possible form."[128]

Far from playing "every phase of the Christian story" or that story "in its completest possible form," the Corpus Christi cycle is in fact highly selective; what is more, it is selective in formally coherent ways. As with the figures of Christ, so too does the drama deal with the ages of the world. No medieval cycle openly develops the theme, and yet it has undoubtedly caused the Corpus Christi drama to find a distinctive protocycle core. The York cycle may be an exception, for it lacks a full-fledged Prophets play in which David and others can come on stage to recite their prophecies. But it has a Prophets prologue instead. Whether that prologue was designed to remedy an earlier omission, to replace another Prophets prologue, or to replace a full Prophets play, we cannot know. Other Old Testament variants are few and easily explained: Chester plays the offering of Melchisedech as part of its Abraham play (two important actions instead of only one); Towneley plays part of the history of Isaac and Jacob, his son (an extension of a generation, as when the first age is represented not only by the Creation and Fall but also by Cain and Abel). At the very least, we may say that the doctrine of figures, and the idea of the world as having seven ages, can together do much to explain the hierarchic importance in the Middle Ages of these specific Old Testament stories. But the correspondence is so exact that something like intention seems implied. Somehow these cycles took form; somehow they took substantially the same form; and the form can best be explained and described in terms of these two organizing ideas. More than that only the dramatists themselves could tell us.

Students of the Corpus Christi drama have occasionally recognized that some episodes had importance as playing *types* of Christ,[129] but no one has ever explored the range of this typological meaning episode by episode, or its effect on action and speech and cycle form, or realized that, on its own, this principle of selection raises more questions than it answers. Only a secondary principle, as suggested above, can explain why certain figures are played and others not. Together they can account for the protocycle of the Corpus Christi drama, the generic thing in itself.[130]

In attending to these principles of selection and to their artistic consequences, we attend to the larger rhythms of the cycle as they exist over and above the steady succession of play following play. These two organizing ideas are, one might say, the beams in the building, largely hidden under decoration and surface detail, but there all the while and of utmost importance. They hold the building together, they give it its shape; and by its shape, we know it.

Chapter Five

Medieval Time and English Place

We have seen that one way of looking at the Corpus Christi drama is as a sequence of plays relating the history of the world in seven ages, offering to its audience, within that framework, an image of all human time. There remains the question of what manner of address this drama makes to *present* time, to that specific portion of the sixth age that comprises the "now" of composition and of performance on Corpus Christi day in the medieval town. The question is central to any full-scale description of this drama's mimesis of historical time.

The Cornish cycle, like the great French plays called *Passions,*[1] concludes with the Ascension of Christ. It does not play Doomsday, but instead opens out into present time, leaving the spectators in the extended moment after, awaiting the conclusion in their own lives to the events they have seen staged. No English cycle that survives, or about which we have trustworthy records, ended in this way: a Doomsday play was essential to Corpus Christi form, and the cycles leap swiftly from the Coronation of the Virgin to the play of the Judgment—or in Chester, to *Antichrist* followed by the *Judgment*— a leap in mimetic time that disdains the moment in which the medieval audience lived. The formal intention is clear: plays called Corpus Christi imitated all time, in chronological sequence and as metaphysical structure, achieving instead of the expressive point of the French and Cornish pattern a formal completeness almost sacramental in its impact.

The Bible, of course, includes no stories from a medieval "present time," but there are other reasons than this to explain the formal omission. We must note, for instance, that about present time the medieval churchman held certain views that deprived it of any specifically

historical interest. If a preacher or teacher wished to address the present moment, he most often would do so in terms of the Four Last
Things and of Everyman's death, in terms of the bridegroom and the
wise and foolish virgins. The present had dignity mainly as a time
for amendment and preparation; its proper use was to earn man a
place in heaven. George Poulet is right, I think, in discerning a new
attitude toward human time as one of the major qualities of the
Renaissance. That period, he says, discovered a joy in being alive in
time that the Middle Ages never experienced: "Temporality then no
longer appeared solely as the indelible mark of mortality; it appeared
also as the theatre and field of action where despite his mortality man
could reveal his authentic dignity and gain a personal immortality."[2]
For the most part, the Middle Ages was chiefly conscious of degenera-
tion, of the times growing ever worse and worse.[3] Only one medieval
conception of present time had an affirmative tone, and its beginning
is staged by the central story of the Corpus Christi cycle: whatever
else "now" might be, it was historically the time of mercy. A passage
from a medieval sermon can usefully illustrate this manner of valuing
present time:

And þer-fore arise, for nowe is tyme for to amend, for now is þe day sterre
vpe.... I vndirstond by þe day sterre no þinge els but þis tyme, þat is now
tyme of grace. For had oon man doon all þe synnes þat all þe world myght
do, and he wolde repente hym and amend hym, he shuld haue grace. But
aftur / þis tyme, when þi bodie is ded, had a man as muche repentaunce as
all þe world myght haue, but he amend hym or þat he die, els he shall neuer
haue grace with-owten ende.[4]

"Now" is the time of grace, and in so recognizing it the medieval cycle
drama makes its only direct address to the present moment. Such a
recognition was necessary because the duration of grace was limited—
it could end at any moment for any man, as for all men at Doomsday.
The Chester play of the *Judgment,* which surpasses all the others in
formal beauty, derives much of its depth and power from its concen-
tration on the old dilemma of Redemptive mercy versus strict justice:
the demons, like lawyers arguing from well-prepared briefs, insist
that though Christ is Mercy, He must in justice grant them the wicked
that He has promised. (Since He is Mercy, they fear all may be saved.)
Christ does not shrink from the philosophic issues involved, nor from

the sternness required to damn the wicked for all eternity. The terms of His resolution are magnificent and simple: "For grace is putt away."[5] The cycle ends with the four Evangelists, in two quatrains each, speaking praise. Luke can represent them:

> And I Luke, on earth lyvinge,
> my lords words in every thinge
> I wrott and taught through my Conninge,
> that all men know[e] might.
>
> And therfore I say forsoth, iwis:
> Excusation none ther is;
> against my talkinge they dyd amisse;
> this Dome it goeth aright.[6]

In terms of drama time, the Evangelists are justifying Christ's judgment by saying that they gave warning to all through their teachings and writings; but in terms of audience time, they are issuing a call for alertness and amendment. The spectators still live in the time of mercy; grace is not yet put away, and they may avail themselves if they will. In leaping from the foundation of the Church (with the *Sending of the Holy Ghost*) to the play of *Antichrist* and the *Judgment,* this cycle, in common with all the others, has formally neglected the audience moment as such, but here with perfect decorum the dramatist makes a gesture backward toward that time. It was understood as a time of mercy, and this understanding involved a certain urgency of action lest one lose one's immortal soul: "Residuum sextae aetatis tempus Deo soli est cognitum," Isidore had written.*[7] The Church and the Corpus Christi drama concentrated alike upon the significant past and the significant future; the drama's addresses toward present time were hortatory and didactic, designed to shape action, not to record it.

But the Corpus Christi drama developed another kind of present relevance as well, and that is my real subject in this chapter. For although the remainder of any age is filled with events wholly inferior in terms of historical significance to those that begin it, yet the remainder of the sixth age has about it this superior subjective importance, for medieval dramatists and their audiences quite as much as

---

* The remaining portion of the sixth age is known to God alone.

for us now: we are alive in it, and thus it matters to us in a very special way. The morality play exploits this fact to great effect: its only address to time is to the present time of its audience. *Everyman* or *The Castell of Perseverance* seem almost as modern today as they did in the fifteenth century, because their message is simple (repent, prepare, think on your end) and because they deal only with things that are universal and unchanging in human experience. They play *only* present action, but of a sort common to every age and every human lifetime. The Corpus Christi drama, in a different way, is formally as timeless—all its actions are past or to come, and we are alive in the sixth age still—but its deeper address to the audience moment has dated it in unique and interesting ways. By means of a pervasive anachronism and anglicization it furnished a critical image of moral and social life as lived in the later Middle Ages. It is possible that these cycles felt no need to stage actions from present time because they staged all past actions as if they were of the present. The Corpus Christi drama managed to hold a mirror to the times while imitating the structure of human time.

A great deal of the anachronistic detail in the drama exists, of course, simply for the sake of convenience. Old Testament speeches liberally seasoned with oaths, "by Christ" or by the saints or even "by Mahound," are undoubtedly the result of nothing more than a wish to write vivid, colloquial dialogue.[8] The York Noah can speak of the rainbow as a token sent "tille all cristen men" and mean something perfectly straightforward, just as the times of day can be reckoned most easily according to a medieval system: the third shepherd will explain that he left the sheep in the corn "when thay rang lawyds."[9] Such anachronism is direct and unselfconscious; as Alan Nelson has written, "Noah is a medieval man acting out the story of the Flood without discarding everything he knows from having lived after the Flood. He does not dissociate himself from his knowledge of Christ and His fulfillment of the prophesies."[10] But elsewhere in these texts, dramatic anachronism involves conscious artistic intention. It is used, for instance, in the service of the medieval poor, registering the wrongs they suffer within the context of an Advent that will ultimately damn their oppressors forever. The two Towneley shepherds' plays, preeminently, are entered in that cause, and they are darkened (to their artistic advantage and their greater social use) by a body of social protest that is anachronistic but in no sense careless or unintended.

Pilate, in the same cycle, is characterized as a corrupt medieval judge—Arnold Williams has written a fine study of the satiric background to that portrait[11]—just as the raging Herods and the proud high priests serve to image the sins of the contemporary rich and powerful. In the *Ludus Coventriae,* the woman taken in adultery and her frightened gallant are fifteenth-century sinners, as familiar to the audience as the women, fashions, and kirk-chatterers discussed in the Towneley *Judgment* (and in many a contemporary sermon commenting on present abuses). This demon, for example, is clearly attacking what we would call the latest Paris "line":

> yit a poynte of the new gett / to tell will I not blyn,
> Of prankyd gownes & shulders vp set / mos & flokkys sewyd
> wyth in;
> To vse sich gise thai will not let / thai say it is no syn,
> Bot on sich pilus I me set / and clap thaym cheke and chyn,
> no nay.[12]

Although Isaac's sacrifice is included primarily for its figural importance, the dramatist will sometimes use it as well to tell young boys they must obey their fathers, and to notice, rather ruefully, how few seem to do so.[13] But the outstanding example of this sort of anachronism is surely the Towneley play of *Cain and Abel,* whose proper subject is that moment in time when the only existing human beings are Adam and Eve and their two sons. The Towneley version allows Cain a boy servant, whom he insults and abuses and cannot entirely control; and after the murder, frightened of the bailiffs, Cain and his boy go through the streets of the town proclaiming a king's pardon for themselves. The first murder is shown as taking place in a highly organized medieval community. Its lesson is about murder, contemporary as well as historical; about unregenerate man, in any age, cut off from God; and, in a smaller, less important way, but also wholly contemporary, about men who cheat the Church in tithing. (This vice was the subject of many a medieval sermon, in part because it so greatly affected the income of the parish priest, and Cain, in his offering with Abel, has been carefully characterized in that way.) The drama, in short, compensated for the formal unimportance of the audience moment by staging the past as though it were largely identical with present time, thereby honoring its specific audience while seeking (among other things) to amend their lives.

The Towneley cycle is particularly rich in this kind of verbal contemporaneity, most notably in the work of the Wakefield Master (who wrote somewhere between 1400 and 1450), although all the other cycles contain a certain amount of medieval reference. But the most pervasive kind of anachronism, equally characteristic of all cycles, was established by the settings and costumes. The *Holkham Bible Picture Book* can give us a fair idea of how the drama might have looked: to cite an extreme example from it, its Harrowing of Hell shows a small, fortified house (Limbo) joined to a blast furnace with an iron chimney—a very up-to-date industrial modification of the older Hell Mouth.[14] Glynne Wickham has concluded from his study of medieval staging that "with the possible exception of representatives of both foreign and ancient founder races, contemporary costume was used to dress all historical characters including figures from Biblical history."[15] (The costumes of Jesus, Mary, and the apostles may have been simpler and more timeless than those of the society in which they move.) This kind of anachronism is of course common to all the visual arts, to every medieval attempt to imagine what characters in biblical history looked like. It is to be explained in part as a lack of knowledge, in part as a failure of the imagination. (How many of us have any confident notion of how Simon of Cyrene may actually have dressed?) Yet there are anachronisms in the drama text wholly different in kind, anachronisms that result from a vivid imagining of similarities, not from a failure to imagine. If Cain murders Abel in a medieval society, we may be sure it is not ignorance but artistic intention that is involved. The anachronism of costume and setting simply reinforced this deeper intention and took on a reflected seriousness from it.

The writers of the great medieval histories, men of considerable learning, in prefaces often address their readers concerning the "uses of the past" in ways fully harmonious with the medieval drama's attitude toward it. Knowledge of medieval conceptions of historiography, the how and why of history writing, can prevent us from being too hasty in regarding anachronisms in the drama as arising merely from the need to make the story comprehensible to an unsophisticated audience. The history writers, seeing these plays, would not have felt themselves patronized or talked down to, any more than would the cobbler or haywainer beside them. The histories, too, begin with the creation of the world by God; they, too, were instruments for remembering the past, and similar things were required of both genres. Higden's *Polychronicon,* of which more than one hundred manuscripts survive, makes an eloquent statement of the historian's practice in its opening pages.[16] Higden, a monk of St. Werburgh's Abbey in Chester, is credited by the post-Reformation Banns to the Chester cycle with being the original author of those plays. This attribution has been convincingly discredited by Salter and Wickham, but the influence of Higden's historical writing was real and widely felt.

Higden praises ancient writers because in their works are recorded "meruailles and wondres, greet berynge and dedes of oure forme fadres, of stalworthe wyt, wise and worthy, and of dyuerse manere men þat were in olde tyme." The purpose of such writings emerges thus: "In our tyme, art, sciens and lawe al were i-falle, ensample of noble dedes were nouȝt i-knowe; nobilite and faire manere of spekynge were all i-lost; but þe mercy of God had i-ordyned vs of lettres in remedie of vnparfiȝtnesse of mankynde."[17]

That this is no mere individual view but the understanding of an age may be seen in comparing it with the preface to the *Flores historiarum,* a chronicle written from St. Alban's and extending to 1235, which was even more influential in England than Higden's considerably later work.[18] The preface begins by addressing those who think historical chronicles are without value, and in defending the uses of history, the author defends the uses of the past:

Now, we would have such persons know that the lives of good men in times past are set forth for the imitation of succeeding times; and that the examples of evil men, when such occur, are not to be followed, but to be shunned. Moreover, the prodigies and portentous occurrences of past days, whether in the way of pestilence, or in other chastisements of God's wrath, are not without admonition to the faithful. Therefore is the memory of them committed to writing, that if ever the like shall again occur, men may presently betake themselves to repentance, and by this remedy appease the divine vengeance.

They are, therefore, not to be heeded, who say that books of chronicles, especially those by catholic authors, are unworthy of regard; for through them, whatever is necessary for human wisdom and salvation, the studious inquirer may be able to acquire by his memory, apprehend by his learning, and set forth by his eloquence.[19]

There is no sense of historical change, no sense of period necessary to
a history devoted to such ends; the interest of the past consists not in
what it can teach us of the past but in how it can remedy the present.
Only the timeless has interest, and only a narrative skeleton of important events is needed to provide a series of occasions in which this
timeless material may be discussed. The interest of history resides in
its reflection of the eternal, unchanging plan of God for the salvation
of man, and in the moral constants of good and evil which reveal
themselves in human behavior. Any event that related to one period
only and not to all time seemed to the Middle Ages not in the highest
sense historical. From this point of view, chronological sequence
chiefly recorded progress toward the millennial release from time and
history. Thus both the *Polychronicon* and the Corpus Christi drama
are built upon a sequence of the seven ages of the world; and in both,
notwithstanding the far greater amount and variety of summary detail
in the *Polychronicon,* the seven ages tend to merge as homogeneous
and undifferentiated. These writers knew there were great gaps in
their knowledge of the past; John Capgrave explained he would leave
many blank spaces on the page in the early part of his *Chronicle of
England,* for anyone to fill in who could:

Also if ȝe merveile that in thoo ȝeres fro Adam to the Flood of Noe sum-
tyme renne a hundred ȝere, or more, where the noumbir stant bare, and
no writing therein, this schal be myn excuse; for soth, I coude non fynde,
not withstand that I soute with grete diligens. If othir studious men, that
have more red than I, or can fynde that I fond not, or have elde bokes whech
make more expression of thoo stories that fel fro the creacion of Adam onto
the general Flod than I have, the velim lith bare, save the noumbir, redy
to receyve that thei wille set in.

He made a similar apology when he came to deal with the life of
Christ:

In all these ȝeres tyl Crist was XXX. ȝere of age the Gospelle makith no
grete declaracion of His dedis; but, with oute ony doute, He lyved a parfit
lyf, and ded many miracles, thou thei be not wrytin in bokis.[20]

But neither he nor his audience were much concerned about the limitations inherent in the quality of their knowledge.

The medieval historian was well aware that his work contained a fair proportion of error, just as the dramatist who set the Cain and Abel story in a medieval village knew that he was filling in the scriptural account with materials of a very different sort. But they could both be confident that such error was not harmful—that is, that it would not teach men wrong moral precepts. Higden says the reader may find inaccuracies, but he quotes St. Paul in his defense: "For þe apostel seith nouȝt, 'All þat is write to oure lore is sooþ,' but he seiþ 'Al þat is i-write to oure lore it is i-write.' "[21] In other words, it may be that not everything written there is true, but everything there written is written in order to teach truth. This view had powerful advocates: Aquinas in his *Summa theologica* quotes Augustine, and gives the statement his own authority in turn: "Not everything of which we make pretence is a falsehood; but when what we pretend has no meaning then it is a falsehood. But when our pretence has some signification, it is not a lie, but a figure of the truth."[22] The context of this statement is, of course, larger than the practice of the historian or the dramatist, but the dramatist, too, like Higden, might confidently have justified his work in its terms.

Though this statement of the goals of medieval historiography misrepresents to some degree its practice, nevertheless it does fair justice to the theory, and it is the theory that is of interest here. The dramatists were not necessarily learned in the way of the historians, but both groups of writers valued the past for its present Christian relevance. The wish to furnish moral lessons from history was important to both forms, and the cycle-drama achieved this by a pervasive anachronism that made those lessons immediately and directly relevant to English medieval life. The technique may seem naïve, but its goal is conscious and sophisticated. There was, of course, great ignorance of the past; not until the Renaissance were men to discover that differences are as important as similarities if one would learn from history. In medieval England no one ever really remarked on the differences.[23]

It should now be clear that the anachronism of the Corpus Christi drama results in part from an attitude toward the past also held by men of high learning, in high places. Among literary men, it is John Gower who furnishes us the clearest explicit statement and defense of this technique, in the Prologue to the *Confessio amantis*. He has been writing of the uses of books that record the past—stories, histories, books like the collection of tales and homilies that he is about to begin:

Thus I, which am a burel clerk,
Purpose forto wryte a bok
After the world that whilom tok
Long tyme in olde daies passed:
Bot for men sein it is now lassed,
In worse plit than it was tho,
I thenke forto touche also
The world which neweth every dai,
So as I can, so as I mai.[24]

The pervasive anachronism of costume and setting, and the occasional imaginative anachronism of a text, allowed these cycles a similar address to that part of the sixth age in which its audience lived, a part which the formal design of the drama neglected. The past was played as an image of present time.

I turn now to a related matter that seems to require a different kind of explanation. Just as in this drama the time is out of joint, so too is the geography of the action dislocated. As *time* was made medieval, so does *place* of action turn out largely to be English.

A good deal of the "Englished" quality of the drama likewise depends on no complex rationale: a certain amount of translation is necessary, as when the Chester cycle interprets Octavian's required penny tax as "the value of tenne pence it shalbe," or when the York cycle makes Pilate hear claims "in Parlament playne."[25] French is spoken as the language of "officialese" because it was so used in medieval England. York and Towneley in their shared play of the *Exodus* substitute pestilence, the most terrible of medieval afflictions, for the biblical death of the first-born of Egypt.[26] All these are simply ways of making a foreign story immediately clear and meaningful to an English audience. Even contemporary gospel harmonies resorted to translation of this sort: the Jewish high priest is called "bisschopp"; the Jewish Passover is referred to as "estren"; the angel sitting beside the sepulchre on Easter morning is "ycladde in a white chesible" as though he were a Christian priest.[27] We all seek to understand the unknown by reference to the known, now as in the Middle Ages.

Such details are, in a sense, inevitable, and of limited significance in themselves. They become important only because they reinforce other kinds of geographical transposition. Although a gospel harmony may tacitly translate, it never purposely alters that which does not need to be changed in order to be understood. The Corpus Christi drama does so quite frequently, and these changes are important to intention and meaning: it often deliberately establishes an English place of action. The undertaking is more subtle than a direct translation of the story into a different time and place, in the manner of Kazantzakis' *The Greek Passion,* where something like the Passion of Christ occurs again among the simple people of a Cretan village. The Corpus Christi drama uses the correct place names—"Iudy," Rome, Egypt, Bethlehem, are all mentioned from time to time, establishing controls, making a gesture toward historical verisimilitude. But the metaphysical "place" of the action becomes blurred because the characters tend to identify themselves with a different native geography.

Examples are easy to find. When Octavian in the Chester cycle sends a messenger to number the Jews, he offers him the "highe horse besides Boughton" as a reward. The messenger replies:

> Graunt mercy, lord, pardy,
> this hackney will well serve me,
> for a great lord of your degree
> shold ryde in such araye.

> The bene high in dignitie,
> and also high and swifte is he;
> therfore that reverance takes yee,
> my deare lord, I you praye.[28]

This makes a good joke, for Boughton is a district outside of Chester, and the "highe horse" is the gallows there,[29] but it does more than amuse—it serves as well to anglicize the scene against which the life of Christ will be staged. Later in the cycle, the shepherds keeping their flocks by night keep them in fields near Chester. The First Shepherd boasts:

> From Comelie Conway unto clyde
> under Tildes them to hyde.
> a better Shepherd on no side
> no earthlie man may haue.[30]

The sulky *Gartius* can insult the Third Shepherd by saying it would be small sorrow to his wife if he were drowned in the river Dee,[31] just as after the Adoration, when they declare firm friendship and love, they can praise each other in terms such as these:

> from London to Louth,
> such an other shepherd I wot not where is.[32]

And when the wicked knights who will slay the Innocents need an image for an ultimate terror which they will somehow find courage to confront, they turn to the north of Chester, toward England's traditional foe: it is "the kinge of Scotis and all his host" that furnishes the object of their boast.[33]

In the Towneley cycle, when Mrs. Noah is angry with her doddering husband, she scolds: "thou were worthi be cled / In stafford blew," offering him a beating that will leave him the color of the famous blue cloth from Stafford, and managing to pun on the word "staff" at the same time.[34] The Towneley cycle is particularly close in its establishment of locale: actions take place in the town of Wakefield proper. Cain, after the murder and the curse, contemptuously requests that he be buried at the head of Goodybower quarry, just outside the town,[35] and the shepherds, who have had a sheep stolen by Mak, make it clear that their loss occurred nearby. One of them says:

> I haue soght with my dogys
> All horbery shrogys,
> And of fefteyn hogys
>   ffond I bot oone ewe.[36]

He has searched Horbury's bushes (or underwood), Horbury being a town some three miles away, where there was in the fifteenth century a chapelry of the Wakefield parish church.[37]

There are other and more suggestive examples of this kind of geographical transposition to be cited, but let me conclude this opening survey with a passage that makes clear how deliberate it is. No dramatist was more consistent in anachronism and anglicization than the Wakefield Master, no shepherds are more English than his (though Chester's are nearly their equal), yet he turns this fact about the drama texture itself into a joke in the *Secunda Pastorum*. The shepherds wake from their sleep, and one says:

Resurrex a mortruis! / haue hald my hand.
Iudas carnas dominus! / I may not well stand:
My foytt slepys, by ihesus / and I water fastand.
I thoght that we layd vs / full nere yngland.[38]

Not only does he employ three oaths meaningless within the historical moment, he also slyly acknowledges that strictly speaking they should not be English shepherds either: it's been a terrible sleep, partly because he dreamed that they were sleeping in England.

The Corpus Christi drama, then, establishes by costumes, settings and verbal reference a time and place that are roughly contemporary, and more or less English. This localizing of place must also be understood as part of the drama's interest in addressing its particular English audience in their particular moment in time, in holding up to them a mirror of their own society and its moral nature. This wish pervades the plays drawn both from the Old Testament and from the New. But there seems to be another factor involved, one that is reflected in the much higher frequency of English geographical reference in the plays of Christ's life than in the Old Testament plays that precede them. I have already examined in some detail the Englishness of the shepherds; here I need only insert a reminder that it is to these English shepherds that the nativity announcement will be made, just as in the *Ludus Coventriae* staging of the *Trial of Joseph and Mary* for fornication, the Summoner convenes a court wholly English and contemporary in its membership. Listen to part of the roll that summons people to attend:

Thom tynkere and betrys belle
peyrs pottere and whatt at þe welle
Symme Smalteyth and kate kelle
    and bertylmew þe bochere
kytt cakelere and colett crane
gyll fetyse and fayr jane
powle pewterere and pernel prane
    and phelypp þe good flecchere.

. . . .

Megge mery wedyr and sabyn sprynge
Tyffany Twynkelere ffayle ffor no thynge
The courte xal be þis day.[39]

Later, in Chester, the tormentors who scourge Christ are English thugs, boasting in this manner:

> In woe shall he be wonden,
> and his graynes grownden;
> no ladd unto London
> such law can him leere!
> (*tunc flagellabunt eum....*)[40]

He is the best torturer from Chester to London, and Christ will feel his blows. The Cornish cycle localizes the action in a way closely akin, for the official patronage in its plays customarily involves the gift of land and rule, and these gifts are always part of Cornwall's geography. When Solomon rewards the carpenters who have put up the main beam in the Temple (it is made of the tree grown from seeds given to Seth in the garden of Eden, and will in time be made into Christ's cross), he gives them the field of Bohellan, the wood of Penryn, Arwinnick, Tregenver, and Kegellik. When Pilate decides to imprison Nichodemus and Joseph of Arimathea to prevent their stealing Christ's body from the grave, he grants the jailer all of Fekenel, Carvenow, and Merthyn; later to the guards who will watch at the tomb, he gives the plain of Dansotha, and Barrow Heath.[41] Something curiously like a Cornish gentry is created out of actions involving Christ.

Obviously, this sort of localization gives great vividness and immediacy to the stories dramatized, but it fulfills needs more important to the history of Christianity as well. The Jews rejected Christ as the expected Messiah, both in His life and after His death, and the drama, in common with other medieval art forms, presents the religion of Christ shorn of its specifically Jewish national character. It makes the Old Testament beginnings relate directly to those peoples who later became Christian, and being an English drama, it sensibly enough is here concerned only with England. The cycles, in the service of the Church, can be seen here and there discreetly shifting the context of the Redemption, showing Christ's earthly parents judged in an English court, and Christ Himself adored by English shepherds, killed by English louts, His tomb guarded by Cornish soldiers. The transition is clearly marked in the Chester cycle when Mary and Joseph arrive in Bethlehem, and Mary has a sudden bewildering vision:

> Ah! lord, what may this signifie?
> some men I see glad and mery,
> and some sighing and sory,
> wherfore so ever yt be;
>
> sithe gods sonne came man to forby,
> is come through his great mercy,
> me thinke that man shold kindlye
> be glad that sight to see.

To which an angel replies:

> mary, Gods mother deare,
> the tokening I shall the leere,
> the common people that thou seest here,
> are glad as they well may,
>
> That they shall se of Abrahams seede
> christ come to helpe them in their need;
> . . . .
> the movrning men—takes this in mynde!—
> are Iewes that shall be put behynde,
> for it passes out of their kinde
> through Christ at his cominge.[10]

This passage is extremely important. It declares Christ lost to the Jews at His birth, not at His crucifixion: they are seen in Mary's vision mourning the loss they will later choose to lose. In their un*kind*ness to Christ, they will separate Him from their kind, and thus the way is open for a life and passion of Christ that will seem at times to be happening in England. The source of the above passage is an apocryphal infancy gospel dating from the second century, known as the *Book of James,* or the *Protevangelium.* It reads thus:

And they drew near (unto Bethlehem) within three miles: and Joseph turned himself about and saw her of a sad countenance and said within himself: Peradventure that which is within her paineth her. And again Joseph turned himself about and saw her laughing, and said unto her: Mary, what aileth thee that I see thy face at one time laughing and at another time sad? And Mary said unto Joseph: It is because I behold two peoples with mine eyes, the one weeping and lamenting and the other rejoicing and exulting.[48]

That is all. The incident is not explained, the two peoples are not identified. Chester includes it and explicates it, and in so doing calls attention to a fact being expressed throughout the cycle by other means.

The dramatists knew that Christ lived His life in Judea, not in England, but some of them blurred the distinction to make a doctrinal point. Among the cycles, Towneley and Chester most consistently transpose history in this way. The Cornish cycle and the *Ludus Coventriae* do so more rarely, and the York cycle alone almost never anglicizes at all—its text is largely unlocalized. But the transposition is common enough to be worth attention, and it can explain much about the "quality" of this drama's world: the Jews are largely expunged from the picture in order that the guilt of Christ's death and the blessing of His sacrifice may both be felt as local. (I shall discuss this more fully in Chapter 8.) What has often seemed to earlier critics a sign of naïveté or carelessness can perhaps better be referred to the long effort of patristic and medieval theologians to make sense of a Messiah promised to the Jews as chosen people, but worshiped only by peoples not designated as "chosen" in the Old Testament.

It is no surprise that the Judgment itself, *dies irae, dies illa calamitatis,* can be held in the immediate area that owns the drama cycle. In Towneley, it declares itself thus in a conversation between two devils about the trumpets that have sounded the call:

> *primus demon.* ffor to stand thus tome / thou gars me grete.
> *secundus demon.* let vs go to this dome / vp watlyn strete.
> *primus demon.* I had leuer go to rome / yei thryse, on my fete,
> Then forto grefe yonde grome / or with hym forto mete.[44]

They go to the Doom up Watling Street. Christ comes to Wakefield to judge.

Implicit in certain scriptural texts is a conception of time that borders upon the mystical, and this has influenced the structure and meaning of the drama cycles as well. When, for example, Christ taught that he who does not believe is already judged (John 3:18), the underlying assumption would seem to be that since the present determines the future, the future can be said to be already present, and that—more significantly—in God there is no distinction of times. Augustine discussed this very fact: "But what is future to God who transcends all time? If God's knowledge contains these things, they are not future to Him but present; therefore it can be termed not fore-knowledge, but simply knowledge."[45] Man's duty, it follows from this, is to understand time as God understands it, to recognize the transient and, turning from it, to prize the eternal. Time was understood to be strictly limited in duration and importance: it differed from eternity, and in eternity lay all human goals. We need to remember that eternity means timelessness, not infinite time, that it involves a release into a different and unimaginable dimension of experience. Augustine's *City of God* approaches its conclusion with this great rhetorical question: "For what other thing is our end, but to come to that kingdom of which there is no end?" Or as the *Golden Legend* expresses it: "We shall be delivered of time, we shall come to him whereas no time passeth, but is perpetuity."[46] Set against eternity, all historical time is but a brief moment,[47] a thousand years as one day (2 Peter 3:8).

Such a manner of misprizing human time certainly played its part in preventing that kind of scholarly and imaginative accuracy about the past which alone can make "anachronism" seem undesirable. But its implications for our study are deeper, for it sets God outside the structure of time, makes that structure small in His eyes, and asserts His total power over it. Augustine defined the difference between time and eternity in just this way, saying that a man may see:

that all time which is past is driven away by that time which is to come; and that all time which is to come follows upon that which is past; and that all which is both past and future is created, and doth flow out from that which is always present. Who shall hold fast the heart of man that it may stand and see how that eternity, which ever standeth still, doth dictate the times both past and future, whilst yet itself is neither past nor future?"[48]

This understanding of temporality as a manifestation of an eternal will took various forms in the Middle Ages. For instance, it permitted (in the absence of specific fact) some very fine symmetries of time, designed to reveal this will at work relating significant event to significant event by making them each other's anniversaries. The *Golden*

Legend, for example, chooses to honor the feast of the Annunciation by referring to mysterious congruities in time:

This blessed Annunciation happened the twenty-fifth day of the month of March, on which day happened also, as well tofore as after, these things that hereafter be named. On that same day Adam, the first man, was created and fell into original sin by inobedience, and was put out of paradise terrestrial. After, the angel showed the conception of our Lord to the glorious Virgin Mary. Also that same day of the month Cain slew Abel his brother. Also Melchisedech made offering to God of bread and wine in the presence of Abraham. Also on the same day Abraham offered Isaac his son. That same day S. John Baptist was beheaded, and S. Peter was that day delivered out of prison, and S. James the more, that day beheaded of Herod. And our Lord Jesu Christ was on that day crucified, wherefore that is a day of great reverence.[49]

This forced and unlikely symmetry represents medieval piety at its worst, and it is not, on the surface, very interesting. But one of the assumptions underlying it has great interest, both in terms of the medieval metaphysic of time and in relation to the Corpus Christi drama. The key is to be found in the phrase, "on which day happened also, as well tofore as after, these things." The Old Testament events cited—all of them, save Melchisedech, a part of our protocycle—along with the Annunciation all happen on the day that will be the day of the Crucifixion; and the events that come after, the martyrdom of James and the delivery of Peter, refer back in the same way to Christ's death. The middle event, the Crucifixion, has affected history both before and after it, not in a causal, serial way—Christ is not crucified in honour of Abel's anniversary—but in a way that involves what we may call time as artifact. Hans Meyerhoff has characterized the modern understanding of time in these terms:

It also happens to be an empirical fact about the world—including our own minds—that the past leaves traces, marks, or records, and the future does not.... There is no memory of the future.... wherever we find traces— whether footprints in the sand, fingerprints on a gun, or faces indelibly imprinted in memory—we assume that these records were caused by events *preceding* them, and are not the result of events coming later.[50]

Causality and chronological sequence supply the secular mind with an objective time-order, but for medieval Christian thought, the dignity of past time consists precisely in those traces of the future written, by God's shaping of events, upon it.

As a result, the progression from episode to episode in this drama is often without consecutive impulse. It is not built upon a theory of direct causation: Noah's thank-offering does not cause the offering of Isaac by Abraham, nor in any sense lead to it, even though the two actions are played in sequence, with complete disregard of the intervening years. (Only the life of Christ has so total a significance that parts of it are staged in directly sequential episodes.) The rationale behind the drama's time structure (see Fig. 2) must be described in other terms.

The events chosen for dramatization are those in which God intervenes in human history; significant time, it follows, becomes simply the point of intersection between these actions, the will of God expressed in time from outside time, by which a connection deeper than temporal causality is stated. Erich Auerbach, in "Figura," compares the conception of time that is based on a strict sequence of causation—which he calls linear, or horizontal—to the time implied in a figural relationship between events—which he calls vertical.[51] His distinctions can provide a useful way of thinking about the larger time structure of the cycle-drama as well. It is like a series of essays into history from the same center, like the casting of a fisherman standing in midstream and making strikes in several degrees of a circle. The sequence of these essays has meaning and moves steadily closer to a goal, but the times between them matter very little. The shape of the drama is a linear progression, a sequence of pageant wagons or self-contained episodes on a stationary stage, but the metaphysic of its structure is centrifugal. The relationship between Noah and Abraham exists in God, not in historical events intervening between them. In the same way, the seven ages are primarily vertical in their connection, initiated by acts of God or by new kinds of covenant with Him; the horizontal connections between them are ignored, a matter of indifference to the Corpus Christi cycle. No age grows by organic development from another; each is abruptly initiated by God, from outside time.

A distinct kind of anachronism is made possible through this conception of time as artifact. We have already looked at an example of it from Chester, when Abraham raises his sword to kill his son and makes this final prayer:

THE SACRED HISTORIES	THE TWO TIMES	THE THREE LAWS	THE SEVEN AGES OF THE WORLD	THE CORPUS CHRISTI PROTOCYCLE
Old Testament	The Time of Misdoing (Justice)	Natural Law	First	Creation & Fall; Cain & Abel
			Second	Noah & Flood
			Third	Abraham & Isaac
		Written Law	Fourth	Moses
			Fifth	The Prophets
New Testament, Apocrypha, and Book of Revelation	The Time of Grace (Mercy)	The Law of Charity (The Law Fulfilled)	Sixth	Nativity; Passion; Resurrection; Ascension; Assumption & Coronation of the Virgin
				CORPUS CHRISTI MOMENT OF PER- FORMANCE
			Seventh	Doomsday

FIG. 2 Time as artifact: some medieval divisions of history.

> Ihesu, on me thou have pittie
> that I haue most in mynde![52]

Only time as artifact permits such anachronism, indeed expresses its most fundamental nature by means of anachronism. The idea underlies, as well, the incident in the Cornish cycle when Maximilla, the first martyr, has her clothing accidentally set on fire in the Temple. In great pain, she cries out to Christ for help, and the Bishop shouts at her (for this being an Old Testament play, Christ has not yet been born nor the doctrine of the Trinity revealed):

> ...O fool's head,
> Where hast thou heard God called Christ
>   By a man in this world born?

She answers with a definition of the Trinity; His name is not written in the law of Moses, but she speaks of His virgin birth, and calls Him Christ. The Bishop in fury commands that she be stoned to death, which action the *tortores* (modeled on the executioners of Christ to come) carry out with savage delight; she cries again to Christ for mercy, and is mocked thus by the Second *Tortor*:

> Do ye hear, comrades,
> How the vile strumpet is
>   Calling on the thing not existing?

Her invocations, as the text emphasizes, are meaningless in that historical moment. But not to us, the audience, nor, more important, to Maximilla. She knows what she knows, and *for* Christ (and as a figure *of* Him) she dies. When she calls out to Christ, it is with this phrase: "As I am for thee tormented."[53]

Hugh of St. Victor wrote in the twelfth century about the kind of anachronism that Maximilla's knowledge represents: "Holy Church began to exist in her faithful at the beginning, and shall last to the end. We believe that, from the beginning to the end, no period lacks its faithful to Christ."[54] Christ exists both before His incarnation and after His crucifixion; His relationship to time is not horizontal but vertical, because of His triune nature in eternity. God is outside time, and knowledge of His workings can transcend the limitations of any single historical moment.

In the Chester *Nativity,* the emperor Octavian is offered the honors due a god, but he rejects them for a reason that is central to this study and can well serve to summarize and conclude it:

> ... godhead asks in all thinge
> tyme that hath no begininge,
> ne never shall have ending;
> and none of these have I.
>
> Wherefore, by verey proofe shewinge,
> though I be highest worldlie king,
> of godhead have I no knowing;
> it were unkindlie.[55]

Human time is the artifact of God; it is shaped by Him and expresses His truth, through a multitude of correspondences, congruences, and paradoxes. In imitating human time, the Corpus Christi drama imitated it as this sort of artifact, in seven ages answering to the seven ages of man and the seven days of creation: at the same time, it furnished a moral image of contemporary English society and instructed men in the instruments of man's salvation, his passage through time into eternity.

The problem of time and place in the Corpus Christi drama is not a wholly consistent one, to which one consistent answer may be found. Much of the anachronism and anglicization requires little explanation: it furnished convenient ways of talking, it saved the trouble of long, complicated expositions of foreign terms and institutions, and it filled some very considerable gaps in knowledge. But certain uses of anachronism and anglicization were deliberate and meaningful in deeper ways, and the ideas I have presented in this chapter seem to me helpful in understanding them. The formal neglect of the audience moment is compensated for by an imitation of past time as contemporary; the biblical past is shown stripped of its specifically Jewish character, in order that it may be seen as significant in its totality to England; and time is displayed as an artifact shaped by God, whose patterns express His eternal truth. Time concerns us because we are alive in it and because God's plan for man's redemption can be worked out only in its terms. But man's real business is eternity, and the drama exists to remind him of that. For several hours of mimetic perform-ance, the audience is invited to contemplate this plan in its temporal sequence, as a thing outside them, as a rhythm that passes by the audience's moment in time in order to talk about times more sig-nificant to the history of the race. In doing this, it achieves something very solemn and beautiful.

Chapter Six

Religious Laughter

In a drama whose subject is Original Sin, the Atonement, and the Judgment, we may well be surprised to find a considerable amount of comedy. Laughter in a medieval religious context is a phenomenon not restricted to the drama, but the drama may reasonably be regarded as its *locus classicus*: in total size, in seriousness of intention, and in the quantity and variety of their comedy, the cycles equal or surpass all other contemporary religious literature. In this chapter and the next, religious laughter will be our single subject, not because I propose to value the comic passages more highly than the rest, but because the problem is fascinating in its own right, because it focuses on a number of the best things in these cycles, and because the mixture of comic and serious is more than anything else responsible for the characteristic "taste in the head" one gets from this drama.

To speak of the relationship of laughter and religion as a problem is not to create gratuitous difficulty out of purely modern notions of religious decorum.[1] The medieval mind was itself much concerned with the seemliness of human laughter under the aspect of eternity, and (by eventual and inevitable extension) within a drama specifically designed to image human life from such a perspective. We shall examine a variety of medieval attitudes toward laughter in the pages that follow, but we can best begin with a view that perhaps little affected the way ordinary men lived, though it was stated many times with conviction and power during the entire medieval period. Just as an artist often prepares his canvas with a ground color that may not appear at all in the finished painting but nevertheless affects the tonal values of all the colors and forms that the eye sees, so the ground color of medieval thought and institutions is an austere asceticism.

It is an essential part of the medieval dialectic concerning religious laughter, and against that total dialectic I shall seek to place the comedy of these plays.

In *Jacob's Well,* a fifteenth-century collection of sermons, there is a tale that illustrates something of this ascetic attitude. It is about a king who never laughed. When an attendant lord reproves him for his somberness, the king has him put on a chair which is then placed above a pit of fire; a sword is suspended over his head, and men on four sides point their daggers at him. The tale continues:

þe kyng bad him leyȝhen, & be merye, & etyn. þe lord seyde, "I may make no merthe for drede of my deth. I may noȝte ete for sorwe; for I se peryles of my deth a-boue me, & be-nethe me, & on iche syde of me." þe kyng seyde: "þou repreuedyst me for I am euere sory & pensyif. my skyl is þis! I am be-set al aboute wyth grettere peryles þan þou seest aboute þe. my chayere is my body of speer brotyl & rotyn bonys, in whiche my soule sytteth. be-nethe is þe pytt of helle brennyng wyth fyir redy to brenne me, whanne my soule partyth fro my body, þat is frele & brotyl. A-boue me hangyth þe swerd of þe wreche of god redy to smyte me."[2]

In such a world, where each action is scrutinized in terms of its eternal consequence, comedy and delight are impossible—even happiness is terrible. A prolonged contemplation of the General Doom must necessarily still all laughter. A story as old as the fourth century had reminded men of this fact throughout the Middle Ages, even into the fifteenth-century *Alphabet of Tales,* a popular collection of sermon *exempla*:

We rede in "Vitis Patrum," how on a tyme ane olde man saw a yong man lagh, & he said vnto hym; "Son, how may þou fynd in þi herte to lagh? Mon not þou & I & we all befor bothe hevyn and erth gyf a rekynyng of all our lyfe? And þerfor me mervels," he said, "at þow may fynde in þi harte to lagh."[3]

Should we forget the Doom, there are other reminders all about us and inescapable. The fact of death was offered as another best teacher of how men should live (the *ars moriendi* is by implication also an *ars vivendi*), for it can teach us how to value life, and, most especially, as Everyman learns in the play called by his name, how to value Fellowship—the mirth, gaiety, and laughter born of good company. Fellowship is the first of Everyman's friends to desert him on his journey to the grave. Christianity told men that they must learn the lesson of Everyman before dying. The multiple traditions of the medieval meditation on death were evolved to teach that lesson, and real life, quite as effectively as any painter or woodcarver, could provide images for contemplation. As a sermon in Mirk's *Festial* teaches, it is better for a man's soul that he visit a house where a corpse is lying and all the folk weeping than that he visit a house of laughter and reveling, for "such worldys murthe makyth a man to forȝete his God and hymselfe alsoo."[4]

On those rare occasions in the Psalms (2:2–4; 36:13; 58:9) when the God of the Old Testament is thought of as laughing, it is in scorn and anger; never does He display a sense of fun. The Middle Ages believed the life of God's Son to have been equally austere. The *Cursor Mundi* says of Christ:

> þat thris he wep we find i-nogh,
> Bot we find neuer quar he logh.[5]

It was commonly understood that Christ lived His life as an *exemplar* for man. In His life every act and every omission had a clear moral implication. Not surprisingly, the Wycliffite critic makes use of this fact as a major part of his attack on the drama: "And therfore it is that seyntis myche noten that of Cristis lawȝyng we reden never in Holy Writt, but of his myche penaunse, teris, and schedynge of blod."[6] The Christian God was never credited with a sense of humor —anthropomorphism stopped short of that. Rather, a powerful case was established and reiterated throughout the Middle Ages that laughter and frivolity, the temporary abstention from involvement in all that is serious in the human condition, was an offense against God, a negation of the example of Christ, and a peril to men's souls. The cycle-drama staged the great events (the Fall, the Crucifixion, the Doom) that gave this ascetic hostility to laughter its urgency and power, and critics who opposed the drama often did so on just these grounds.[7] But it seems not much to have inhibited the drama's practice.

Medieval physiology had carefully identified the physical source of laughter—it came from the spleen[8]—and was interested in it because laughter was considered a characteristic *proprium* of mankind, an idea deriving ultimately from Aristotle's *De partibus animalium*.

Laughter was thought to distinguish man from all the other animals, and Notker Labeo, who translated many important works at St. Gall before his death in 1022, had formulated that fact thus: "Quartum est in quo concurrit soli homini risibile esse. Quamvis non semper rideat, tamen naturam habeat ridendi. quia quicquid risibile est, homo est, et quicquid homo est risibile est." Or as he wrote elsewhere, "homo est animal rationale, mortale, risus capax."*⁹ The idea had a long life and may be found in the works of Quintillian, Julius Pollux, Porphyry, Marcianus Capella, Boëthius, and Alcuin; the full Middle Ages continued it, cautioning that though important as *proprium,* it was not of man's essence.¹⁰ Rabelais, too, worked in this tradition, as when he prefaced his *Gargantua* with this verse:

> Mieulx est de ris que de larmes escripre,
> Pour ce que rire est le propre de l'homme.

It was possible to believe that the faculty of laughter was one of the results of the Fall of Man, and that in our original perfection we voiced our higher joys in less carnal ways;¹¹ but man as an animal who laughed was a fact independent of anyone's approval or disapproval. Most medieval teaching took positions much less severe than the one we have been examining, recognizing laughter to be widely present in human life, and acknowledging its considerable delight. *Ratis Raving,* a courtesy book designed to instruct a Christian youth in proper social conduct, discusses the subject in an illuminating way. The reader is advised to be:

> Nocht loud of lauchtyr amang men,
> Thar smylyng scantly may men ken.
> Bot syk a bourd may quhilum fall,
> That al men lauch, baith gret & small.¹²

Moderation is best, but some jokes no man can resist. It is sound advice, in touch with reality, and it was not restricted to secular manuals alone. The Benedictine Rule, for instance, defined *moderate* laughter as one of the twelve degrees of humility:

---

* The fourth part involves the fact that it is consonant with the nature of man alone to be capable of laughter. Although he is not always laughing, laughter is nevertheless among his natural traits; because whatever creature is capable of laughter is human and whatever is human is capable of laughter.

Man is a rational, mortal animal, capable of laughter.

> The x degre es þus to lere:
> Not to lagh with ouer-lyght cher
> Ne with laghing our voce to raise.
> For hali writ þus leres & sais:
> "A fole," he sais, "bi day & nyght
> In laghyng rais his vose on hight."
> Þarfor es gude to man & childe
> For to ler at be laghter-myld.[13]

Pecock's *Reule of Crysten Religioun* suggests, in a discussion of penance, that even vital things such as food and drink can be renounced in part, and it includes laughter in that category:

> Also euery day in ech houre of þe day we mowe forbere certeyn vsis of oure outward wittis, as is of siʒt, of speche, of taast, of þouʒt, of lauʒing, of japing and of bourding; þouʒ not al, ʒit sum; þouʒ not alwey, ʒit at certeyn tymes; now oon, now an oþer; and neuer fare þe worse.[14]

It is pleasing to God that we forbear from much laughing, but there is no suggestion that we renounce it altogether. We are made as we are made: the need is central to our psychological structure, and we repress it at our peril.

Indeed, the Middle Ages frequently used images of breaking or bursting to express this need for relaxation into laughter. Such an image occurs in a letter issued by the Theological Faculty of the University of Paris on March 12, 1445, indicting the feast of Fools and seeking to put an end to it forever. The argument that man must laugh is specifically mentioned as a defense often made by proponents of the feast,[15] and it is rejected; but one suspects it is the particular instance that has caused its rejection here, since the same argument is cited with approval by good churchmen in other contexts, its authority referred back to St. Anthony himself. *An Alphabet of Tales* recounts the story in a form that would have been used in church and cloister pulpits through much of England:

> We rede in þe life of Saynt Anton how on a tyme ane archer, þat was a gude sh[oter], fand Saynt [Anton] syttand emang his brethir makand merie with þaim. And þis archer was displesid þerwith & þoght þai sulde hafe bene in þer clostre, & tente þer bukis & þer serues, & nott hafe bene att no sporte nor no welefare. And onone Saynt Anton purseyvyd his menyng, and callid hym to hym, & bad hym putt ane of his arows in his bow, & shote

als fer as he myght, & he did so; and þan bad hym take a noder, and do on
þe same wyse, and he did as he bad hym; & þan he bad hym take a thrid,
& draw hys bow als fer as he myght, at it mott fle far fro hym. And þan þis
archer [ansswerd] hym agayn and said, "Sir, I dar nott, for I may happen
draw so fer þat I may breke my bow, & þat wold I nott, for þan I monde
make mekull sorow." Than Saynt Anton sayd vnto hym agayn, "loo! son,
þus it is in þe werke of allmyghtie God; ffor and we draw it oute of mesur,
we may sone breke itt; þat is to say, and we halde our brethir so strayte in
aw þatt þai com to no myrth nor no sporte, we may lightlie cauce þaim to
breke þer ordur. And herefor vs muste som tyme lowse our pithe, & suffre
þaim hafe som recreacion & disporte emang all þer other chargis, as Caton
says, Interpone tuis interdum gaudia curis.[16]

The same image of a bow under great strain also occurs, alongside a
motto from Aesop, in the Prologue to Robert Henryson's *Fables*.[17] It
is one of the central images by which the Middle Ages understood the
human psyche.

Laughter was respectable in the Middle Ages partly because it could
teach. Notwithstanding its value as entertainment, it seldom wholly
neglected this other function, as even genres less obviously didactic
than the cycle-plays can testify. We may look briefly to the *100 Mery
Talys* for an especially interesting instance of this double address. Although it was not published until the end of the medieval period, its
matter was traditional and long familiar. Today we would call it a
joke book, but it has features no longer characteristic of that kind.
Four tales near the middle of the collection (numbers 54–57) are
included chiefly for doctrinal purpose, to teach in English the basic
items of the Christian faith. Tale 56, which sets out the Creed, makes
no gesture toward humor at all, nor does it make any excuse for being
there, but the other three all use humor as part of the lesson. To be
sure, the jokes in tales 54 and 55, which teach the Ave Maria and Pater
Noster, are somewhat weak, but they are as "mery" as many in the
collection.[18] Tale 57, however, is genuinely funny, and it manages to
teach two doctrinal lessons at the same time. It concerns a friar who
knows how to preach only one sermon, and that on the Ten Commandments. (These are set down in the course of the tale.) But its
apparent subject is the embarrassment of the friar's servant at this
poverty of matter: someone tells him his master is called "frere Johnn
.x. commaundementys," and he is ashamed that his master is so simple.

He goes to him and begs him to preach about something else. The friar challenges him, saying, since you've heard this one so many times, recite the Ten Commandments for me:

Mary quod yᵉ seruaunt these be they. Pryde Couetyse Slouth Enuy wrath Glotony and Lechery.
By redynge this tale ye maye lerne to know the .x. commaundementes and the .vii. dedely synnes.[19]

Such laughter could be put to good use: it could make doctrine memorable.

Medieval writers who used laughter as a technique of teaching were, at the same time, rarely asleep to its possible dangers. Their caution was not conceived in ascetic terms—rather it grew from practical experience of the delightfulness of comedy, sometimes so great as to submerge serious meaning and doctrinal instruction. G. R. Owst, who has demonstrated the kinship of the sermons with the drama in the use of humor as a mode of instruction, cites a complaint from the *Summa predicantium* that focuses on the problem:

If anyone tells some open folly in the pulpit (in predicatione apertam fatuitatem diceret), they retain it in the memory well enough; not so the useful things.
...these folk hearken with the greater zest for vain, quaint and laughable matter in the sermon, which may provoke them to mirth.

The good things they fail to bring away. The remarks that were out of place, they are all too ready to seize upon, to repeat them again and again with glee.[20]

An incident in the history of the York cycle can illustrate a comparable concern on the part of the drama. Among the plays lost from that cycle is the play of *Fergus,* once the charge of the Masons. We know it was a source of great embarrassment to them, for they complained to civic authority in 1431 that it caused more laughter and clamor than devotion.[21] They were given *Herod* to perform instead. The guild itself sought the change—the lay people too wanted a dignified and useful entertainment. Anyone reading the description of the lost play from Burton's list of 1415 would be hard put to say why it was found objectionable: "Quatuor Apostoli portantes feretrum Marie, et Fer-

gus pendens super feretrum, cum ij aliis Judeis [cum vno Angelo]."*[22]
But by reference to other sources it is possible to guess at the reason.
In apocryphal accounts, the enmity of the Jews is particularly focused
upon Mary after the death of Christ; when she is dead and the apostles
carry her bier through the streets, a last attack is made upon her. Mirk's
Festial narrates the event thus, in a sermon on the Assumption:

And when þay of þe cyte herd hom make such melody, þay ren toward
hom wyth bottys, and staues, and oþer wepon, yn ful purpos forto haue
drawyn downe þe bere, and cast þe body yn þe fenne. But he þat layde
fyrst hond on þe bere, anon boþe hys hondys wern puld of by þe elboues,
and hongyt soo styll on þe bere; and he wyth hys stompes stode soo, cryng
and ӡellyng for ake and sorow þat he suffyrd. Then sayde Petyr: "Kys þe
body of oure lady, and knowlech welle wyth trew hert þat Crist, veray God
and man, was borne of þat same lady, and þou schalt be hole."[23]

A drama that offered game equivalents for reality would not have
hesitated to dramatize this incident in detail: if God can come down
in a cloud made of sheets and a basket, if the Holy Ghost can appear
as tongues of real fire, so can Fergus' arms come off at the elbow and
stick to the bier. But this last action, in real life so horrible, would
translate into a game-version undoubtedly comic: its literalness would
make it ludicrous, and attention would be focused far more on the
costuming and the trick, and on Fergus' humiliation, than on the
serious miracle it was supposedly enacting. Because the story of
Fergus was apocryphal and inessential to the larger design, it was
simply dropped from the cycle, thus ensuring that the "useful things,"
the "good things," were not lost from the entertainment as a whole.

These, then, are some of the ways the Middle Ages, at its most serious, thought about laughter—its peril, its necessity, its potential usefulness. With this survey behind us, establishing perspectives, we may
turn to the most extensive defense of mirth within Christian life that
has survived from the English Middle Ages. It is from a work known
as *Diues et Pauper,* and it offers a defense of the miracle plays specifically as a source of mirth and gladness. Among contemporary
notices of the drama, it is second in length only to the Wycliffite Sermon, and has been as little used, probably because it has not been

---

* Four Apostles carrying the bier of Mary, and Fergus hanging upon the bier, with
two other Jews [and with one angel.]

printed since 1536. First written sometime between 1405 and 1410, and first printed in 1493, it is available only in great libraries, and I shall therefore quote from it extensively here.[24] The problem of laughter is included in a discussion of the Third Commandment, concerning the kinds of behavior proper on the Sabbath. It is a difficult place in which to make such a defense, but with considerable skill and conviction the author turns that very difficulty into his strongest argument. Dives has asked whether miracle plays and dances are lawful on Sundays and great feast days, and to this, Pauper replies:

Miracles pleyes & daunces that ben done principaly for deuocion honestye and myrthe. to teche men to loue god the more. and for no ribaudrye / ne medlyd with rebawdrye ne lesynges. been leful / so that the people be nat lettyd therby from goddes seruyse / ne fro goddes worde hering and that ther be no erroure medled in suche miracles and pleyes ayenst the feith of holy churche. ne ayenst gode lyuynge. Alle other ben forfendyd both haliday and Werkday.... where the glose saith that for to represente in pleyng at Cristmasse Heroude and þe thre kynges. and other processe of þe gospel bothe thanne and at ester. & in other tymes also / it is leful. and commendable. *Diues*. Than it semyth by thy speche þat in halidayes men may lefully maken myrthe. *Pauper*. God forbede elles For as I saide the haliday is ordeyned for reste and releuing bothe of body and of soule. And therfore in lawe of kynde / in lawe writen / in lawe of grace / & euyr from the begynnyng of the World. the haliday hath ben solaciouse with onestie / both for soule and body / & for worship of god whos day is that daye.... And therfore the prophete saith. Hec dies quem fecit dominus: exultemus et letemur in ea This is the day þat god made / make we nowe mery & be we glad. *Diues*. Contra. Seynt austyn saith þat it were lesse wycked to go at the plough and at the carte / & carde and spynne in the sundaye than to lede daunces. *Pauper*. Seynt austyn spekith of such daunces and pleyes as was used in his tyme / whan cristen peple was moche medlyd with hethen peple / and by olde custome and example of hethen people used unhonest daunces and pleyes that by olde tyme were ordeyned. to stire folk to lechery and to other synnes And so if daunsyng and pleynge nowe on the halidayes stire men & wymen to pryde to lechery glutonye and sleuthe / to ouir longe wakynge on nightes. & to ydelship on the werk daies. and other synnes / as it is righte likly þat they do in our daies than ben they unleful both on the haliday and on the werke day. And ayenst al suche spake seynt Austyn But ayenst honest daunces. and pleyes done in due tyme and in gode maner in the haliday. spake nat seint austyn. *Diues*. Contra te. we fynde in holy wryt þat god badde his peple turmente their soules and yeue them to sorowe and mournynge in the haliday.... *Pauper*. Salomon saith. Spes que differtur affligit animam. Prouer. xiii.c [*sic*]. The hope the desire and the longynge þat is delayed turmentithe the soule. For the more that man or woman longith after a thing the more it is disease / tyl he hath his disese and his longynge. But nowe it so that the rest the mirth the ese and the welfare / that god hath ordeyned in the halidayes. is token of endlesse reste ioye and myrthe and welfare in heuenes blisse that we hope to haue withouten ende. For there men shalle halowe withouten ende / from al maner trauayle thought & care. And therfore as I saide first god wole that we thynke on the haliday of the reste ioye and blysse / þat the haliday bitokneth and haue it in thought / in desire in longing & hope to come therto.... Nat to shewe greate heuynesse outwarde / and to doo bodily penaunce in any grete haliday.[25]

In the following chapter, Dives asks to hear scriptural proof that God wishes mirth and gladness from his creatures. Pauper discusses several texts, among which this is perhaps the most interesting (the story is taken from 2 Kings 6):

But michol saules doughter and Dauydes wyf scornyd dauyd for his daunsynge and for his skyppynge / & said. that it was nat semely to a king to skippe & daunce as a knaue. bifore the people & bifore her maydens. Dauyd saide to her. I shal pley and daunce bifore my lorde god þat hath chosen me to be a kinge. & put thy fader & al thy kyn from þe crowne I shal pley bifore my lorde god / & put me in lower degre for his loue / and be lowe and meke in myn owne sight to plese god þat made me king And for þat mychol scornyd so dauyd for his skippynge & his daunsynge and his lownesse / therfore god made her bareyne.[26]

The argument is clear and consistent, and does honor to both God and man. Certain elements in this defense should be noted, for they draw together many ideas I have already developed in this book. The medieval author is aware of the considerable difference between the theater of Rome as known by Augustine and the theater of the Christian community in his own time; because he knows that Augustine and the early Fathers spoke of another *kind* of entertainment, he would have rejected as irrelevant most of the patristic condemnations of theater so frequently cited in the Middle Ages. He believes mirth to be necessary for both body and soul (going further than the physiologists and their interest in the spleen), and what is more, he believes it to have been divinely authorized in all three periods of human time, those three already discussed as the law of nature, the law of Moses, and the law of Grace or Charity. We should note as well his assertion that mirth and recreation are among the major purposes of this drama, not merely by-products or incidental "goods": he sees them as ends important in their own right. He holds (on scriptural authority) that to play *to* God and *for* God is to please Him, that human joy and such humility as chooses to express joy in play and game are acceptable to heaven. And most interesting of all, he uses an argument that combines physiology, psychology, and the technique of figural explication to justify this mirth as particularly suitable for Sundays and high feast days. Dismissing out of hand the ascetic argument for anguish and self-torment, he assumes as self-evident that we all long for eternal rest and joy—the Sabbath of the world, the end of human time—and that longing deferred does us physical and spiritual harm. Therefore, he says, God, knowing this, has ordained a "figure" of that eternal rest for us, as a recurring medicine to our longing: the weekly Sabbath is our foretaste of the joy that will have no end. We honor it and God, and we do ourselves good, by celebrating it with mirth such as miracle plays and honest dances.

The case for laughter in a religious context was reasonably coherent and convincing: against those who urged sorrow and anguish as man's proper spiritual bread, promising the release of laughter only at the moment of release from life,[27] there were men to argue that man's body was built with the need for laughter, and even some to argue that his very soul was made for mirth and happiness, on earth as much as in heaven. They argued that too much seriousness could breed despair and madness, and that laughter should therefore be allowed, as a thing neutral in itself and convertible to good end. The Corpus Christi drama is an institution of central importance to the English Middle Ages precisely because it triumphantly united man's need for festival and mirth with instruction in the story that most seriously concerned his immortal soul.

There is current another theory concerning laughter in the medieval drama, too important to be passed over in this discussion. Its most eloquent spokesman was the late A. P. Rossiter, who suggests that the cycle-plays involve a comic mockery of sacred personages, a kind of compulsive ritual defamation of those things that medieval society normally held most sacred. His argument is based upon both anthropology and psychology: he believes that the veneration in pre-Christian fertility rituals took the form of mirth or mockery,[28] and that in this drama, too, the audience was invited to show disrespect for the things it ordinarily most revered. This view involves important questions of interpretation, for if it is true, the tormentors, the crucifiers, the doubting midwife, all perform actions that engage at some profound level the sympathies of the audience: the audience must join them spiritually in their jokes, their taunts, their scorning. Furthermore, it depends on evidence that has long and, I think, too uncritically been assumed to relate to this drama. For both these reasons, it demands close scrutiny.

The evidence in question has been printed or described in Chambers' *The Mediaeval Stage,* where nearly a hundred pages are devoted to two feasts that are considered to embody this mockery: the feast of Fools, and the feast of the Innocents, commonly known in England as the feast of the Boys or of the Boy Bishop.[29] Rossiter's study devotes a chapter to these festivals, as proof of the "Ritual Comic Relief" which also informs the Corpus Christi cycles. And a student as cautious as A. C. Cawley continues the tradition in his recent edition of the *Wakefield Pageants* when he concludes that "it is plain that the spirit of nonsense has infected the Wakefield playwright, who wrote his pageants for Corpus Christi day, just as it did the subdeacons who played the fool on the feast of the Circumcision."[30] He does not intend a direct relationship, yet any reader would find it difficult to state what the limits of such a relationship as he implies might be. I should like to try and do that here. The essential confusion is born when we link the feast of Fools with the feast of the Innocents; they are different in name, in nature, in geographical occurrence, and they bear differing relationships to the Corpus Christi drama. Chambers kept them scrupulously separate, but his conclusions are made so quietly amid pages and pages of documentation that their effect is finally somewhat unclear. The feast of Fools allowed the inferior clergy (the subdeacons) one day in the year in which they took control of ritual observances within the cathedral. The result was often a full-scale burlesque of sacred ceremony: for example, Beauvais service books indicate a drinking bout on the church porch, censing with pudding and sausage, introducing a live ass into the church, and using a specially written *ordinale* where parts of the Mass ended with brays and were answered with braying responses from the congregation.[31] In other places in France, it involved the wearing of monstrous masks and women's clothing, dicing at the altar, and comic processions through the market place.[32] From Chalons-sur-Marne in 1570, we have a full description of the *maîtrise des fous* and his costume, and of the inferior clergy singing gibberish, grimacing, and leaping about the cathedral.[33] There was considerable opposition to this feast from high ecclesiastical authority, and it was in some places difficult to put down. Two facts particularly concern us. The celebration was considered an abomination by high Church authority, and more important, it was confined almost entirely to France; in England the feast of Fools had little importance. Chambers tells us that in England the feast apparently was never widespread, and even within its limited area of observance little subject to the kind of abuse that attracted official censure. The English records are few. An Inventory (1245) from St. Paul's mentions the Fools' scepter (the *Baculus stultorum*); an Inventory (1222) from Salisbury records the same; in Lincoln, Bishop Grosseteste forbade this celebration in 1236, incorporating the prohibition in his formal *Constitutions* of 1238. These are thirteenth-century records, distant in time from the vernacular drama. Two later records, however, are possibly relevant and come from cities with drama cycles: the custom seems to have grown up again in Lincoln, for a Visitation in 1390 denounces it; and the Statutes of Beverley Minster drawn at the end of the fourteenth century also prohibit the feast.[34]

The feast of the Boys is quite different in nature and importance. It was celebrated on Innocents' day, when, in honor of the young martyrs, the boys of the cathedral choir were ceremonially installed in office and authority over the senior clergy. The feast grew from an important biblical text—"He hath put down the mighty from their seat, and hath exalted the humble"—and it was conceived as a reverent celebration of this Christian truth. It may occasionally have passed into excessive revelry, but evidence of this is rare; even in France it seldom got out of hand, for it entailed in essentials merely the selection of a Boy Bishop from the ranks of the young choir, a procession of choir boys through the cathedral, and the transference of a *baculus* as a symbol of power from the elders to the bishop-for-the-day. The ceremony was common and well loved in England, far more common than the feast of Fools. If it sometimes led to excess, the revelry was merely accidental to its serious ecclesiastical purpose. Boys are more easily kept in order than are adults of low education and humble station, and ecclesiastical discipline was hardly threatened.[35] These distinctions turn out to be important: the feast of the Boys is geographically relevant to a study of medieval English culture and, as we shall see in the next chapter, to certain English Shepherds' plays; the feast of Fools, at least as described by French documents, is probably not. Again there may be two documentary exceptions, this time from two southern cities that had no cycles: at Wells in 1331 and 1338 and at Exeter in 1360 there are complaints against shameful *ludi* in the Cathedral during the Nativity season, with Bishop Grandisson complaining that the celebrations at Exeter mock divine service and damage church vestments and ornaments.[36] It is unlikely that the feast of the Boys is the particular subject of either complaint, but one cannot be sure: if it is not, something like the feast of Fools may be. These documents are also possibly relevant, and I do not wish to understate their interest or significance.

But we need to be cautious about the interpretation of these few records; we must not confuse the natures of the two feasts, nor their areas of significant occurrence. The Boy Bishop ceremony was probably never comic, and the feast of Fools was probably not known to the writers and audiences of most of these plays. Furthermore, the Church opposed the feast of Fools with its gravest authority, and in England only Lincoln seems to have resisted censure for a time. It is unlikely that ceremonies thus prohibited would serve either as models or as authorizations for a drama sanctioned and supported by the Church. But the drama texts themselves offer our best proof that neither in detail nor in spirit do the cycles display any tendency to mock, blaspheme, or make merry with the sacred characters of the story, and to this more important source of evidence we may now turn.

We can avoid a great deal of confusion in this matter by first excluding from our discussion things that are *not* comic. In drama there are always two areas of emotional response to an action, the response made within the world of play and game, and the response that the audience makes to the entire play world of which the action is a constituent part. The comic in the drama is that which makes the audience laugh; it has nothing to do with the laughter of personae in the play itself. Audience and stage characters may sometimes laugh together, but they need not always do so: the medieval cycles often dramatize incidents where these responses are different. The failure to recognize this distinction is, I think, the real source of Rossiter's shadowy antinomies and ironic ambivalences. The only real feelings present in a theater, or in a medieval marketplace on Corpus Christi day, are those induced in the audience; the rest is feigning, whether it accords with the audience's response or not.

The test case for such a theory must be, as it is in Rossiter's book, the crucifixion of Christ. The *Meditations on the Life and Passion of Christ*, a narrative poem, characterizes the mood of the historical moment in its full complexity:

> Whan dom was ȝiue aȝeyn þat kyng,
> þere was lauȝtre, cry, and scornyng.[37]

These emotions are also created within the dramatic situation, but it is unlikely that they indicate audience response. The *tortores* find for themselves a great deal of amusement in the torturing of Christ; they make jokes, they think each other very funny. But we are separate from them. These dramatists presented the death of Christ as a thing of consummate horror and shame, clearly intending that the violence and laughter on stage should be answered by silence and awe in the audience, and if recent productions of these Passion episodes may offer a guide, they succeeded. The Chester plays are the equal of any in their gusto and vitality, yet the Banns to that cycle charge the responsible guilds thus:

> You ffletchers, bowyers, Cowpers, stringers, and Iremongers,
> see soberly ye make of Christes dolefull death,
> his scourginge, his whippinge, his bloudeshett and passion
> and all the paines he suffred till the last of his breath.[38]

Regardless of how the spectacle is constituted, it is "soberly" presented. These Passion episodes will be studied in detail in a later chapter, where a very different explanation will be offered there for the jokes, the games, and the stage laughter. Here we need only notice that never in these plays is one invited to laugh at God the Father, Christ, or the Virgin.[39] They move in a mimetic world which includes the comic, the violent, the noisy, the grotesque, but though that world acts upon them, it never really touches their characters. They were reverently conceived and have about them a sanctity that defies circumstance. This is so even in the two comic episodes that usually attach themselves to the life of Mary: Joseph's troubles over Mary's pregnancy, which turn into a kind of *fabliau* farce, and the midwives' testing of Mary's virginity after the birth of Jesus. Both these scenes are, at least in part, comic. But the comedy is not the reason why they are included in the cycles, and in neither episode is Mary a comic character—that is to say, the audience never laughs at *her*. Joseph's doubts *are* funny, because of his grumpy, aged incomprehension, and his insinuations to the audience that there have been cuckolds before him. But Mary knows she is pure, and so do we—she is untouched by our laughter. The gynecological probing of the midwife is a terrifying action and so the audience would understand it; indeed, it is precisely (and intentionally) parallel to the action of Thomas when he thrusts his fingers into the wounds of Christ. (The two central mysteries of Christianity, the Incarnation and the Resurrection, are thereby formally "doubted.") And it has a terrible end: the midwife withdraws her hand to find it paralyzed, and a miracle of Jesus is needed to make it sound again.[40] Even the *Ludus Coventriae* episode in which is staged a virginity trial of Joseph and Mary (based on *Protevangelium* 16 and *Pseudo-Matthew* 12) carefully preserves Mary's dignity.[41] Far from witnessing the trial of a servant girl who has slipped up, as Rossiter suggests,[42] we are watching the trial of the Virgin, whose character and history are known to us from sources outside the play. The inquisitors may behave absurdly and create a context slanderous and coarse, but Mary stands among them like a green island in a turbulent and dirty sea; though the audience may find the episode intermittently funny, never is she the source of their amusement. Laughter in these cycles was never, in an empirical sense, irreverent. That charge could only be made in metaphysical terms.

In saying that laughter is carefully controlled in the Corpus Christi drama, I do not mean to imply a polite, sophisticated amusement. It often sought the vulgar guffaw, the laugh from the belly rather than the smile. And on occasion it valued this kind of laughter as an indication of sanity, indeed almost of holiness. A story much current in the English Middle Ages will furnish an excellent illustration, the more valuable because it discusses laughter within a church service (I quote the version in *The Knight of Tour-Landry*). St. Martin of Tours was saying mass one day assisted by his godson, St. Brice, who laughed heartily in the midst of it:

And whanne the masse was done, seint Martin asked hym whi he laughed, and he ansuered, that he saw the fende write all the laughinges that were betwene the women atte the masse, and it happed that the parchemyn that he wrote in was shorte, and he plucked harde to haue made it lengger with his tethe, and it scaped oute of hys mouthe, and hys hede had a gret stroke ayenst the wall, "& that made me to laugh." And whan seint Martin herde hym, he knewe that seint Brice was an holy man.[43]

The approval is the key: St. Brice's laughter at the devil's ridiculous desperation is a sign that St. Brice is holy, that is to say, on the side of God. He sees from a *fully* Christian point of view: God is in control, the evil and the demonic behave stupidly because that is their nature, and the proper reaction to this example of the rightness of things is laughter. In the Corpus Christi drama, as in the sources it drew upon, the severance from God is chiefly a result of man's stupidity, of his failure to be intelligent. Lucifer falls from heaven as a fool who has attempted the impossible and who could have known (had he but considered) its fundamental impossibility. Cain thinks God can be cheated in offering. Satan makes a fatal mistake in setting under way the plot to kill Christ, and hell is harrowed as a result. Anti-Christ is likewise a buffoon, a confidence man. Stupidity, even in social terms, is funny, but when it willfully expresses itself in opposition to God's plan—a plan not only intelligible but known—it becomes more than merely laughable. It is also, in some outrageous sense, perverse, and the laughter it attracts is correspondingly unrestrained and unsympathetic. This Christianity has nothing in common with the Indian mystic who said she would never accept individual salvation as long as one single human soul remained outside the gate of heaven. Rather it is one with that terrible episode in the *Inferno* in which Dante sees the place called Ptolomaea, wherein are punished the traitors to hospitality. These sinners against the sacred host-guest relationship lie on their backs in a frozen lake, weeping but unable to weep, for the tears freeze in their eyes and their anguish can find no outlet. One of them, Friar Alberigo, promises to tell Dante his history if he will take the ice from his eyes for just one moment; they will freeze again, but for that moment he will be able to weep. Dante agrees, the friar recounts his story, and then asks that the merciful act be performed:

> "And now, do thou stretch forth thy hand to me,
> Undo my eyes." And I undid them not,
> And churlishness to him was courtesy.[44]
> [*e cortesia fu in lui esser villano.*]

The role of man is to concur with the judgment of God, never to seek to be more merciful than his Creator. Whatever the modern mind may think of this idea, it was part and parcel of medieval religion. With the 57th Psalm as warranty—"The just man shall rejoice when he shall see the revenge"—the author of the *Ancrene Riwle,* for instance, had explained its propriety to his anchoresses thus:

On the day of judgment God will act as though He were saying: "Daughter, did this man injure you? Did he make you stumble. . . ? Look, daughter, see how he shall pay for it." And there you shall see him beaten with the devil's mallets until he wishes he had not been born. You will be well pleased at the sight, for your will and God's will shall be so joined that you shall will all that He ever wills, and He all that you will.[45]

Though this speaks of enemies, a saying of Augustine's that was much quoted by preachers and religious poets, made explicit the harsher implications of such a view. Here is how it occurs in *The Pricke of Conscience*:

> He says, "if my fader or moder ware
> In helle, and I wist þam þare,
> I wald nouther nyght ne day,
> For þam byd bede here, ne pray."[46]

In a recent production of the Towneley cycle at the Mermaid Theatre in London, the driving of the damned into hell at the end of the *Doomsday* play proved to be triumphantly funny still. In part we enjoyed the way the devils rolled, shoved, pricked and tossed the damned into Hell Mouth unceremoniously, as one might toss coal into a furnace; but far more than that we enjoyed a comedy of victory. In this action, the damned have no character as human beings: they appear merely as the balance sheet of their good and evil deeds, judged against a standard that is wholly acceptable (the Seven Corporal Acts of Mercy); and we are content they should go as booby prize to the devil. The rude laughter and humiliating action thus focused on the very wicked is the drama's version of the philosophic cruelty that underlies the teachings I have quoted above.

Laughter of this sort was almost the only laughter to get into the Latin drama of the Church, as we can demonstrate from two late texts. The feast of the Presentation of the Virgin in the Temple, celebrated officially in the West for the first time in 1372, includes in the Avignon *ordo* this action: Mary has mounted the fifteen steps and each of the characters in turn ascends the stage to praise her:

Synagoga, however, after a tearful lament, is pushed down the west steps of the stage by Gabriel and Raphael, lets fall her banner and the tables of the Old Law, and flees crying from the church. After the laughter of the people has subsided (*tantum quod populus quietetur a risu*), Michael ascends the platform leading the howling and unwilling Lucifer (*inuitum incedentum et ululantem*). After Michael has delivered his verse of praise, and has humbled Lucifer to the extent of making him Mary's footstool, Michael, Gabriel, and Raphael unite in thrusting *rebellator Dei* to the ground by way of the west steps.[47]

The Benediktbeuern Christmas play uses rough comedy and violence in the same insulting way. It begins with a modified *Ordo Prophetarum,* Augustine seated in the nave of the church, with Isaiah, Daniel, the Sibyl, Aaron, and Balaam on his right. On his left sit the chief of the Synagogue and a group of Jews. When the prophecies are over, Archisynagogus becomes loud and obstreperous, behaving "just like a Jew" (*imitando gestus Iudei in omnibus*), and heaps ridicule upon the prophecies. He singles out for especial scorn the notion that a virgin can bear a child. The Boy Bishop intervenes to say that these "drunken sotteries" will be easily refuted by the intellectual arguments of Augustine, and a kind of *flyting*-debate is staged, its outcome just as predicted.[48]

The characters most closely related to Lucifer and Archisynagogus in the vernacular drama are the Jews, the easily corrupted knights, the devils, and the wicked rulers. This latter group especially, with their raging Herods, inherit equal riot and scorn. They alternate between the highest boasting and the lowest fury, speaking alliterative encomia to their own majesty at one moment and behaving like madmen the next. In the Chester play of Balaam, for example, Balaack the King has been suitably regal until Balaam refuses for the third time to bless his people; suddenly his dignity disintegrates into this:

> What the Devilles! eyles the poplart?
> thy speach is not worth a fart,
> doted I wot well thou art,
> for woodlie thou hast wrougt.[49]

With the exception of the Chester Octavian, there are no good rulers in the cycles save the King of Kings. Denying a higher kingly authority, they cannot themselves manage to be kingly. Instead they behave ludicrously, ranting about their power and magnificence, easily frightened, out of their wits if their will is crossed, and struggling desperately to keep a semblance of control over their kingdoms. They excite rough, bawdy laughter, of the sort their stupidity and pretension deserve. The devils alone elicit worse treatment. There are here no fallen magnificences, no Miltonic rebels trailing remnants of their former glory. The *Ludus Coventriae* Satan has about him a particular dark coarseness, saying, after the fall from heaven:

> Now to helle þe wey I take
> in endeles peyn þer to be pyht
> Ffor fere of fyre a fart I crake
> In helle donjoon · myn dene is dyth.

And again after he has successfully tempted man and God has once more banished him to hell:

> At þi byddyng ffowle I falle
> I krepe hom to my stynkyng stalle
> helle pyt and hevyn halle
> xul do þi byddyng bone
> I ffalle down here a ffowle freke
> ffor þis ffalle I gynne to qweke
> with a ffart my brech I breke
> my sorwe comyth ful sone.[50]

His exits are grotesque, sprawling, obscene—and undoubtedly, to the Middle Ages, funny. The truly unregenerate are handled roughly in these plays, a festival equivalent in play of the treatment they may expect from God when He comes to judge at the end of time.

This is not the comedy we value most in these cycles, though it is an important part of medieval religious laughter. There was also comedy of a more genial sort—warmer, funnier, more human—and in the pages that follow we shall examine some of the ways in which it too relates to serious meaning.

Chapter Seven

The Invention of Comic Action

Medieval dramatists were rarely called upon to invent original dramatic action. They worked with a known story, and their business was to invent dialogue, to shape the story into formal, self-contained units, to find ways of turning it into play and game. The few actions that appear to be of their own invention are therefore of particular interest. They are almost entirely comic actions, and they grow out of two episodes above all others—the play of Noah's Flood and the Adoration of the Shepherds. Because these plays concern ordinary people who find favor before God, they pose questions I shall reserve for a later chapter called "Goodness and Natural Man"; here I wish to examine not the characters but the shapes, the configurations, of the action alone. I shall concentrate on six comic actions, chosen because they can illustrate a range of medieval techniques and procedures, and because they can cast further light on the question with which we have been dealing—the proprieties of medieval religious laughter. All six are actions for which one would search in vain the Bible, the Apocrypha, and related vernacular sources; and for the most part, they have not had proper critical explanation.[1]

A recent study of the Abraham and Isaac plays, to my mind a model of learning and literary perception, has stated clearly the difficulty these other plays present, and it can serve us as a point of departure:

Although [other plays] such as the famous *Secunda Pastorum* or the Towneley Play of Noah may be more lively, they are less integrated: they are diverting in both the modern and original meaning of the word, for they interest and amuse by characterization and action which have no relevance to the religious meaning of the story.[2]

I want to look at possible ways in which these surprising inventions may relate to the major action that gives them their formal place in the cycles. I want to isolate those elements that are apparently arbitrary and gratuitous, in order to discuss the ideas that may lie beneath and constitute their relevance. The comic surfaces of these plays are, of course, valuable in their own right, and it is our first privilege as audience to respond to them; if I seem to devote little space to recreating the comedy of these actions, it is only because that comedy is still alive and apparent to anyone, reader or spectator, whereas its origins and theological resonance are no longer so. Without intending to substitute "deeper meaning" for the delightful humor of these plays, I nevertheless want to suggest some possible relationships between them. Though these dramatists invented, they did not invent *ex nihilo.*

Noah had a wife. From this bare scriptural fact, a comic character and a dramatic tradition were born, so familiar and loved in the English Middle Ages that she became a kind of paradigm of human character: she was the root-form of the shrewish wife, and her relationship with Noah became the archetype of everyday marital infelicity. Chaucer's "hende Nicholas" in *The Miller's Tale* refers to her, in plotting the seduction of his landlord's wife:

> "Hastou nat herd," quod Nicholas, "also
> The sorwe of Noe with his felaweshipe,
> Er that he myghte gete his wyf to shipe?
> Hym hadde be levere, I dar wel undertake
> At thilke tyme, than alle his wetheres blake
> That she hadde had a ship hirself allone."[3]

At the level of this interpretation, Noah's wife might be a character out of the *fabliaux,* the usual genre for such character studies. But her inclusion in the drama serves some very different ends, and one of the actions traditionally associated with her will furnish our first example of the way in which comedy in these cycles can be born of serious and central meaning. In both Chester and Towneley, there is staged before the ark a knockabout battle between Noah and his wife: she opposes his will, refuses to come on board, and gives him a sound beating on the banks before she is finally subdued and made conformable. It is a great comic battle, but its moment in history, properly considered, is tragic and awesome—God, in His wrath, is about to purge the world of sin, and only Noah and his family are to be saved. In such a context, the domestic comedy has perplexed many readers.[4]

We can best avoid that perplexity by paying close attention to certain repeated words and ideas in these plays, most especially to the words "servant" and "stable," and the way they relate to a conception of "maistrye" that serves as a major principle of relationship in the cycles. Briefly stated, it is simply the notion that all things exist in their proper degree, and that the lower shall be subject to the higher. God is greater—stronger, more worshipful—than the angels; the angels, in turn, are above man, man is above woman, human beings above animals. So the progression goes, with obedience as its binding force, and stability as the proper condition within it. The alternative was understood to be chaos and sin. *Purity,* a long homiletic poem of the fourteenth century, describes the condition of the world that caused the Flood in just such terms:

> Þat watz for fylþe upon folde þat þe folk used,
> Þat þen wonyed in þe worlde wythouten any maysterz.[5]

Thus the Towneley *Flood* play can begin with perfect relevance by having Noah recall the rebellion of Lucifer and his presumption to God's mastery, with God in turn justifying the Flood in terms of a sovereignty disdained by man, speaking to Noah as "noe my scruand," and explaining to him why he will be saved:

> Thou was alway well wirkand / to me trew as stele,
> To my bydyng obediand / freudship shal thou fele.[6]

The York play, too, centers on these terms:

> Nooe, my seruand, sad an cleyn,
> For thou art stabill in stede and stalle.

And the York Noah begins to build the ark in confidence, "Thurgh techyng of god maister myne."[7] The characters of the sons are similarly conceived: they are as obedient to their father as Noah is to God. The *Ludus Coventriae* shows the entire family of Noah praying to God, vowing their fidelity and lamenting the contrary way of the world, all as a means of establishing the obedience that was the received notion of Noah's condition in Grace.[8]

The brawling of Mrs. Noah is directly related to Noah's fidelity to God in ways that, without at all lessening the humor of the piece, add to its intrinsic vitality that final relevance of meaning that a work of art demands. Mr. and Mrs. Noah, though at the remove of many generations, are still the children of Adam and Eve, still the offspring of that initial mistake in marital "maistrye." It had been punished by God's curse (Gen. 3:16), which a prose life of Adam and Eve translated as woman being "vnder monnes heste,"[9] and which the Chester cycle takes care to have spoken in its *Fall* play, with God addressing Eve:

> And for thou hast done so to daye,
> the man shall mayster thee alwaye,
> and vnder his power thou shalt be aye,
> thee for to drive and deere.[10]

This establishes, clearly enough, a theological norm for marriage,[11] but equally clearly, one often at odds with empirical fact. A lively fifteenth-century carol with the refrain,

> Nova, noua, sawe yow euer such?
> The most mayster of the hows weryth no brych,

relates this abuse, as the drama does, to its scriptural background:

> Nat only in Englond, but of euery nacion,
>   The femynyng wyl presume men for to gyd;
> Yet God at the tym of Adams creacyon
>   Gaue man superiorite of them in euery tyd;
>   But now in theys women is fyxyd such pryd,
>   And upon themself wyl tak so mych
>   That it constreynyth the most mayster to wer no brych.[12]

But whereas the carol starts with present facts, referring them to sacred history, the drama begins with history, imagining it in present terms. The Chester Noah addresses his wife thus:

> Good wife, let be all this beere
> that thou makes in this place here;
> for all they wene thou art master,
> and so thou art by St. John.[13]

In the Newcastle Play (of which only Part I survives) there is an interesting anomaly—the devil is introduced into the action to guide

Mrs. Noah in her shrewishness. But even this variation grows from the same parent tree. Just as God has designated Noah and his family as His only true servants, so the *Diabolus* interferes to protect his, those about to be drowned:

> I wene there has been none alive,
> Man, beast, child nor wife,
> But my servants were they.[14]

And his advice to Mrs. Noah (patterned on the traditional tempting of Eve) is to ignore her husband's counsel and commands, to oppose her will to his for their common good:

> And thou do after thy husband read,
> Thou and thy children will all be dead,
>   And that right hastily.[15]

"Maistrye" is, then, the key to the brawling, and both Chester and Towneley do something fine with it. In Chester it is subsidiary to a theme I have reserved for later discussion; but in Towneley it is used for its own sake, for the shape of its action. Not only does the Towneley cycle stage a better brawl than any of the others, and find a racier, more colloquial language to fit to its intricate stanza pattern, but it pushes deeper into the philosophical implications of this battle fought out at the moment of mankind's destruction.

The impending doom is created by the Wakefield Master in verse that effectively contrasts an ominous, swelling rhythm with the plain-spoken, tetchy replies of the reluctant *Uxor:*

> *prima mulier.*   Good moder, com in sone / ffor all is ouer cast,
>   Both the son and the mone. /
> *Secunda mulier.*   and many wynd blast
>   fful sharp;
>   Thise floodis so thay ryn,
>   Therfor moder come in.
> *Vxor.*   In fayth yit will I spyn;
>   All in vayn ye carp.[16]

The battle that develops when she is forced along is splendidly comic, the *Uxor* crying out that her heart's desire is for a mess of widow's soup, addressing her husband as "wat wynk" and "Nicholl nedy," and behaving so outrageously that Noah complains to the audience, "Se how she can grone/ and I lig vnder."[17] On the level of comic entertainment this is not different in kind from the other versions, but its art is finer. For the Wakefield Master adds to the serious context a new detail and uses it to make explicit a philosophic significance merely latent in the others. It is signaled by Noah's speech concerning the urgency of departure, made before what we may call the "domestic storm" begins:

> Behold to the heuen / the cateractes all,
> That are open full euen / grete and small,
> And the planettis seuen / left has thare stall,
> Thise thoners and levyn / downe gar fall
>   ffull stout.[18]

The seven planets have left their places in the sky; all is chaos and lack of order. (The Vulgate speaks simply of torrential rains.) And to this macrocosmic anarchy the drama relates the microcosm. God's great world is turned upside down just as is man's little world, and for the same reason: proper *maistrye* has been destroyed. Just as fallen man is rebellious to his master, God, so too is the wife rebellious to her husband, and only when the proper human relationship is re-established does the universal order begin to reconstruct itself. When all have finally entered the ark, it is a new Mrs. Noah who speaks, in a voice chastened in tone and moving to a graver rhythm. Her first speech after she is on board makes the deeper meaning clear; the progression toward it is worth quoting in full for its art is not mean:

> *Primus filius*. A! whi fare ye thus? / ffader and moder both!
> *Secundus filius*. Ye shuld not be so spitus / standyng in sich a
>   woth.
> *Tercius filius*. Thise ar so hidus / with many a cold coth.
> *Noe*. we will do as ye bid vs / we will no more be wroth,
>   Dere barnes!
>   Now to the helme will I hent,
>   And to my ship tent.
> *Vxor*. I se on the firmament
>   Me thynk, the seven starnes.[19]

With the restoration of domestic order and degree, the seven planets again find their place in the universal order, and man and the universe move together toward the rightness of new beginnings. An interesting statement of the assumptions that underlie this Towneley play may be found in St. Augustine's *De Genesi contra Manichaeos,* where the Flood, which begins the second age of the world, is compared to the second day of the creation, when the firmament was made by God from chaos and disorder:

Et incipit mane a temporibus Noe secunda aetas.... Et bene comparatur secundo diei quo factum est firmamentum inter aquam et aquam; quia et arca in qua erat Noe cum suis, firmamentum erat inter aquas inferiores in quibus natabat, et superiores quibus compluebatur.*[20]

The ark *was* the firmament. It enclosed the living world, and the larger progression from disorder and violence in the universe is given its domestic equivalent within the family world of the survivors.

The other actions I wish to examine in this chapter all come from the plays in which the shepherds adore Christ. They are among the finest achievements of the cycles and they have been much studied, but they are probably the least understood. Although there was available little theological commentary on the shepherds as such, there was, of course, a vast amount of commentary on the Nativity and Incarnation, and it was from this that the dramatists worked, transforming its detail into action wholly at ease within plays about ordinary herdsmen. This fact may help to explain the surprising importance given the episode of the Shepherds in the cycles, in contrast both to the Latin liturgical drama, which played the episode briefly if at all (preferring the Adoration of the Magi), and to a work as comprehensive as *The Stanzaic Life of Christ,* which barely mentions the announcement to them.[21] The vernacular drama seems to have allowed the shepherds this greater importance because they could serve to establish the significance and meaning of the birth that they witness. What is surprising to us is that the actions which establish this meaning should be comic actions. York and the *Ludus Coventriae* dramatize the episode briefly and in a straightforward manner, but the Chester and Towneley versions pose complex problems for the modern reader or audience.[22]

---

* And with the morning there begins the second age, extending from the time of Noah.... And it is well compared to the second day, in which the firmament was created dividing water from water; because the ark which contained Noah and his people was the firmament between the lower waters on which it floated and the upper waters from which it was raining.

The Chester shepherds begin by boasting at great length of their skill in curing the diseases of their sheep. Their catalogues of ailments and remedies are tedious, repetitive, and funny—a comic exploration of the obsessive way in which simple men talk about the thing they know best. The Towneley shepherds define themselves as watching over their flocks; these in Chester talk mostly of their veterinary skills. Says one:

> my tytefull tuppes are in my thought,
> them to saue and heale
>
> from the shrewd scab it (?) sought,
> or the rot, if it were wrought,
> yf the cough had them caught,
> of it I colde them heale.

Another boasts:

> Hemlockes, and herif—take keepe!—
> with Tarboyst most bene all tamed,
> penigras, and butter for fat sheepe;
> of this salue am I not ashamed.
>
> ashamed am I not to showe
> no poynte that longes to my crafte.[23]

He comes from boiling a salve for his sheep, and is scouring with gravel the pan he used so that his wife will not know. They are real shepherds talking of real sheep diseases, and they spend a long time at it. What can be the relevance of such an action?

I think its ultimate source must be traced to a tradition deriving from statements of Christ, as in Matthew 9:12, that He has come as a physician or healer. From this grew a metaphor that found varied expression in the Middle Ages, as when *The Mirrour of the Blessed Lyf of Jesu Christ* states:

Goddes sone toke man. and in hym he suffred that longeth to man / and was made medecyne of man: and this medecyne is so mykel that it may not be thouʒt. For there is no pride / but that it may be iheled thoruʒ the mekenes of goddis sone: there is no couetise / bot that it may be heled thoruʒ his pouerte.[24]

The *Stanzaic Life of Christ* focuses more particularly on the dying:

As to the secund nedeful thing
that come of Cristesse passion,
medicyn moost acordyng
hit was to bring vs of baundoun.[25]

And the *Golden Legend,* Englished by Caxton, speaks of the deadly sins as diseases and Christ's name as healing medicine:

It is medicine whereof saith S. Bernard: This name Jesus is such a medicine that refraineth the strength of wrath, it appeaseth the swelling of pride, it healeth the woundys of envy, it restraineth the fire of lechery, it distraineth the flame of covetousness, it attempereth the thirst of avarice, and it dryeth all rotten wretchedness.[26]

Examples could be multiplied almost indefinitely from contemporary treatises,[27] from the Cornish play cycle,[28] and from the *Ludus Coventriae,* in which Peter preaches a magnificent sermon identifying Christ as both bodily "leche" (healing the lame and blind) and as "gostly" healer (curing mortal sins).[29] But I am, for the moment, chiefly interested in the Chester plays, which develop the theme at length. When Mary comes to be purified, Simeon says:

for nowe I see my savyour
is comen to leech my langoure,
and bringe me unto blesse

. . . .

thou arte mankindes heale.[30]

Jesus describes Himself to the doctors in the temple in these same terms,[31] and in the Chester ministry play He makes a central speech in which ideas of the shepherd and the healer are carefully united:

for I am the good sheapheard, that putteth his lyfe in Ioperdy
to save his flocke which I loue so tenderly,

. . . .

Go we therfore, Brethren, while the day is light,
to doe my fathers workes, as I am fully minded
to heale the sick and restore the blynd to sight,
that the prophesy of me may be fulfilled,
for other sheep I haue, which are to me committed,
they be not of this flocke, yet will I them regarde,
that ther may be one flocke and one shepheard.[32]

This moment, which recalls the boastings of the shepherds, is directly anticipated within the shepherds' play itself, when the angel has made the announcement of the birth and the *Gartius* (the shepherds' boy) recalls:

> he sang also of a "Deo"
> me thought that healed my hart.[33]

The Latin *salus* could mean both health and salvation; and so the second of these is spoken of in terms of the first.[34]

So far the matter is simple: two parallel themes, the shepherds as healers of sheep, and Christ (who spoke of Himself as a shepherd) as healer of men. But this alone would not justify so long a dramatic exposition; its final propriety depends on the two being made one. It is achieved by extending further the sickness-medicine theme, in ways we may instance from a treatise (*c.* 1400) on how to receive the Eucharist: "I aventure me to resceyue þee, swete lord, as a syke man resseyueþ a medcyne. þou art a sooþfaste leche, lord, and soþely I am syke. þerfore I take þee. for to be maad hool þorouʒ þee."[35] The connection seems to be this: Christ, as healer of Adam's wound, left behind Him the power to work healing miracles, His life as a pattern of goodness, and His body and blood in the Sacrament as sovereign medicine for sin. He taught His disciples "leche-crafte"[36] and they taught the priests after them. Christ passed on the cure of souls. The Chester play dramatizes this by establishing first the literal term of the metaphor (the shepherds talk of real sheep diseases and sheep medicines); later, when they have seen Christ, their identity is altered, and these shepherds of sheep become shepherds of men. The Second Shepherd says, after seeing the infant Christ,

> vnkind will I never in no case be
> but preach Ever that I can and crye,
> as Gabryell taught by his grace me,
> singing alway hethen will I.

and the Third Shepherd follows:

> Over the sea, and I may have grace,
> I will gange and about goe now
> to preach this in everye place;
> and sheepe will I kepe no more nowe.[37]

He will give up sheep-herding for a different kind of pastoral care. The Boy says he will become an anchorite, and the First Shepherd says he will become a begging friar.[38] It is to these three kinds of religious vocation that the earlier action has led, and the completion of this metaphor is thus a major unifying element of the Chester play, furnishing its beginning and its end.[39] The medieval Church thought it particularly suitable that Christ's birth should be first announced to shepherds, because of a congruity we can find stated in a twelfth-century homily:

ure louerd ihesu crist . . . þat is alre herdene herde. and alre lechene leche. þe com to helen þe wundes. þe þe deuel hadde on mancun broht.[40]

He was the shepherd of shepherds, the healer of healers, and the Chester dramatist found his own way of revealing this *sensus* in action. In final support of this reading, one may refer to the long poem called *The Southern Passion,* which discusses papal responsibilities in precisely the terms (actual sheep diseases) that the Chester shepherds use. The poet there says of the Pope:

> He shal answerie at domes-day · of eche soule ffor-lore.
> And so him hadde beo betere · habbe ywist by-fforc
> A ffold ffol of ffale sheep · þey hi were half y-schore,
> Oþer skabbede in þe pokkes · oþer hare ryg al to-tore,
> And bydde crist at one word · þat he were him-sulf vnbore.[41]

Christ's Vicars and the shepherds of Chester join hands.

Equally puzzling in these plays is the common staging of some sort of altercation, be it a "flyting" or wrestling or both together. In the Chester cycle, it is precipitated by the invitation of the shepherds to their boy, Trowle, that he should eat of their feast. He, lying far off, superbly rude and darkly rebellious, will pay homage to no man:

> if any man come me by,
> and wold wit which way best were,
> my leg I lift up, where I lie,
> and wish him the way by east- and west-where.
>
> and I rose when I lay,
> me wold thinke that traveyle lost were:
> for King nor Duke, by this daye,
> rise I will not but take my rest here.

He scorns their food as dirty and grubbed; and in cursing the items of the feast, he simultaneously pronounces a curse on their own bodies and organs:

> Fye on your loynes and your lyveray,
> your lyveras, lyvers, and longes,
> your sawce, your Iawce, and your saveray,
> your sitting without any songes.[42]

The slanging goes on and on, its ostensible purpose a protest against poor wages. But then it takes a strange turn. Trowle wrestles with the shepherds one after another and successfully throws them all.[43] The action is strong, the rhetoric vivid, the comedy knockabout and vulgar, and its relevance (today) obscure. How did this action find its way into a play of the Adoration of the Shepherds?

To consider first the actual wrestling. The essential action is one in which a boy (Trowle, *Gartius*) forces to the ground three older men, who are also his masters. This notion of youth overcoming age, of the servant overcoming the master, must be referred to a theme pervasive in the religious life of the Middle Ages, deriving from the Magnificat spoken by the Virgin to Elizabeth at the Salutation. The verse that concerns us is from Luke 1:52 and had been used as the Canticle for Vespers throughout Roman Christendom since the sixth century: "He hath put down the mighty from their seat, and hath exalted the humble." It was used every day of the year, but the text came into special prominence (as we noted in the last chapter) during the Christmas season at the feast of the Innocents, when the custom grew up of electing from the choir a Boy Bishop for the day and allowing the boys to sit in the seats of their elders and superiors and to conduct certain of the divine offices.[44] The truth enshrined in that custom was felt to be a part of the deepest significance of the Incarnation. England took the festival to its heart; it seems to have been more common there than anywhere else in Europe. And thus, this theme of the exaltation of the humble had a particular Nativity reference. Though it originally concerned the Virgin, it came to apply to the Innocents slaughtered by Herod, and directly to Jesus Himself: on Christmas a babe is born in a mean stable who will displace the powerful and privileged. An Egerton Manuscript poem on the birth of Christ makes just this point:

Miȝti men he haþ · al a doun ido
Of here sege, & mekliche men · iheiȝed he haþ also;

.   .   .   .

Israel he haþ vnderfonge · & is child al so.[45]

We see here wedded the two ideas: the humble overthrowing the
mighty; the young overthrowing the old. It is a profound part of the
meaning of the Nativity, and no Corpus Christi cycle neglects it. Each
has Mary speak or sing the Magnificat at the close of her visit to Elizabeth,[46] and in the plays of the Magi, Herod rants fiercely on the same
theme. In the *Ludus Coventriae* he goes on in this way:

> how xulde a barn wax so bolde
> be bestys yf he born be
> he is yong and I am old
> An hardy kyng of hye degre.[47]

In the Towneley play:

> Alas, that euer I shuld be knyght,
> Or holdyn man of mekyll myght,
> If a lad shuld reyfe me my right
>   All thus me fro.[48]

And in Chester:

> what the Deuill shold this be!
> a boy, a groome of Low degree
> shold raigne aboue my Roialtie
> and make me but a goose![49]

The overthrow that Herod fears is in essentials like the overthrow
in play of the old shepherds at the hands of their boy. Trowle is
humble only in station, not in spirit, but it is enough to satisfy the
requirements of the comic design. Only the mode of the two actions
is different. If the words that the First Shepherd uses to describe their
defeat at wrestling, "Fellowes, this a fowle case is/that we bene thus
cast of a knave,"[50] seem parallel to those Herod uses to describe his
predicament, it is because they both ultimately derive from the theme
of *Deposuit potentes* and its Christmas liturgical connotations. The
one is an action found in the Bible, the other is invented, but both
grew from the same seed. I am not suggesting that we read the shep-

herds' wrestling match as an allegory for, or a figure of, the overthrow of Herod or—a better parallel—for the Harrowing of Hell. Trowle is not Christ, not by a long way, nor a figure of Him; the shepherds are neither Herod, nor Jewry about to lose its Messiah, nor Satan. They are simply men—men of good-will, for the angel appears to them—who are having a little sport. Significantly, it is the Third Shepherd who suggests the action:

> Trowle, boy, for Gods pitty,
> come, Eate a morsell with me
> and then wrastle wil we
> here on this would.[51]

And Trowle, too, understands it as sport, though he wrestles fiercely, and continues to insult them sullenly. "Have done! begin we this game,"[52] he says, and the action is under way. But it is a "deposing" only in play—Trowle remains the shepherds' boy, and they his masters. It serves to create festival mirth, and to sketch in, by comic means, a serious part of the larger theological meaning of the episode.

We may now include the quarreling in a larger definition of this action as a discord between the shepherds. Viewed in this way, it bears a close kinship to Towneley I as well, which includes a slanging and a brawl over the grazing rights of an imaginary flock of sheep.[53] Scholars have discovered several folktale analogues, the basic story being identified within the play itself as that of the Fools of Gotham,[54] in which two fools are condemned in their folly by a third man, who himself does a foolish thing in demonstrating to them their witlessness. As is perhaps too often the case, scholars, having discovered an analogue, conclude that the work of understanding is done. In fact, the place of this episode in a *Pastorum* play has never been satisfactorily explained.[55] It is there, I think, simply in order that contention and discord may be established as a dramatic fact, as mood, so that a dramatic progress from it can be made. The motive for such a progress is to be found in the angel's song, *Gloria in altissimis Deo, et in terra pax in hominibus bonae uoluntatis.* The announcement is *of peace* and it is made *to men of good-will.* (It is perhaps for this reason that these shepherds quarrel *in play* and over mock-issues.) The bringing of peace was considered a most important part of Christ's mission, as the *Speculum Sacerdotale* in a Nativity sermon explains:

For fro the tyme that Adam hadde synned vn-to the tyme that the saveoure come there was grete discorde be-twix God and man, betwix man and angels, betwyx man and man, betwix spirit and flesche.[56]

Mirk's *Festial* states the same theme more forcefully:

At mydnygh[t] Crist was borne, for þen alle þyng be kynd taketh rest yn schewyng þat he ys prynce of pes, and was comen to make pes.[57]

And it found its way into carols of Christmas, as verse and as refrain:

> Nowel syng we now al and sum,
> For Rex Pacificus is cum.[58]

The playwrights have created a world of discord and strife in order that the King of Peace may be born into it and reveal His nature by His effect upon that world. It is an object lesson in how to give an epithet, as well as the theological idea behind it, dramatic life in action. The Chester wrestling is particularly successful, for in it "natural man" exhausts his energy and is finally quiet:

> *2nd Shepherd:* therfore will I wayte on this wold
> upon the wedder, for I am weary.
> *3rd Shepherd:* Though we be weary, no wonder,
> what betwene wrastling and waking!
> ofte we maye be in thoughte, we be nowe under,
> god amend it with his making![59]

At this precise moment, the star appears and the announcement of peace is made. God has come to amend it all. The plays go on to dramatize friendship and good-will in the journey to Bethlehem, the adoration of the child, and the parting kiss of peace. As a Chester shepherd expresses it:

> we haue bene fellowes, I wis,
> therfore lend me your mouth,
> and frendly let us kisse![60]

Man becomes friend of man; the angel comes in friendship *to* man, and announces (as in Towneley II): "God is made youre freynd/now at this morne."[61] Out of discord have come harmony and love.

We move on. In the Shearmen and Taylors' Pageant from Coventry there is a straightforward stage direction: "There the scheppardis drawys furth there meyte and doth eyte and drynk; and asse the drynk, the fynd the star, and sey thus."[62] The action serves to characterize the shepherds' lives very simply: they eat and drink in the fields at their work. In the French *Passion de Semur* they boil milk and cook eggs.[63] But two of the English plays greatly expand this conventional action, for another purpose. In Towneley I, almost a hundred lines of dialogue (ll. 191–286) are devoted to the action, most of them spent in describing the various items of the shepherds' meal. They produce boar's brawn with mustard, a cow's foot in sauce, a leg of pork, two blood puddings and a liver pudding, beef, mutton from a "rotted" ewe, a boiled oxtail, a pie, two pig's jaws, most of a hare, the leg of a goose, more pork, a partridge, a tart, chickens, a calf's liver scored with fruit juice, and a good deal of ale. When they have finished, they propose to collect the remains and give them to the poor or to mendicant friars, thus ending their preposterous feast with charity. Chester develops a similar action (ll. 101–72) in which the shepherds produce a feast consisting of bread, onions, garlic, leeks, butter, green cheese, ale, meat, pudding, a "ianock" (? oatcake), a sheep's head, a pig snout, some sour milk, a pig's foot, a "panch cloute" and a "womb clout" (? tripe), a liver, a boiled chitterling, pig's-foot pudding, gammon and other meat, another pudding, and an ox tongue. Some has been concealed under a cloak, some is shaken out of satchels.[64] Carey documents the fact that such a pooling together of food was common, and cites a "gossip myne" carol that mentions such a custom.[65] But major questions remain. We need to decide first of all what exactly is comic about this action. One critic has focused on the Towneley juxtaposition of proletarian and aristocratic dishes as a source of grotesque humor,[66] but if this is in fact a joke (I shall later give reasons for doubting it) it is a very small one, not in itself enough to justify the action or to explain the feast in Chester, which is homely in every way. Surely the humor lies in the sheer size of the meal: what in the Coventry cycle and the French plays is a kind of medieval box lunch is here a gargantuan banquet. And there is further laughter in the way in which the shepherds produce the feast, like conjurers, pulling out this and that from all corners of their clothing.[67] Medieval feasts were known for their lavishness, but this is a meal for only three men, and it is served in the fields out of pockets and packets. The manner of its making and its disproportionate size constitute the comedy of *both* versions. All this seems simple enough, but there is a more difficult problem still to be considered: how does this action come to be associated with the plays of the Shepherds' Adoration, and in what way is it relevant to the total action?

We should remind ourselves that the play comes immediately after the birth of Christ in the cycle sequence, for I think it seeks not merely to represent the historical action (the shepherds' adoration) but to invest that action with some of the mood and custom of medieval Christmas celebration, familiar in every detail to its original audience. We must approach the season as they did, through the keeping of Advent fast.

Advent is the period before Christmas in which Christians make themselves ready to celebrate the first coming of Christ and in so doing to prepare themselves also for His second coming as Judge. It is a time of prayer, repentance, and amendment. Our first records of Advent observance in the West date from the latter half of the sixth century. In the diocese of Tours, fasting three times weekly was ordered from the feast day of St. Martin (November 11) until Christmas, and after the synod of Mâcon (583), the rule was generally accepted and given liturgical expression. In the Middle Ages, these weeks were observed as a time of fasting, analogous to Lent although not usually so strictly kept.[68] We can trace the observance in English documents such as the *Penitential of Theodore* (emanating from Theodore of Tarsus, Archbishop of Canterbury, 668–90), the *Penitential* ascribed by Albers to Bede, the *Stanzaic Life of Christ,* and the *Golden Legend.*[69] But it is the *Speculum Sacerdotale,* a fifteenth-century collection of *sermones de tempore et de sanctis* which includes a treatise on penance as part of its pages on Lent, that can best instruct us:

There bethe in the yere foure lentyns, *scilicet,* one afore Paske, the whiche is comen to alle men. And in this Quadragesime it is inioyned to manye for to faste to brede and to water the Wedenysday and Friday. The secunde Quadragesime is after the vtas of Pentecost. And some fasteþ al this Quadragesime iii. dayes in the weke. The thridde Quadragesime is the myddis of heruest, but it is noзt vsid in many countres. And the fourthe Quadragesime is before the Natiuite of oure lord.

And of Seynt Thomas is no fastyng, for his feste is in the tyme of the Aduent when tyme is of contunuall fastyng.

All this seems clear enough: Lenten fast is "comen to alle men," and the Advent fast is clearly kept in England, though the Harvest fast is not. But when the treatise begins to specify penances for various sins, the matter becomes confused:

ʒif a man trespas twyse or somwhat ofter in fornicacion, let hym do the forsaide penaunce with this addicion, *scilicet,* that he faste the | Quadragesime be-fore the Natiuite of oure lord, *scilicet,* the Aduent or ellis the half of it, or ellis let hym absteyne hym fro flesche yche Wedenysdaye.[70]

Here it seems that the observance of the fast may serve also as a special penance, i.e., that the fasting enjoined for a particular sin may run concurrently with regular liturgical fasts, just as a prisoner may serve two jail sentences concurrently. The matter is not wholly clear, but in some sense or other—probably subject to local custom, and exercised in different degrees among laity and clergy—Advent was a time of fasting.

Certainly, the week before Christmas was particularly austere in diet, for the fasting of the Ember Days includes an Advent occasion:

The fowre tymes of the yere are these: wynter, somer, heruest, and veer. And yche tyme hath thre monethes. And for we synne and trespas in yche tymes and monethes, therfore it is ordeyned in holy churche that in yche of these iiii. tymes we faste thre dayes in waschynge of oure synnes þrouʒ prayingis, fastyngis, almes dede, and wakyngis.

the fourthe thre dayes schuld be fastid in the weke before Cristenmasse, so that when it happeneþ that the vigele of the Natiuite of oure lord falle in the Satturday, then that the thre dayes be fastid in the weke goynge a-fore, for that vigele and þe fastynge of the foure tymes schall neuer falle to-geder in oo weke.

The night before Christmas day, then as for Catholics now, was an obligatory fast:

We forbede that ye yeten no maner of flesche or fleschely metes in that worshipful nyʒt.[71]

Medieval fasting was, furthermore, very severe, forbidding all flesh, including "melted" flesh (butter, milk, cheese) and all fowl.[72] It is small wonder that carols were composed to bid Advent a gay, if slightly bitter, farewell. We may enjoy a spirited fifteenth-century example:

[Refrain] Farewele, Aduent; Christemas is cum;
    Farewele fro vs both alle and sume.
With paciens thou hast vs fedde
And made vs go hungrie to bedde;
For lak of mete we were nyghe dedde;
    Farewele fro [vs both alle and sume.]

While thou haste be within oure howse
We ete no puddynges ne no sowce,
But stynking fisshe not worthe a lowce;
    Farewele [fro vs both alle and sume.]

There was no fresshe fisshe ferre ne nere;
Salt fisshe and samon was to dere,
And thus we haue had hevy chere;
    Farewele [fro vs both alle and sume.]

Thou hast vs fedde with plaices thynne,
Nothing on them but bone and skynne;
Therfore oure loue thou shalt not wynne;
    Farewele [fro vs both alle and sume.]
. . . .
Come thou no more here nor in Kent,
For, yf thou doo, thou shallt be shent;
It is ynough to faste in Lent;
    Farewele [fro vs bothe alle and sume.]
. . . .
This tyme of Cristes feest natall
We will be mery, grete and small,
And thou shalt goo oute of this halle;
    Farewele [fro vs both alle and sume.][73]

The tradition persists even into Ben Jonson's *Christmas his Masque,* in which Christmas (personified) orders, "nor out of neither of the Fish-streets, admit not a man; they are not Christmas creatures: Fish and fasting dayes, foh! Sonnes, sayd I well? looke too't."[74]

But if Advent meant fasting and privation, Christmas meant feasting and plenty. Says the *Speculum Sacerdotale*: "The feste of Seynt John the Euaungelist is euer in Cristenmasse wyke, and then is no tyme to faste."[75] In representations of the months of the year, whether in carvings or in stained glass, feasting scenes for December and January abound.[76] It was a continuing tradition, as Thomas Tusser indicates in *Five Hundred Pointes of Good Husbandrie* (1557): "At Christmas, we banket, the rich with the poor."[77] At Christmas, all work ceased for twelve days. The cattle, sheep, and swine had just been slaughtered, and great feasts were made of this temporary surfeit. Tenants bore obligatory gifts of food to the lord, and with them he organized a great feast, adding food of his own, since the right of a peasant to a Christmas feast from his lord was often contractual.[78] A boar's-head carol of the fifteenth century indicates the kinds of food an aristocratic banquet would include: boar's-head with mustard, crane and heron with "bytteris," partridges, plovers, woodcocks, snipe, larks, good wines, bread, furmentye, venison, capons, peas, raisins and currants, etc.[79] Against this "noble" bill-of-fare might be set this account of an annual Christmas dinner due to John de Cnappe, of Somerset, from a customal of 1314 listing his rights as a tenant:

> ... his *gestum* at Christmas with two others, namely two white loaves, as much beer as they will drink in the day, a mess of beef and of bacon with mustard, one of browis of hen, and a cheese, fuel to cook his food and that of the other tenants of the king's ancient demesne, and to burn from dinner time till even and afterwards, and two candles of assize to burn out while they sit and drink one after the other if they will sit so long.[80]

This feast is similar in kind to the fare of the Chester shepherds, and the items listed in the boar's-head carol, if added to this, would create a banquet not unlike that in Towneley I. When the rich and poor banqueted together, it is likely that the feast was made up of both the plain and the fancy. Thus to call the Towneley feast "grotesque" because of its great variety is perhaps to mistake the matter; rather it is comic because of its size and its locale.

In Chester, the custom of the Christmas feast was so popular that in Tudor times authorities had to legislate against it:

> Whereas heretofore of late tyme yt hathe been used that dyverse of the worshipfull of this citie haue caused breckfasts to be made in ther houses upon Christenmas daie in the mornyng before Dyvyne service endyd by reasone wherof manye dysorderid persons have used themselves rayther all the daye after idellie in wyse and wantonnes then geven them selves holy to contemplacion and prayre.... Mr. Mayre by the advyse of his worshipfull Brethren thaldermen of this cytie have thought good that those breckefasts, banckytts the same Christenmes daie in the morning shall not be used and

kept herafter and you shall understand that this ys not meynyd but that every man y^t wyll upon other dayes convenyent may bestowe the same coste upon ther frinds and pore nyghbours as lyberally as thaye have byne accustomyd other yeres before tyme.[81]

The Chester Corpus Christi cycle, it is to be noted, staged the best shepherds' feast of them all. By reducing the observance of a society to the observance of three men, and by treating this great annual feast as an ordinary meal in the fields, the Chester and Towneley cycles together make the episode one of mirth and gaiety.

The staging of this action may, however, involve still another level of meaning. In the offices for Christmas Eve according to the usage of Sarum, a Post Communion prayer speaks of Christ, "cujus coelesti mysterio pascimur et potamur.*[82] Christ's body and blood, the spiritual food of the Christian, are born that night, and the Sacrament of the Altar was often spoken of as a kind of banquet which had its beginning on Christmas Day. Witness this fourteenth-century poem on the festivals of the church:

> Viij feestis oure lord gan dresse,
>   And all be newe euery ȝere.
>
> . . . .
>
> His fleissh fediþ more and lesse,
>   And fendiþ vs from feendis fere;
> Þe kirnell sprang at Cristemasse
>   Þat now is crist in a cake clere,
>   Þe preest drynkeþ blessyd bere,
> Goddis blood in sacrament.
> Almyȝty god omnipotent,
> Hys blessyd body haþ sent
> To fede hys freendys here.[83]

The *Golden Legend* in turn states the relationship in terms so reminiscent of the cycle plays that some attention to the tradition must be paid:

O precious feast and convive and verily full of great wonder, the feast healthful and replenished of all sweetness. What thing may be more precious than the noble convive or feast in which not only the flesh of calves ne of oxen like as was given in the old law for to taste, but the proper body of Jesu which is very God, is presented for to receive and assavour devoutly.[84]

* From whose heavenly mystery comes our food and drink.

This passage occurs in the discussion of Corpus Christi feast day, the very day on which these dramas of Christmas feasts were originally played in cycle-sequence: the contrast between the two feasts is therefore strong. But the idea is subtle and difficult, at very best only contributory—the audience would chiefly have recognized in these plays an outlandish Christmas banquet in the fields.

The actions we have been examining are perfectly accorded to the peculiar drama-time of the cycles, in which the past is played out as present in an English town, and the metaphors, motifs, and moods are contemporary in relevance. The diseases of sheep and their remedies, the insolence of shepherds' boys, the transition from Advent fast to Christmas feast—all these are vividly alive in their fourteenth- and fifteenth-century contexts. But deeper than this, serious work is being done: the banquet in the fields serves as a dramatic metaphor of plenty, the vaunting of medicinal skills serves as a dramatic metaphor of healing, and the ending of some form of altercation serves as a dramatic metaphor of peace. These motifs, translated into comic action, create a mimetic world for Christ to be born into: the significance of that birth—health, abundance, peace—is established by actions invented within richly articulated theological traditions.

We are now in a position to understand why both Towneley plays begin with extensive formal complaints against poverty, the indifference of the rich, the insolence of office, the harshness of nature, and the mutability of all things. Towneley I devotes 100 lines to establishing these facts, Towneley II nearly 170 lines, and there are traces of the motif in the Chester play as well.[85] The abuses spoken of are contemporary evils, the mood is satiric, but somehow a deeper note is often struck, as in this passage expressing distrust of the world and envy of the dead:

> Lord, what thay ar weyll / that hens ar past!
> ffor thay noght feyll / theym to downe cast.
> here is mekyll vnceyll / and long has it last,
> Now in hart, now in heyll / now in weytt, now in blast,
> 　　Now in care,
> Now in comforth agane,
> Now is fayre, now is rane,
> Now in hart full fane,
> 　　And after full sare.

And in Towneley II, the weathers, merely sharp and cruel in the first play, become ominous in an apocalyptic way:

> Was neuer syn noe floode / sich floodys seyn;
> Wyndys and ranys so rude / and stormes so keyn;
> Som stamerd, som stod / in dowte, as I weyn;
> Now god turne all to good / I say as I mene.[86]

The purpose served is deeper than satire. These opening soliloquies define a world at its worst—aged, cruel, full of suffering—in order that a dramatic (and theological) progress might be made therefrom. A twelfth-century homily for Christmas preaching can furnish a useful commentary on the dramatic moment:

Al mankin was wunende on muchele wowe · sum on þisse worelde . and sum on helle pine · forte þat ilke time · þat ure louerd ihesu crist hem þarof aredde · and turnede swo here wowe to wele · and here sor to muchele blisse · and of þesse blisse specð þe engel · [87]

Christ came to end man's most extreme misery, and therefore even the time and hour of His birth were understood to have symbolic meaning, as in "The Mirror of St. Edmund":

Þe tyme was in myd-wyntter, when it was maste calde; þe houre was at mydnyghte, þe hardeste houre þat es.[88]

The Towneley plays establish such a world through complaint speeches. Closely allied are the shepherds' attacks upon the rich, the powerful, the fashionable, included not merely because the Wakefield Master was committed to a kind of Christian social reform (which he was) but because whatever the sufferings of the poor, they are about to be given notice of their one great boon, Christ born poor *like them* and *to them*. The *Mirrour of the Blessed Lyf of Jesu Christ* comments upon this fact most powerfully:

And also the aungels in cristes Natiuite apperynge to the wakynge scheephirdes conforten none othere but the pouere trauailloures · and to hem tellen they the ioye of newe liȝt / and noȝt to the riche men that hauen her conforte here.[89]

In the Towneley plays, the rich are described, satirically, in their worldly comforts, prior to the action that will announce to the poor a comfort that is beyond the world and time. The anachronistic elements of the complaint establish that these ills are still with us and must be remedied; but equally important is the contrast drawn between suffering without knowledge of Christ's birth, and the same sufferings made endurable by that knowledge. A shepherd in Towneley II expresses it thus:

> lord well were me / for ones and for ay,
> Myght I knele on my kne / som word for to say
>   To that chylde.[90]

The angel's song marks the change, a change that is decisive to history, and to each play. Mary signals it explicitly in the York version, after Joseph has spoken of the wretchedness of their arrival in Bethlehem:

> And yf we here all nyght abide,
> We shall be stormed in þis steede;
> Þe walles are doune on ilke a side,
> Þe ruffe is rayned aboven oure hede,
>   als haue I roo,
>   . . . .
> For in grete nede nowe are we stedde,
> As þou thy selffe the soth may see,
> For here is nowthir cloth ne bedde,
> And we are weyke and all werie,
>   . . . .
> It waxis right myrke vnto my sight,
>   and colde withall.

He goes off to find light and fuel to make their situation a little more comfortable, while Mary, alone, speaks of a joy that transcends all this, a comfort beyond all care:

> Nowe in my sawle grete ioie haue I,
> I am all cladde in comforte clere,
> Now will be borne of my body
> Both God and man to-gedir in feere.[91]

The medieval world as established by the complaint speeches of the Towneley shepherds is not unlike the world inhabited by Joseph and Mary here; but Christ comes to alter it and to give them joy. The First Shepherd in Towneley I expounds the Virgilian "prophecy" of Christ

in a way that sums up what I take to be the deeper formal intention
of these plays:

> / that Saturne shall bend
> > vnto vs,
> > With peasse and plente,
> > with ryches and menee,
> > Good luf and charyte
> > > Blendyd amanges vs.[92]

In the discovery and adoration of the infant Christ, these various comic
actions, which have seemed to many students so independent and arbitrary, find their unity and conclusion. The "Mumming at Eltham"
which Lydgate wrote for presentation before the King and Queen
at Christmas should probably be interpreted in terms of this Christian
understanding, too, even though its terms are classical. In this piece,
Bacchus, Juno, and Ceres bring gifts of wine, olive oil, and wheat to
the King and Queen; the gifts are then moralized in several ways:

> Þey wol þeyre gyfftes with you and youres dwelle
> *Pees, vnytee, plentee* and *haboundaunce,*
>
> . . . .
>
> But care and sorowe for ever sette asyde,
> *Happe, helthe* and *grace* chosen to be youre guyde.[93]

The sophistication of the court permits a learned mythological language, but the meaning that this language expresses is part of the traditional understanding of the Incarnation and its Christmas anniversary.

The angel's song itself becomes the object of comic action, the last
that we shall study in these pages. In almost every extant version, the
shepherds after hearing the song try to imitate it, producing a bizarre
parody of both Latin text and "angelic" singing. In essentials this is
not new: in the liturgical *Pastores* from Rouen, the canons who represent the shepherds sing *Pax in terris nuntiatur,*[94] and in the Shrewsbury Fragments there occurs this sober usage:

> Ȝone brightnes wil vs bring
> > Vnto þat blisful boure;
> For solace schal we syng
> > To seke oure Saueour.[95]

In these plays, the two motifs are unrelated: the angel sings a message, and men respond to it in song. But in the mature vernacular drama such material is more tightly organized, and the one becomes a curious parody of the other: the shepherds imitate badly, hence comically, the song of the angel. Is this irreverent, uncontrolled burlesque, or has it, too, its own propriety?

We may begin by noting that in the Middle Ages shepherds were traditionally thought of as musicians. As late as 1555 it was customary for shepherds to provide music at weddings in Beverley, and the *Holkham Bible Picture Book* shows one of the shepherds entertaining at the Adoration by blowing his bagpipes and dancing to his own tune as Mary lies giving suck to the infant Christ.[96] It is perhaps in recognition of this fact that five of the six extant Shepherds' plays include more than one episode of singing: along with the attempt to sing the angels' song, Towneley I and II both allow the shepherds a song before the announcement, and the York, Chester, Towneley II, and true Coventry all provide that they sing another song after it has been made. The angel sings because song is itself harmony and perfect accordance, and such is his message: form and content are there one.

But we must distinguish between their *kinds* of music, for the angelic song would be drawn from the liturgical music of the Church, it would be sung by trained singers, and its total effect would be complex, ornate, and beautiful. The music of the shepherds would be simpler in both its ends and its means. In both Towneley I and Towneley II the shepherds engage in some admiring, if bumptious, discussion of the singer's technique,[97] but it is Chester that develops the scene most imaginatively. It stages a kind of idiot critical-panel, convened to adjudge a performance, awarding praise and disputing about what it is precisely that they have heard. There is a double joke in this long passage (ll. 369–458)—the difficulty that unlearned men have with a Latin text, and the enthusiastic appreciation, but faulty understanding, that they bring to a higher musical art than their own:

> *I Pastor:* Naie, on a "glore" and a "glare" and a "gli"
> good Gabriell when he so glored,
> when he sang, I miht not be sory,
> for through my breast-bone bloting he bored.
>
> *II Pastor:* Naie, by my faith! it was a "gloria,"
> said Gabriell, when he sang soe,

> he had a much better voyce then had I,
> as in heaven all other haue so.[98]

They set about formally approving such words as *bonae voluntatis* and *terra* and *pax*. Unlike their counterparts in the Towneley plays and the York play, they do not actually sing the same song, but they make as merry with it in their discussion. The alternative handling can be represented by Townley II:

> *primus pastor.* ffor to syng vs emong / right as he knakt it,
>   I can.
> *ijus pastor.* let se how ye croyne.
> Can ye bark at the mone?
> *iijus pastor.* hold youre tonges, haue done!
>   *primus pastor.* hark after, than.[99]

Angelic song rendered as badly as a barking at the moon would be improper were they actually imitating angelic song: but they are imitating an imitation, and the original is so wholly of another order that no insult can touch it. Richard Rolle wrote that the angel's song "may noghte [be] dyscryuede be no bodyly lyknes, for it es gastely, and abown all manere of ymagynacyone and mans reson. It may be perceyuede and felide in a saule, bot it may noghte be spoken."[100] We must understand that, on stage, regardless of the differences in subtlety between the angel's song and the shepherds' imitation of it, both are entirely gross in comparison with the beauty of the song the original shepherds heard. The laughter concerns the gap between these two, not the gap between the shepherds' singing and the ghostly beauty of the angelic original. The words of Shakespeare's Theseus apply: "The best in this kind are but shadows, and the worst are no worse, if imagination amend them."

Though this can establish a possible propriety for such an encounter between man and angel, we are still left wondering about its necessity: why does this human parody of the angelic message occur in some form in every extant English version of the Shepherds' play? The best clues, of course, are to be found in the plays themselves, most clearly perhaps in Towneley I, where one shepherd charges another:

> now, in payn of a skelp
> This sang thou not lose.[101]

Beneath the comic surface, this is an action of considerable urgency:

the shepherds have just been given a message of the highest importance, and they want to remember it whole—not just the meaning but
the message itself, of which the music was an expressive part. And
as these shepherds of sheep are "translated" into shepherds of men—
that is, as they become priests—the song serves to signal that change
without violating the essential limitations of their dramatic characters.
They will preach *by singing* to men this song. Thus the Chester Second Shepherd departs, saying:

> brethren, let us all three
> Singing walke homewardes,
> vnkind will I never in no case be
> but preach Ever that I can and crye,
> as Gabryell taught by his grace me,
> singing alway hethen will I.[102]

In Towneley II, also, the shepherds depart singing. It becomes their
means of bearing witness, as the two unidentified Prophets of the true
Coventry cycle make clear:

> *II Profeta.* Whatt, seycretly?
> *I Profeta.* Na, na, hardely;
> The made there-of no conseil;
> For the song ase lowde
> Ase eyuer the cowde
> Presyng the kyng of Isaraell.[103]

The idea may occasionally be found in related vernacular forms, as in
this fifteenth-century lyric describing a dream vision:

> And þoroght þat frythe as I can wend,
> A blestfull [song] ȝit hard I mo;
> And þat was of threo scheperdus hend,
> "Gloria in excelsis deo."
> I wold noght they had faren me fro,
> And eft-hyr þem full fast I prest;
> Then told þei me þat þei sange ssoo
> ffor verbum caro factum est.[104]

In the Shepherds' plays we are given a comic glimpse of their first
rehearsal of that song.

Certain patterns of comic invention emerge from this series of
analyses. It can be seen that sometimes the cycle dramatists work

from a traditional epithet such as "prince of peace" or "healer of men" and invent an action that amuses while establishing at the same time the significance of these attributions to the infant who has just been born. Sometimes they incorporate customs of the medieval Christmas feast into their representation of the first Christmas day, using the feast as a metaphor of plenty and abundance. Sometimes they work from a liturgical commonplace, such as the *Deposuit potentes,* in order to suggest the mystery of the Incarnation. And sometimes they invent a comic action simply in order to parallel the central action of the play, to honor and adumbrate that action by playing it twice, in different modes: Mak, Gill, and a stolen sheep anticipate the true nativity adoration of Joseph, Mary, and the infant Jesus; a brawl between Noah and his wife briefly images the kind of relationship between God and man that will cause the world to be destroyed. The one thing all these have in common is their formal seriousness: however funny, bumptious, coarse, or improvisatory these comic actions may seem, they have their roots in serious earth; they are intimately and intricately involved in their play's deepest meanings.

All this we must today reconstruct, for we are no longer commonly in possession of certain necessary facts—we are no longer alive to certain liturgical and patristic traditions that were the stuff of ordinary medieval churchgoing. For example, few of us are deeply familiar with all the verses of the Magnificat, and probably none of us has ever seen a Boy Bishop. But even the simplest member of the Corpus Christi audience, though he might have been hard put to explain the precise relevance, would have felt an instinctive "rightness" about Trowle's wrestling and throwing old men in connection with the Nativity event. I suspect the more sophisticated in the audience, and certainly the dramatist himself, could have furnished an exact explanation. We lack, then, certain information; but more important, we have lost the habits of mind, the ways of honoring, that fostered this kind of comic invention. We have all heard of Christ as healer, or prince of peace, but we do not readily perceive the relevance of the resulting drama action, because we would not ourselves any longer establish serious meaning in this way. This has been a real barrier to understanding.

So wholly are these actions allowed to exist in their own right, as comedy, that excellent scholars have assumed they were created for the sake of amusement only. This can no longer be maintained, for we have seen that these actions, when properly understood, far from diverting, concentrate and define the Flood or Nativity moment. They are like mirrors arranged in a circle around one center. Nor can we any longer agree with those scholars who would explain the presence of these actions by reference to their realism. The new material, wrote Samuel Hemingway many years ago, "consists of realistic descriptions of the life of the shepherds on the hills."[105] It is of course true that the cycles sought to make the scriptural story immediate and real. But as a total explanation, this is to put second things first, to underestimate greatly the achievement of the men who wrote these plays. For they imagined so generously, so fully, and with such respect for their dramatis personae that these invented actions, born of theology, seem as natural to the life of the characters as to the doctrinal life of the story. So thoroughly is the theological background assimilated that we seem to be in the presence of nothing more than ordinary life, closely observed and represented. But the realism of these comic actions is, as a medieval metaphysician might say, accident, not substance, the effect of the dramatist's expense of art, not his reason for it.

Chesterton once wrote, concerning medieval churches:

We talk of the inimitable grandeur of the old cathedrals; but indeed it is rather their gaiety that we do not dare to imitate. We should be rather surprised if a chorister suddenly began singing "Bill Bailey" in church. Yet that would be only doing in music what the medievals did in sculpture. They put into a Miserere seat the very scenes that we put into a music-hall song; comic domestic scenes similar to the spilling of the beer and the hanging out of the washing.[106]

The cycle drama grew out of this same cultural milieu, and displays a similar gaiety. Its achievement is, if anything, greater, for the business of playmaking is a contextual one. The dramatist did not put two wrestlers on a pillar and leave the viewer to ponder, unaided, their relationship to the scriptural stories in stained glass which gave them light. Instead he guided the spectator in understanding the comedy as part of a coherent and reverent whole. The centuries that intervene between his art and our experience of it have dimmed and partly muted his voice, but by attending to the nuances of his art, to the serious meaning behind the laughter, we can restore something of its original resonance.

Chapter Eight

The Passion and Resurrection in Play and Game

In the twelfth century, the characteristic representation of the Crucifixion showed Christ in majesty, ruling from the cross. The cross functioned as a kind of earthly throne, rather than as the instrument of His dying. In the thirteenth and fourteenth centuries, as we have already noted, this image changed greatly, in response to new meditational modes, new theological ideas, new fashions in sensibility: Christ is depicted suffering on the cross, His body broken and bleeding.[1] This transformation of Christianity's central image affected all art forms, the drama not least among them: the Corpus Christi cycles show Christ "don on þe rood" in greater circumstantial detail, and with greater force and artistic complexity, than any other art form of the Middle Ages.

The vernacular drama had to find its own ways of dealing with this new and supremely difficult subject, for the Latin drama of the Continent, even had it been available, had little to offer. Karl Young, the best student of this Latin drama, has written:

In comparison with the multitude of medieval Church plays treating events relating to the Resurrection, the number of dramatic representations of the Crucifixion is astonishingly small. We hear of no dramatization of the Passion earlier than the beginning of the thirteenth century, and even after that date evidences that such plays were promoted within the church are extremely rare. We must infer, therefore, that the representation of the last occurrences in Christ's life was deliberately avoided. We may also surmise, if we wish, that for bringing vividly before the medieval worshipper the great Immolation, the Mass itself was felt to be sufficiently effective.[2]

The usual means of avoiding direct dramatic treatment was to include a *planctus Mariae* in the dramatic text, for a narration of the Crucifixion could easily be spoken as part of the mother's grief. But such laments had gone no further than an occasional quotation from the words spoken by Christ, as in this example:

> Jesus matri loquitur
>   totus vulneratus:
> "Cur tam doles, mulier?
>   ecce tuus natus,
> Johannes discipulus,
>   tibi commendatus."*³

Apart from an Italian fragment of the fourteenth century, the only extant Latin plays in which the death of Christ is enacted are to be found in the thirteenth-century Benediktbeuern manuscript—a short play mostly in mime, and a fuller dramatization which includes among many prior episodes the anointing by Mary Magdalene, the Last Supper, and the Betrayal.⁴ Both plays crucify Jesus, but they do so without violence, never going beyond the scorn of the crowd specifically recorded in Scripture, as when the Jews cry *"Si filius Dei es, descende de cruce"* and *"Alios saluos fecit, seipsum non potest saluum facere."*†⁵ The mood is grave and decorous, quite unlike the mature vernacular drama, in which the torturing and killing are greatly prolonged and horribly detailed.

The Latin drama, then, had little or nothing to offer in the way of tradition. In the related literature, such as the *Northern Passion,* the *Cursor Mundi,* the *Stanzaic Life of Christ,* or the *Meditations on the Life and Passion of Christ,* the problem does not really arise, and for reasons worth noting. The difference is not merely due to medium, although it is true that human actors involve possibilities and problems not encountered on the manuscript page. More important than this is the uniquely "specific" nature of the drama: every action is precise and limited, the audience judges from what it *sees* and *hears.* The narrative poem is more free; it can hint, can estimate, can be indefinite, if this will best serve its purpose. Indeed, narrative poems such as those mentioned above almost invariably trail off into a kind of in-

---

* Jesus, gravely wounded, spoke to his mother: "Woman, why do you grieve so? Behold your son, the disciple John, entrusted to you."
† "If thou be the Son of God, come down from the cross," and "He saved others; himself he cannot save" (Matt. 27: 40, 42).

definite superlative when they seek to describe the anguish of Christ. The *Northern Passion,* for instance, tells us:

> Ihesus sufferd with gud will
> All payns þat þai wald putt him tyll,
> And so þai fore with him þat nyght,
> Vn-to þat it was day full lyght.[6]

But the drama cannot hint at "all payns" in this way: it must show the specific suffering Christ endured, and its actions effectively stop when they stop on stage—they cannot vaguely occupy all "þat nyght." Here are two related examples from the *Cursor Mundi:*

> þe scam þai on þair lauerd soght,
>   ful tor it war to tell!
>
> .   .   .   .
>
> þe teind part o þair despitt,
>   i mai noght tell to yow![7]

An over reliance on this rhetorical device is one of the reasons these poems lack any final claim to literary merit: in trying to convince us that the pain and grief were past telling—an emotional infinity—they all too frequently fail to move us at all. The expressive power of art depends on particulars. The Corpus Christi drama nowhere pretends that the grief was greater than it can show.

The necessity of having to imagine the whole Passion of Christ in full detail brought the vernacular dramatists face to face with a number of obtrusive problems. One of these we have already discussed at length: in order to enact the Crucifixion, a clear conception of dramatic genre and its relation to reality—a conception of theater as *play or game*—was necessary. But there were other problems as well, chief among them the need for much new dialogue in order to sustain so lengthy a dramatic action. It is obvious that certain actions take longer to enact than to narrate, and the Crucifixion of Christ is preeminently one of these. The *Northern Passion* describes at unusual length the putting of Christ on the cross, but 58 lines of verse suffice for the whole. The *Cursor Mundi,* a leisurely poem of nearly 30,000 lines, devotes only 10 of these to a description of this action and the raising of the cross. In the York play, on the other hand, the dialogue accompanying these actions amounts to more than 250 lines of text: one cannot convincingly crucify a man in the twinkling of an eye, though one can read about it in that time. The difference in genre necessarily involves a different disposition and proportioning of material, for while the action is being accomplished, the characters must talk. In none of the narrative poems are the *tortores* given any clear, sustained motivation or any real dramatic "character"; because there is no need for them to speak, they need only be identified as agents in the action. Once they are set talking, however, everything they say becomes a clue to their emotional and intellectual relationship to the action they are performing. (Even apparently irrelevant discourse implies a certain kind of motive.) The method of the two Latin plays and of the narrative poems had been to restrict their speech to those few scornful remarks attributed to them in the Gospels, but such a method was suitable only for a brief, stylized Crucifixion; it was totally inadequate to communicate the full horror and shame of its detailed circumstance. So the executioners must talk, but with that decision new problems arose: What shall they actually say? How shall they relate to what they do?

The dramatists' problem was twofold: they required some coherent characterization for the tormentors, out of which dialogue could grow; and they needed to shape the Passion into strong dramatic patterns. Their subject was the most terrible and shameful action in human history, but for it to communicate as such, it had to be artistically controlled, effectively terrible; they needed action at once formal and violent. To understand the drama's most original contribution to the "realization" of the Passion in the Middle Ages, we must begin by determining what materials were available to its authors, what facts, in other words, they could work from.

Most obviously, there were the formal charges against Christ made by the high priests and testified to by false witnesses. The drama could let the *tortores* themselves summarize this case against Christ, as the Towneley play does in this speech by the *primus tortor:*

> ffor all thise dedys of great louyng / fower thyngys I haue fond
> certanly,
> > ffor which he is worthy to hyng: / oone is oure kyng that he
> > wold be;
> > Oure sabbot day in his wyrkyng / he lettys not to hele the seke
> > truly;

he says oure temple he shall downe bryng / and in thre daies
byg it in hy
All hole agane;
Syr pilate, as ye sytt,
looke wysely in youre wytt;
Dam ihesu or ye flytt
On crosse to suffre his payne.[8]

For these claims they are shown genuinely to hate Him, and in their brutal fashion to take pleasure in His pain. Taken together, the statement of one, "Bot more sorow thou hase / oure myrth is incresyng," and this confession from another, "Nay, I myself shuld kyll hym / Bot for sir pilate,"[9] represent this hatred at its most savage and uncompromising, clearly directed at the man who claimed to be king. Throughout the Passion, there will be moments of this kind of conscious cruelty, and they deepen the horror and pity with which we respond to the action. But this accounts for relatively little of the tormentors' dialogue and of the invented action as a whole. For the dramatists were guided by another fact about the *tortores,* greater in importance, and richer in meaning: they had to develop characterization and dramatic action which could accord with (and make clear the meaning of) Christ's direct statement to them of forgiveness. Christ had said, "They know not what they do," and this imposed strict limits on how far the tormentors could be presented as counsel for the prosecution, as in the Towneley play. On one level, there is perhaps no contradiction: Christ's statement can be taken to mean simply that they have not believed His claims, and therefore what they do they do to their idea of Him, not to the Son of God. This interpretation of Christ's forgiveness flickers through the cycle texts and can explain a fair amount of textual detail. But the dramatists found yet another solution to the problem, one that managed at the same time to suggest ways of shaping the action into vital dramatic form.

Christ was killed by those He loved and came to save—by those he loved, not by those He hated. The *Stanzaic Life of Christ* discussed the paradox this way:

For las wonder had ben i-wys
ȝif he of enmys suffride hade
to quych he done hade er amys,
sich manas thaȝe he hade made,

Or of aliens & straungers
that had not knowen hym bifore,
but of his frendes & verray feres
he tholet that greuet mich þe more.[10]

The Towneley play incorporates this same idea into the speech of
Christ in which He asks God the Father to forgive those who kill
Him. It begins:

My brethere that I com forto by,
has hanged me here thus hedusly,
And freyndys fynde I foyn.[11]

The men who should be His friends, though they scorn Him and kill
Him, are not aware of what they really do. This fact, central to the
mystery of the Passion, decisively shaped the cycle-drama's characterization of the *tortores*. They are shown killing Christ in outbursts of
great energy, violence, laughter, and delight; they are shown turning
the tasks assigned by their masters into a sequence of formal games,
into a changing metamorphosis of play, and adding to them further
games of their own devising. The *tortores* are dramatized as too self-
aware, too conscious of their own need for amusement, distraction,
and gratification, to be more than sporadically aware of the man they
kill. This technique offered a way of making meaningful Christ's
judgment on His tormentors—for that judgment is also a statement
of their intentions, and a description of their actions—and it suggested a dramatically exciting mode into which the humiliation and
death of Christ could be translated. The drama, alone among medieval religious writings, sought to reveal as much about the men
who scorn and kill Christ as about the pathos and dignity of His suffering.

A new set of game words becomes important at this point—mainly
the words "jape," "jest," "bourde," and "layke," all of which are used
again and again to describe the actions by which Christ is captured,
brought to trial, buffeted, scourged, and killed. Before we begin to
examine in detail the ways in which the Passion and the Resurrection
are translated into game, it will be useful to make clear just what
these terms have in common. To begin with, all indicate action in
some sense arbitrary and formal. Once a game or play is begun, its
inherent form governs the action; to begin it, game identities are

superimposed upon real identities, and the object of the action is simply the game itself. One can illustrate this with an ordinary children's game, such as hide-and-seek. The game exists in itself, prior to, and independent of, the children who decide to play it: it is "known," that is, it has certain rules and requires a certain formal sequence of actions. It is begun by a contract: someone is designated as It for the duration of the game; in accepting this game identity (which has nothing to do with his real person), he who is It will cover his eyes while his fellows go and hide. These arbitrary actions give form to the play—without them such play could not be a game. The object of the game is similarly contractual: it is agreed that he who is It will try to find the others, and that they will try not be found. The game is at an end when all have been discovered, but it can begin again with a simple shifting of game identities: someone else can be declared It. For the duration of the game, the only meaningful identities are as hiders and seeker. The medieval dramatists show Christ killed as a figure in a series of such games; only a few times do the *tortores* define Him in their action as a man who claims to be the son of God, and never is He defined *as* the Son of God. The *tortores* can be said to kill only what they understand.

Thus we shall find the terms "jape," "jest," and so on used in the text to signal a series of game substitutions made *in the minds* of Christ's opponents. The substitutions seem to be of two major kinds. First of all, there is frequent substitution of a game figure for Christ as a real person, as when the Towneley Caiaphas in the *Buffeting* names Christ as "kyng copyn in oure game."[12] In such instances, the *tortores'* actions then become governed by the game rather than by any direct awareness of Christ; He serves as a passive figure in a series of games largely played for their own sake. Second, there is a frequent substitution of game action for essential parts of the *tortores'* assigned task, as when they turn the raising of the cross into a contest of strength, thus separating themselves slightly but significantly from the real and terrible purpose of the action. The focus of attention is altered. If, for example, a soldier shoots a criminal by official order, he has performed a straightforward execution; but if four men are ordered to shoot the criminal and they decide in their shooting to see who can hit a small brass button on the criminal's jacket, the direct object of their action becomes success in a competitive game rather than the execution of the criminal. The results are the same, of course, but the way in which the executioners relate to the action is different. We shall find that the *tortores* who kill Christ turn almost all their necessary actions into competitive games; these, taken together with the games they play simply for amusement's sake, fundamentally affect the way Christ dies in this drama and determine what we understand about the men who kill Him. The idea is a bold and interesting one; its detailed working-out is equally worth attention, for it is tough-minded, energetic, and inventive. The exact variations played upon this game motivation vary from cycle to cycle, but we can examine here the most important details they have in common, and some of the more interesting anomalies. These two categories of game substitution will provide, I think, a key to the whole, and their detailed illustration can indicate something of the brilliance with which this drama staged its central story.

In York, a strange and disturbing mood is created the minute Christ is captured and the Passion begins: the stage is suddenly filled with noise, violence, rough laughter, talk of game. The soldiers who have taken Christ in the middle of the night set up a cry in the streets, and are reprimanded by Caiaphas' servants:

> Gose abakke, bewscheres, ȝe both are to blame,
> To bourde whenne oure Busshopp is bonne to his bedde.[13]

We have seen Caiaphas put to bed in great luxury and have heard his orders that he is not to be disturbed: noisy riot in the street is here judged to be mere "bourdyng," just as it will be later when Christ is brought before Pilate (also in bed asleep) and his servant commands the soldiers cease their noisy "jappis" and "gawdes."[14] But when the servants learn that it is Christ who has been brought before their masters, they wake them gleefully. The soldier shouts his news to Caiaphas:

> My lorde! my lorde! my lorde! here is layke, and ȝou list![15]

Later, Herod is told of Jesus' arrival in very much the same way:

> My lorde, þei bryng you yondir a boy boune in a bande,
> Þat bodus outhir bourdyng or bales to brewe.

And Herod shows pleasure at being sent such good game:

> And in faith I am fayne he is fonne,
> His farles to frayne and to fele,
> Nowe þes games was grathely begonne.

He has earlier warned his men that he must be amused or both the soldiers and Jesus will pay heavily:

> Go ynne, and late vs see of þe sawes ere,
> And but yf þei be to oure bordyng, þai both schall abye.[16]

Here he echoes the words of Christ's earlier examination before Caiaphas and Annas, when Annas wants Christ beaten straightway but Caiaphas urges a slower pace as being more amusing:

> Nay, sir, none haste, we schall have game or we goo.
> [*To Jesus.*] Boy, be not agaste if we seme gaye.[17]

Caiaphas wants his fun quite as much as the others, but he has more discriminating ideas about what constitutes a good joke. He stops a soldier from beating Jesus like an animal because this particular "animal" has His hands tied: "Itt is no burde to bete bestis þat are bune."[18] Jesus in these early trials gives answers too deep for man's comprehension, and He is beaten for thus joking with the High Priest:

> *Jesus.*   My reasouns are not to reherse,
> Nor they þat myght helpe me are noȝt here nowe.
> *Anna.*   Say, ladde, liste þe make verse,
> Do tell on, by-lyffe, late vs here nowe.
>
> . . . .
>
> *i Miles.*   What! fye on þe beggarr!
> who made þe so bolde
> To bourde with oure Busshoppe?
> thy bane schall I bee.[19]

It is in the trial before Herod, however, that the York cycle shapes the action most elaborately into game, beginning with Herod's decision to address Jesus in French. A soldier remarks that the joke is useless: "Nay, my lorde, he can of no bourdyng, þis boy." But Herod is inventive and eager for fun:

> O! my harte hoppis for joie
> To se nowe þis prophette appere,
> We schall haue goode game with þis boy,
> Takis hede, for in haste ȝe schall here.[20]

He understands Jesus to be a boaster, and he has long looked forward to hearing His tall tales. Jesus refuses to speak, and Herod becomes very angry. Since Jesus is neither deaf nor mute, Herod concludes that He is sporting with them, and His silence becomes the object of a new and insulting game in which Herod pretends that Jesus' replies are deafening ("sirs, he dethis vs with dynne!") and begins shouting at Jesus as if in answer to the volume of His speech; he is pleased with this game, calling it "a bourde of þe beste."[21] And another game is then begun, as a scepter is placed in Jesus' hand and Herod's men do mock-reverence to Him. When Jesus still remains silent despite their goading, they lose all patience, and a soldier tells an interesting lie to feed Herod's wrath: he says that Jesus has "played" before, while He was being taken from Pilate to Herod. "ʒa, lorde, and made many gaudis as we haue gone."[22] This lie, of course, makes Jesus' present refusal to play seem the more grudging, and in punishment they devise an even crueler sport—dressing Him in the white robes of a fool and displaying Him in the marketplace.[23] When Jesus is finally taken back to Pilate, Annas makes clear the immediate rationale behind all this game action when he denounces Him as "Jesus þat japer þat Judas ganne selle vs."[24] In the earlier examination, Pilate had become angry only once—when told that Jesus calls Himself King of the Jews—and had said ominously, even then, "þat borde to bayll will hym bryng."[25] In the York trial sequence this conception of Jesus as joker is uppermost, as when Pilate's son, reprimanding Jesus for failing to bow to his father, says, "O Jesu vngentill, þi joie is in japes."[26] The same conception underlies Judas' description of Christ to the Jews in the Cornish cycle:

> It is good for you to be cautious;
> The fellow is very sharp, without a doubt,
> And he knows many tricks.[27]

From the very beginning we can see two kinds of "substitution" shaping the action: these men decide in advance that Jesus is a joker, a trickster, an absurd imposter, and never properly see Him or hear Him as a result; and they constantly substitute games and jokes for the serious religious and legal examination that it is their proper duty to conduct. They examine Him, it is true, but they turn the examination into a witty and insulting series of games, with a few blows thrown in for good measure. The York Christ only once makes an explicit comment upon their action, but it puts the whole mood and manner of the trials in true perspective:

> And if my sawes be soth þei mon be sore solde,
> Wherfore þou bourdes to brode for to bete me.[28]

Quietly He reminds them that if He is telling the truth, their "answering" jests are too broadly conceived. The dramatist has shown us the judges and soldiers creating the character of Jesus in their own image.[29]

Christ's claim to prophetic powers engenders the cruelest of the early games: the tormentors blindfold Him and beat Him with sticks, charging each time that He use his supernatural vision to declare which of them has hit Him. This action is taken from the Bible (Luke 22:63–65), but it is translated into everyday medieval terms, into a common children's game, called "papse" in the York cycle, "whele and pylle" in the *Ludus Coventriae,* and "a new play of yoyll" (identified by Cawley as the game of Hot Cockles) in Towneley.[30] Its names are many, but it seems to be always the same game, and indeed survives to the present day. In the Bodleian manuscript of the fourteenth-century *Romance of Alexander* there is a border illumination of children's games, among them one in which a veiled young woman stands with her legs stretched wide apart, bracing herself, while a girl to her left prepares to deliver a stout blow to the head with a long, heavily knotted cloth.[31] An English alabaster table of the same period presents the scriptural scene in almost exactly the same way, the only difference being that Christ is seated.[32] A comparison of the two can show better than any words how the scriptural act of scorn was translated into a contemporary game. G. R. Owst quotes an interesting passage from a fifteenth-century sermon:

A common game in use nowadays is that which the soldiers played with Christ at his Passion: it is called *the bobbid* game. In this game, one of the company will be *blindfold* and set in a prone position; then those standing by will hit him on the head and say—

> "*A bobbid, a bobbid, a biliried:*
> *Smyte not her, bot thu smyte a gode!*"

And as often as the former may fail to guess correctly *and rede amys,* he has to play a fresh game. And so, until *he rede him that smote him,* he will be *blindfold stille and hold in* for the post of player.[33]

This and the throwing of dice for Christ's robe are the only parts of the Passion that are commonly described in medieval narrative poems as games;[34] the rest they treat simply as direct action. But again the drama goes beyond mere discription: it actually plays the game with Christ, in a long Passion sequence dramatized as a series of games and jokes. Here is the dialogue spoken during the action by a tormentor from the *Ludus Coventriae:*

> A and now wole I a newe game begynne
> þat we mon pley at all þat arn here-inne.
> whele and pylle · whele and pylle
> comyth to halle ho so wylle
> ho was þat.[35]

When the York tormentors have tired of their game of papse, they vary it with another, reminiscent of a drinking ceremony, "Wassaille, Wassaylle."[36] Finally they have done and take Jesus back to Caiaphas, reporting that his orders have been carried out but with little success:

> *iii Miles.* My lorde! we haue bourded with þis boy,
> And holden hym full hote emelle vs.
> *Cayph.* Thanne herde ye some japes of joye?
> *iv Miles.* The devell haue þe worde, lorde, he wolde telle vs.[37]

Their noise and violence and rowdy amusements all serve to define and make dramatically distinct the silent, patient endurance of Jesus, but in addition this other purpose is being served: the judges and tormentors are shown substituting in their minds a game figure for the real person of Jesus. The entire mock-reverence in the York play occurs simply because once the tormentors have dressed Christ as a fool, a game spontaneously suggests itself:

> To clothe hym and to croune with thorne,
> As falles for a fole kyng.[38]

Only intermittently do the tormentors actually focus upon Him as He really is, charged with certain specific crimes; for the most part He is simply a person in their power, from whom they derive such amusement and diversion as they can. We are shown Christ's death, in respect to its human motivation, as gratuitous. W. L. Hildburgh has written of an interesting alabaster carving of the Scourging of Christ:

The torturer who holds his scourge in his teeth while he adjusts his hose is—although something corresponding may occasionally be seen in continental art—so far as I know, unique in "Scourging" tables, a bit of rough clowning according well with the torturers' boastful threats. I have, however, no texts to indicate whether his action is due to an excess of zeal or to a feeling of compunction towards a task become distasteful to him.[39]

The tormentor in question has turned his back on the scourging and is looking out of the frame, staring straight into the eyes of anyone viewing the carving. The fact that he has momentarily forgotten the central action in order to pull up his hose should not surprise us: far from feeling any revulsion or distaste, he is attending to his own propriety and fashion, concerns for him fully the equal of any other at that historical moment. The motivation implied is wholly in accord with that developed by the drama, in which the tormenting is a game played all the more savagely because it is disinterested action. The Cornish cycle can furnish further evidence of this, in the scene in which the executioners receive the order to crucify Christ and go to the blacksmith to get the necessary nails. The blacksmith believes in Christ as the son of God and refuses to help them, but his shrewish wife, after cursing him roundly for his refusal, joins the executioners in a clumsy attempt to forge the nails themselves. None of them knows anything about the smithy's craft, but they turn this fact into a kind of challenge and game, boasting loudly of their skill, though he who wields the bellows puts the fire out in his enthusiasm, and he who tempers the nails has not much greater success. All is noise, violence, laughter; in the end, though they admit the nails are badly made, they console themselves that Christ's hands will be hurt the more because of that.[40] Until this moment, Jesus has been almost entirely forgotten. A subordinate, engrossing action, a game of skill and ingenuity, has been interposed.

Both of these—the tormentor who stops to adjust his hose and the Cornish executioners who play at being blacksmiths—are wholly at one with the way in which the English cycles shape the action of the Crucifixion, and the way in which they understand the relation of the executioners to their task. After the *tortores* discover what a difficult job they have been charged with, they are noisily boastful of their cleverness in overcoming its difficulties and are determined to enjoy themselves as they work. In the Towneley play, for instance, the decision to blindfold Jesus while they buffet Him is quickly made, but the action is slow in getting under way because of a good-natured eruption of private grievances:

> *Secundus tortor*. I wold we were onwarde. /
> *primus tortor*.   but his een must be hyd.
> *Secundus tortor*. yei, bot thay be well spard / we lost that we dyd;
> Step furth thou, froward! /
> *ffroward*.   what is now betyd?
> *primus tortor*. Thou art euer away ward. /
> *ffroward*.   haue ye none to byd
>   Bot me?
> I may syng ylla-hayll.
> *Secundus tortor*. Thou must get vs a vayll.
> *ffroward*. ye ar euer in oone tayll.
>   *primus tortor*. Now ill myght thou the!
>
> well had thou thi name / for thou was euer curst.
> *ffroward*. Sir, I myght say the same / to you if I durst;
> yit my hyer may I clame / no penny I purst;
> I haue had mekyll shame / hunger and thurst,
>   In youre seruyce.
> *primus tortor*. Not oone word so bold!
> *ffroward*. why, it is trew that I told!
> ffayn preue it I wold.
>   *Secundus tortor*. Thou shalbe cald to peruyce.
>
> *ffroward*. here a vayll haue I fon / I trow it will last.[41]

Once the buffeting is under way, it becomes a contest of skill to see who buffets best, whose technique is most praiseworthy.

This habit of turning tasks into competitive games also shapes what is dramatically the most difficult, and aesthetically the most precarious, action in these cycles: the actual stretching and nailing of Christ to the cross, and the raising of the cross on high. Devotional tradition held that holes were drilled in the cross in advance of the Crucifixion, but were drilled to the wrong size. When Jesus is put upon it, the executioners find He does not fit. And so He is made to, by nailing one hand fast and pulling the other by ropes until it is long enough.[42] The narrative poems on the Passion often describe this action in a restrained way, as yet another piteous detail in Christ's suffering. The Bodley play of the *Resurrection* narrates it in retrospect;[43] since the action is not played, there is no *game* shaping of the action. But the Chester dramatist had to allow time for this action to be actually performed, and he had to give his actors something to talk about as they do it. And so the Fourth Jew boasts:

> ffellows, will ye see
> how sleight I will be,
> this fyst or I flye,
> here to make fast?

as the Second Jew triumphantly solves the problem of the arms that are too short to fit the holes:

> ha! therfore care thou nought,
> a sleight I haue sought,
> Ropes must be brought,
> to strean him with strength.[44]

The operative word in both instances is "sleight," indicating skill, cunning, and crafty, clever devices. Once the arms have been fastened, the Second Jew names the whole action a "game":

> ffellows, by this light!
> now if his feet were pight,
> this Gommon went aright,
> and vp he should be raysed.[45]

There is no pretense that the games they play as they work are nice games, but there is a kind of distancing involved: in so far as what they do is done in game, it is not done *directly* in hatred of Christ.

The York executioners offer an interesting variant on this same theme, in their first, unsuccessful, attempt to raise the cross with Christ on it:

> *iv Mil.* Þe deuill hym hang!
> *i Mil.* For grete harme haue I hente,
> My schuldir is in soundre.
> *ii Mil.* And sertis I am nere schente,
> So lange haue I borne vndir.
>
> *iii Mil.* This crosse and I in twoo muste twynne,
> Ellis brekis my bakke in sondre sone.
> *iv Mil.* Laye doune agayne and leue youre dynne,
> Þis dede for vs will neuere be done. [*They lay it down.*]
> *i Mil.* Assaie, sirs, latte se yf any gynne,

May helpe hym vppe, with-outen hone;
For here schulde wight men worschippe wynne,
And noght with gaudis al day to gone.
ii Mil. More wighter men þan we
Full fewe I hope ȝe fynde.
iii Mil. Þis bargayne will noght bee,
For certis me wantis wynde.[46]

They are chiefly aware of their own aches and pains, and of their victim as the cause of these: "He weyes a wikkid weght."[47] Their attention is only now and then directed at Christ; for the most part they
are simply concerned with the job at hand, one that exercises their
highest ingenuity, and whose accomplishment is a cause for rowdy
self-congratulation. In the Towneley play this action is interrupted
by a quarrel as to whether they are all pulling equally or whether
someone is only pretending to pull while taking his ease. The third
tortor begins the argument, refusing to continue until it has been
settled:

Nay, felowse, this is no gam!
we will no longere draw all sam.[48]

They are stupid men who have no real consciousness of Christ's suffering; to them, He seems more an animal than a human being, and thus
the explanation of their intense cruelty is not sadism but unawareness.
The craft of the *killing* is revealed dramatically, step by step, and
furnishes them with a subject of conversation, and a focus of interest;
their deepest emotions relate to that, rather than to the other object
of *our* attention, the grief and the shame of the *dying*.

Scripture itself supplies the next game that is played: after the cross
has been erected, the executioners fall to dicing for the robe of Christ,
and this game easily takes its place in a sequence of other games invented by the dramatists to accompany the death of Christ. Only Chester does something strange. The sequence is deliberately altered, so
that here the dicing interrupts the killing: *before* Jesus is mounted on
the cross, the executioners abandon their main task in the interests of
greed and pleasant pastime. Their single concern is the ownership of
the cloak, and once they have decided to determine this matter by a
game of chance, the game effectively diverts their full attention and
energies. Only the furious intervention of Caiaphas gets the Crucifixion under way again:

> Men, for Cockes face!
> how longe shall poydrace
> stand naked in this place?
> goe, neyles him to the Tree![49]

This dicing, so obviously a game drawn from real life, is neverthe-less not given game treatment in all the narrative poems. Lacking the drama's interest in the motives of the *tortores,* the poems often use the episode to different end, as when the *Southern Passion* con-cerns itself with a fulfillment of prophecy:

> "We nolleþ nouȝt his curtel kerue · þey he beo odde yffalle,
> Ak caste we lot who shal hit haue · on among vs alle."
> Þo was hit ffolffuld þat Dauid · in his sauter seyde,
> Þat hi delde his cloþes · and vp his cloþes þe lot leyde.[50]

The difference in genre is one source of this difference in interest.

The Towneley cycle develops its Passion games with greater verbal brilliance than does any other cycle; its *tortores* often turn their actions into jests, as when they choose to drive Jesus from Caiaphas to Pilate like an animal, saying:

> *primus tortor.*   Com furth, old crate,
>   Be lyfe!
> we shall lede the a trott.
> *ijus tortor.* lyft thy feete may thou not.
> *ffroward.* Then nedys me do nott
>   Bot com after and dryfe.[51]

But I want to examine here the joke they choose while mounting Jesus on the cross, for it serves as a transition between the games that Jesus has apparently been losing and the game He is about to win. The mood is set early in the play of the *Crucifixion*:

> Now ar we at the monte of caluarye;
> haue done, folows, and let now se
>   how we can with hym lake.

The *primus tortor* is first to define the game figure they will substitute in their minds for the real Jesus:

> In fayth, syr, sen ye callyd you a kyng,
> you must prufe a worthy thyng
>   That falles vnto the were;
> ye must Iust in tornamente.[52]

The others take this up and develop it further: they converse as if they were servants arming and horsing a great lord before he rides to joust in battle. They find the joke very funny, for the figure of Christ in these circumstances accords ill with the aristocratic metaphor:

> *iijus tortor.* If thou be kyng we shall thank adyll,
> ffor we shall sett the in thy sadyll,
>   ffor fallyng be thou bold.
> I hete the well thou bydys a shaft;
> Bot if thou sytt well thou had better laft
>   The tales that thou has told.

> *iiijus tortor.* Stand nere, felows, and let se
> how we can hors oure kyng so fre,
>   By any craft;
> Stand thou yonder on yond syde,
> And we shall se how he can ryde,
>   And how to weld a shaft.

> *primus tortor.* Sir, commys heder and haue done,
> And wyn apon youre palfray sone,
>   ffor he [is] redy bowne.
> If ye be bond till hym, be not wrothe,
> ffor be ye secure we were full lothe
>   On any wyse that ye fell downe.

They have great trouble in getting Him "horsed," and contests of strength are necessary to get the cross into place:

> do rase hym vp now when we may,
> ffor I hope he & his palfray
>   Shall not twyn this nyght.[53]

In earlier centuries, when Christ was customarily shown as victorious *on* the cross, the Crucifixion was chiefly understood as a theological rather than human event. By the time of the cycles, the dying and the victory were conceived separately: victory was postponed until Christ harrowed hell, and a traditional statement of His triumph there was as a knightly combat in which He jousts with Satan for man's soul. The Towneley dramatist has simply—and brilliantly—displaced that metaphor into the Crucifixion itself, to create a powerful dramatic irony: he makes the *tortores* dress Christ, in their game figure, for just such an encounter. They think it a joke—the cross is not a horse—not knowing that this joke will be realized in that later pageant whose action begins with this declaration by Christ:

> Therfor till hell now Will I go,
> To chalange that is myne.[54]

The idea was a common one—indeed, the dramatist's irony depends on its being so—and it had found its way into other late medieval literature. A Dispute between Mary and the Cross uses it thus:

> On a stokky stede
> He Rod we Rede,
> In Red Array.[55]

A fourteenth-century sermon extant in three English manuscripts describes the armor worn by Christ in this encounter and includes this detail: "Pro equo habuit crucem super quam pependit; pro scuto apposuit latus suum, et processit sic contra inimicum cum lancea, non in manu sed stykand in his side."*[56] The Towneley irony centers on the fact that the real battle is to be fought not against the executioners —they are, though they do not know it, Christ's armorers and accomplices—but against the devil. The executioners think the action is over when Christ dies, but the audience knows that it is really just beginning. Satan knows this too, and after abusing the other demons for their weakness in dealing with the foe, he calls for his armor in a way that extends this tournament metaphor further:

> ffy, fature! wherfor were ye flayd?
> haue ye no force to flyt hym fro?
> loke in haste my gere be grayd,
> my self shall to that gadlyng go.

> how! thou bclamy, abyde,
> with all thi boste and beyr!
> And tell me in this tyde
> what mastres thou makys here.[57]

---

* For a horse he had the cross upon which he hung; for a shield he offered his side, and he advanced against the enemy so, with a spear not in his hand but sticking in his side.

Behind this speech lies the patristic idea that the Redemption was a contest of power with the devil,[58] and it turns on the custom, familiar from chivalric romance, by which a renowned knight enters a tournament in disguise so that the opponent he seeks will not evade an encounter with him in the lists. This conception of the Harrowing of Hell as a tournament in which Christ is man's "campioun" was particularly vital in the later Middle Ages, and it lies at the center of some of the finest medieval poems about the Redemption.[59] Here, we are particularly concerned with those works that connect the knightly victory with the Descent into Hell. Among the earliest of these is a poem, in French, written around 1320 by an Englishman named Nicholas Bozon,[60] but surely the most famous is this magnificent passage from *Piers Plowman*:

> One semblable to the Samaritan · and some-del to Piers the
>   Plowman,
> Barfote on an asse bakke · botelees cam prykye,
> Wyth-oute spores other spere · spakliche he loked,
> As is the kynde of a kynʒte · that cometh to be dubbed,
> To geten hem gylte spores · or galoches ycouped.
> Thanne was Faith in a fenestre · and cryde *"a! fili Dauid!"*
> As doth an heraude of armes · whan auntrous cometh to iustes.
> Olde Iuwes of Ierusalem · for Ioye thei songen,
>   *Benedictus qui venit in nomine domini.*
>   Thanne I frayned at Faith · what al that fare be-mente,
> And who sholde Iouste in Iherusalem · "Iesus," he seyde,
> "And fecche that the fende claymeth · Piers fruit the Plowman."
> "Is Piers in this place?" quod I · and he preynte on me,
> "This Iesus of his gentrice · wole Iuste in Piers armes,
> In his helme and in his haberioun · *humana natura*;
> That Cryst be nouʒt biknowe here · for *consummatus deus*,"
> . . . .
> "Who shal Iuste with Iesus?" quod I · "Iuwes or scribes?"
> "Nay," quod he, "the foule fende · and Fals-dome and Deth.
> Deth seith he shal fordo · and adown brynge
> Al that lyueth or loketh · in londe or in watere.
> Lyf seyth that he likth · and leyth his lif to wedde,
> That for al that Deth can do · with-in thre dayes,
> To walke and fecche fro the fende · Piers fruite the Plowman,
> And legge it there hym lyketh · and Lucifer bynde,
> And forbete and adown brynge · bale and deth for euere."[61]

A little known alliterative poem called *Death and Liffe, c.* 1450, develops the theme with equal force. In it, Life is sent from Heaven to dispute with a brazen, personified Death, and to reassure God's people. The crucial point in their argument is reached when Death claims to have won on Calvary, and Life counters:

> Of one point lett vs proue or wee part in sunder:
> how didest thou iust att Ierusalem with Iesu my Lord?
>
> . . . .
>
> When thou saw the King come with the crosse on his shoulder,
> on the top of Caluarye thou camest him against.

Once the spear had pierced Christ's side (Life continues) His godhead shone out, and Death ran to his hell hole to hide from the wounded Knight, but the Knight followed him there and defeated him decisively.[62] In the York *Agony in the Garden,* Christ anticipates His death in just such terms:

> I fele by my ferdnes my flesshe wolde full fayne
> Be torned fro this turnement, and takyn þe vntill.[63]

Many other treatments could be quoted here, but these few will suffice to indicate the background against which the Towneley dramatist has worked.[64] It is a measure of his genius that he alone discovers in this traditional metaphor a dramatic irony that can serve to characterize the tormentors (they once again substitute a game figure for Christ) and at the same time can define, even in the midst of apparent defeat, the true nature of Christ's victory.

In poems, sermons, and drama the Harrowing of Hell is always treated as a contest of power.[65] The metaphor used may vary—sometimes it is a knight jousting in tournament, sometimes it is a town under siege—but the decisive *action* always turns on whether or not the gates of Hell will hold. Christ three times commands these gates to open and then He bursts through. The correct staging of the Cornish version is made explicit in this speech by Satan:

> Put beams against the gate;
> Your shoulders, every fellow,
>   Thrust against it also.[66]

The forces of Hell push hard to hold the gate firm, but Christ, outside, quickly breaks in and sends Hell's minions sprawling. Their power is no match for His. It is likely that the other cycles staged a similar action. In the *Ludus Coventriae,* Christ declares that such opposition is futile:

> Aȝens me it wore but wast
> to holdyn or to stondyn fast
> helle logge may not last
>   Aȝens · þe kynge of glorye
> þi derke dore down I throwe.[67]

In the York cycle the battle metaphor is extended further (the Towneley play is borrowed, with only minor changes, from York):

> We! spere oure ȝates, all ill mot þou spede,
> And sette furthe watches on þe wall.
> And if he call or crie
> To make vs more debate,
> Lay on hym þan hardely,
> And garre hym gang his gate.

and:

> ...boldely make youe boune
> With toles þat ȝe on traste
> And dynge þat dastard doune.[68]

But Jesus breaks the doors, though they are bound with brass, proving His superior strength (a game or battle objective) and leading forth the patriarchs into Paradise. The apparent loser is now demonstrating His victory.[69]

The circumstantial resurrection of Christ follows immediately. Neither the Gospels nor, to my knowledge, the narrative vernacular treatments actually describe how Jesus arose from the tomb. Instead, the story resumes, through the eyes of the three Marys, with the discovery of the empty sepulchre. The scene is extensively treated in the visual arts, however, and often in this manner: Jesus, with a staff in the form of a cross, steps down from the tomb onto the body of one of the stunned or sleeping guards.[70] The drama cycles, too, show Jesus rising;[71] some of them certainly (and maybe all) showed Him stepping down in that same way. Stage convenience may be partly responsible, but the audience would have understood the action just as the graphic artists intended it to be understood—as a gesture signifying victory in physical combat. It has always been such: to place your foot on the prostrate body of a vanquished foe is the strongest possible demonstration of success in combat or game. Thus the game metaphor for the Passion is continued, but now reversed unmistakably, as a Chester soldier recalls:

> He sett his foote vpon my Backe,
> that every lith began to cracke;
> I would not byde such another Shacke
> for all Ierusalem.

It is the end of a contest for "maistrye," as the Third Soldier has previously explained:

> stryve with him we ne may,
> that maister is and more.[72]

The outcome is finally clear to everyone involved, and in a manner organic to a game shaping of the whole Passion that seems to be unique to the cycle-drama.

The *Ludus Coventriae* must be distinguished from the other cycles in this respect, for although its extremely detailed stage directions indicate all the major games with Christ, and although game words are used to describe certain other actions, it contains relatively little new dialogue for the *tortores*. By speaking little, they reveal little about themselves, their moral natures, and how they feel about the job they are given to do. Twice, however, they are described in terms that are to be found in no other cycle, and that seem to evade the real question. Jesus says to them in the Capture:

> ... now as woodmen ȝe gynne to Rave
> And do thyng þat ȝe notwth knove.[73]

An earlier stage direction has defined their action in the same way: "A-noon Alle þe jewys come A-bowth hym and ley handys on hym and pullyn hym as þei were wode."[74] We are told that their actions are like those of madmen—admittedly one way of making intelligible Christ's judgment that they know not what they do—and some of the later action would seem to grow from this, as when, suddenly, just after they have fitted Christ to the cross, a stage direction says, "Here xule þei leve of and dawncyn a-bowte þe cros shortly."[75] It seems doubtful that the dramatist intended to put much weight on such a description of their action, for taken literally, it provides too easy an answer, reveals too little about fallen man and his relation to God. But even if we do not take it literally, we are left with the fact that he has provided too little dialogue for us to learn anything very coherent about their motives. This is not the case in the other three English cycles nor in that from Cornwall: they shape the scorning and death into a sequence of games and answer that sequence with a sudden and surprising victory—in terms of game—by the man who seemed to be the victim of the torturers' action.

The many contemporary vernacular accounts of the Redemption seem never to *develop* their subject in anything like the drama's way: only the buffeting, the dicing, and sometimes the dressing of Jesus in the white robes of a fool, are called game, play, or jape. But a vernacular "Evangelie," a long narrative poem similar in nature to a gospel harmony and existing in two versions, one *c.* 1300, another *c.* 1410, twice uses game words in a larger way in passages that are worth entering here. This is the description of Jesus before Herod:

> & herode sawe ihesu be stille /
> And to him gyf none ansuer ·
> sone he him droof by bysmere /
> And of him þan made his game ·
> as he a fole were & did him shame.

And this a description of man's behavior once Jesus is on the cross:

> While ihesu crist þus hanged on þe rode ·
> þe wikke men þat aboute stode /
> Scornyng him did & shame ·
> & of him made al her game /
> And shoke her hedes & lough & pleied.[76]

Richard Rolle wrote in the *Psalter*, "Now thai haf vmgifen me in the crosse hyngand, as foles that gedirs til a somere gamen,"[77] and the *Meditations on the Life and Passion of Christ* also uses the word once in a general way:

> Þat fayre face wax red for shame;
> Scornyng þey made of hym hure game.[78]

These four instances, the only important ones I have found in the related literature, lend significant support to the reading proposed in this chapter. They document such an understanding of the Passion from sources outside the drama; and they suggest (in their brevity) the

real achievement of the dramatists who, working from this generalized understanding, actually invented the games, the jokes, the play
figures by which Christ's death could be mimetically represented.

In no other medieval genre, then, could one learn so much about the
characters of the tormentors, their motivations, and the details of how
they went about their task. Because the drama, unlike the visual arts,
is an imitation of a total action, and because its important actors must
speak, the cycle-plays were forced to develop a characterization for its
tortores and to invent a formal mode for its action. The result is a
Passion that proceeds with a vast expenditure of noise and energy and
activity, only a small part of which is effectively focused upon Christ.
He dies the victim of a playful, uncommitted, sham enmity; the tormentors are shown as supremely *self*-aware and constantly aware of
one another, but only from time to time aware of Christ, the mute
center of their activity. At such moments they see Him as a braggart,
as a man not unlike themselves who pretends to be something greater,
and this draws from them great scorn and savagery. But they are incapable of sustaining even this awareness, and may be said to kill
Christ literally, as well as generically, in play. Thus these dramatists
understood and gave dramatic expression to Christ's statement of forgiveness: "They know not what they do" (Luke 23:34).

We shall examine further the nature of the torturers' responsibility
in the following chapter, when we consider the ways in which the
Corpus Christi drama apportions the real guilt for Christ's death.
Here our concern has been with the contours of action itself, the shaping of the whole Redemption into a dramatic sequence, and with the
purpose behind the jokes and games that are embedded in that action.
These jokes and games have been interpreted as inventions designed
to elicit *our* laughter, as part of the comedy of these cycles. I have here
sought to provide a better explanation. Whether or not the dramatists
were consciously striving for this end, the use of game and play in the
Crucifixion scenes does also serve to make the physical horror tolerable
as an aesthetic experience. The drama sought to serve the devotional
life of its audience by making the Crucifixion imaginatively vivid and
memorable, but it was important, too, that the experience be kept
under control, so that it could be understood as well as felt, so that
feelings would not numb themselves through excess. The action is
deeply shocking, there is that in these texts which approaches the
intolerable; and yet they are not so, not even in a fiercely realistic per-

formance. The horror of the Passion is controlled by constantly breaking the flow of its action. As the judges, scorners, tormentors, and
executioners become totally absorbed in each new and limited game
which they take up, so too is our attention diverted in turn: the Cornish making of the nails, and the premature Chester dicing, are notable examples. Christ remains almost entirely silent and still throughout these proceedings, and our attention moves from Him to the
games of His murderers and back. The Crucifixion is thereby made
the more shattering as an experience of theater, for this mode of action
much lengthens its playing time, but it is made effectively terrible, that
is to say, aesthetically controlled. We never cease to feel and respond
through too concentrated a demand being made upon us at any single
moment.

Even more important is the way this game shaping takes a "known"
action—the Passion and Resurrection, familiar from countless sermons, poems, and pictures—and makes it fresh, energetic, new. It is
able to command an audience's attention absolutely, not by an appeal
to the piety of the spectators, but by sheer theatrical power: Christ dies
in a chaos of noise, violence, jests, and laughter, in a series of spon-
taneous, improvised games. Though we know the essential action of
the play, we never know precisely what the *tortores* will do, or forget
to do, next: game blends into game in an endlessly changing series.
The sequence is conceived in such particular and convincing detail
that it is always surprising, seems always to be experienced for the
first time.

The *tortores* play with Christ, but we must not forget that Christ
is playing too—that He is in the game, by His own choice, to serve His
larger purposes. And the game must go as God intends. Thus in the
Towneley play, angels announce to John the Baptist that he is to bap-
tize Christ in the river Jordan, and this conversation ensues:

> *Iohannes.* Shuld I abyde to he com to me?
>   That that shall neuer be, I traw;
> I shall go meyt that lord so fre,
>   As far as I may se or knaw.
>
> *Secundus angelus.* Nay, Iohn, that is not well syttand;
>   his fader will thou must nedys wyrk.
> *primus angelus.* Iohn, be thou here abydand,
>   Bot when he commys be then not yrk.[79]

Conditions are often created for no other purpose than to demonstrate or advance these stages in the larger game. When Jesus restores the blind boy's sight, in the Chester cycle, the disciples ask whether the boy was born blind for his own sins or because of the sins of his parents. Jesus says it was neither:

> But for this cause specially,
> to set forth gods great glory,
> his power to shew manifestly,
> this mans sight to reforme.[80]

He was born blind in order that Christ's power might be demonstrated. When Peter is grief-stricken at his betrayal of Christ, Christ tells him that the threefold denial was ordained in order that Peter (who will be Pope) might learn mercy:

> Therfore I suffered thee to fall,
> that to thy Subiects, hereafter, all
> that to thee shall cry and call,
> thou may haue minning.
>
> Sithen thy self so fallen hase,
> the more inclyne to graunt Grace![81]

Free-will in these plays is, in some sense, an illusion: the judges themselves choose to doom Christ, and the executioners think they are serving only their official masters, but all this is ironic in meaning. They do not know what we know as audience, that they are playing essential roles in a divine game.

The Passion of Christ is particularly interesting in this respect. Regarding the Crucifixion, the *Southern Passion* states directly what the plays allow to emerge from the pattern of the action: "By his owen wil to ham he com · and þorw non oþer strengþe ybrouȝt."[82] The Chester cycle alters the sequence of the betrayal of Christ by Judas in a way that seems meant to demonstrate this fact. In three of the Gospels, Judas identifies Christ with the agreed sign of a kiss and Christ is then taken by the Jews. Chester chooses to follow the version in the Gospel of John, which has Christ identify *Himself*, but it also retains Judas' kiss and places it in the sequence in a very subtle way:

> *Iesus:* You, men, I aske: whom seek ye?
> *Malchus:* Iesus of Nazareth; him seck we.
> *Iesus:* here, al ready; I am he!
> what haue you for to say?

Iudas:	A! swet maister, kyssë me,
	for it is long sith I thee see;
	and, togeather we will flee,
	and steal from them away.[83]

The kiss is necessary in order to preserve the full integrity of the biblical story—Judas *does* betray Christ. But the dramatist seems also to
be concerned that we understand Christ is not in the final sense betrayed, that He is taken only because He is ready to be taken. Christ
openly declares his presence—and by that His assent to the action—
and thus Judas' kiss has no real meaning. Judas is allowed to believe
that his actions and decisions determine the course of the game, but
he is deceived: everything that happens is part of God's plan. The same
sequence is followed in the *Ludus Coventriae*.[84] In the *Ludus breviter
de Passione* from the Benediktbeuern manuscript, the Last Supper
precedes the bargaining of Judas with the Jews, an alteration in sequence that makes the betrayal known before it has apparently been
conceived. Again, the reason is probably a wish to demonstrate Christ's
superiority to the schemes of man, to show God as the ultimate leader
of the game.[85] It is like that moment in the *Northern Passion* (following John 18:6) when the first attempt of the Jews to take Christ leaves
them stretched out on the ground:

> "I say yhow sothely I am he."
> And als he said þir wordes ryght,
> He schewes þare som dele of his might,
> And so astond þam in þat stound
> þat doun þai fell all to þe ground;
> And styll þai lay and dared for drede,
> Vn-tyll he with-drogh his godhede.
> . . . .
> þan godhede to þam shewed he nane,
> ffor tyme was comen he wald be tane.[86]

Having demonstrated His power—His potential freedom from their
designs—He allows them to take Him, for that is part of *His* design.
The York cycle shows the Jews stunned and blinded by a great light
shining from Jesus when they first attempt to capture Him, and in
the final trial before Pilate it provides a dazzling demonstration of
the immediate victory that could be His: the banners of the Jews dip

in homage to Jesus when He is brought into the judgment hall, and though burly men are brought in to try to hold them erect (once again the action is translated into a game or contest of strength), the banners remain down, until even Pilate is forced to rise and do homage to Christ's power. Only when Jesus wishes is the trial allowed to get under way.[87] Later in this same cycle the soldiers who crucify Christ notice an extraordinary thing (the dialogue serves as a stage direction):

> Byhalde, hym-selffe has laide hym doune,
> In lenghe and breede as he schulde bee.[88]

Christ puts Himself on the cross, for—as we have noticed earlier in the Towneley tournament figure—Christ and His executioners are finally both working toward the same end. In a fourteenth-century "Dialogue Between Jesus and the Blessed Virgin at the Cross" (a lyric that may in fact be a dramatic fragment), Christ speaks of the whole Passion as just such a formal, contracted action, as a game that *He* must play:

> Alone i am with-oten make,
> On rode i hange for mannis sake,
> Þis gamen alone me must pleyȝe,
> For mannis soule þis det to deyȝe.[89]

It is rare to find a game word used in this religious sense outside the drama, but in such an instance, as here, it is used to describe a quality inherent in the basic story.

Prophecy is constantly referred to in these cycles, and in the sources they draw upon, not merely because it proves Christ to be a Messiah but because it foretells the whole game, laying down its method and procedures in order that we, as audience, may understand that nothing crucial in importance here happens by caprice or accident. The plays of The Prophets exist formally in order to represent the fifth age of the world, but they have another function equally important, and that is to define the game that will take place. Chester, for example, includes very full prophecies, and an exposition of each in turn; they are carefully selected so that the Incarnation, Passion, Resurrection, Ascension, and Sending of the Holy Ghost, are all prophesied and explained in advance, just as the Three Kings in presenting their gifts foretell the Babe's full career.[90] The effect of this on the drama may be seen most clearly in a French medieval *Jugement de Jésus,* in which the Virgin pleads for her Son before a court of the prophets; they refuse to change a single detail in their prophecies according to which the Redemption must be accomplished.[91] The other Old Testament plays in the cycles are concerned with prophetic event rather than prophetic statement, but (as we have seen) they too set up their own causal necessity: the figures must be fulfilled.

In short, the whole of human history can be understood as a game in which the opponents are the Triune God and Satan, and it is in such terms that Satan, in the *Ludus Coventriae,* realizes that if Christ is killed, he will have lost:

> A · A · than haue I go to ferre
> but som wyle help I haue a shrewde torne
> My game is wers þan I wend here
> I may seyn · my game is lorne.[92]

The game has reached its decisive moment and he makes a bold bid to avert disaster: he goes to Pilate's wife in a dream and tells her that if Pilate dooms Jesus he will be sorely punished. But the game is under way and cannot (as he soon learns) be halted or turned aside, for God is in control and His strategy will lead Him to a victory for mankind.

Not all games are for children, and many of those played by the *tortores* are full of adult cunning and savagery. And actions shaped like game, played as though they were game, can in fact be serious and real. Though the medieval drama, as we have seen, defined itself as play and game, as something therefore not "in ernest," its great subject was a struggle for power played out as game but in fact historically real and deadly serious—a battle between God and Satan for man's soul, in which the outcome is never in doubt, but where the price of victory is a terrible one.

The basic simplicity of this game shaping allows the drama to ignore such thorny theological questions as the free-will of the *tortores* in an action foreknown and preordained by God. Instead of doctrinal explanations, it offers a drama-world analogous to the world it imitates: in it the *tortores* have free-will, yet what they do must be done and has been ordained from the beginning. The game is God's at every stage, but only three times does He reveal Himself as its leader—

at the Fall of Lucifer, in the Harrowing of Hell, and at the Final Judgment. And so there are two complementary game elements, the one gratuitous and improvisatory, apparently conceived and necessarily acted by man, the other preordained and inescapable, God's plan made known through the prophets, in which everything goes exactly as intended. Their effect is very subtly balanced. On the one hand, we feel the suffering to be unnecessary and terrible, and our pity goes directly to Christ as human scapegoat and victim. But on the other, at the level of the preordained, we feel how necessary and inevitable is the whole; our sympathy goes to God and fallen man together, as partners in an essential enterprise; and we—together with Christ in these plays—assent to His death, in order that we may later rejoice in His resurrection, in the victory He wins on man's behalf. A fifteenth-century lyric can define the complex emotional and intellectual response that this drama sought and achieved:

> My wofull hert is baith reiosit and sade,
>   Thy corps, lorde Iesu christ, quhen I behalde.
> Of my redempcioun I am baith blyth & glaid;
>   Seand þi panis, sorelie weip I walde.[93]

Chapter Nine

Natural Man and Evil

The Corpus Christi drama, in playing actions where God and man confront each other in ways so momentous as to begin new ages of the world, presents their relationship with a greater variety and force of circumstantial detail than any other art form of the Middle Ages. Every character who appears on the pageant stage is implicitly defined in terms of his relationship to God. Taken together, these characterizations amount to a composite portrait of humankind.

The chief scene of this drama, significantly, is earth. Heaven is a "high place" from which God speaks to humanity below. Hell Mouth is an entrance built like the yawning maw of leviathan, from which fiends come forth to sport with sinners and to which they carry off the damned. The torments of hell are never enacted, though such a performance could have been both sensational and instructive; indeed, the descriptions of hell's horror are almost as perfunctory as the descriptions of heaven's bliss. In Chester, Jesus has little to say about heaven more precise than this:

> Ther neither honger is ne could,
> but all things as your selues would;
> euerlasting ioy to yonge and owld
> that in earth pleased me.[1]

Instead the focus is on earth and human life, the things we can know about.[2]

In narrative and encyclopedic poems of the time, the essentials of sacred story are expanded upon by detailed doctrinal instruction or by lyric exclamations intended to inspire the soul with a deeper love of God. In either case they focus (as Milton was to do some centuries later) on the great figures, on God, Satan, Christ, and generalized

Man. The drama shows far less interest in extensive doctrinal instruction or lyric apostrophe, though it includes something of both. Chiefly it expanded from its basic story by characterizing the men among whom these great figures move. In doing so it marked an important change from the earlier Latin liturgical drama as well. As Glynne Wickham has remarked:

The liturgical drama of the Church interior seems clearly to have had its origin in thankfulness for the miracles of Christ's Nativity and Resurrection. Dramatically, however, thanks for these two mysteries cannot develop very far, no matter how often the thanks are reiterated. Concern for man's inadequacy, on the other hand, and the means of his redemption lends itself dramatically to limitless development. [3]

In time, the liturgical drama went on to dramatize other actions, but these two visitations, one to a sepulchre, the other to a stable, furnish the vast majority of extant Latin texts. Rejoicing and thanksgiving are not the only emotions aroused, but common to all these Latin plays is an interest restricted to the central action, the thing that is done, and an almost total lack of concern with the sources and impact of that action. The result is a drama that chiefly celebrates mystery: things happen in a graphic and isolated way, their theological significance is briefly indicated, and a *Te Deum* may be sung. But the human coherency of these actions is little attended to: no one could ever discover from the Latin passion plays *why* Christ was killed, except in terms of redemptive necessity; that alternate source of the action, its human inevitability, was left obscure. The interaction of the Messiah and fallen man, the claims, challenges, and affronts implicit in that relationship, remain in shadow. And as the drama developed in its vernacular form, a new intention and a new achievement were added: the attempt to understand in his full empirical complexity the creature we shall call natural man.

The dramatic treatments of the Slaughter of the Innocents can illustrate the change very clearly. In Matthew 2:16–18, the slaughter is recorded and mention is made of the prophecy of Jeremiah concerning the lamentation of Rachel for her children. The Latin drama presents the murder of the children in a formal, stylized way, and concentrates on the theological element in its source: Rachel becomes the central character, though she was dead long generations before the birth of Christ. In a Freising manuscript the play is designated as an *Ordo Rachelis*;[4] in the *Magi* play from Laon (which includes the Slaughter) there is only a formal lament between Rachel as figurative Jewish mother and a "Consolatrix";[5] in the Fleury version, the natural mothers are allowed on the stage to sing, *"Oremus, tenere natorum parcite uite,"*[*][6] but their presence is purely formal. And (in common with a version from Compiègne) this play ends with an angel speaking words of Christ which cause the Innocents to be immediately resurrected:

> *Sinite paruulos [venire ad me, talium est enim regnum coelorum].*
> Ad uocem Angeli surgentes Pueri intrent chorum dicentes:
> *O Christe* [etc.]†[7]

In enunciating sublime theological mystery in terms of a formal grief which is turned to joy, this handling of the episode attains considerable beauty. But it is not the way of the vernacular drama. The vernacular drama faces all the questions that the Latin plays ignore in order to maintain their grave and exalted tone. It studies the character of Herod, who must command the action. It examines the motives of the knights who agree to carry it out. It knows that children under the age of two are not to be found away from their mothers, and it dramatizes the mothers' response to the murder. It enters into the historical moment sufficiently to admit that the innocents died real deaths and did not stand smilingly upright at the convenient words of an angel. In the presence of these new concerns, grief and terror remain, but they are of an immediate, unformal kind. In addition there will be outrageous anger, cowardice, farce, a free-for-all battle with distaffs and fists, and wild lament. The drama has become aware of society and interested in the psychology of non-theological man: the background to the action is suddenly painted in color and vigorous detail. The Latin liturgical drama was, by comparison, like the great Byzantine mosaics: its foreground figures were given a certain somber and magnificent life, but only against a flat curtain of gold.

The cycle-drama's portrait of man *sub specie aeternitatis* shows him in many postures. He wrestles with angels, he hides from God, he cheats his fellows, he kills his Saviour; he prays, he distributes alms,

---

* Let us pray: spare the tender life of our children.
† Suffer the little children to come unto me; for of such is the kingdom of heaven. At the voice of the Angel let the Boys rise and enter the choir saying, O Christ [etc.].

he becomes a disciple of Christ. But even in these latter actions, when
his will harmonizes with the will of God and he becomes true servant
to his master, he remains wholly human. The imaginative basis of
Corpus Christi drama is an awareness of man's dual severance from
God—a *categorical* severance deriving from man's identity as creature,
which permits the good people to be godly without allowing them to
be god-like, and a severance that is *willful,* that superimposes upon
the categorical difference an estrangement whose origin is not in
creaturely definitions but in the perversity and rebellion of the individual human life. The Chester cycle's Octavian carefully defines
human nature as his reason for rejecting the religious homage that
the Senators of Rome have come to offer him. I shall quote it in full,
for it defines clearly what I mean by *categorical* severance:

> but folly it were, by many a waie,
> such soveraingtie for to assaie,
> sith I must dye I wot not what daye,
> to desire such dignitye.
>
> for of fleshe, blood, and bone
> made I am, borne of a woman;
> and sicker other matter none
> sheweth not right in me;
>
> nether of Iron, tree nor stone
> am I not wrought, you wot each one;
> and of my life most parte is gone,
> age shewes hym so, I see.
>
> and godhead askes in all thinge
> tyme that hath no begininge,
> ne never shall have ending;
> and none of these have I.
>
> Wherefore, by verey proofe shewinge,
> though I be highest worldlie king,
> of godhead have I no knowing;
> it were unkindlie.[8]

It is difficult to find an exact name for this twofold severance from
God, for the dramatists were content to give it mimetic life rather than
an appellation. We need a word to indicate man in his non-theological

identity, to stand for the part of his nature that is his first discovery—his awareness of himself as microcosm—before loneliness and misery and terror lead him to postulate his gods. We shall call this creature "natural man," following Tyndale's use of the term in his 1526 translation of the Bible (I Cor. 2:14): "For the naturall man perceaveth not the thyngs off the sprete off god."[9] From that moment in these cycles when man falls from his original innocence and perfection, the basic datum about all human personality is its fallen nature: the good men as well as the evil descend from Adam. Alexander Neckham wrote in *De naturis rerum* (early thirteenth-century):

That man therefore is said to be an animal tamed by nature should not be referred to the original state of his nature, boasting of its great worth, but to a state of his nature already damaged and disturbed. For the subtle investigation and laborious diligence of physicians do not consider the state of his first nature but that of his second. And so there would have been no disease, no disturbance of health, if man had remained in the state of his glory.[10]

It is man in the second state of his nature who occupies the dramatists' attention, the man of whom William Blake remarked in a well-known aphorism: "There is no such thing as natural piety, because the natural man is at enmity with God." The Corpus Christi drama shows the interventions of the divine in the purely human, and it gains in warmth, energy, and robustness as a result.

The most striking characteristic of natural man as disposed toward evil is his exuberant vitality: the drama presents him as an anarchy of stored-up energy seeking a release in any direction. The York Herod demands his obedience thus: "All renkkis þat are renand to vs schall be reuerande."[11] Man is a "rennyng" creature; even his repose is restless. When the executioners in the Cornish dramatization of Pilate's death grow impatient, one of them says to the Emperor:

> I do not like to stay long,
>   Nothing to do nor to look at;
> Hasten to say
>   What is needful for us to do.[12]

They are quite ready to be led—whether toward good or evil matters not. They await a decision, for they lack inner direction and a capacity for private judgment. Their pleasure in action is closely akin to the surprise shown by the Towneley Cain when his knave sulks at having been beaten. To beat him without cause seems to Cain perfectly natural; he is merely keeping his hand in ("Peas, man, I did it bot to vse my hand").[13] In his clouting of the angel, in his energetic cheating at tithes, and in the murder of his brother, one has a masterly portrait of a creature cut off from God by his own unregenerate vitality. He has many brothers in the drama, among them the *primus Tortor* of the Cornish cycle, apologizing to Pilate for his tardy arrival:

> Sir Justice, joy to thee!
> I was, on my soul,
> > Wrestling till I was very much tired.
> I could not run immediately,
> As I was panting,
> > And sweat all my neck and back.[14]

He interrupts his violent sport to begin the games that kill Christ. A little earlier, Pilate has had to reprimand the Jailer and his boy, distracted by a kind of sword practice, for failing to bring Jesus to court as they were told:

> How, jailor, make good haste,
> Bring the prisoners here;
> > He does not hear a bit.
> O ye two Knaves, evil be to ye!
> It is to you a great delight
> > To beat each other.[15]

Natural man can be made to take orders, but he has so little understanding of their necessity that attention must be constantly paid to his performance. All action is equally welcome and one sort is easily put by for another. This portrait of "renand" natural man is made particularly vivid in the early scenes of the Passion plays, where the furtive scurryings and machinations of Judas are contrasted with the weary stillness of the disciples in the Garden. Jesus, in the *Northern Passion,* describes in two lines of verse the exact dramatic effect of this episode when staged:

> And all if yhe haue sleped wele,
> Iudas has sleped neuer a dele.[16]

The inherent defect of such superabundant energy is that it easily becomes anarchy, canceling itself out in cross-purposes. It was perhaps

such a recognition that suggested to the *Ludus Coventriae* dramatist
that Jesus be led to trial "with gret cry and noyse some drawyng cryst
forward and some bakwarde and so ledyng forth."[17]

Noise, brawling, and a chaos of intention characterize the natural
world of men, and there are in the plays numerous impatient commands for silence and attention, commands that serve as implicit stage
directions for crowd or court. The York Herod begins his trial with
these words:

> Pes, ye brothellis and browlys, in þis broydenesse in brased,
> And frekis þat are frendely your freykenesse to frayne,
> Youre tounges fro tretyng of trifillis be trased,
> Or þis brande þat is bright schall breste in youre brayne.
> Plextis for no plasis, but platte you to þis playne,
> And drawe to no drofyng, but dresse you to drede, with dasshis.[18]

The Towneley Pilate begins a pageant thus:

> Peasse I byd euereich Wight!
>   Stand as styll as stone in Wall,
> Whyls ye ar present in my sight,
>   That none of you clatter ne call;
> ffor if ye do, youre dede is dight,
>   I warne it you both greatt and small,
> . . . .
> What! peasse in the dwillys name!
>   harlottys and dustardys all bedene!
> On galus ye be maide full tame,
>   Thefys and mychers keyn!
> will ye not peasse when I bid you?[19]

Long speeches of this sort are common, defining the natural condition
of men in society: before anything can happen, order has to be imposed from above. Their leaders speak to them insultingly, for they
are noisy and simple, like children or low-born servants. The Towneley Pilate says: "By youre mad maters I hald you bot boyes."[20] But
they possess a worldly cynicism that is fully the equal of their moral
simplicity. The Digby *Mary Magdalene* (a dramatized Saint's life)
shows the King of Marcylle, wishing to go on pilgrimage to the Holy
Land with his Queen, contracting for a boat to make the journey. The
shipman doubts the King's legitimate intentions:

I trow, be my lyfe,
þou hast stollyn sum mannes wyffe;
þou woldyst lede hyr owt of lond.
never-þe-les, so god me save,
lett se whatt I xall have,
or elles I woll nat wend.[21]

He is perfectly willing to be corrupted, but with his eyes open. No
one tricks this kind of man, though he can be easily bribed if the sum
is large enough. Too much knowledge about the way of the world has
distorted his vision: he is as incapable of recognizing goodness as he
is of preferring it in his own life. And underlying this moral simplicity
is the thing that makes it so dangerous a quality—the vast resources of
energy we have been examining. However little is understood, that
understanding is always implemented in action. In the Towneley play
of *The Talents* the *tortores* arrive breathless from running; the statement of one may stand for all:

war, war! within thise wones,
ffor I com rynyng all at ones!
I hauc brysten both my balok stones,
    So fast hyed I hedyr;
And ther is nothyng me so lefe
As murder a mycher and hang a thefe:
If here be any that doth me grefe
    I shall them thresh togedir.[22]

The good people in this drama are much less active: they lack this
galvanic vitality. One singular exception is the "rennyng" joy of the
apostles after Christ's resurrection, as they hasten to view the empty
sepulchre and then run off to tell their fellows. Here their joy is so
great that only release in physical action can answer to it. The *Ludus
Coventriae* Proclamation describes the scene (in advertisement) thus:

than petyr and johan as ȝe xal se
down rennyn in hast ouer lond and wolde.[23]

But their gaiety here has a religious propriety—it is in response to the
triumph of God. The "rennyng" energy of the other kind, our present
subject of discussion, is turbulent, undirected, undiscriminating, existing prior to any cause. It is an important part of the drama's conception
of human nature after the Fall.

These plays, like the *fabliaux,* never forget the ordinary man's ha-

tred of pretension: he cannot bear that another human being, one of
his kind, should presume to a high destiny. There is a comic statement of this in the York *Flood* play, when after a hundred years of
labor, the ark is finished and Mrs. Noah is allowed to see it for the
first time. She is furious:

> *Vxor.* Noye, þou myght haue leteyn me wete,
>   Erly and late þou wente þer outte,
>   And ay at home þou lete me sytte,
>   To loke þat nowhere were wele aboutte.
> *Noe.* Dame, þou holde me excused of itt,
>   It was goddis wille with-owten doutte.
> *Vxor.* What? wenys þou so for to go qwitte?
>   Nay, be my trouthe, þou getis a clowte.   [*Strikes him.*]
> *Noe.* I pray þe, dame, be stille.
>   Thus god wolde haue it wrought.
> *Vxor.* Thow shulde haue witte my wille,
>   Yf I wolde sente þer tille,
>   And Noye, for þat same skylle,
>   þis bargan sall be bought.²⁴

It is bad enough that she didn't know what was going on, but when
Noah justifies his secrecy (and the very act of building the ark) as
God's will and command, she hits him for thinking that an explanation. In this drama, mention of God always brings out the worst in
natural man, for at such moments the "good" people seem to be giving themselves airs. She is further grieved that he didn't ask her assent
—as far as she is concerned, God's permission temporarily counts for
nothing. But this aspect of the natural character of man, here so warm-
ly and amusingly detailed, takes on a sinister tone in the Passion episodes. Guided by scriptural source, the dramatists turn it into the single
conscious hatred directed at Christ by His tormentors. Working from
texts such as John 10:33, they make their *tortores* treat Christ's claim
to theological kingship as an idle boast in bad taste; He must be
cut down to size, and they implement a sort of rough proletarian justice to this end. In Chester, for example, a Jew explains why they are
scourging Jesus:

> Passe he shall a pace now,
> for god he him makes now;
> getts he no grace now,
> When I begyle him.²⁵

Folly and pride are to be cured by public indignity, and, as in the *fabliaux,* humiliation is the obvious means of recalling man to his human size. The technique does not need to be taught—it is a skill man is born with, as a soldier in York boasts:

> Vs nedis nought for to lere,
> Suche faitoures to chastise.[26]

In so far as those who actually kill Christ ever really are aware of Him, it is in terms such as these. They are not engaged in torturing their God, they are simply teaching a braggart a country lesson in humility.

We have spoken of natural man's lack of inner direction and have seen how he takes orders from those above him in a joyful, unconsidering way. Characteristic too is his habit of suddenly declaring at an end his responsibility to carry out those orders, if given what seems to him adequate cause. It is worth looking at his ultimate declarations of irresponsibility, of non-involvement, for they are acutely observed. They may relate to nothing more extraordinary than his basic human needs, as in the *Ludus Coventriae* when the knights charged with guarding the sepulchre make a formal round of speeches declaring they will fend off anyone who attempts to violate that ground, and then follow this with another round of speeches in which they proclaim their need for sleep, totally denying the duties they have just boasted they will perform. We need quote the transition stanzas only, where the contrast is most heightened. The First Knight is the last to issue his personal threat:

> He þat wyll stalke
> be brook or balke
> hedyr to walke
> þo wrecchis be wood.

And he follows it straightway with the first in a round of disclaimers:

> Myn heed dullyth
> myn herte ffullyth
> of sslepp
> Seynt Mahownd
> þis bereynge grownd
> þou kepp.[27]

There are for them obligations that override those of contract: if they need sleep, all else will be put aside. Similarly, they are easily halted in a course of action by physical pain or defeat. In the Digby *Mary Magdalene,* the cheekiness of the Shipman's boy is finally subdued by a sturdy beating administered by his master:

> for all my corage is now cast;
> alasse! I am for-lorn![28]

A more telling instance may be found in the York *Betrayal.* When Jesus is taken, Peter draws his sword and cuts off the ear of Malchus, one of the most energetic and determined of the conspirators. Malchus cries: "We! oute! all my deueres are done."[29] His duties and obligations are all ended, for the violation of his body brings a despairing separateness. He now has no identity save that of a man who has lost an ear, and that identity recognizes no outside responsibilities. He becomes the thing itself, a naked, forked animal, a creature uninvolved.

The mere fact of mortality itself puts human obligations in a shifting perspective. Because man is "deadlish"[30]—the moment of his birth is the commencement of his dying—all his human relationships, and the duties they imply, are necessarily finite. What is ultimately limited by external circumstance, man may choose to limit by his will. The fright of the soldiers who have failed to prevent Christ's resurrection leads to differing notions about what their report to Pilate should be. Some advise truth, while others opt for lying. In the Cornish cycle, the Third Soldier suggests they tell the truth, at least at the beginning:

> If he begin to be angry,
> We will lie to him,
> For all love to live.[31]

Life is his only moral good, truth, honor, integrity are insubstantial and readily to be discarded for its sake. But the fact of mortality can be used to justify a different kind of "irresponsibility" as well—that of self-*disregard* in favor of truth and honor. The Towneley dramatization of this same episode has a soldier refer to death in order to draw a conclusion exactly opposed to its Cornish counterpart:

> *primus Miles.* why, and dar thou to sir pilate go
> with thise tythyngys, and tell hym so?
> *Secundus Miles.* So red I that we do also,
>   we dy bot oones.[32]

But both are alike in this: they spring less from any ethical concern with good and evil than from a simple, instinctive response to the fact that natural man is mortal.

But there are declarations of irresponsibility that go deeper still. They are categorical, and hold that because man is different *in kind* from God, God's commands may be disregarded. Such a consciousness underlies, for example, the extraordinary speech of Cain in the *Ludus Coventriae,* to justify the bad tithing he intends to make:

> what were god þe bettyr þou sey me tyll
> to ȝevyn hym awey my best sheff
> and kepe my self þe wers
> he wyll neyther ete nor drynke
> Ffor he doth neyther swete nor swynke.[33]

The Towneley Cain asserts this disjunctiveness even more richly and darkly. Whatever else the supernatural ambience may be, it is non-human; the pastures of heaven and the fields of Cain exist in no obvious relationship to each other. At certain times, natural man is categorically at enmity with the divine; at other times (and they are more dangerous to theological order), he simply holds the divine to be categorically irrelevant to him.

But the Christian version of the history of the world insists that God sometimes intervenes in human affairs, and when this happens, natural man is shocked out of his complacency to testify to the awful otherness of God. He is ill at ease in the presence of his Creator. In the Chester play of *Balaam and Balak,* when God speaks in His proper person to the Israelites, they are terrified, and the *Princeps Sinagogue* on their behalf begs Moses to be their intermediary:

> Ah! good lord, much of mighte,
> thou comes with so great lighte;
> we bene so afraide of this sighte,
> no man dare speak ne looke.
>
> God is so grym with us to deale,
> but Moyses, master, with us thou mele;
> els we dyen many and feele,
> so afrayde bene all wee.[34]

It is a dreadful thing to hear the voice of God—do not speak to us, lest we die—but Moses, being man, can bring the message back to them: no one minds a few words from the vicar. The potential terror of the divine when it intervenes in human society leads Simeon in a Digby play to rejoice that Christ has come as a gentle baby, and not in any of the awful forms that are His as readily:

> My spretes Ioyen // thou art so amyable
> I am nat wery / to loke on thi face.[35]

But even this, as it turns out, is an illusion: Christ comes in the form of Goodness, of perfect Innocence, and this is more disturbing to a society of fallen men than any other possible manifestation. Because it cannot be endured, they kill him. In the words of the *Cursor Mundi*:

> þai had leuer se find of hell,
> þan him bituix þam forto duell.[36]

This presumptive portrait of natural man emerges most clearly in response to the great central action of the cycles, the killing of Christ, and it can clarify further the judgment made upon the *tortores* from within this drama. Other writers, other genres, were prepared to judge the executioners harshly. The narrative *Southern Passion* says that not only could Christ see who hit Him during the Buffeting, but He can see them now in hell:

> Þou couþest, ham þouȝte, to lute goed · whanne hi hudde þin eye,
> And who þe smot hi wende þat þou ne miȝtest ywite · bote þou him seye;
> Ak ich wot þou seost ham now · in helle in al hare teone.[37]

The *Speculum Gy de Warewyke (c.* 1300) in its discussion of the Judgment says Christ will turn then to that company who drove nails through His hands and feet, and will say to them:

> "Corsede gostes, ȝe beþ me loþe!
> Goþ anon, goþ nu, goþe
> In-to þe stronge fyr of helle,
> Euere more þer to dwelle.[38]

But this was not the judgment of the drama cycles, nor was it (according to the dramatists' understanding) the judgment of Christ. The drama saw these men as implicated in the guilt, but not as doomed to eternal perdition.

In the three cycle plays that deal most clearly with the question of guilt, the key to understanding proves to be Longinus, the knight who lances Christ's side. The authorities, in order to make certain that

Christ died, had ordered a soldier to open His side with a spear, and from that wound came blood and water. The Gospel gives no details concerning the soldier, but medieval tradition had supplied him with a name, Longinus, and a disability—he was blind. The dramatists of the Towneley, Chester, and Cornish cycles make use of the blindness to rid Christ's judgment on the tormentors of any ambiguity.

The speech, "Father, forgive them, for they know not what they do" (Luke 23:34), in the Bible is spoken from the cross, and is perhaps most easily read as being general in its reference: from His tree Christ seems to forgive fallen man at large. The Cornish version displaces it in such a way as to make it refer specifically to the executioners. As they stretch Christ with ropes to make Him fit the cross, He prays:

> O sweet Father forgive them,
> For they know not really
>   Whether they do evil or good;
> And if they knew in truth
> They would not destroy me;
>   O Father dear, forgive them for that.

To which the third executioner, as if in demonstration of this, replies scornfully:

> I care not a crumb for his forgiveness.[39]

Though the prayer is immediately and savagely denied by one of its subjects, that very denial is included in the prayer, anticipated and harmonized. They use the blind Longinus as a final game or trick, the crowning jest in their play:

> ... I know no better trick in the world
> For us to make to the dirty fellow.[40]

And when Longinus pierces His side, the stage direction and following speech read thus:

> *tunc fluat sanguis super lancea usque ad manus longii militis et tunc terget oculos et uidebit et dicit**

> Lord, forgive me, · as I pray thee
>   On my knees;

---

* Then let the blood flow over the lance all the way to the hands of Longinus the soldier, and then he will rub his eyes and will see and say ...

What I did · I knew not,
   For I did not see.
And if I had seen, · I would not have done it,
   Though I had been killed.[41]

The verbal parallels with Christ's speech from the cross, quoted above, are numerous and intentional; the function of Longinus is to contribute in dramatic terms a metaphor of blindness which will apply ultimately to the *tortores*. They do not see, and if they did, they would not do what they do. They themselves do not achieve Longinus' recognition, but his salvation (signaled by his restored sight) is potentially theirs, for their actions are spiritually and psychologically akin, and Christ's prayer has included them too. Where Christ has pardoned, these dramatists do not presume to condemn. But they are concerned to understand the pardon, just as much as the action it concludes, and it is here given a dramatic expression that is supremely clear.

This was not the only medieval view of Longinus. The *Meditations on the Supper of our Lord, and the Hours of the Passion,* for instance, treats him as neither blind man nor dupe. Mary has pleaded with the soldiers not to break Christ's legs and has begged them to allow her and her friends to bury Him:

Þan longeus þe knyȝt dyspysed here pleynt,
Þat þo proude was, but now, be mercy, a seynt.
A spere he sette to crystys syde,
He launced and opun[de] a wounde ful wyde.[42]

Here he fully intends what he does, in spite of Mary's plea. Nicholas Love's fuller translation of the same source[43] gave further currency to this tradition, making Longinus a conscious sinner who is converted to good living by his role in Christ's passion. The *Ludus Coventriae* does not include the episode at all, though Jesus on the cross very specifically forgives "þese jewys þat don me wo."[44] York apparently combines the two traditions: Longinus is blind, and he is *told* that he is to stab Jesus. When the blood restores his sight, it brings with it new knowledge: he realizes that the man he has stabbed is God, and he repents. York does not use the event as a means of defining unawareness,[45] but the Towneley play, like the Cornish, uses Longinus' blindness, enforced by verbal parallels, to image the spiritual condition of those who kill Christ. "Thay wote not what thay doyn" is set against Longinus' plea, "Gar me not do but I wote what."[46] In Chester, too, Christ says of the *tortores,* as He prays for their forgiveness, "they be blynd, and may not see,"[47] so that later Longinus may say as he prepares to thrust the spear:

> what I doe I may not see,
> wher it be ill or good.[48]

His movement into awareness, into "sight," might have been theirs. Their sin is no worse than his, and its causes are metaphorically identical. The dramatists show Christ's judgment upon his executioners as pardon, and they allow us to understand why.

Such care is expended upon the executioners in part because they figure more than themselves. The crowd that cries *crucifigatur* and prevents Pilate from freeing Christ is like them;[49] so also, in the most fundamental and dangerous potentialities of its nature, is the English Corpus Christi audience itself. The *tortores* mirror a common human nature.

The Seven Deadly Sins, with their numerous branches, are of course large enough to explain the *tortores'* guilt as well. "Wrathþe" can account for it in part, since it includes "Hate of herte, Malys of mowþ, Werchyng of wreche, Hastynesse or fershed, Manslawhtre, Vnpacyence, Blasfemye."[50] And "Enuye" can also furnish something of an explanation.[51] But the dramatists give one little lead in searching for such categories: the common people in these plays seem to have been created at a level closer to experience than to theories, and their characters are drawn instead in terms of ideas such as natural energy, animal cunning, moral simplicity, and unawareness. The very lack of moral consciousness in the wholly ordinary man, itself a most comprehensive sin, is best expressed in terms of *traits.* In sharp contrast, the leaders of the people are shown on these stages in ways which constantly make us think of certain specific sins, and for reasons which suggest that the dramatists consciously created them in that way. It is among these more sophisticated men that we find the specifically guilty: they are shown taking counsel, assessing expediency, bribing soldiers, giving false judgment; they are distinguished from those they lead by a reasoned awareness of what they are doing. The most chilling sentence in Scripture is that of John 18:14, which records Caiaphas' decision that it is expedient that one man should die for the people. In the *Ludus Coventriae,* Jesus at the Last Supper admonishes Judas when He identifies him as His betrayer-to-be: "þou art of grett Age and wotysst what is reson."[52] His guilt will be greater because he knows what he does; and in this category may be found all the leaders. They have the power of decision, and the natural capacities of simple men, who obey their orders without question, are entirely at their disposal. Listen to the speech of the York cycle's porter when he pledges his obedience to Pilate:

> I am fayne,
> My lorde, for to lede hym or lowte hym,
> Vncleth hym, clappe hym, and clowte hym,
> If ȝe bid me, I am buxhome and bayne.[53]

He is speaking of Christ, and the differing moral responsibilities are powerfully pointed: the porter is sinful, for no man has a right to be so indifferent to the ethical meaning of his action; but granted this condition of moral simplicity, the leader who uses him to a wicked end is himself the more grievous sinner. And in contrast to the judgment made on the *tortores,* the rulers in these cycles (all of them men who pervert intellect and power) are damned. In the Chester *Emmaus* play, Lucas says to the traveler who is the risen Christ, but who is unrecognized by them:

> To god and man wyse was he,
> but Bishopps—cursten mott they be!—
> damned him and nailed him on a Tree,
> that wronge neuer yet wrought.[54]

And Christ, who ought to know, does not contradict him. Similarly, the Centurion in the Cornish cycle speaks with almost visionary sureness after his conversion to belief:

> Black they shall be accursed
>   Who decreed to kill him;
> Truly they are condemned
>   To the fire of hell, the very bad place.[55]

A deeper guilt than the *tortores'* is here being made known, and one of the ways in which this drama insults these others and assesses their character is to caricature them unmistakably as exemplars of the Deadly Sins, most especially Pride and Anger. Here is part of the ranting of

Herod the Great in the Towneley cycle—occupying, in sum, more than sixty lines:

> I wote not what dewill me alys,
> Thay teyn me so with talys,
> That by gottys dere nalys,
>   I wyll peasse no langer.
>
> what dewill! me thynk I brast / ffor anger and for teyn;
> I trow thyse kyngys be past / that here with me has beyn;
> Thay promysed me full fast / or now here to be seyn,
> ffor els I shuld haue cast / an othere sleght, I weyn.[56]

Twice Herod in his ranting himself names his spiritual condition:

> My myrthes ar turned to teyn / my mekenes into Ire.
>
> . . . .
>
> The payn can not be told / that thay shall haue ilkon,
>   ffor Ire.[57]

In every cycle, Herod the Great and Herod the Judge are created chiefly in the "character" of *Ira,* but they serve as examples of *Superbia* as well, boasting of their power, their beauty, their wealth. Sermons and confessional techniques played a prior role in making this meaning clear, as when the *Instructions for Parish Priests* directs confessors to ask this sort of question about the sin of pride when examining a penitent: Have you been proud of your beauty, your strength, the trust of great ones, your high birth or high office, your great wealth?[58] The list is long. In the York cycle even Pilate temporarily serves this end. He introduces himself to the audience at the beginning of the *Second Trial of Jesus* in this way:

> For I ame þe luffeliest lappid and laide,
> With feetour full faire in my face,
> My forhed both brente is and brade,
> And myne eyne þei glittir like þe gleme in þe glasse.
> And þe hore þat hillis my heed
> Is even like to þe golde wyre,
> My chekis are bothe ruddy and reede,
> And my coloure as cristall is cleere.
> Ther is no prince preuyd vndir palle
> But I ame moste myghty of all,
> Nor no kyng but he schall come to my call,
> Nor grome þat dare greue me for gold.[59]

This is undoubtedly funny, it being unlikely that the dramatists intended Pilate in his stage person to possess the beauty he so immodestly describes; and the pride stated here is not really consistent with his character in the rest of this cycle. But for a brief moment, this tradition of using main characters to illustrate certain sins is the pageant's only concern. At these moments, the cycle-drama veers dangerously near the native weakness of its sister form, the morality play, in whose earliest extant English example, *The Pride of Life,* we can see a certain generic unreality already present. The central character in this play is called King of Life, and he lives wholly and unashamedly in worldly pleasure. When others attempt to caution him about his way of living and his coming end, he only replies:

> I ne schal neuer deye
>   For I am King of Life.[60]

He exists on stage less as a mimesis of a human being than as a spokesman for an abstract truth. For even though it is true that many of us live as though we shall never die, we never actually admit to believing this—we merely live as though we do. This final silence, to the world and to ourselves, is what makes the attitude human and real, alive in the way a copybook maxim is not. Only in certain portraits of the leaders does the cycle-drama violate this verisimilitude, and even then it does so only briefly. Eventually, these men, too, move on from exaggerated self-description into the specific actions that require their presence in the drama. The only occasions on which the cycle-drama *consistently* uses types instead of people associated with specific historical circumstance is in its plays of the *Last Judgment,*[61] and then it does so with full Christian propriety: in that last moment of historical time, we cease to be persons and become only the moral sum of our actions.

If, as I believe, the evil rulers, judges, and priests are less acutely observed and less interesting than is the common man in this drama, their deficiencies must be explained in part by the decision to humiliate them through caricature and to use them as a warning chiefly against Pride, the root from which the other Sins grow. Judas is also made to serve too clearly as a warning example and as a result is somewhat diminished in stature: because he must represent the sins of covetousness and wanhope, the deeper implications of betrayal from within the chosen twelve are little developed. These other explanations were at hand and could serve a useful didactic purpose, and so they were used. The drama gives Judas' betrayal a logical motivation by making him Christ's purseman and a thief, accustomed to taking for himself one-tenth of anything that comes into the coffers. When Mary pours ointment worth three hundred pence over the feet of Christ, Judas falsely reproves his master, saying that it could have been sold and the proceeds given to the poor. Consumed by resentment and greed, he sells Christ to the Jews for thirty pence, the exact sum he considers due him from the ointment. The story may be found everywhere in the literature associated with the drama and takes its origin from John 12:3–6, even though that merely identifies Judas as purseman and thief and recounts his anger at this use of Mary's gift. There is nothing about stealing one-tenth of all goods, and no specific connection of this anger with the betrayal. In Matthew, *all* the disciples are described as indignant at the wasting of the ointment, and in Mark *some* (unspecified) are mentioned so. Three of the English cycles restrict that indignation to Judas, and determine that he should steal exactly one-tenth, an idea used elsewhere to represent those who do not tithe honestly to God.[62] In choosing to explain Judas' betrayal in terms of "couetyse," the three cycles define his character and actions clearly enough, but at the same time they diminish the mystery and terror of his evil.[63] The *Ludus Coventriae* alone never allows him to rationalize his betrayal in this way.[64]

Judas' other major action is also made to serve a homiletic purpose. He is damned, in harmony with the usual pulpit view, not because of his treason to Christ but because of his suicide. His ultimate sin is wanhope, that despairing of the mercy of God that offends the Holy Ghost. The *Southern Passion* makes the point clearly:

> Goed ensaumple he vs ȝaf · aȝen wanhope echone.
> ffor non oþer þing he nas ffor-lore · bote ffor wanhope al-one.[65]

The Towneley cycle devotes an entire play to Judas' hanging, and in the *Harrowing of Hell* play which follows soon after, Christ assures Satan that some souls shall remain in his keeping:

> thou shall haue caym that slo abell,
> And all that hastys theym self to hang,
> As dyd Iudas and architophell.[66]

We should not complain that this treatment of Judas' death lacks moral profundity, for wanhope was considered the greatest of sins.

To turn Judas' ending into its greatest historical example does not precisely minimize his crime,[67] but it does tend to divert attention from the act of betrayal itself, and from the specific guilt that might derive from it—a guilt implied by Christ Himself when He said (Mark 14:21) "But woe to that man by whom the Son of man shall be betrayed. It were better for him, if that man had not been born." The York cycle's bargaining between Judas and the Jews is effective chiefly because it finds other means to establish the terror of the action: it includes the fact of Judas' greed, but it does more. When Judas knocks at Pilate's gate, the porter refuses to let him in, for he reads strange and ugly passions in Judas' appearance:

> Go hense, þou glorand gedlyng!
> God geue þe ille grace,
> Thy glyfftyng is so grymly
> Þou gars my harte growe.
>
> .　.　.　.　.　.　.　.
>
> ʒa, som tresoune I trowe,
> For I fele by a figure in youre fals face,
> It is but foly to feste affeccioun in ʒou.
> For Mars he hath morteysed his mark,
> Eftir all lynes of my lore,
> And sais ʒe are wikkid of werk,
> And bothe a strange theffe and a stark.
>
> .　.　.　.　.　.　.　.　.　.　.　.
>
> Full false in thy face in faith can I fynde
> Þou arte combered in curstnesse
> And caris to þis coste.[68]

The condition of Judas' soul can be read in his face, and what it reveals preserves more of the mystery of Christ's betrayal than a categorical statement of it as deriving from "couetyse." It relates directly to the nature of fallen man rather than to a schematic analysis of that nature.

Having examined some of the ways in which the Corpus Christi drama understood the characters of the *tortores,* of the leaders, and of the disciple who betrayed his master, we may now pose one final question about the guilt of the Crucifixion: How much of it is Satan's, and how much of it is man's?

The visual arts of the Middle Ages often show a kind of pandiabolism, with earth and the lower sky full of black demons intervening in human affairs. In *Queen Mary's Psalter,* for example, there is an illustration of the Fall which shows Adam considering whether or not to eat the apple proffered by Eve. Three demons are in the scene as secondary actors: one has his hand on Eve's shoulder, encouraging her; another is urging on Adam; the third ludicrously braces his buttocks against Adam's to prevent Adam's exit from the scene.[69] But even here the demons cannot make our first parents sin; the impulse to that is in some mysterious way discovered within man himself. A piece of religious instruction called "Craft of Deyng" shows what the ordinary Christian was taught to believe, whatever the subtleties of the theologians in the matter: "A man suld think, that all his euill dedis cumys of hyme self, and all his gud dedys cumys of grace, and the gyft of god."[70] Even though Scripture is perfectly clear about Satan's part in the Crucifixion, the Corpus Christi drama does not speak with one unanimous voice on the matter. The Gospel of St. John says (13:2, 27): "And when supper was done, (the devil having now put into the heart of Judas Iscariot, the son of Simon, to betray him) ... And after the morsel, Satan entered into him." Only Chester works entirely along these lines. Towneley includes this same Satanic ascription[71] but shifts the responsibility elsewhere; York, the *Ludus Coventriae,* and the Cornish cycle all agree in doing something profoundly different, which vitally affects the moral meaning of the Passion. They all show Satan at a crucial moment expending considerable energy in an attempt *to prevent* the crucifixion of Christ. To establish the difference, it is worth quoting the boasts that Chester has Satan make just before the Harrowing of Hell:

> Against this Shrew, that comes here,
> I tempted the folke in fowle manere;
> ayesell and Gall to his Dinner
> I made them for to dight,
>
> And hange him on a Rood Tree.
> Now is he dead right so throw me,
> and to Hell, as you shall se,
> he comes anone in height.[72]

This foolish boasting serves to make Satan suitably ludicrous as a dramatic character. The devil is exposed as unwittingly working his own downfall, and the alarm of the other demons when they hear this serves as prelude to the defeat soon to be suffered by all the forces of hell. But York, *Ludus Coventriae,* and the Cornish cycle use an ambiguous detail from only one gospel (Matt. 27:19) to do something far more interesting. In the gospel, Pilate's wife sends her husband a message saying he should have nothing to do with the just man, Jesus, for she has suffered in a dream about him. In these three cycles, Pilate's wife takes the stage solely to have this dream.

In Matthew (as well as in the apocryphal Gospel of Nichodemus[73]) the source of the dream is unnamed: we do not know if it came from God or the devil, for either is possible. *Handlyng Synne* (citing St. Gregory) says that a dream can come in one of these ways:

> And sum beyn þe fendes temptacyoun
> Þat to þe trowþe ys fals tresoun;
> And sum come of ouer mochyl þouʒt
> Of þyng þat men wuld hauë wrouʒt;
> And sum beyn goddys pryuyte
> Þat he shewyþ to warnë þe.[74]

Modern readers of the Bible easily assume that the dream was sent by God, for the Crucifixion was evil and anything designed to halt it would seem to have been on the side of good; witness Allardyce Nicoll's discussion of the incident:

In the mystery cycles the Devil is continually being dragged in, even where he is not strictly required, and scenes of diablerie are introduced purely for their own merriment.... So anxious were the dramatists to make use of this material that they even made the Devil responsible for the dream of Pilate's wife, which ought to have been a divine dispensation.[75]

But since there are no grounds for saying it "ought" to be divine in origin, the dramatists' interpretation is perfectly legitimate. They dramatize it so, not simply to pad the devil's role and thus please the audience, but above all to make a final and unequivocal statement concerning the sources of this ultimate act of evil.

This version of the event depends, of course, on Satan's being made to realize that if Christ is killed his kingdom is lost. Earlier, he has had opportunity to test Christ in the wilderness, and he ought there to have learned a lesson about Christ's superhuman nature. These three cycles also enjoy humiliating Satan by showing him having to learn this lesson again, but they differ from Chester in allowing him to learn it *before* the Crucifixion takes place, a recognition made possible by postulating a division in hell. The devil who breeds the hatred of the Jews against Christ in these cycles does so without the knowledge and counsel of his fellow-demons. If he boasts of his deeds in time, they can warn him of disaster, and he can go to Pilate's wife and attempt to halt the adventure so foolishly begun. Thus the dream, apparently sent in aid of Christ, is really sent in scorn of man: Satan seeks to prevent man's redemption. The *Miroure of Mans Saluacionne* describes the purpose behind the dream in just that way:

> Y^t wroght the dyvel wilnyng / to lette crists passionne
> To lette so of mankinde / the preciouse saluacionne.[76]

One of the taunts hurled at Christ on the cross, usually ascribed to man's spite and meanness, is interpreted by the *Southern Passion* as a serious plea expressed through the mouth of a *tortore* by Satan:

> "And ȝif þou art godes sone · adoun of þe rode aliȝt."
> Ak þat hi sede þorw þe deuel · ffor þe deuel hit nolde
> Þat he were ded, ffor he wiste wel · þat his deþ him schende
>   sholde.[77]

Satan seeks to save himself by reminding Christ that He has the power to come down from the cross.

The York cycle treats the attempt to halt the Passion in a straightforward manner,[78] as does the Cornish version, but the latter moves into irony when the Second Executioner dedicates the raising of the cross to the devil:

> In the name of the father Satan,
> Raise the cross up,
>   And deliver it to its place.
>
> Ho! haul every one,
> Let it, on Malan's part,
>   Into the mortise, crack to fall.[79]

Satan has tried, unsuccessfully, to prevent this very thing; the measure of his failure (and of man's lack of awareness) is that the unwanted deed is performed in his name. It is the *Ludus Coventriae,* however, that most clearly reconciles the Satanic origin of the event, as it is made explicit in the Gospel of St. John, with this later Satanic attempt to halt the tragic progress. Its Satan muses on the rebuff Jesus gave him in the Temptation, and on the measures of revenge he has taken:

> Som what I haue be-gonne · and more xal be do
> ffor All his barfot goyng · fro me xal he not skyp
> but my derk dongeon I xal bryngyn hym to.
>
> I haue do made redy his cros · þat he xal dye up-on
> And thre nayles to takke hym with þat he xal not styrte.[80]

A demon speaks to him from hell to warn him they are lost if Christ dies, and Satan immediately recognizes the fearful truth of this. His dream warning is given very clever dramatic life:

here xal þe devyl gon to pylatys wyf · þe corteyn drawyn as she lyth in bedde and he xal no dene make but she xal sone After þat he is come in · makyn a rewly noyse · comyng and rennyng of þe schaffald and here shert · and here kyrtyl in here hand · and sche xal come beforn pylat leke A mad woman.

The stage direction directs that Satan make no noise, but she describes his warning as a terrible roaring cry:

> As wylde fyre and thondyr blast
> he cam cryeng on to me
> he seyd þei þat bete jhesu · or bownd hym fast
> with-owtyn ende dampnyd xal be.[81]

Pilate heeds her advice, thanking her for her good counsel and promising that all will be well. The devil's last hope has been fulfilled: Pilate resolves not to sentence Jesus to death. But events have gone too far, and neither Pilate nor Satan himself can stop man now. Whatever master man obeyed at the beginning, he has thrown off that servitude and now serves only his own nature. The vicious element in man has been awakened, put on a course, and nothing can turn it aside. Pilate learns that lesson, and explains his helplessness to Jesus thus:

> Busshoppys and prestys · of þe lawe
> þei love þe not as þou mayst se
> and þe comon pepyl A-ȝens þe drawe
> In pes þou myth A be for me.[82]

In medieval Christianity, Satan was implicated in every sin because of his having officiated at the Fall that brought sin into the world.

But his prior guilt does not lessen man's moral responsibility. Only a man could eat the apple, and only men can kill Christ. The cycle dramatists here deliberately exempt Satan from the final stages of that appalling action, in order to emphasize the more strongly that man's natural traits alone can explain the killing of a man perfectly good. We have come full circle: those qualities we discussed in the early pages of this chapter become their own adequate cause of the Passion. "Þai had leuer se find of hell / þan him bituix þam forto duell." The causes of the event had been analyzed by St. Thomas Aquinas, in answering the question "Whether Christ was slain by another or by Himself?" and his statement there can summarize for us this version of the Redemption:

I answer that, A thing may cause an effect in two ways: in the first instance by acting directly so as to produce the effect; and in this manner Christ's persecutors slew Him because they inflicted on Him what was a sufficient cause of death, and with the intention of slaying Him, and the effect followed, since death resulted from that cause. In another way someone causes an effect indirectly—that is, by not preventing it when he can do so ... and in this way Christ was the cause of His own Passion and death.... since Christ's soul did not repel the injury inflicted on His body, but willed His corporeal nature to succumb to such injury, He is said to have laid down His life, or to have died voluntarily.[83]

In this discussion, the devil is not specifically mentioned at all—not because he was unimportant but because his work was done long ago in Eden. Man's fallen nature is one of the two adequate causes of the Passion; God's plan to redeem man is the other.

All the English cycles except Towneley work basically within a "good Pilate" tradition, according to which Pilate is a troubled judge, one who has no wish to condemn Jesus, and in whose mouth the great question recorded by John 18:38—"What is truth?"—seems natural and necessary. This is the point of view of the four Gospels, as well as of the apocryphal Gospel of Nichodemus (known also as the Acts of Pilate).[84] Pilate's failure as a man lay in too great a regard for expedience: as a leader he was content to be led. But as the centuries passed, he came more and more to share in the odium attaching to those associated with the killing of Christ, and a full "life and death of Pilate" legend developed which treats him very harshly indeed.[85] The cycles are not wholly consistent in their attitude to him: at times, as we have seen, he is satirized in the character of Pride; and after the Resurrection, when he becomes aware of what really has happened, his dignity falls to pieces and he becomes very much a harried provincial governor. But during the trials of Jesus, which alone involve him in Christ's death, he is shown as steady, reasonable, and without hatred. The Cornish cycle treats him sympathetically in the *Passion,* even though the *Resurrection* play on the following day actually stages from the legend his trial before Tiberius and his terrible death. At that trial, Veronica charges:

> Pilate killed him; without fail
> Take retribution of him,
>   For he was Christ, the King of heaven.[86]

York, Chester, and the *Ludus Coventriae,* on the other hand, present only the part of Pilate's life that directly crossed the life of Jesus, and though he is undoubtedly among the drama's evil men, he takes his place gravely and soberly among them. Unlike the Cornish cycle, these English cycles direct no specific vengeance at him.

The Towneley cycle builds upon a conception of Pilate's character that has no parallel in the related literature. It makes Pilate the chief opponent of Jesus, a kind of arch-hypocrite who announces early to the audience that he intends to kill Christ, and that to achieve this end the more subtly and delightfully, he will feign sympathy and friendship:

> I shall fownde to be his freynd vtward, in certayn,
>   And shew hym fare cowntenance and wordys of vanyte;
> Bot or this day at nyght on crosse shall he be slayn,
>   Thus agans hym in my hart I bere great enmyte.[87]

To shape the dooming and death of Christ in this way is to alter deeply the meaning of the Crucifixion as understood by the other cycles: not natural man, but one particular historical character becomes finally responsible. The contrast between Pilate and the crowd is lost,[88] for, whatever his pretense, he and they seek the same decision—*crucifigatur.* Arnold Williams, in an otherwise helpful study, *The Characterization of Pilate in the Towneley Plays,* seems to me mistaken in his main conclusion: that the Towneley modification of Pilate's character is a great stroke of genius, the highest achievement of the English medieval drama. This view is based on assumptions about dramatic art and moral meaning that are perhaps irrelevant to the Corpus Christi drama.

Williams values, above all, economy of effect and consistency of character:

The supreme achievement of Towneley is that there is no wavering between the two competing conceptions of Pilate's character. He is bad, all bad.... The Towneley method is the true dramatic method. Starting with a concept of Pilate as a tragic villain, not very different from the Machiavellian of Elizabethan drama, Towneley built up this character as a dramatic contrast to the suffering Christ.[89]

But this is consistency purchased at a high price. It is an aesthetic weakening of the dramatic genre, whose special gift is to imitate life, for life notably displays a mixture of good and bad in all men. To present a character as "bad, all bad" is a dramatic fiction, and an uninteresting fiction at that. When the Towneley dramatist chose to fit Pilate, potentially the most complex figure in the scriptural account of the Passion, to this artistic oversimplification, the cycle's total imitation of the Passion became less convincing. Aesthetic conviction, after all, is related to the depth of moral understanding that a work achieves; as an author pushes deeper and deeper into the ultimate mystery of the human personality, his audience comes to understand that in some profound sense the artifact is a convincing analogue to real life. This polar opposition of Pilate and Christ may be economical, but it is perhaps morally inconsequential as well. It avoids the real question about the death of the man who was God: that is, what degrees of guilt adhere to the various men implicated in that action. This chapter has sought to show the way in which these cycles—Towneley among them —are interested in such problems. But Towneley alone, by making Pilate a smiling, posturing villain, provides another sufficient cause of Christ's death. In view of the length of the cycles (the York performances lasted more than fifteen hours; Cornwall and Chester both took three days), we may legitimately doubt that economy of effect is their "true dramatic method." In a drama so spacious, there was ample time and opportunity for a larger investigation.

Williams goes on to discuss the weakness of the dramatic organization in the other cycles:

Though the simple religious intensity of the Chester passion and the stir and movement of Ludus Coventriae are impressive, one gets the sense that

Christ is the only unifying figure. The Jews, Pilate, the torturers or soldiers, Herod—all take turns in the role of antagonist, and the result is a one-character-at-a-time organization, such as Marlowe's *Edward II,* rather than the development by opposition and contrast of a Shakespearian tragedy.[90]

It seems to me that the unifying figure which these other cycles contrast to Christ is something like a portrait of fallen man, and the great range of his collective characterization is an artistic strength. Pilate, as pure villain, can represent only one marginal aspect of this human condition. The effect of multiplicity is in truth as much spatial as it is sequential: it presents Christ as meeting opposition not one character at a time but antagonists everywhere he turns. Towneley, in fact, is not so very different. What has happened is merely that upon a collective portrait of natural man observed with a psychological acuteness fully the equal of the other cycles, the reviser known as the Wakefield Master has placed two pageants (*The Scourging* and *The Talents*) which present at the crisis of the cycle action a character who claims in asides to the audience to be its whole explanation. This dramatist, Williams notes, leaves out Pilate's wife and her dream: "Obviously, the action does not fit the Towneley conception of Pilate, and it is somewhat uncontributory wherever it occurs."[91] In failing to understand its contribution elsewhere, he has missed the deepest implication of these other dramatists' meaning: that natural man—not Pilate and not Satan—is ultimately guilty of Christ's death. To disagree with Williams' concluding judgment, which holds that Towneley is "not truer to Scripture, but, in terms of the level of the audience, a truer exposition of that conflict between good and evil which is the essential meaning of the passion and the resurrection,"[92] is not merely to value less highly the Towneley Passion episodes as art; it is also to make clear the higher moral seriousness that emerges from the alternative characterization of Pilate, a characterization that focuses our attention instead on natural man, the creature on this stage who images us all. For the real meaning of the Crucifixion is Christ dying to save those who kill Him. A strict contest between good and evil is the dramatic point of the *Harrowing of Hell,* but those actions that happen on earth are subtler and morally complex; they are not well expressed in the blacks and whites of chiaroscuro.

Christ came to redeem our nature rather than our specific deeds. As Aquinas had written, Christ's redemption was made chiefly in respect to the original sin of Adam rather than to the actual sins of Adam's descendants:

... Christ assumed human nature in order to cleanse it of corruption. But human nature did not need to be cleansed save in as far as it was soiled in its tainted origin whereby it was descended from Adam. Therefore it was becoming that He should assume flesh of matter derived from Adam, that the nature itself might be healed by the assumption.

... original sin, whereby the whole human race is infected, is greater than any actual sin, which is proper to one person. And in this respect Christ came principally to take away original sin, inasmuch as *the good of the race is a more Divine thing than the good of an individual.*[93]

And so it is in the drama. In the *Ludus Coventriae* Christ says to His mother, from the cross: "And woman þou knowyst þat my fadyr of hefne me sent / to take þis manhod of þe · Adam ys rawnsom to pay."[94] The Towneley Christ addresses the audience from the cross in much the same way: "Thus by I adam blode."[95] In York, the fact not only is stated by Christ but is echoed immediately in scorn by His executioners:

> *Jesus.* Almyghty god, my Fadir free,
> Late þis materes be made in mynde,
> Þou badde þat I schulde buxsome be,
> For Adam plyght for to be pyned.
> Here to dede I obblisshe me
> Fro þat synne for to saue mankynde.
> . . . .
> *i Mil.* Wel herke, sir knyghtis, for mahoundis bloode!
> Of Adam-kynde is all his þoght.
> *il Mil.* Þe warlowe waxis werre þan woode,
> Þis doulfull dede ne dredith he noght.[96]

Christ came to die for Adam's sin, and the legacy of Adam to his descendants—man's fallen nature—has been shown on the Corpus Christi stage in its total range, and under the figure of history. In the sixth age of the world, Christ Himself comes to walk the earth as a man, and we see the children of Adam uncomfortable in His presence, just as the Israelites were frightened of God at Sinai.

In my view, the Corpus Christi drama succeeds best in its characterization of evil when it is showing the energy, the wiles, the playfulness and moral simplicity of ordinary men at their most instinctive and creaturely. Its portrayal of the evil leaders, those who have intellect and power, is less interesting but wholly consistent: it shows these same instincts made subtler by reason, smoother by hypocrisy, steadier and more sustained through intellectual hatred. The cycles are able to make comprehensible the sullen indifference of the crowd, the savagery of the executioners, and the hatred and cunning of the leaders, for they are rooted in the place where all explanations must start, in our metaphysical identity *ni l'ange ni bête*. The Corpus Christi drama looked hard and deep into human nature.

Chapter Ten

Goodness and Natural Man

Perhaps the greatest strength of the Corpus Christi drama as well as the strongest claim it has to our attention and sympathy lies in its manner of showing human goodness. Its good people are not pale abstractions, idealized and saintly, but creatures of flesh and blood, recognizably members of the same family as the rulers, the knaves, and the executioners we have been examining. The same instincts, passions, and creaturely limitations descend from Adam to both groups alike. The good people, too, are characterized as fallen, though not as evil; as a result they have a kind of sprawling existence which is larger than categories, and which is not judged harshly. God has patience with them. Human goodness is of an earthly sort, and in this chapter we shall look at the qualities and limitations of that goodness as embodied by characters on the Corpus Christi stage.

In the earlier episodes of these cycles, the need for ideas about the natural *kind* of human virtue was particularly pressing, for it is apparent to anyone that the God-favored in the Old Testament are nothing like divinely good. John Fisher, Bishop of Rochester, had analyzed the career of Jonah in seven stages, as an example of how a man who breaks a commandment of God falls further and further toward hell. He anticipates an important objection to his example thus:

It forceth not for our purpose at this season though Ionas in holy scrypture sygnefy Cryst. For one & the same thynge by a dyuers consyderacyon may be taken fyguratyuely for two contraryes. Somtyme in holy scrypture the lyon sygnefyeth Cryst, and somtyme by the lyon is sygnefyed the deuyll, as in the epystle of saynt Peter. *Tanquam leo rugiens circuit.* It sygnefyeth Cryst as in the appocalypse. *Vicit leo de tribu Iuda.* What thynges be more contrary than god and the deuyll. For as moche therfore as one thynge may betoken Cryste and the deuyll, why may not Ionas somtyme sygnefy Cryst and somtyme the synner.[1]

He faces the difficulty openly, but his analysis is slightly confusing: the dual meaning of Jonah's life does not so much derive from two ways of looking at it (a "dyuers consyderacyon") as from the fact that it, like any human life, was a mixture of both good and evil. Jonah, chosen by God as prophet, used all his energy and cunning to try to escape that dread command, but in the end he obeyed.

The example of Jonah is instructive, though his story is never dramatized in the cycles, because it focuses attention on the one good quality that is shared by all of God's chosen. That quality is obedience, and until Christ's ministry, human goodness is made known chiefly in its simple terms.[2] The steadfastness of Noah has already been discussed, as has the obedience of Abel, and of Abraham and Isaac; Moses and the prophets, too, spoke as God commanded them to speak. This necessity to obey continued into New Testament times. Mary accepted the message of the angel with the words, "Behold the handmaid of the Lord," and Christ in Gethsemane affirmed that not His natural will, but the Father's, would be done. At Christ's incarnation, however, new patterns of goodness were established, for Christ was understood by St. Paul, and by the Fathers after him, to be the first "spiritual" man. Augustine discussed the change in his *De Genesi contra Manichaeos*:

Yet in that age, as in the old age of a man, a new man is born who now lives spiritually. For on the sixth day it was said, "Let the earth bring forth the living creatures." But on the fifth day it was said, "Let the waters bring forth," not living creatures but "creeping things that have life." For bodies are creeping things and up to now that people had been serving the Law with bodily circumcision and sacrifices.... It says that those creatures are alive, because in this life eternal things began to be desired.[3]

In the sixth age, Christ established new sacraments—Baptism and the Eucharist—potent to change any man's nature;[4] likewise He ordered His life on earth as a model of how a man should live. Where before there had been only the law, there was now an *exemplar* of goodness. One of the services of the Corpus Christi play was to present that new pattern of goodness in dramatic terms. In the York *Judgment,* God the Father begins with a long recapitulation of history, in which this part of Christ's mission is given great importance:

> Sethen in erthe þan gonne he dwelle,
> Ensaumpill he gaue þame heuene to wynne,
> In tempill hym-selffe to teche and tell,
> To by þame blisse þat neuere may blynne.[5]

The example of Christ's life redefines the goodness acceptable to God, and as a result we have in the plays of the Final Judgment little reference to the written law, or even to man's obedience, but instead a more searching examination of the individual soul in terms of the seven deeds of corporal mercy. The saved are those who fed the hungry, gave drink to the thirsty, clothed the naked, visited the sick—those, in short, whose lives followed Christ's example of perfect charity. In the cycle-drama, the *Expositor* or *Poeta* figure often appears to comment on an action that Christ performed *in example* for us; so, too, does the morality play, *The Castell of Perseverance,* narrate Christ's life as an example for Mankind to follow when the Deadly Sins besiege the Castle.[6] Mary's life came to be understood in the same way, for as Christ allowed Satan to tempt Him in order to teach men how to withstand temptation, so Mary, after the birth of Christ, performs the ceremony for the Purification of Women, not because she was impure but "for a sample of mekenesse."[7]

A most important aspect of human goodness as shown on the Corpus Christi stage is thus seen to be the ideal form that Christ and Mary demonstrate as a new goal in human life. But they are as masters, and the rest as pupils. The other good people on this stage will reveal virtue in smaller and less perfect ways; their goodness is achieved in spite of their fallen nature, and the signs of struggle are usually visible. They are not remarkably spiritual men, nor is the word "grace" used often in its full theological sense, except to distinguish the time of grace from the time of misdoing in dramatizing the history of the world.[8] Even those chosen twelve who follow Christ and see His example often find goodness difficult, and there is no suggestion that the audience will find it easier than they. Because the good people in this drama remain human, they lack the copybook simplicities, but they are meant to reassure us as audience that in our own imperfect lives their example can be found relevant. We are expected to be good, but not good beyond our capacities. This didactic end, so modest and sensible, demanded of the dramatists that they imitate human life in recognizable ways; the result was a religious drama that pays tribute to every man's right to existence and idiosyncracy, while insisting that he serve God.

We may begin, as in the last chapter, by examining a series of incidents in which the good people reveal more of themselves than abstract virtue requires—incidents which reveal virtue as a plant growing in human soil. We shall see how that soil relates them more closely to their evil brothers than to God: we shall examine the goodness that is possible to natural man.

Good men, like evil, live in society and are engrossed in themselves and in human affairs. The shepherds chosen to receive the first announcement of Christ's birth live wholly in the world: they quarrel, they make jokes, they have shrewish wives, they like a good round of ale. They are not pale watchers, waiting only for this night of nights, but when the announcement comes they are able to recognize its importance. In at least one version, their lives are changed irrevocably by it. In York, they present their homely and touching gifts to the Infant—a brooch with a tin bell, two cobb-nuts on a ribbon, a horn spoon capable of holding forty peas at once—and a sly hint that He might think to reward *them* with gifts at a later time. Even in this most devotional moment, there is an amusing touch of naïve self-interest. Says one:

> Loo! here slyke harnays as I haue,
> A baren broche by a belle of tynne
> At youre bosom to be,
>   And whenne ʒe shall welde all,
> Gud sonne, for-gete noʒt me,
>   Yf any fordele falle.

And another:

> Loo! litill babe, what I haue broght,
> And when ʒe sall be lorde in lande,
> Dose goode agayne, for-gete me noght.
> For I haue herde declared
>   Of connyng clerkis and clene,
> That bountith aftir rewarde;
>   Nowe watte ʒe what I mene.[9]

The purpose of these speeches may be to invoke the idea of the Messiah as a temporal ruler (one of the Jewish conceptions of His possible role) and of temporal benefits, but the idea is presented in psychological terms appropriate to simple men: they give presents, and they expect to get presents in return. Like the corrupt knights who will later kill Christ and guard His sepulchre, they are interested in rewards—such is man's nature—but these shepherds look to the giver of all gifts, to the King of Kings, and those others to masters as corrupt as themselves.

In Chester, Balaak offers Balaam great riches if he will curse God's chosen people; God forbids Balaam to do so, and hears this reply:

> Lord, I must doe thy byddinge,
> thoughe it be to me unlykeing,
> for truly much wynninge
> I might haue had to daye.

But he does get God's permission to go to Balaak and then confides to the audience, as he rides away, that he intends to disobey for the money's sake:

> they shalbe cursed every one,
> and I ought wyn maye.

> If Balaak hold that he has heighte,
> Gods hest I set at light,
> warryed they shalbe this night,
> or that I wend awaye.[10]

Balaam's arrogance earns him a richly comic humiliation. His ass suddenly goes down on its knees in the road and refuses to move; when Balaam begins to beat it, the ass speaks in reproof until Balaam sees what the ass has seen already—the angel of God, sword in hand, blocking the way. Balaam learns his lesson, and in Balaak's company he blesses Judea each time he is ordered to curse its people. What is more, his blessings prophesy the great joy soon to come to the Jews. Though Balaam is perverse in mind and easily tempted by money, he does finally *obey* God, and his reward is a prophetic knowledge of the Messiah. God has used him to comfort the Jews and to confound their enemies. He uses men so, and calls their service goodness.

God chooses His men from out of a busy and demanding world, and often that choice falls on men as little concerned with Him as are their more evil fellows. Simon of Cyrene is a prosperous man of affairs, hurrying about important business, when his path happens to cross that of Christ on the way to Calvary. At first he makes excuses:

> [*iii Miles.*] We pray þe, sir, for-thy,
> That þou wilte take þis tree,
> And bere it to Caluerye.
> *Symon.* Goode sirs, þat may nouȝt be,
> For full grete haste haue I.
> My wayes are lang and wyde,
> And I may noght abide,
>   For drede I come to late;
> For surete haue I hight
> Muste be fulfillid þis nyght,
>   Or it will paire my state.
> Therfore, sirs, by youre leue,
> Me thynkith I dwelle full lang,
> Me were loth you for to greue,
> Goode sirs, ȝe late me gang.[11]

But the executioners will have their way, and he is won from his affairs to the affair of man's redemption. Chester makes its Simon seek to avoid carrying the cross because he does not assent to the Crucifixion;[12] since he is among the good people in this drama, Chester ranges him on the side of goodness from the first. The other cycles use him as a man engrossed in the world who is brought to the service of God. Initially as unaware as the *tortores* will remain, he comes to share willingly Christ's burden.

The spiritual danger of society is that the distraction and turbulence of its relationships may overwhelm or put from mind the quieter but more imperious relationship that exists between man and God: the three foes to man's soul were traditionally defined as the world, the flesh, and the devil. But to be man is necessarily to live among men, to enjoy and have place in society, and the good people are as social, as concerned with their kind, as are the evil. Mrs. Noah and her gossips offer a lively example, and so does this charming passage from the Towneley *Salutation of Elizabeth*. It delays the actual salutation (marking a decisive change in the relationship of God and man) until some purely human matters have been dealt with:

Elezabeth. ffull lang shall I the better be,
That I may speke my fyll with the,
   My dere kyns Woman;
To wytt how thi freyndys fare,
In thi countre where thay ar,
   Therof tell me thou can,

And how thou farys, my dere derlyng.
Maria. Well, dame, gramercy youre askyng,
   ffor good I wote ye spyr.
Elezabeth. And Ioachym, thy fader, at hame,
And anna, my nese, and thi dame,
   how standys it with hym and hir?

Maria. Dame, yit ar thay both on lyfe,
Both ioachym and anna his wyfe.
   Elezabeth. Els were my hart full sore.
Maria. Dame, god that all may,
yeld you that ye say,
   And blys you therfore.

Elezabeth. Blyssed be thou of all women,
And the fruyte that I well ken,
   Within the wombe of the.[18]

The real business of the play finally gets under way with the words "Blessed art thou among women," and the Magnificat that follows, but the delay is beautifully handled, and much of the play's effectiveness depends on this opening. Its warm and gossipy irrelevance make the two women real people, behaving as women do when they meet; Elizabeth's purpose is to salute the child in Mary's womb, but she must first know how things are at home. The dialogue eventually becomes purely lyric utterance, like a liturgical play in the vernacular; but in its opening thirty lines, it creates a society and places its characters within it. The tone of all that follows gains in warmth and tenderness as a result.

When characters in this drama are called upon to play exalted roles in divine history, the dramatists never forget that they will perform them in the manner of men. This fact modifies the exaltation without in any way diminishing it. Thus, the York Noah will agree to build the ark before he remembers he has no knowledge of how boats are built, and his counterpart in Towneley will be forced to hear his wife's laughter at the results:

> I was neuer bard ere / As euer myght I the,
> In sich an oostre as this.
> In fath I can not fynd
> which is before, which is behynd.[14]

Yet this ark will serve to carry all of the old world worth saving into a new beginning. Similarly, in the York *Flight into Egypt,* Joseph and Mary are warned in a dream to flee, but even this action, performed under such high command, is also full of human uncertainties and incapacities:

> *Maria.* Allas! Joseph, for greuaunce grete!
> Whan shall my sorowe slake,
> For I wote noght whedir to fare.
> *Joseph.* To Egipte talde I þe lang are.
> *Maria.* Whare standith itt?
> Fayne wolde I witt.
> *Joseph.*   What wate I?
> I wote not where it standis.
> *Maria.* Joseph, I aske mersy,
> Helpe me oute of þis lande.

They will go to Egypt without question, though they do not know the direction, much less the road. And though Mary is not an accomplished horsewoman, yet some good advice from Joseph will see her through:

> And yf þou can ille ride
> Haue and halde þe faste by þe mane.[15]

It is like that moment in the Coventry *Weavers' Pageant* when Simeon prepares for the purification of Mary and the presentation of the infant Christ by instructing his two boys, one of them clever, the other not, in their proper duties:

> And when he aprochis nere this place,
> Syng then with me thatt conyng hasse
> And the othur the meyne space
>   For joie rynge ye the bellis.[16]

Each serves according to his skill; the devotion of the clerk who sings the service is no more and no less valued by God than that of the boy who can only ring bells to express his gladness. God is content to find his witnesses and worshipers as they are.

Like those more evil than good, those more good than evil find life a misty, perplexing experience. They are distinguished from the others in their capacity for witnessing as much of the truth as they can understand. In the Chester ministry play, the Pharisees are greatly angered by a boy who claims to have been healed by Christ. They interrogate his parents to learn if he was truly blind before, and they try to change his story by telling him that if he *was* healed on the holy day, the healer must have been a servant of evil. This argument confuses the boy, but he will not recant his fundamental certainty—that he was blind and now can see:

> If he be sinnfull, I doe not know;
> but this is truth that I doe show.[17]

Like those of their fellows devoted to evil, the good people too are not very brave. Isaac warns his father before the sacrifice that he must be bound, for natural fear will make him oppose both God and his father's will:

> I knaw myselfe be cours of kynde,
> My flessche for dede will be dredande,
> I am ferde þat ȝe sall fynde
> My force youre forward to withstande.
> Ther-fore is beste þat ye me bynde.[18]

The finest medieval study of a good person's instinctive cowardice is perhaps the portrait of Jonah in the fourteenth-century poem called *Patience,* but there are several fine studies of the reluctant-prophet type in the drama as well. Among them is the York Moses, struggling to escape the order to prophesy to Pharoah and his people:

> A! lord syth, with thy leue,
>   Þat lynage loves me noght,
> Gladly they walde me greve,
>   And I slyke boodword brought.
>
> Ther-fore lord, late sum othir fraste
>   Þat hase more forse þam for to feere.[19]

Even those whom Christ chooses for his own, the twelve he loved best, are imperfect: among them are numbered a traitor, and two who defect through fear. The cowardice of John is treated in an undignified way, as when the Cornish drama directs: "tunc II^s tortor accipiet iohannem apostolum et ipse relicto syndone nudus fugiet."*[20] He is so eager to escape that he loses his linen in the process. But Peter's denial of Christ, which follows, is treated more gravely, for it amounts to a betrayal made consciously three times. Christ is saddened by it, but He is not surprised. Even the best of them are not very brave, and Christ Himself, through the mystery of His incarnation, knows what it is to fear.[21] In the Towneley cycle, after the Resurrection, the disciples are shown doubting the truth of the miracle. Despite Christ's prophecies and teachings, their faith wavers and they scoff at Mary Magdalene when she tells them that she has seen Christ in the garden:

> *petrus.* Do way, woman, thou carpys wast!
> It is som spirite, or els som gast;
>   Othere was it noght;
> we may trow on nokyns wyse
> That ded man may to lyfe ryse;
>   This then is oure thought.[22]

But though they doubt, they are able to believe when they see, and afterwards to repent and rejoice. There is an important difference between their doubt and the doubt of Caiaphas or Herod, just as there is between the fearfulness of the good people and the cowardice of the bad: their immediate response to a surprising or frightening situation may be the same, but the good grow into courage by an effort of the will (as with Isaac, Moses, and Christ at Gethsemane) or into repentance and increased understanding (as with Peter destined to be Pope).

Taken together, these examples can illustrate in lively detail the drama's understanding of that truth expressed in two great medieval commentaries concerning the goodness that caused Noah to be saved. The *Historia scholastica* of Petrus Comestor defines it so: "*Noe vero erat perfectus in generationibus suis (Gen.* vi), quasi non illius perfectionis, quae est in patria, sed secundum modum generationis suae,

---

* Then the second executioner will take hold of the apostle John and the latter will flee naked leaving his garment behind.

scilicet terrenae."*[23] And Rabanus Maurus, in his *Commentariorum in Genesim,* offers a similar account: "Perfecti hic aliqui dicuntur, non sicut perficiendi sunt sancti in illa immortalitate, qua aequabuntur angelis Dei, sed sicut esse possunt in hac peregrinatione perfecti."†[24] These examples, taken together, can epitomize accurately enough this drama's version of the goodness that is possible on earth, in our pilgrimage here.

But it is to the character of Joseph that we must look for the cycle-drama's most substantial comment on the dual role of natural man and servant of God. It is scarcely surprising that the Holy Family should provide the best examples of good people: Jesus is God as well as man, and Mary is highest among women, the chosen vessel of the Incarnation. But Joseph is also chosen, not some chance neighbor who has wandered into the family photo. (In the *Ludus Coventriae* there is a *Betrothal* play, in which all the sons of David assemble in order that Mary may be given a husband, and God indicates by a miracle that Joseph is His choice.) We can profitably approach him through the visual arts, for they use him in similar ways. For example, a four-teenth-century Nativity painting in the museum at Anvers shows a midwife tending the infant Jesus, while Mary in blue robes lies resplendent on cloth-of-gold spread out on the hillside. High above, God holds a planet in His hand and looks down upon the scene, while in the lower left corner, Joseph, with one boot off, is busy cutting open his leather sock with a knife. His feet have been hurting him, and though Christ has just been born, this is his chief concern.[25] In most English medieval alabasters of this scene, Joseph is caught in an old man's sleep; one shows Mary handing the baby to the midwives, while Joseph off to one side makes a meal with a pot and spoon over a small brazier;[26] in a fifteenth-century Burgundian Book of Hours, he is shown drying swaddling-clothes by the fire while Mary holds the child.[27] Even at this most exalted birth, someone must attend to the food and blankets, and Joseph is there to turn the theological mystery

---

* Noah was in truth perfect in his generations, which is not to say of that perfection that is found in man's true homeland, but perfect within the limits of his generations, i.e., earthly in his perfection.

† Certain persons are here called perfect—not perfect in the way the saints are to become perfect in that immortal state in which they will be made equal with the angels of God, but perfect in the way in which men can be perfect in this earthly pilgrimage.

of the Incarnation into a homely, human event. Whatever action he is called on to play, he is always shown bent with age and burdened with the special cares that God has given him. The Chester shepherds describe him thus:

> *Primus pastor.* what ever this olde man, that heare is,
> take heede howe his head is hore,
> his beard like a buske of breeres
> with a pownd of heare about his mouth and more.
>
> *Secundus pastor.* more is this marvaile to me nowe,
> for to nappe greatlie he nedes;
> hartles is he nowe,
> for aye to his heeles his head is.
> *Tertius pastor.* why! with his beard though it be rough,
> right well to her he heedes.[28]

When troubled by Mary's pregnancy, he goes into the wilderness and falls asleep; an angel awakens him and the York Joseph is allowed a confused and grumbly old man's response:

> *Angelus.* Waken, Joseph! and take bettir kepe
>   To Marie, þat is þi felawe fest.
> *Joseph.* A! I am full werie, lefe late me slepe,
>   For-wandered and walked in þis forest.
> *Angelus.* Rise vppe! and slepe na mare,
> Þou makist her herte full sare.
>   Þat loues þe alther best.
> *Joseph.* We! now es þis a farly fare,
> For to be cached bathe here and þare,
>   And nowhere may haue rest.
> Say, what arte þou? telle me this thyng.
> *Angelus.* I Gabriell, Goddis aungell full euen.[29]

If one sets against this the episode in which the Towneley Cain clouts an angel over the head, one has two complementary portraits of natural man, one good, one evil, but brothers nonetheless in their categorical separation from the angelic orders.[30]

The only detail in the canonical gospels concerning Joseph's character is the fact that he was "troubled" by Mary's pregnancy, and thought to put her away quietly to spare her shame. The early Church had to fight heresies arguing the earthly paternity of Christ, and so Joseph was given only a minor place. The apocrypha chiefly affirm his old age (he must be too old for "preuay play"), his chastity (which in some versions is represented as lifelong), and his own astonishment at Mary's childbearing. For such reasons, the cult of St. Joseph was late in developing in the West: it first appears in the twelfth century, and until the late fifteenth century its manifestations were purely private and local. In 1481 Sixtus IV introduced March 19 as the feast day of St. Joseph, and in 1621 it was made a holy day of obligation.[31] Because this emphasis on his sanctity was so late in developing, medieval art was allowed much greater freedom with his person than with either Mary or Christ. And so these dramatists used him as a "type" of natural man, his presence in the Holy Family affirming that the miraculous happens in a natural world: were the miraculous not defined in relation to that world, it would have no extraordinary quality.

Joseph is given larger independent life in the true-Coventry play of the *Purification* than anywhere else in the medieval drama. His treatment in this play has been described by a learned critic as irreverent and objectionable exploitation, but that is an opinion I do not share.[32] Most versions of this incident simply detail the fact (drawn from Luke 2:24) that two doves were presented in offering; in both the Chester and the Digby dramatizations, they are gladly obtained and offered by Joseph. But the Coventry *Weavers' Pageant* turns the occasion into a domestic crisis, for when Mary asks Joseph to find two doves as the law requires, he refuses with grumpy ill-grace:

> *Josoff.* Nay, nay, Mare, thatt wol not be.
> Myne age ys soche, I ma not well see;
> There schall noo duffus be soght for me,
>   Also God me saue!
> *Mare.* Swette Josoff, fullfyll ye owre Lordis hestes.
> *Josoff.* Why and woldist th[o]u haue me to hunt bridis nestis?
> I pray the hartely, dame, leve thosse jestis
>   And talke of thatt wol be.
>
> For, dame, woll I neuer vast my wyttis,
> To wayte or pry where the wodkoce syttis;
> Nor to jubbard among the merle pyttis,
>   For thatt wasse neyuer my gyse.

Now am I wold and ma not well goo:
And small twyge wolde me ouerthroo;
And yche were wons lyggyd aloo,
    Full yll then schulde I ryse.

. . . .

    You mynde nothynge myne age
But the weykist gothe eyuer to the walle:
Therefore go thyself, dame; for me thow schall,
    Ye, or ellis get the a nev page.

. . . .

Mare. Now, gentyll Josoff, when wyll ye goo
    To make an ende of this owre jurney?
Josoff. That shal be or I have any lust thereto
    And thatt dare I boldely sey.[33]

The mood is surprising: Joseph knows God has commanded that the doves be offered, but still he grouches, as if it were all a foolish whim of Mary's. And he goes on to address the audience in the *mal marié* complaint which earlier has been his characteristic utterance in doubting Mary's virginity:

How sey ye all this cumpany
Thatt be weddid asse well asse I?
    I wene that ye suffur moche woo;
For he thatt weddyth a yonge thyng
Mvst fullfyll all hir byddyng,
Or els ma he his handis wryng,
Or watur his iis when he wold syng;
    And thatt all you do knoo.

To this stock complaint Mary makes a reply that can guide us in its interpretation:

Leyve of these gawdis for my lowe;
    And goo for these fowlys, Sir, I you pray.[34]

They are "gawdis"—that is to say, "jests, jokes, merry sport"—belonging to a sort of marriage game. Joseph has said to his wife, "Dame, leve thosse jestis," and now she answers him in kind. His charges are traditional and, in that sense, gratuitous; they are not a bitter heart's truth being uttered. An old man who likes attention, he grumbles not darkly but in a kind of joy, giving expression to that part of natural man which loves self-dramatization[35] or delights in raising objections for their own sake. And Mary, like any good housewife who knows how husbands are, turns it aside lightly, saying in effect, "Stop fussing and get on with it." Off he goes, still grumbling:

> Now, Lorde God, thow sende me feyre weddur,
> And thatt I ma fynd those fowlis togeddur,
> Whytt or blake, I care nott wheddur,
>   So thatt I ma them fynde!
>
> . . . .
>
> Then I woll goo by and by,
> Thogh hit be not full hastely.[36]

The self-dramatization is here made explicit: he will go, but under protest—just as he has really meant to do all along.

So far the episode has been largely comic. The scene in which Joseph actually hunts for the doves was no doubt intended to be played straight, for the statement of his weakness, his age, his weariness can be very moving, and it is made to a serious end:

> For-were I ma no lengur stond;
>   These buskis the teyre me on eyuere syde.
> Here woll I sytt apon this londe,
>   Oure Lordis wyll for to abyde.[37]

Earlier he has set up his infirmities in playful opposition to his wife's will; here he rests them in the will of the Lord. They are more real here, less a catalogue of complaints, and a serious action answers them —an angel appears to bring him the two doves. He is wonderfully happy, for fear of failure seems to have been the one real reason behind his reluctance to search for them. He brings them to Mary, and the self-dramatization is resumed, this time in a new mood and voice:

> Now rest well, Mare, my none darlyng!
> Loo! dame, I haue done thy byddyng
> And broght these dowis for oure offeryng;
>   Here be the bothe alyve.
> Womon, haue them in thy honde,
> I am full glade I haue them fond.
> Am nott I a good husbonde?
>   Ye! dame, soo mot I thryve![38]

For the earlier figure of the *mal marié,* Joseph now substitutes that of the "good husbonde"; in the course of the scene he projects himself into both. (And what is more, he never tells her how he got the doves.) He plays this new role of the skillful provider with great relish, particularly since it allows him to revert to his earlier role with apparently increased cause when Mary says they must go at once. He cannot resist one final contrary remark:

> Aftur my labur fayne wolde I rest;
> Therefore goo thyselfe thow schalt for me,
> Or tarre att whome wheddur thou thynkist beste.[39]

But of course neither of them can tarry at God's command: it is a token resistance merely, and Joseph knows that as well as Mary. He extracts as much amusement and distraction as he can from necessary actions; on this level of the human psyche, he joins hands with the *tortores* who hang a braggart in a similar manner. The ethical difference lies in the actions themselves, not in the manner of their doing. In this play there is a remarkable ebb and flow of gentleness and assumed surliness, a contrasting rhythm and tone which reveal considerable dramatic art. It serves a serious didactic purpose, as does the rather similar cherry-tree episode in the *Ludus Coventriae,*[40] allowing God to provide for His own, to honor Mary with doves (as with cherries) in the manner of miracle. But beyond that, it offers a way of characterizing the domestic life of the Holy Family. Joseph and Mary are charged with the rearing of Jesus, and though God and his angels may intervene at will, it remains a human marriage. The medieval dramatist thought that to conceive it so was to do it honor, and the characterization of Joseph decisively determines its "natural" character. In the episode of Jesus and the Doctors which follows, Mary and Joseph express their wonder at the way Jesus grows, how big and fair he is becoming, and Joseph concludes proudly:

> I kno non soche on of hys age;
> I pra God make hym a right good mon.[41]

It is a stroke of great daring, and enormous comic power: no one but Joseph could say anything at once so irrelevant and tender as this pious blessing. It is impossible not to love him. And just as the married life of Joseph and Mary has been given a delightful dramatic statement, so too the adolescent reality of the twelve-year-old Christ is not forgotten here. They exhibit normal parental care and pride, as though He were just a boy and not the Incarnate Word: the silences of Scripture are filled in with details designed to show the Incarnation happening among, and for, people like those in the audience. In its portrayal of human goodness, the Corpus Christi drama furnishes an object lesson in the art of making religion relevant; and both terms of that lesson, the art and the relevance, may be admired.

It was possible for the drama to show human goodness in relation to human nature only by allowing the good people an imaginative life larger than doctrine and story strictly require. They are given a certain independent dignity, most highly developed at those moments in which man serves God, but serves Him critically, not opposing His will, but reserving the right to voice a human judgment upon it. At such moments the medieval drama became most strongly an act of piety to man as well as to God, a religious drama written from *within* the human condition.

This final element in the character of natural man emerges most clearly in dramatizations of two terrible actions of God: His decision to destroy the world by flood, preserving only Noah and his family, and His command that Abraham sacrifice his son. There are several versions extant of each episode, and each finds an individual life and interest within the story. Some of these we have studied in earlier chapters. Here we shall look only at those that discover part of their dramatic life in man's reservations about the necessity and goodness of the actions of God.

The awkwardness attending the biblical account of the Flood must be traced to its particularly anthropomorphic God: God in Genesis 6 "repents" that He made man; He "sorrows" in His heart; and after He destroys the world, He makes a new covenant with man for a reason that was perfectly adequate to explain man's condition before the Flood (Gen. 8:21): "I will no more curse the earth for the sake of man: for the imagination and thought of man's heart are prone to evil from his youth: therefore I will no more destroy every living soul as I have done." The Chester dramatization includes this bewildering rationale without comment,[42] and it uses two other details, anomalous in the drama, to give man an enhanced human dignity within the action. The first occurs when Noah explains to God why it has taken him so long to build the ark (other treatments attribute his slowness to old age):

> A 100 wynters and 20
> this shipp making taried haue I,
> if through amendment any mercye
> wolde fall vnto mankinde.[43]

He is not questioning God's judgment, nor opposing His will; but his first sympathy is with his fellowman, and he has worked slowly in order that man's potential amendment and (or) mercy from God might avert the human catastrophe. Similarly, God, in explaining to Noah the meaning of the rainbow, seems to recognize that man needs protection from His power and the vicissitudes of His will:

> The stringe is turned toward you
> and toward me is bent the bowe
> that such wedder shall never showe,
> and this behett I thee.[44]

The bow, here a symbol of destruction, is carefully pointed at heaven, not earth. These details, small in themselves, modify only slightly the traditional tone of the Chester *Flood* play. But there are other medieval versions that travel a further journey down this road, versions that recognize in the story an ultimate mystery about the will of God which admits of no human resolution. The ancient poem of the Babylonians called the *Epic of Gilgamesh* recounts a Flood sent to destroy the human world, and this story is related, as source or analogue, to the Flood in Genesis. But *Gilgamesh* resolves the ethical difficulties of its subject by postulating many gods, among them one hostile to man (who sends the Flood) and one friendly (who saves man's seed by a timely warning).[45] The Judaic version presupposes a single God who alternately loves man, hates man, and loves him again.[46] On that apparent caprice in His will is centered the Flood narrative in the fourteenth-century poem called *Purity* and the dramatization of the Flood in the Cornish cycle.

In *Purity*, God is imagined in the character of a courtly prince or king, passionate, aristocratic, authoritarian; the effect of altering His character to suit the ethos of a particular poetic form (in this case, alliterative romance) is to emphasize even more strongly the all too human inconsistency of His actions. The poet describes God thinking on man's unclean living, and says:

> For, as I fynde, þer he forȝet alle his fre þewez,
> And wex wod to þe wrache for wrath at his hert.[47]

His courtly courtesy and noble customs are forgotten as anger wells up inside Him, and as His survey of sin continues:

> When he knew uche contre coruppte in hitselven,
> And uch freke forloyned fro þe ryȝt wayez,
> Felle temptande tene towched his hert;
> As wyȝe, wo hym withinne werp to hymselven:
> "Me forþynkez ful much þat ever I mon made."[48]

The poet expressly describes God's anger as being like that of a man, and the picture that emerges is of a king who is ruled by his passions. His speech to Noah is described as "Wylde wrakful wordez,"[49] and His change of heart after the Flood has abated and all save Noah and his family are destroyed, is set down powerfully (and without any attempt to explain it):

> Now, Noe, no more nel I never wary
> Alle þe mukel mayny [on] molde for no mannez synnez,
> For I se wel þat hit is sothe, þat alle mannez wyttez
> To unþryfte arn alle þrawen wyth þoȝt of her herttez,
> And ay hatz ben, and wyl be ȝet, fro her barnage;
> Al is þe mynde of þe man to malyce enclyned;
> Forþy schal I never schende so schortly at ones
> As dysstrye al for manez [dedes], dayez of þis erþe.[50]

In this poem the focus is almost entirely on the world that is lost— an epic panorama of death and the destruction of everything accustomed and dear—and the effect of such words is very strong. In all save His power, which is infinitely vast, God is shown to be much like man. Like a man, He has second thoughts: He repents that He made man, and He repents that He destroyed man; He judges His own action as "hard."

> Hym rwed þat he hem uprerde and raȝt hem lyflode,
> And efte þat he hem undyd, hard hit hym þoȝt.[51]

I have discussed the *Purity* version of the Flood both as an introduction to, and corroborative proof of, the sophisticated attitudes behind the Cornish drama's staging of this action. In this cycle, Noah so profoundly identifies himself with his fellowman that even the gracious decision by God to save him and his family seems capricious in his eyes:

> What is the need for us
>> To have such labour?
> Since thou wilt kill every one
>> Who is on the face of the world,
> Save only my people and me,
>> Kill us with them as well.

God finds this humility good, but Noah's incomprehension remains. And though he and his family will carry out God's orders, they are uneasy about His promises. Ham gives clear voice to this doubt about God's real intentions, as he helps cover the ark with a cloth roof to keep out the rain:

> In the name of God, be he praised,
>> Cover what we call our grave.

He doubts they will survive. But it is in the negotiations after the Flood has ceased that natural man rises to his greatest dignity. God promises that He never again will take "Heavy vengeance on all the world," and Noah responds, out of despair at a human condition so entirely at the mercy of the divine:

> What avails it to us to cultivate,
>> If thou be angry with man, without a lie.
> When all is laboured by us,
>> Our work will be failing.
> By heavy vengeance on the world,
>> Thou wilt make all dead.

God, trying to reassure him, reiterates his promise, but Noah refuses to grant his unconditional trust:

> *God.* Noah, for love to thee,
>> I will make a good promise to thee;
> Full vengeance on the whole world
>> I will not take ever.

> *Noah.* Promises made by the mighty,
>> Are no law to them;
> Though they be broken in anger,
>> I am unable to resist.[52]

Not until God gives the rainbow as a surety is Noah convinced and ready to resume his cultivation of the earth. The speeches (quoted above) that precede this settlement have a kind of grandeur: they show natural man aware of his station and fragility, not pretending that he can bargain on equal terms with God, willing to accept as necessity any settlement given, but at the same time insisting that he is not deceived. Noah participates in this action as a true servant of God, continuing to work God's will in the manner that earned his escape from the Flood; but though he participates, it is with a profound unease. The play is a singular essay in the relationship between the human and the divine.

The episode in which God orders Abraham to sacrifice his son is comparable to that of the Flood in the possibilities it offers for an art at once generous, sophisticated, and humane. The two finest Abraham and Isaac plays may or may not have been played in cycles, though they would grace any of those extant; through an accident of their provenance, itself a matter of dispute, they may have taken the pageant stage simply as single plays. We shall follow their editor in identifying them by the place in which the manuscripts were found, Brome and Dublin.[53]

These versions are alike in their respect for human love, and in dramatizing a test designed to prove that Abraham's love for God is greater than his love for his son, the medieval drama achieves its moment of greatest pathos—greater even than that associated with the death of Christ, for we can feel and understand the redemptive necessity of that later death. Neither Abraham nor Isaac can understand the necessity of the command that is given to them. They only know that it is given and must be obeyed. The perplexity and pathos are developed by the Dublin version in such pleas of Isaac as the following:

> Alas, gentyl fader, why put ye me in þis fere?
>   Haue I displesid you any thing?
> ʒif I haue trespast, I cry you mercy;
> &, gentil fader, lat me not dye!
> Alas, is þer none oþer beste but I
>   Þat may plese þat hy king?
>   . . . .
> Alas, what have I displesid þis lord of blisse,
> Þat I shal be martyred in þis mysse?[54]

The cosmic questions are here asked of the earthly father, Abraham, in pathetic expectation of an answer; they are only briefly referred to

the heavenly father—and then rhetorically—knowing no answer need
be expected from that quarter. But Abraham cannot answer either,
except to say that God has ordered it. Isaac is obedient to his father
as Abraham is to God, and neither will resist; that fact is of greatest
importance, but it is important too that they pass this test as human
beings. Isaac speaks a moving farewell to his mother (who is absent)
in which his love and the perplexity of his human situation are beautifully mingled:

> She was wont to calle me hir tresoure & hir store;
> But farewel now, she shal no more.
> *Here I shal be dede & wot neuer wherefore,*
> *Saue þat god most haue his wille.*   [my italics]

So too Abraham reveals a contrary movement within him:

> Þe hye lord bad me to do þis dede,
> But my hert gruccheþ, so god me spede.[55]

Obedience is shown as a triumph over nature: Isaac will submit,
though he does not understand; Abraham will sacrifice his son, by
exercising the will against the natural affection of the heart. Their
eyes are resolutely open: God may command a sacrifice, but Isaac
will not indulge in liturgical euphemism: "Fader, shal my hed of
also?"[56] At the last possible moment, the angel intervenes, and the
tragic movement is turned into a happy ending; but they do not pretend that this release negates the suffering and anguish they have
undergone. When Abraham thanks God, the strain shows, and there
is, I think, an element of rebuke in his speech of gratitude:

> & lord, I thank þe þat Isaac is not killed.
>   Now, lord, I know wele þou dydest but asay.
>   What I wold sey þerto, ouþer ye or nay.
> Þou knowest myne hert now, & so þou didest afore;
>   Haddest not sent þyn aungil, Isaac had died þis day.
> But, goode lord, saue þi plesaunce, þis pref was riȝt sore.[57]

Not only was it a cruel test, but it has proved nothing that was not
already certain: "Þou knowest myne hert now, & so þou didest afore."
The idea is important, for it echoes the statement God makes at the
beginning of the play, in which He decides on the testing:

Of al þing erþely, I wot wel, he loueþ him best;
  Now he shuld loue me moste, as reson wold & skylle,
& so, I wot well, he doþe, I dyd it neuer mystrest.
  But ȝit, for to preue hym, þe truþe wol I fele.[58]

God rewards Abraham generously for his obedience, but the testing in this Dublin version has no motivation whatever. The action is imitated from within the human condition. The dramatist no more understands the necessity of the action than do its human participants: like them, he knows only that man must obey.

The Brome play follows the tradition that Isaac was a young child at the time of the sacrifice,[59] and consequently its tone is rather different. Isaac's instinctive reaction to the test is that of a dutiful child, and his joy at the release from it has a child's gaiety. From time to time, however, the dramatist allows him a precocious comment on God's will, as when this Isaac, too, recognizes the arbitrary quality of his fate:

Now, fader, aȝens my Lordes wyll,
  I wyll neuer groche, lowd nor styll;
He mygth a sent me a better desteny
Yf yt had a be hys plecer.[60]

A choice has been made which determines his destiny, and for which there is no apparent reason. God's pleasure might as easily have meant life for him as death. To recognize the arbitrary caprice of God in His dealings with men constitutes knowledge so terrible that man can scarcely endure it; though Abraham and Isaac will find the strength to do so, Isaac begs that his mother be protected from that knowledge:

But, good fader, tell ȝe my moder no thyng,
  Sey þat I am in a-nother cuntre dwellyng.[61]

In no other dramatic version does Isaac express such joy at the reprieve from heaven. He praises the sheep that will replace him in the sacrifice, thus:

A! scheppe, scheppe! blyssyd mot þou be,
  That euer thow were sent down heder,
Thow schall thys day dey for me,
  In the worchup of the Holy Trynyte,
    Now cum fast and goo we togeder

> To my Fader of Heuyn;
>   Thow þou be neuer so jentyll and good,
>   ʒyt had I leuer thow schedyst þi blood,
>   Iwysse, scheppe, than I.[62]

The result is less a celebration of the mystery of God's mercy than it
is an image of a young boy exuberantly aware he has missed death
and is still alive. Significantly, he takes no more chances. When he
has to bend down in preparing the sacrifice, he first makes certain he
can do so safely:

> But fader, wyll I stowppe downe lowe,
> ʒe wyll not kyll me with ʒour sword, I trowe?
>
> . . . .
>
> . . . I woold þat sword wer in a gled,
>   For, iwys, fader, yt make me full yll agast.[63]

This amusing precaution is not without a deeper seriousness. He is
not really sure that it was God's command at all: it may simply have
been a notion that could come again into his father's mind.[64] Isaac
has been through an extraordinary ordeal—one that, in human terms,
had neither cause nor consequence. It merely happened, unmerited
and therefore not really understood:

> I wos neuer soo afrayd before,
>   As I haue byn at ʒyn hyll.
> But, be my feth, fader, I swere
> I wyll neuermore cume there
>   But yt be a-ʒens my wyll.[65]

The hill of the sacrifice is the place of his highest spiritual achievement, for he consented to his death. Yet as natural man, he will never
visit it again. Its meaning in remembrance is only terror.

The Towneley version also honors human priorities. When its
Abraham learns that Isaac will be spared, he says:

> I thank the, lord, well of goodnes,
> That all thus has relest me this;
>
> To speke with the haue I no space,
>   with my dere son till I haue spokyn.[66]

There is some doubt about who has largest claim to Abraham's attention at this moment: he will give full thanks to God but only *after*
he has spoken to Isaac.

Dublin and Brome both draw the same didactic moralization from the episode, a moralization wholly inadequate. The Brome *Deus* may be allowed to speak for both:

> I schall asay now hys good wyll,
>> Whether he lovyþ better hys chyld or me.
> All men schall take exampyll be hym
>> My commawmentes how they schall kepe.[67]

This is spoken near the beginning of the play; in the Dublin version it is expressed at the end. The moral is apposite, of course; and as we saw earlier, the story finds its place in the cycle by virtue of its figural connection with the sacrifice of Christ (the Son) by God (the Father). But we must guard against thinking that the dramatists understood its significance solely in these terms. The medieval habit of finding a moral in every story was never very rigorously disciplined:[68] so long as it was suitable and useful, the medieval writer held it to be proper and was content that the larger life of the story should reside in the full narrative or dramatic presentation itself. Such capsule lessons were never intended to limit the resonance of the action, nor was the dramatist interested only in ethical or formal meaning. In these two versions of the Abraham story, there is also a response to the terror and inscrutability of God's will. Pecock, in his *Reule of Crysten Religioun,* cites the sacrifice as an example of actions *against nature* which may be performed only under the highest authority. He has already discussed Peter walking on the water, at Christ's command, and says Peter rightly never attempted it again; he continues:

Whanne abraham was bede to offre his sone, he was redy to do it; if he wolde haue do it wiþout such special biddyng or aftirward whanne he was not boden, he schulde greuoseli haue synned—as is open ynouȝ to ech mannys resoun—And þerfore to attempte forto worche or suffre aboue or aȝens kinde and resoun ouȝte no man take ensaumple of oþere mennys doyng.[69]

Abraham and Isaac, in these versions, recognize the un*kind*ness of God's command as well as the necessity of obeying it. In their goodness, they retain their dignity as natural men.

This brings to a close the second of our two portraits labeled "natural man." We have examined his physiognomy when out of a proper relationship to God, for as Chesterton once wrote, "There is no value

in a version of the brotherhood of men which does not cover troglo-
dytes and cannibals."[70] And we have set against that a survey of his
features when in God's proper service; for there is no value either in
a version of the brotherhood of man that does not include the three
Marys or Simon of Cyrene. All men are profoundly linked by their
creaturely limitations, by their difference in *kind* from any other
state of being. Indeed, the brawling of Mrs. Noah in the Chester cycle
is on behalf of the world that will be destroyed. She refuses to board
the ark without her gossips, saying:

> But I haue my gossips everichon,
> one foote further I will not gone;
> they shall not drowne, by St. John,
> and I may save their lyfe.
> they loved me full well, by christ;
> but thou wilt let them in thy chist,
> els rowe forth, Noe, whether thou list,
> and get thee a new wife.

The gossips plead confidently for such comfort as they can, hoping to
enter the ark or at least to have some pleasure together in their accustomed ways:

> The flood comes in, full fleetinge fast,
> on every side it spredeth full fare;
> for feare of drowning I am agast,
> good gossip, let us draw neare.
>
> and let vs drinke or we depart,
> for often tymes we have done soe;
> for at a draught thou drinkes a quarte,
> and so will I doe, or I goe.

And three of the extant Chester manuscripts then record the song
that the gossips and Mrs. Noah sing:

> here is a pottell of malmesy, good and stronge,
> it will reioye both hart and tong;
> though noy thinke vs neuer so long
> yet wee will drinke alyke.[71]

It is a look backward, at the unworthy, the unviable; but more important than that, it is also a declaration of identity. In Chaucer's

Miller's Tale, old John the Carpenter is deceived into thinking God has decided to send another Flood, and that he and his winsome young wife and the clerk who "reveals" this destiny to him, alone are to be saved. In a wonderfully comic conclusion, he breaks an arm and is made publicly a cuckold, in part for his credulity, but even more for his presumption. John the Carpenter never for a moment thinks it odd that God might choose him to begin a new world. Mrs. Noah is *like* her gossips, and her dignity consists in knowing this to be so. The Chester play establishes by other means a critical sense of evil—of a world deservedly lost—but it intends one to experience a sense of human loss as well. This stretching out of hands takes two forms in medieval versions of the Flood: one is an elegaic sadness for that which is to be destroyed; the other is a temporary participation through laughter in the corrupted world at its last moment of being. The former finds masterly expression in *Purity* and some extended and very moving use in the York cycle as well. There Mrs. Noah speaks three times on behalf of those lost, though they do not appear in person on the stage:

> My commodrys and my cosynes bathe,
> Þam wolde I wente with vs in feere.

She remembers them as the flood rises:

> My frendis þat I fra yoode
> Are ouere flowen with floode.

And laments them again when the ark touches land:

> But Noye, where are nowe all oure kynne,
> And companye we kn[e]we be-fore.[72]

The other form of identification—a farewell fellowship of drink and song and laughter—is uniquely represented by the Chester play. But whatever the method, the resulting sense of community is very important to the meaning and achievement of the Corpus Christi drama. It imitates existence as divided into three "worlds" of creatures: God and His angels, Satan and his devils, and men. The disciples are more closely akin to the *tortores* than either group is to devils or angels. They are recognizably members of the same family, not merely because they all lack wings, halos, or black feather-coats, but because the dramatists show their actions as originating in the same fallen nature. The good men, like the evil, live in society, are self-engrossed and busy with affairs; they are troubled by their wives, their poverty, the oppression of their masters; they are fearful, sometimes cowardly, and prone to doubt; they all find life a dark and confusing experience. They too seek amusement and distraction; their performance of tasks assigned them is, at best, barely competent; they are troubled by youth or age or simplemindedness. Cain's boy and the shepherds' boy are brothers; Noah makes his ark as crudely as the *tortores* make the cross and nails; the knights who lie about Christ's resurrection are no more cowardly than John fleeing naked from the scene of Christ's capture; Judas, Balaam, and the shepherds who adore Christ, are all interested in rewards. They like gossip and games, a curse and a good drink of ale. Humankind is a single estate, defined by the instincts and limitations of a fallen nature, and it is imitated in this drama with sympathy and inclusive detail. Thomas à Kempis wrote in *De imitatione Christi*:

For ȝiftes of nature are comoun to good & to evel, but þat þe propre ȝifte of þe chosen children is grace or charite, wherwiþ who þat be nobleied shal be worþy euerlastyng lif.[73]

He intends a distinction between grace and nature which is theologically too complex to be useful in our reading of the drama, for the ultimate mystery of how it is possible for a fallen man to do good is never posed by this drama in abstract terms. It more simply and usefully imitates historical actions that have pleased God, and shows their origin in a common human nature. The ultimate virtue of the good is obedience, and later, charity; whatever their initial instinct, in the end they bend themselves to God's will, and though they remain categorically separate from Him, they become His good and chosen servants. We are shown men instead of saints, and a modest phrase that Gabriel uses in the *Ludus Coventriae* play of the *Annunciation* might stand for all. He tells Mary that she is to bear One who will redeem:

> ...Adam · Abraham · and davyd in fere
> And many othere of good reputacion.[74]

Chapter Eleven

Conclusion

Because nearly six centuries stand between us and the original audience of the Corpus Christi drama, a certain amount of learning has been necessary to reconstruct the information and kinds of awareness that we must have if we are to respond to this drama fully and easily. One of my aims has been to supply some of this necessary information, but this should not be taken to imply that the Corpus Christi drama was therefore a learned drama for learned people. Nothing drawn from other sources overshadowed in importance or effectiveness the basic Christian story which the dramatists inherited and passed on. The men who wrote these plays were educated, though not necessarily learned, in a complex and sophisticated religious tradition. That distinction, between knowledge and learning, is crucial in discussing the background of this drama. It is unlikely that anyone in the audience, and probably not even the dramatist himself, could have discussed at length the history and development of the Flood story as a *figure* of the baptism, the cross, and the end of the world. They knew it figured such things, and the dramatist could perhaps have mentioned an authority or two; but such knowledge would not have been (and did not need to be) of a learned sort. To return to an earlier metaphor, if sacred history is here seen through an arch of scholasticism and commentary, we must understand it as a finished and perfected arch: it forced one to look through it, to the scene it framed. The machinery of learning is little evident in these plays, though subtleties of theological understanding are apparent everywhere, determining the choice of an episode, the manner of its staging, the shaping of its action, the textures of its language, and even the invention of new action. Though I have had to support my readings with a burden of learned reference, the purpose of all this material has been simply to alert our eyes and ears: it is meant to be remembered in substance, not in scholarly detail; it should be kept at the back of the mind, not the front. Once the play has begun, or we have opened a text to begin reading, we must put ourselves entirely into the dramatist's hands. He will make such demands upon our knowledge of these traditions as serves his specific end; our duty and privilege is to attend to the immediate address of the work of art.

The medieval dramatist would have reassured his audience, as John Donne reassured members of his congregation, that every response to the Christian story, from the most simple to the most complex, is valid and useful:

S. *Matthew* relates Christs Sermon at large, and S. *Luke* but briefly, and yet S. *Luke* remembers some things that S. *Matthew* had left out. If thou remember not all that was presented to thy faith, all the Citations of places of Scriptures, nor all that was presented to thy reason, all the deducements, and inferences of the Schooles, nor all that was presented to thy spirituall delight, all the sentences of ornament produced out of the Fathers, yet if thou remember that which concerned thy sin, and thy soul, if thou meditate upon that, apply that, thou hast brought away all the Sermon, all that was intended by the Holy Ghost to be preached to thee. And if thou have done so, as at a donative at a Coronation, or other solemnity, when mony is throwne among the people, though thou light but upon one shilling of that money, thou canst not think that all the rest is lost, but that some others are the richer for it, though thou beest not ... thou broughtest a feaver, and hast had thy Julips, another brought a fainting, and a diffident spirit, and must have his Cordials.[1]

The function of theological understanding is to interpret the Christian story, not to replace it by another thing. The attentive and the educated among the Corpus Christi audience did not understand *differently* from their fellows, but they understood more.

In these chapters, I have sought to furnish for this drama a more comprehensive commentary from medieval sources than has hitherto been available—to place the drama in its time, to let its voice be heard in harmony with the voices of other genres addressing the same audience with the same Christian truths. But I have tried equally to distinguish the drama from its sources and analogues, to discover the kinds of intention and achievement that are uniquely its own. It is not enough to conclude with Hardin Craig that "The medieval religious drama existed primarily to give religious instruction, establish faith, and encourage piety,"[2] for this statement, though true as far as it goes, could apply equally well, and without further qualification, to sermons, to religious lyrics, to encyclopaedic and narrative poems, even to wall paintings in parish churches. I have read widely in this related literature, and I should like to conclude by offering two large (but I think not misleading) generalizations about what makes the cycle-drama itself, and not another thing.

The first of these concerns, quite simply, artistic merit. The Corpus Christi drama far surpasses in interest and achievement the vast majority of its cousin works, and this despite the fact that some of the poems and some of the drama texts may have been written by the same authors. The difference is finally not one of talent (though some of the dramatists, such as the York alliterative reviser or the Wakefield Master, are among the best writers of their age), but one of generic discipline. For the drama necessarily concentrates attention on the main action—there is little room for digression in either the episode or the cycle form as a whole—and it makes necessary the composition of verse that can imitate, at some remove, the sound of people talking. There is relatively little use of lengthy description, emotional apostrophe, or pious doggerel. The whole story had to be told, and time was strictly limited; as a result the dramatists were forced to select rigorously, and the patterns implicit in their material are thrown into bolder relief by an absence of intervening matter. Because all the characters must speak, and reveal in their speaking what they think about the action they perform, the dramatists were forced to motivate action, and this involved, in turn, an imitation of human behavior based as much upon experience and observation as upon schematic categories. The cycles presented so great a range of action, with such a variety of rhythms and textures, that even those quiet, formal episodes that seem at first glance undramatic are found in performance to be essential to the whole. They are points of introduction, rest, and recapitulation, which serve to establish the solemnity of the whole. The formal soliloquy of God as He creates the world, the patient expectancy of the prophets, the grave formality of Christ's post-Resurrection appearances to His disciples, are examples of these. The cycles not only "survive" such formal and static episodes, they in truth depend upon them for their full beauty and richness of texture and mood. The need to select and concentrate, the need to make every line suitable for human speech and more or less natural to a human event, and the need to find rhythms and patterns of action that could hold the attention of an audience for a period of many hours, saved the drama from the characteristic defects of most religious writing contemporary with it. It was concise, robust, and imaginative; and these qualities, so rare among the related writings, grew from the demands of the genre itself.

The other major source of the cycle-drama's uniqueness is its mood of celebration. This intrinsic joyfulness is due in part to the Corpus Christi feast-day occasion, ordained as a time in which Christians specifically rejoice at God's greatest gift; and it is also due to the fact, probably closely related to the feast-day from the very beginning, that the Christian story is staged entire, building to an ultimate triumph and joy. Unlike the morality plays, which demonstrated the urgent need for everyman to amend his life lest he lose his individual salvation, the Corpus Christi cycles celebrated the salvation of men—the action of redemption achieved by Christ and available to all. They were carefully designed as festival drama, to give form, beauty, and color to a day consecrated by Church and society to rejoicing. The words of Huizinga describing the nature of medieval festival may be recalled here:

Modern man is free, when he pleases, to seek his favourite distractions individually, in books, music, art or nature. On the other hand, at a time when the higher pleasures were neither numerous nor accessible to all, people felt the need of such collective rejoicings as festivals.... Now festivals, in so far as they are an element of culture, require other things than mere gaiety. Neither the elementary pleasures of gaming, drinking and love, nor luxury and pomp as such, are able to give them a framework. The festival requires style.... In the Middle Ages the religious festival, because of its high qualities of style founded on the liturgy itself, for a long time dominated all the forms of collective cheerfulness. The popular festival, which had its own elements of beauty in song and dance, was linked up with those of the Church.[3]

Properly to assess the importance of its festival occasion, we need to picture in our mind the effect of a Corpus Christi performance in a medieval town such as York or Chester. We need to see, in our mind's eye, the crowded streets, the summer sunshine, the people resting from their labor in fellowship and good company; and we need to see, all day long, the pageant wagons moving through the crowd, halting at their assigned stations and performing their play in sequence with the rest of the cycle. In York, forty-eight sumptuous wagons played at twelve stations throughout the city, from dawn to dusk, enclosing the spectators themselves in a play representing the seven ages of the world, shown as happening there and then in England, and demonstrating God's love for fallen man.

It is in this mood that the Cornish cycle concludes its third day of performance with the Ascension of Christ, His entry into Heaven wearing robes the color of His blood, and God's welcome to Him to sit at His right hand until the ending of the world. A brief epilogue is spoken, summarizing the play of the Resurrection, and the whole is brought to a close with these verses, uniting the religious and the social festival in one speech:

> And his blessing on you every one.
>   Now let all go to the side of home.
> Now minstrels, pipe diligently,
>   That we may go to dance.[4]

On whatever days this Cornish cycle played (we have no records), it too benefited from a festival occasion, and its mood of celebration grew easily back into the festival it was staged to honor. We can no longer experience the Corpus Christi drama in a day-long, community, festival performance, but knowledge of this setting can aid us in understanding the nature and achievement of the drama in its own time, as well as explain certain qualities apparent in the drama text even now. Its subject was triumph, its mood celebration, and this is perhaps the key to its success in harmonizing a large number of actions widely different in tone and rhythm: the savagery of the *tortores* and the comedy of Mrs. Noah are united into a single affirmation of God loving man even in his sin, and redeeming him from that sin's just punishment. Though the total design of the Corpus Christi cycle is incomparably grand, it seeks no answering sublimity of local detail, and this apparent contradiction is the true source of its artistic life: its theological elements are given warmth, immediacy, and human relevance, while its portrait of humanity, drawn with an eye fixed firmly on the actual condition of men, gains in dignity and importance from being shown under the aspect of eternity. The good and the bad people, as we have seen, are very closely related in this drama, and though even the best are not very good, they are good enough: they obey God, they hear and see Christ's example of perfect charity, they do what they can. Nowhere in the related literature, not in sermons or narrative poems nor in books of religious instruction, is there communicated a comparable affirmation of human life within the schema of theology. It is thus (at its largest) that I would modify Craig's formulation of the drama's intention and achievement: the medieval religious drama existed to give religious instruction, to establish faith, to encourage piety, and to celebrate man as loved by God.

The play and game nature of this drama contributed much to its festival quality, for there is something intrinsically joyful about that unspoken contract between audience and dramatist-producer that agrees to the temporary establishment of a game world which is not "in ernest" but which can be used to imitate imaginatively something other that is both real and existential. By reducing to play and game equivalents those actions held by theology to be the most important in the total history of the world, those actions were made human-sized, and what may properly be called joyful. Whereas the Flood in *Purity* frightens and appalls, the Flood in the cycle-drama largely reassures. The difference is intentional, and in no small part it is due to these very game qualities and limitations: there can be no real focus on the doomed and dying, because there is no room for them on the pageant stage—at best, we may have three gossips of Mrs. Noah to stand for them all. There can be no panoramic views of waters rising, animals running, lovers making their last farewells. Instead, we see the ark assembled before our eyes in a few minutes' time, as Noah complains of the weariness of his labor; the animals are brought on in pairs, painted on boards; and Mrs. Noah, everyman's wife, is, like almost every man's wife, finally subdued. They enter the ark, they close the windows, they sing a hymn from within; they open the windows, they find ground again and give thanks. Our focus is on those who will be saved, and we are able to affirm them as an image of ourselves. The Flood itself is supplied by us in our minds—we must share in the game and play our parts. This lively contract between audience and player, this delight in the openly unreal, is at the core of the medieval experience of theater. Only in such terms could actions of such magnitude and importance be played at all.

When we speak in later centuries of the limitations of the medieval stage, we speak after the fact, judging its adequacy against very different conceptions of the nature and purpose of drama. To enact *Hamlet* on forty wagons in forty scenes with forty different casts would limit the effect of the play very greatly; plays such as *The Enemy of the People* or *The Cocktail Party* would have been equally impossible. But the medieval theater was perfectly designed to perform the tasks required of it: indeed, its conventions seem to have grown less out of a wish to explore the full possibilities of drama than out of the needs and problems inherent in its one great story. The interplay between Corpus Christi story and the dramatic genre has been a frequent object of attention in this book, and though habits, customs and conventions were passed on to the secular stage, I have tried to show that their original rationale was in large part grounded in the nature and needs of the Christian religion. The Greek stage was far more austere in its means and requirements than the medieval, but we do not much discuss Aeschylus in terms of the "limitations" of his theater. We acknowledge that it was adequate to do the things he needed to do, and move on to the more important business of understanding his intentions and achievement. The medieval stage used play and game conventions, multiple casts, and discontinuous staging to thread pageants of sacred history through the streets of the medieval town on Corpus Christi day, revealing in these small, pageant units the grandeur of God's continuous care for man, and the progress of His plan to redeem him.

In this study we have been concerned with the total richness of the four extant English cycles—a richness greater, of course, than that of any single cycle text. So too was the achievement of the Corpus Christi drama as a whole greater than that of those cycles that have come down to us. The remainder of the true-Coventry cycle, the cycles of Newcastle, Norwich, Beverley, and many others—all these have been lost to time. To make value judgments among the four extant cycles is extremely difficult, for the Corpus Christi drama varies from the superb to the perfunctory—in meaning, interest, and beauty—and it varies within cycles, not merely between them. They vary as cathedrals vary: their ground-plans are much the same, they were created for the same purpose, their common medium exercised certain generic disciplines and presented certain inescapable generic problems. And they grew as cathedrals grew, over a period of many decades, each new dramatist guided by the past but not constrained by it, inventing always in his best contemporary mode. One will not find perfection in these cycles any more than one does in cathedrals—to ask for that is to ask for the wrong thing. Both kinds of structure are too large and too various; too much has been brought in, too much has been revised at too many separate times in their history. But there is magnificence in their design, and life in their detail. Despite occasional flaws and inconsistencies, these plays are unlike anything else in the history of English drama, and the sympathetic reader, Christian or non-Christian, will find they repay any attention he may give. The Corpus Christi cycles satisfy two of the deepest needs any audience brings to an experience of theater: they embody both a criticism and an affirmation of human life.

Notes

Notes

The following abbreviations and shortened titles have been used in the Notes:

Two Coventry Plays: Two Coventry Corpus Christi Plays, ed. Hardin Craig, 2d ed., 1957, EETS e.s. 87.

Chambers, OHEL: E. K. Chambers, *English Literature at the Close of the Middle Ages,* Oxford History of English Literature (corr. ed.; Oxford, 1947).

Chester: The Chester Plays, ed. Hermann Deimling and J. Matthews, 1892, 1916, EETS e.s. 62, 115.

Craig, *English Religious Drama:* Hardin Craig, *English Religious Drama* (Oxford, 1955).

Cornish Drama: The Ancient Cornish Drama, ed. and trans. Edwin Norris, 2 vols. (Oxford, 1859).

Digby: The Digby Plays, ed. F. J. Furnivall, 1896, EETS e.s. 70.

EETS e.s.: Publications of the Early English Text Society, Extra Series, London.

EETS o.s.: Publications of the Early English Text Society, Original Series, London.

Ludus Coventriae: Ludus Coventriae or The Plaie Called Corpus Christi, ed. K. S. Block, 1922, EETS e.s. 120.

Macro Plays: The Macro Plays, ed. F. J. Furnivall and Alfred W. Pollard, 1904, EETS e.s. 91.

Mediaeval Stage: E. K. Chambers, *The Mediaeval Stage,* 2 vols. (Oxford, 1903).

Patrologia Latina: Patrologiae cursus completus: Patrologia Latina, ed. J. P. Migne, 221 vols. (Paris, 1844–64).

Non-Cycle Plays: The Non-Cycle Mystery Plays, ed. Osborn Waterhouse, 1909, EETS e.s. 104.

O.E.D.: The Oxford English Dictionary, ed. James A. H. Murray, Henry Bradley, W. A. Craigie, C. T. Onions, 12 vols. and Supplement (corr. ed.; Oxford, 1933).

Towneley: The Towneley Plays, ed. George England and Alfred W. Pollard, 1897, EETS e.s. 71.

Wakefield Pageants: The Wakefield Pageants in the Towneley Cycle, ed. A. C. Cawley (Manchester, 1958).

Wycliffite Sermon: "A Sermon against Miracle-plays," ed. Eduard Mätzner, *Altenglische Sprachproben,* I, Part II (Berlin, 1869), 222–42.

York: York Plays, ed. Lucy Toulmin Smith (Oxford, 1885).

Young: Karl Young, *The Drama of the Medieval Church,* 2 vols. (Oxford, 1933).

JEGP: *Journal of English and Germanic Philology*
Med.Aev.:   *Medium Aevum*
MLN: *Modern Language Notes*
MLQ: *Modern Language Quarterly*
MLR: *Modern Language Review*
MP: *Modern Philology*
PMLA: *Publications of the Modern Language Association*
RES: *Review of English Studies*
SP: *Studies in Philology*

CHAPTER ONE

*Introduction: The Medieval Dramatic
Image and Its Audience*

1. Chapter 3 will define with greater precision what a Corpus Christi play, in its essentials, seems to be.

2. Throughout this book, I refer to the cycles according to the titles of the editions I use. Though the *Ludus Coventriae* has nothing to do with Coventry, that name at least refers readers to the right book, whereas the alternative "Hegge cycle" or "N-town cycle" serve no very useful purpose. (I describe the *Two Coventry Corpus Christi Plays* always as the "true Coventry" cycle.) Similarly I speak of the *Towneley Plays* because they are edited under that name (of the family who owned the manuscript), rather than under the name Wakefield, which indicates their probable home. The titles are unfortunate; the best one can do is to make one's actual references clear. A "second generation" of editions, with full apparatus, is much to be desired. A. C. Cawley's excellent 1958 edition of the six *Wakefield Pageants in the Towneley Cycle* makes one hope he will someday undertake to edit the remainder of that cycle text; Arthur Brown has a new edition of the York cycle in preparation for the Early English Text Society; the Chester cycle, too, needs editorial attention beyond transcription and collation. Meanwhile we must work with what we have.

3. An excellent introduction to some of this material may be found in Part III of W. A. Pantin's *The English Church in the Fourteenth Century* (Cambridge, 1955).

4. Many studies have sought to establish one or more possible sources for a drama text, relying chiefly on brief verbal parallels, the ordering of events, and repetitions and contradictions as evidence of indebtedness. See, for instance: Marie C. Lyle, *The Original Identity of the York and Towneley Cycles* (Minneapolis, 1919), pp. 4–46; Robert H. Wilson, "*The Stanzaic Life of Christ* and

the Chester Plays," *SP*, XXVIII (1931), 413–32; Eleanor G. Clark, "The York Plays and the *Gospel of Nichodemus*," *PMLA*, XLIII (1928), 153–61; Carleton Brown, "The Towneley *Play of the Doctors* and the *Speculum Christiani*," *MLN*, XXXI (1916), 223–26; George C. Taylor, "The Relation of the English Corpus Christi Play to the Middle English Religious Lyric," *MP*, V (1907), 1–38; *The Northern Passion*, ed. Frances A. Foster, 1913, 1916, EETS o.s. 145, 147, II, 81–101; *The Life of Saint Anne*, ed. Roscoe E. Parker, 1928, EETS o.s. 174, pp. xxxiv–liv; *York*, pp. xliv–xlv; *Ludus Coventriae*, pp. xliv–lx. Such studies have their value, and establish beyond any doubt that the drama is directly related (as well as generally indebted) to the vernacular religious literature contemporary with it.

5. See *The Lay Folk's Catechism*, ed. Thomas F. Simmons and Henry E. Nolloth, 1901, EETS o.s. 118, p. 2 (8–18).

6. *Chester*, p. 448 (579–80).

7. *Ludus Coventriae*, p. 269 (9–12). See also *York*, pp. 94 (29–32), 94–95 (42–48) for instances of the audience being invited to contemplate mysteries.

8. See John Mirk, *Instructions for Parish Priests*, ed. Edward Peacock, rev. F. J. Furnivall, 1902, EETS o.s. 31, p. 48 (1555–64), for a list of narrative or emblematic subjects, all imaged by the Corpus Christi drama, that could be usefully assigned for contemplation, as penances against the sin of pride.

9. John Mirk, *Festial: A Collection of Homilies*, ed. Theodor Erbe, 1905, EETS e.s. 96, p. 171 (18–29).

10. *Cornish Drama*, I, 389 (2091–96).

11. *Towneley*, pp. 265–66 (233–43). See also *York*, pp. 357, 363. The laments of Mary serve the same devotional end.

12. *Diues et Pauper*, printed by Pynson, 1493, Precept 1, Chap. 1.

13. *Mediaeval Stage*, II, 357–58, 381.

14. As this book will demonstrate again and again, the cycles could only have been written by men schooled in theological traditions and trained by the pulpit in the techniques of holding the attention of a large and heterogeneous audience. This point has been made unequivocally by G. R. Owst, *Literature and Pulpit in Medieval England* (2d ed.; Oxford, 1961), pp. 480–88, and by Grace Frank, *The Medieval French Drama* (Oxford, 1954), p. 173. For further evidence, see the London records printed in *Mediaeval Stage*, II, 380–82; *Wycliffite Sermon*, p. 233 (18–19); the poem against the friars in *Historical Poems of the XIVth and XVth Centuries*, ed. Rossell H. Robbins (New York, 1959), pp. 163–64; and the Beverley record, 1423, printed by A. F. Leach, "Some English Plays and Players, 1220–1548," in *An English Miscellany Presented to Dr. Furnivall* (Oxford, 1901), p. 215. Throughout this book I shall speak of "the dramatist" as standing for that single writer, or collection of writers and revisers, responsible for the passage under discussion, for, in truth, the last reviser to have worked over a play is finally responsible for it all. The decision to retain some features and verses from the existing version is his, as is the task of harmonizing them with whatever new verses and action he himself contributes. I am interested in the texts as they stand, as they would have communicated in performance.

CHAPTER TWO

The Corpus Christi Drama as Play and Game

1. The most convenient summary is in Frank, *Medieval French Drama,* Chap. 1.

2. For detailed evidence, see Mary H. Marshall, "Boethius' Definition of *Persona* and Mediaeval Understanding of the Roman Theatre," *Speculum,* XXV (1950), 471–82.

3. Etienne Gilson, *Painting and Reality* (London, 1958), p. 266.

4. *Chester,* p. 20 (1–4).

5. *Ibid.,* pp. 13–17.

6. *Cursor Mundi,* ed. Richard Morris, 1874–92, EETS o.s. 57, 59, 62, 66, 68, 99, p. 1078 (18817–24). [Cotton MS.]

7. Young, II, 412.

8. *Wycliffite Sermon,* p. 233 (26–27, 29–30); see also the "Pley not with me, but pley with thi pere" idea, developed on p. 226.

9. In the sixteenth century, the conviction that man cannot play God or holy actions without being blasphemous was, for the first time, allied to a strong political interest, and that alliance killed the Corpus Christi drama. The whole of this fascinating history has been studied by Harold C. Gardiner, S.J., *Mysteries' End* (New Haven, 1946).

10. *"Presepe sit paratum retro altare, et Ymago Sancte Marie sit in eo posita"* (Young, II, 14). The Padua play may have used the same technique (*ibid.,* pp. 9–10). The use of an image for the Virgin and Child may, however, represent a dramatic tradition that began with the crèche and later added human actors, rather than one that began with human actors and stopped short of the Virgin and Child. The *Magi* play from Rouen also uses a crèche.

11. Craig, *English Religious Drama,* pp. 4–5, 9. Yet in the same paragraph (p. 9) he talks of its "symbolic distances" and its "symbolic time."

12. *Mediaeval Stage,* II, 309.

13. See especially Young, II, 407–10.

14. *Ibid.,* p. 397.

15. *Ibid.,* p. 408; see also I, 684.

16. *Mediaeval Stage,* II, 104.

17. Young, II, 408.

18. *Digby,* pp. 1 (20), 23 (559), 33 (155–57).

19. *Chester, passim; Digby,* p. 52 (657); *Ludus Coventriae,* "Proclamation" and also p. 187 (287–88).

20. See *O.E.D.* "pageant" (sense 1c); also *A Hundred Mery Talys,* ed. Herman Oesterley (London, 1866), pp. 67–68.

21. See, for instance, *Chester,* p. 6 (118), *Ludus Coventriae,* pp. 1 (10–11), 2 (28).

22. The evidence is set out by George R. Coffman, "The Miracle Play in Eng-

land—Nomenclature," *PMLA,* XXXI (1916), 448–65. He emphasizes that "miracles" was a popular, not an official, word for the plays. Because he fails to take the Wycliffite's categories seriously, his paper reaches (rather bewilderingly) what he calls "negative results."

23. Erwin Wolff, "Die Terminologie des Mittelalterlichen Dramas in Bedeutungsgeschichtlicher Sicht," *Anglia,* LXXVIII (1960), 1–27, fails to notice this central fact. He, too, has been misled by the infrequency of the Latin *ludus* into thinking its English derivatives unimportant. He concludes that "pageant" represents the greatest liberation of the drama from its liturgical beginnings, simply because it means both wagon and spectacle.

24. *Chester,* p. 7 (133–35); see also p. 16 (185–88).

25. *Ibid.,* p. 101 (409–12); see also p. 112 (177–79).

26. *York,* p. 133 (211–12); see also p. 432 (191–92).

27. *Ludus Coventriae,* p. 10 (308–9).

28. *Ibid.,* p. 10 (314).

29. *Ibid.,* p. 355 (25).

30. *Ibid.,* p. 287.

31. The *O.E.D.* records a possible theatrical sense in contexts relating to Greek and Roman antiquity (4b); two special combination-forms, "game-play" and "game-player" (17), and the entry given for "gameley" are unequivocally so defined. But "game" in the fully naturalized, theatrical sense displayed here is unrecorded. The *Middle English Dictionary,* ed. Hans Kurath, Sherman M. Kuhn, and John Reidy (Ann Arbor, 1954——), published its letter G just before this book went to press; it records the meaning "a play" (sense 2a) but its only citations are from *The Castell of Perseverance* and the *Ludus Coventriae.* Rossell H. Robbins, "An English Mystery Play Fragment Ante 1300," *MLN,* LXV (1950), 30–35, points out some "game" occurrences in his discussion of the nature of the fragment. He does not speculate on the significance of the term, nor does Chambers, though he mentions it with regard to *Pride of Life* in *OHEL,* p. 53. Glynne Wickham's first volume of studies of the Elizabethan stage has an interesting discussion of *plega, pleg stów,* and *pleg-hús;* see his *Early English Stages 1300 to 1660* (London, 1959, 1963), II (Part I), 166 ff., and my note 41 below.

32. *Ludus Coventriae,* p. 2 (46–48).

33. *Ibid.,* p. 16 (518–21).

34. *Non-Cycle Plays,* p. 91 (109 12); see also p. 88 (5–8).

35. *Macro Plays,* p. 186 (3644–46). "Game" words are used to describe the main action of the play as well, p. 157 (2688, 2697); for other examples, see *York,* p. 188 (103–4) and *Everyman,* ed. A. C. Cawley (Manchester, 1961), p. 24 (808–9).

36. In *Specimens of Old Christmas Carols,* ed. Thomas Wright, Percy Society 4 (London, 1841), p. 28.

37. John Skelton, *Magnyfycence,* ed. Robert L. Ramsay, 1908, EETS e.s. 98, p. 80 (2566–67).

38. *Mediaeval Stage,* II, 343.

39. This record for 1543, which Chambers overlooked, was noticed by Lawrence Blair, "A Note on the Relation of the Corpus Christi Procession to the Corpus Christi Play in England," *MLN,* LV (1940), 93.

40. *Mediaeval Stage,* II, 368.

41. Wickham, *Early English Stages,* II (Part I), 361, n. 21. Wickham has fascinating material in this volume on the multiple function of the Elizabethan theaters as "game-places," with records demonstrating the currency of that word for theater right up to the contract (1613) for the building of the Hope as "one other Game place or Plaiehouse." (See pp. 165–69, 332, 361–62.) In this contract, we can perhaps see the word "play" beginning to develop its more modern and specialized sense, implying a distinction between activities within the same structure: "for players to playe In, And for the game of Beares and Bulls to be bayted in the same" (p. 168), a distinction also made by Henslowe (see p. 169, and p. 362, n. 25). It is clear from the records that this rather tentative distinction between play and game was a new development. Wickham and I discovered the importance of "game" independently, each of us having finished our work before learning of the other's researches. We use very little of the same material, though our findings reinforce each other; for students of the later period, and for anyone interested in the continuity of the tradition I attempt to define here, Wickham's study is essential.

42. Lily B. Campbell, *Divine Poetry and Drama in Sixteenth Century England* (Berkeley, 1959), p. 225.

43. "An English Mystery Play Fragment Ante 1300," p. 32 (1–8).

44. "A Sixteenth Century English Mystery Fragment," ed. Rossell H. Robbins, *English Studies,* XXX (1949), 135.

45. Skelton, *Magnyfycence,* p. 61 (1948–49).

46. *Cursor Mundi,* p. 168 (2815–16). [Cotton MS.]

47. *Sir Gawain & The Green Knight,* ed. J. R. R. Tolkien and E. V. Gordon (Oxford, 1930), p. 22 (691–92).

48. Cited by the *O.E.D.* under "earnest" (sense 2) and "play" (sense 7), respectively.

49. Skelton, *Magnyfycence,* pp. 14 (427–28), 61 (1947–49), 80 (2548). The whole sequence of speeches from p. 79 (2505) to the end is interesting in its use of new generic terms.

50. *Wycliffite Sermon,* p. 229 (2, 18–21).

51. *Ibid.,* p. 241 (13–18). An earlier preacher also held all play to be potentially a snare of the devil in that it fostered idleness; see *Old English Homilies of the Twelfth Century, Second Series,* ed. R. Morris, 1873, EETS o.s. 53, p. 211.

52. Coffman, "The Miracle Play in England—Nomenclature," p. 458.

53. Quoted by Mary H. Marshall, "*Theatre* in the Middle Ages: Evidence from Dictionaries and Glosses," *Symposium,* IV (1950), 380.

54. J. Huizinga, *Homo ludens* (London, 1949), pp. 13, 8. Benjamin Hunningher, in *The Origin of Theatre* (Amsterdam, 1955), pp. 14–16, has also used Huizinga, along with Frazer and others, in order briefly to suggest the con-

nection between play, ritual, and theater in primitive cultures, in connection with his study of the origins of the early Latin drama of the Church.

55. See, for example, the Beverley records printed in *Mediaeval Stage,* II, 340.

56. *A Hundred Mery Talys,* pp. 7–11.

57. From the "Intermeane" after Act I. Quoted in A. P. Rossiter, *English Drama from Early Times to the Elizabethans* (London, 1950), p. 62.

58. *Wycliffite Sermon,* p. 231 (20–22), and pp. 230 (24) to 231(1).

59. Quoted by Bertram Joseph, "The Elizabethan Stage and Acting," in Boris Ford (ed.), *The Age of Shakespeare* (Penguin Books, 1955), p. 150. This admirable essay should be read by anyone interested in the history of theatrical conventions.

60. Richard Southern, *The Medieval Theatre in the Round* (London, 1957), Appendix, p. 236.

61. *Two Coventry Plays,* pp. 87 (11), 100 (12–13), 107 (3–5).

62. *York,* pp. xxxvii–viii.

63. Eleanor Prosser, *Drama and Religion in the English Mystery Plays* (Stanford, 1961, pp. 54–55), notes that any major character would have been played by several persons, and suggests that this should prevent us from speaking of any complete cycle as "one play." I think this perhaps posits too modern (and relative) a notion of dramatic unity. The need to divide production responsibility among the guilds was an immediate cause, but it happily suited the needs of the genre and story as well, creating a different but not necessarily inferior kind of dramatic coherence.

64. *Chester,* p. 52 (textual notes to l. 112). MS Harl. 2124 has it in Latin some few lines earlier.

65. *Ibid.,* p. 54.

66. *Two Coventry Plays,* p. 97 (33–34). This record first came to my attention in the notes of Martial Rose, *The Wakefield Mystery Plays* (London, 1961), p. 146.

67. *Wycliffite Sermon,* p. 234 (8).

68. Arnoul Greban, *Le Mystère de la Passion,* ed. Gaston Paris and Gaston Raynaud (Paris, 1878), p. 6 (239–48).

69. Northrop Frye, *Anatomy of Criticism* (Princeton, 1957), p. 135.

70. See the Chester records printed by F. M. Salter, *Mediaeval Drama in Chester* (Toronto, 1955), p. 76.

71. *Chester,* pp. 379–80 (199–202).

72. *Ibid.,* p. 381.

73. *York,* p. 461 (175).

74. Representations of the Creation by manuscript illuminators could easily have been translated into stage devices, at once simple and beautiful. See for example, Margaret Rickert, *Painting in Britain: The Middle Ages* (London, 1954), Plates 92 and 101; also M. R. James (ed.), *Illustrations of the Book of Genesis* (London, 1921), fol. 1a, 1b. Items in Coventry records concerning the "makyng of iij worldys" and a fee for "settyng the world of fyer" and for "kepyng fyre" clearly suggest that the end of the world was shown literally; see

Two Coventry Plays, p. 102 (6–10). See also Frank, *Medieval French Drama,* p. 172, and M. D. Anderson, *Drama and Imagery in English Medieval Churches* (Cambridge, 1963), pp. 141–42.

75. John Stevens, "Music in Mediaeval Drama," *Proceedings of the Royal Musical Association,* LXXXIV (1958), 83.

76. The miniature, which shows a performance of the *Martyre de Sainte Apolline,* is reproduced in Gustave Cohen, *Le Théâtre en France au Moyen Age* (Paris, 1928), Vol. I, Plate III. See also Anderson, *Drama and Imagery,* pp. 47–48.

77. Frank, *Medieval French Drama,* p. 170.

78. P. B. Salmon, "The 'Three Voices' of Poetry in Mediaeval Literary Theory," *Med. Aev.,* XXX (1961), 5.

79. *Chester,* p. 225 (201–4).

80. Alan H. Nelson, " 'Sacred' and 'Secular' Currents in The Towneley Play of Noah," *Drama Survey,* III (1964), 399.

81. *Wycliffite Sermon,* p. 241 (1–13).

82. *Historical Poems of the XIVth and XVth Centuries,* p. 163 (7–16). Against the judgment of previous editors, Robbins (p. 335) takes this poem, "On the Minorites," to refer to wall paintings rather than to miracle plays. This seems unwarranted: the poem is clearly laughing at "crude" dramatic conventions. Robbins did not know of work by Lawrence G. Craddock, O.F.M., "Franciscan Influences on Early English Drama," *Franciscan Studies,* X (1950), which includes a valuable discussion of this poem, pp. 399–415. Craddock cites St. Bonaventura to explain the second stanza quoted above: one of the seraphs appeared to St. Francis in the form of the Crucified, but retained his identity as angel, a fact clearly evident from his six seraph's wings.

83. *Historical Poems,* p. 163 (19–20).

84. *York,* p. 408 (225–28). Something like this happens in *Chester* as well, p. 344 (341–44).

85. *Diues et Pauper,* Precept 1, Chap. 8. Lollard opposition seems to have had little effect on the confidence of the drama. In *Towneley,* p. 374 (213–14), there is a rare satirical joke against the Lollards, in which a devil claims to be their chief.

86. W. W. Greg, *The Trial & Flagellation with Other Studies in the Chester Cycle* (Oxford, 1935), p. 159 (294–304).

87. Or the MS abbreviation "F." *Le Mystère d'Adam,* ed. Henri Chamard (Paris, 1925), pp. 2, 10, *et passim.*

88. *Chester,* p. 362 (261–76).

89. *Ludus Coventriae,* p. 209 (293–96). But see also p. 187 (281–88), where this kind of dramatic awareness is not specifically written into the text.

90. *Towneley,* p. 278 (661–66). I suspect there is a similar displacement from the dramatic moment in the York play of Thomas, pp. 454–55 (187–92). The Sykes MS of this play alters the "þou" to "þey" and the game-distancing is lost.

91. See *Macro Plays,* p. 186 (3650), and Frank, *Medieval French Drama,* p. 177.

CHAPTER THREE

Corpus Christi Feast and the Impulse toward Cycle Form

1. See a contemporary description of these plays, quoted by E. K. Chambers, *Mediaeval Stage*, II, 77–78, n. 3, and the discussion by Glynne Wickham, *Early English Stages*, I, 140–42. Wickham uses these records to argue that a similar cycle in Latin, performed by the clergy, was possible in Chester in the early or middle fourteenth century. One cannot deny the possibility, but there is no evidence to support it.

2. See, for example, texts in Young, I, 413–19, 518–33.

3. *Non-Cycle Plays*, pp. xvii–xxiii and 1–7. Also in Young, II, 514–23.

4. *Digby*, p. 171. The play dates from the early fifteenth century. The manuscript begins with a "Prologe of this treyte or meditatione off the buryalle of criste & mowrnynge therat," but there are instructions that the prologue (meant for a reader) is not to be spoken when the text is played. The generic term used to describe it should not surprise us; *Everyman*, too, is called "a treatyse ... in maner of a morall playe" (see the edition by A. C. Cawley, p. 1). Part I is certainly very static, though stageable. Part II is unmistakably intended for playing: there are stage directions and songs, and a closing address to the audience.

5. The records may be consulted in *Mediaeval Stage*, II, Appendix W.

6. This is true even of the two Old Testament plays that survive in complete form: the two Daniel plays, one written by Hilarius, the other by an unknown writer at Beauvais, both conclude with an address to a Christmas occasion, of which Daniel is a major prophet. (See Young, II, 286–87, 301–3.) Both the incomplete *Ordo de Ysaac et Rebecca* and the Laon *Ordo Joseph* lack endings, where an address to the occasion might have been made. It is possible that these plays were integrated into the Church year—the second and third Sundays in Lent would furnish suitable occasions, for their stories are read on those days— or they may simply represent an eccentric development. The evidence does not allow any confident conclusion. (*Ibid.*, pp. 265, 275.)

7. Craig, *English Religious Drama*, p. 140. Detailed records are given in *Mediaeval Stage*, II, Appendix W.

8. The London records may be found in *Mediaeval Stage*, II, 379–82. Chambers, OHEL, pp. 16–17, mentions a record from 1300, in which the Abbess of Clerkenwell complained to the King of damage done her fields and crops by crowds attending the "miracles." There is no hint concerning the subject or extent of those plays. The first explicit notice of a *cycle-play* in that locality (Clerkenwell is near Skinners Well) is dated 1384.

9. Clear and comprehensive categories are certainly needed. For instance, Craig, *English Religious Drama*, pp. 142–43, postulates a bewildering number of *major* kinds of drama. The New Romney Resurrection play and Interlude of the Passion, the Leicester Passion play, and the Aberdeen Nativity group should probably all be called liturgical plays or sequences, since they are anchored in their respective anniversary occasions (Good Friday, Easter, Whitsun, Candle-

mas). The Aberdeen *Haliblude* play is admittedly a problem, since nothing is known about it. If it was performed on Corpus Christi Day, as Craig thinks, there is nothing about the name that necessarily restricts it to the Passion: "Haliblude" may be Middle Scots for "Corpus Christi." (Still another possibility is discussed on pp. 47–48, and in note 44 below.) The London cycles are indeed different (see my discussion, p. 36) but not for the reasons Craig gives. He assumes that they lacked Nativity and Doomsday plays, yet he quotes a record referring to a Doomsday play as part of the subject matter (p. 153). It is difficult to believe that cycles as long as these would neglect the Nativity: the description "in quo tam vetus quam novum testamentum oculariter ludendo monstrabant" certainly does not exclude the possibility; moreover, this is almost identical with a 1425 description of the York cycle, which had a Nativity, as "ludum sumptuosum, in diversis paginis compilatum veteris et novi testamenti representacionum." See *York Memorandum Book*, Vol. II, ed. Maud Sellers, Surtees Society, No. 125 (London, 1915), 156. Records of this sort must be used for what they tell us specifically; they are too brief and perfunctory for one to read much significance into their omissions.

10. From the *Historia Monasterii Sancti Petri Gloucestriae*, quoted in Craig, *English Religious Drama*, p. 128.

11. It used to be held that the 1378 record was the first in York, and was thus anticipated by Beverley one year earlier. A. C. Cawley noticed the 1376 record in the *York Memorandum Book*, and corrected the received chronology in his edition of *Everyman and Medieval Miracle Plays* (London, 1956), p. x.

12. Craig, *English Religious Drama*, p. 130. The recent researches of Salter and Wickham have finally discredited the tradition that the Chester cycle had its beginning in 1327. It, too, seems to have taken shape in the late 1370's or early 1380's. See Wickham, *Early English Stages*, I, 133–37.

13. *The Holkham Bible Picture Book*, ed. W. O. Hassall (London, 1954), pp. 27–30.

14. Carleton Brown, "Caiaphas as a Palm Sunday Prophet," in *Anniversary Papers by Colleagues and Pupils of George Lyman Kittredge* (Boston, 1913), pp. 105–17.

15. Craig, *English Religious Drama*, p. 130.

16. Carleton Brown, "Sermons and Miracle Plays," *MLN*, XLIX (1934), 394–96.

17. See Wickham, *Early English Stages*, I, 145–46, and May McKisack, *The Fourteenth Century* (Oxford, 1959), pp. 331–33, 336–40, 373–78, etc.

18. Hardin Craig, "The Corpus Christi Procession and the Corpus Christi Play," *JEGP*, XIII (1914), 597.

19. This is the classic view, to be found in most standard accounts of the drama. See *Non-Cycle Plays*, p. xvii, and for a recent example, worthy of respect, Mary H. Marshall, "The Dramatic Tradition Established by the Liturgical Plays," *PMLA*, LVI (1941), 962–91, where much detailed evidence is set down. See also note 25 below.

20. Young, I, 665–66. The other plays are a *Conversion of St. Paul* and four plays concerned with St. Nicholas.

21. Frank, *Medieval French Drama*, p. 67.

22. *Mediaeval Stage*, II, 399.

23. Virginia Shull, "Clerical Drama in Lincoln Cathedral, 1318 to 1561," *PMLA*, LII (1937), 966. This has much material missed by Chambers.

24. Marshall, "The Dramatic Tradition," p. 991. We should remind ourselves, too, that liturgical drama was sung, not spoken.

25. Craig, "The Corpus Christi Procession," pp. 590, 598–99. Page 597 makes it clear that "plays" in the last two quoted sentences means plays developed from local, Latin originals. Arnold Williams, in *The Drama of Medieval England* (East Lansing, 1961), pp. 52–54, also adopts this account of the cycles' development.

26. Hardin Craig, "The Origin of the Passion Play: Matters of Theory as Well as Fact," in *Studies in Honor of A. H. R. Fairchild,* ed. Charles T. Prouty, (Columbia, Mo., 1946), pp. 88–89, argues that the Benediktbeuern *Passion Play* is the original form of all Passion plays, though it occurs (along with a briefer treatment of the same subject) in only one manuscript, and that German.

27. The essential structure of all the cycles may be reduced to the Creation, the Passion, and the Judgment—three plays largely without antecedent in the Latin drama of the Church. Though the German MS noted above does contain two plays of the Passion, no record (much less a text) of a Creation or a Judgment play is known. The Cividale records (no texts are extant) are obviously of interest here, but the plays they mention were performed in the Court of the Archbishop and are not really part of what Young calls "the drama of the medieval Church."

28. Edward M. Clark, "Liturgical Influences in the Towneley Plays," *Orate Fratres,* XVI (1941), 69–79.

29. The only scholar to dissent from the views attacked above is Wickham, who offers a guess as to what was happening, and works out a "presumptive chronology" for the period in *Early English Stages,* I, 315–17. His guess is considerably different from mine, and his reasons for doubting the tradition are not the same. In particular, Step II of his chronology fails to convince me: it assumes that plays of the Fall, Crucifixion, Antichrist, and Judgment must have been written between 1225 and 1350, furnishing the initial form, after which other liturgical plays of the Nativity and Resurrection were gradually translated and assimilated into it. But there is no English evidence at all for the four essential plays mentioned, nor for such a sequence; nor is there any necessary a priori reason for assuming one. Indeed, a single decision could easily have led to the creation of an entire cycle text, though probably a text simpler and shorter than those that have come down to us. (The 1298 cycle at Cividale, for example, seems to have had no evolutionary, agglutinative history.) Wickham offers his sequence as a "guess," which is all anyone can do, given records as scanty as these. But I prefer a guess that does not involve postulating a whole class of

plays for whose separate existence we have no evidence in England, and which are represented on the Continent only by isolated examples. We must be wary of our natural wish to find a gradual, patterned, and logical development of these cycles: their history seems at least as likely to have been sudden and disjunctive, two terms that can be suitably applied to the surviving records of their performance.

30. Shull, "Clerical Drama in Lincoln Cathedral," p. 966.

31. *The Golden Legend: or Lives of the Saints as Englished by William Caxton,* ed. F. S. Ellis (London, 1900), I, 169, 181, 187, 207, 228, 256.

32. *Ibid.,* II, 1–2.

33. Paul E. Kretzmann, *The Liturgical Element in the Earliest Forms of the Medieval Drama* (Minneapolis, 1916), pp. 13–15.

34. *Breviarium ad usum insignis ecclesiae Sarum,* ed. Francis Proctor and Christopher Wordsworth, I (Cambridge, 1879), cols. xx–xxiii, lxxxii–iii, c–cii, cxxxiii–v.

35. See, for example, the Sermon for Advent Sunday in Mirk, *Festial,* pp. 1–5, which concerns the 15 Signs and the Day of Doom.

36. The custom of a Corpus Christi procession also grew up without papal specification; it consisted of bearing the Host in splendid ceremony through the streets of the town, often stopping at churches on the way, and then returning with it to the home church. The guilds seem quickly to have assumed responsibilities in this observance. There has been much speculation about the Corpus Christi procession as a source of the plays, but no convincing evidence has been found. Merle Pierson, "The Relation of the Corpus Christi Procession to the Corpus Christi Play in England," *Transactions of the Wisconsin Academy of Sciences, Arts, and Letters,* XVIII (1915), 110–65, has made the definitive study. Blair, "A Note on the Relation of the Corpus Christi Procession to the Corpus Christi Play in England," contributes some further records and endorses Miss Pierson's conclusions. In his words (pp. 94–95), "No church record here of a Corpus Christi procession mentions a play in any form. No church record here of a play shows any definite connection of the play with a Corpus Christi procession."

37. Printed in *Textus antiqui de festo Corporis Christi,* ed. Petrus Browe, S.J., Fasc. IV of *Opuscula et textus* (Münster, 1934), p. 31 (1–6).

38. *Ibid.,* pp. 28 (20–29), 32 (8–13).

39. *Missale ad usum insignis et praeclarae ecclesiae Sarum,* ed. Francis H. Dickinson, I (Burnt Island, 1861), col. 457.

40. *The Golden Legend,* I, 143.

41. Mirk, *Festial,* pp. 170–75; *The Minor Poems of the Vernon MS,* ed. Carl Horstmann and F. J. Furnivall, 1892, 1901, EETS o.s. 98, 117, pp. 174–77, 183–85; William of Wadington, *Handlynge Synne,* trans. Robert of Brunne, re-ed. F. J. Furnivall, 1901, 1903, EETS o.s. 119, 123, pp. 309–35 (a version of six miracles is also found in *Minor Poems of the Vernon MS,* pp. 198–221); *The Mirrour of the Blessed Lyf of Jesu Christ,* trans. Nicholas Love, ed. Lawrence F. Powell (Oxford, 1908), pp. 301–24.

42. Karl Young, "An *Interludium* for a Gild of Corpus Christi," *MLN*, XLVIII (1933), 84–86.

43. These lines were erased, presumably after 1531, but can still be read. Printed in Wickham, *Early English Stages*, I, 347.

44. The Aberdeen *Haliblude* play may also have been a play of the sacrament.

45. The Banns speak of a Monday performance; the play is dated 1461. The best available text is in *Chief Pre-Shakespearean Dramas*, ed. Joseph Quincy Adams (Cambridge, Mass., 1924), pp. 243–62.

46. See Cecilia Cutts, "The Croxton Play: An Anti-Lollard Piece," *MLQ*, V (1944), 45–60. Love's indignation is apparent in *Mirrour of the Blessed Lyf*, pp. 304–5, 320–21, and elsewhere.

47. *Minor Poems of the Vernon MS*, p. 199 (57–70).

48. Eleanor Prosser, in *Drama and Religion in the English Mystery Plays*, especially pp. 16–25, has suggested central and far-reaching relationships among the doctrine of repentance, the feast of Corpus Christi, and the drama cycles, but this part of her book fails to convince me. The decree of the Fourth Lateran Council in 1215, in its provisions for an increased religious education for the laity, undoubtedly displays interests that are (among others) reflected in the cycle-drama; but the connection is too distant, too slow in being realized, to be termed causal. The Council's decision to require all members of the Church to attend confession and communion once a year, with the new emphasis upon the efficacy of repentance that this implied, did influence a number of individual plays from the cycles, and Miss Prosser has written an illuminating study of these. But repentance is not the informing lesson of the Corpus Christi drama— the morality plays preeminently teach that—nor is it the central subject. The cycle-plays concern something larger; their subject is human history and God's interventions in it.

49. According to Craig, *English Religious Drama*, pp. 269–70, the change at Lincoln probably took place in the 1470's. At Chester the change may have been made in 1447 (p. 166). In addition to frequent performances of the whole cycle, Chester occasionally played a single episode for a special purpose: Lord Strange in 1488 and Prince Arthur in 1497 were both shown the play of the *Assumption* (*Mediaeval Stage*, II, 355). Old Testament plays were used freely: the maritime guild of Hull played Noah on Plough Monday, co-opting Noah as a kind of patron saint (*ibid.*, pp. 370–71); there are two texts of Abraham and Isaac plays that may never have been attached to a cycle (*Non-Cycle Plays*, pp. 26–53); Reading had a play of Adam and Eve in 1507, a play of Cain in 1512 and 1515 (*Mediaeval Stage*, II, 392). These are all late developments, and probably stem from, or were suggested by, Corpus Christi traditions, since they are all subjects that had long been played in the cycles.

50. This outline is based on material that can be most conveniently consulted in *Mediaeval Stage*, II, Appendices T and W, although descriptions in T are not always accurate.

51. The Chester version of the Assumption and Coronation of the Virgin has been lost, but it is mentioned in the early Banns. We know that it was performed

as part of the cycle in 1477 and separately in 1488, 1497, and 1515. It was unique in being the only episode acted not by a guild but by "the worshipfull wyves of this towne." W. W. Greg, *Bibliographical and Textual Problems of the English Miracle Cycles* (London, 1914), p. 49.

52. *Towneley*, p. 366.

53. The nature of the Towneley MS as "register," made from unique originals possessed by the crafts, allows another possibility: a play not at hand may have been intended for later addition. The *Lazarus* and *Hanging of Judas* both came into the manuscript this way. But the twelve missing leaves hint at a better explanation.

54. All the prophecies are recited by one actor. This prologue is indicated by an interlined entry in Burton's 1415 list of the pageants (*York*, p. xx); it seems to have been written in the play text without any disruption of the manuscript (dated by Miss Toulmin Smith as *c.* 1430–40, and by Greg *c.* 1475, in *Bibliographical and Textual Problems*, p. 28, n. 1). But a marginal note in sixteenth-century script at the beginning of the play calls attention to it with some surprise, "Doctor, this matter is newly mayde, whereof we haue no coppy" (*York*, p. 93). We know that York in 1415 had a cycle of fifty-one plays, that somewhat later it had fifty-seven, and that the manuscript contains only forty-five. There is no record of an earlier play of the Prophets that has been replaced or abridged; on the other hand, the current Prophets' prologue seems to be at least contemporary with the manuscript version. In short, the formal status of this passage is extremely confused; we may hope that Arthur Brown, in his forthcoming edition of the York plays for the Early English Text Society, will be able to throw light on it.

55. *Two Coventry Plays*, pp. xv, xl–xli. The continuous Old Testament group, from the Fall of Lucifer through the Sacrifice of Isaac, which was absorbed into the *Ludus Coventriae*, seems to me exactly the kind of play we might have seen in the true Coventry cycle; a second could have been a play of Moses and the Prophets. See Esther L. Swenson, *An Inquiry into the Composition and Structure of Ludus Coventriae* (Minneapolis, 1914), pp. 5–8.

56. *Non-Cycle Plays*, pp. xxxix–xl.

57. *Ibid.*, p. xxx. M. D. Anderson, *Drama and Imagery in English Medieval Churches*, pp. 87–104, attempts to reconstruct what some of the lost Norwich plays—those concerning the Nativity, Childhood, and Ministry of Christ—might have looked like, using evidence from the roof bosses of Norwich Cathedral. Her discussion is extremely interesting, but it can offer us little help here. Even if we could prove that many of the bosses reflect stage procedures, the sheer number of them—more than four hundred in all—would make them of little use in determining which subjects were staged as part of the full cycle.

58. See Joannes Vriend, S.J., *The Blessed Virgin Mary in the Medieval Drama of England* (Purmerend, 1928), and Evangeline G. Weir, *The Vernacular Sources of the Middle English Plays of the Blessed Virgin Mary* (unpublished Ph.D. dissertation, Stanford University, 1941).

59. Frank, *Medieval French Drama*, p. 176.

CHAPTER FOUR

Corpus Christi Form: Principles of Selection

1. *Chester,* p. 87 (69–72).
2. *Middle English Sermons,* ed. Woodburn O. Ross, 1940, EETS o.s. 209, p. 314 (16–20).
3. *Golden Legend,* I, 10. Medieval orthodoxy associated Christ with the creating Logos (*ibid.,* p. 148).
4. *Ibid.,* p. 25.
5. *Ibid.,* p. 13.
6. Jean Daniélou, S.J., *From Shadows to Reality. Studies in the Biblical Typology of the Fathers,* trans. Dom Wulstan Hibberd (London, 1960), p. 30. The French title is *Sacramentum futuri.*
7. *Textus antiqui de festo Corporis Christi,* p. 29 (26–29).
8. *Towneley,* pp. 86–87 (30–34).
9. *Chester,* p. 224 (161–68).
10. I have been privileged to see J. Martin Evans' studies-in-progress on the history of the doctrine of the Fall of Man, and these brief remarks are based on his work.
11. *Golden Legend,* I, 172.
12. *Chester,* pp. 27–28 (169–204).
13. *Speculum sacerdotale,* ed. Edward H. Weatherly, 1936, EETS o.s. 200, p. 18 (24–28). The exact "significance" given is rather curious (the resurrection of us all). Possibly the author is thinking of an ending common to some of the Latin plays of the Innocents in which an angel appears and commands the little ones to come to him, and they all rise. See Young, II, 113, for an example.
14. Reginald Pecock, *The Reule of Crysten Religioun,* ed. William C. Greet, 1927, EETS, o.s. 171, p. 209.
15. Erich Auerbach, "Figura," trans. Ralph Manheim, in *Scenes from the Drama of European Literature* (New York, 1959), p. 29.
16. Quoted in Daniélou, *From Shadows to Reality,* p. 188.
17. Louis Réau, *Iconographie de l'Art Chrétien* (Paris, 1955–59), I, 192.
18. *The Miroure of Mans Saluacionne,* ed. Alfred H. Huth (London, 1888), pp. 1–2.
19. *Towneley,* p. 345 (196–99).
20. Réau, *Iconographie,* I, 198–200. Compare the accounts of Christ's death with Psalms 22:1, 17, 19, and 69:21 (Vulgate numbering).
21. Auerbach (quoting Augustine) in "Figura," p. 39. The preceding discussion of Philo and Tertullian is drawn from pp. 31–36.
22. *Ibid.,* p. 41.
23. For a fuller background to the discussion that follows, I recommend my own chief sources: Beryl Smalley's *The Study of the Bible in the Middle Ages* (2d ed.; Oxford, 1952), Auerbach's essay "Figura," and Daniélou's *From Shadows to Reality.* For the full medieval figural inheritance, a student should

consult Henrik Cornell, *Biblia pauperum* (Stockholm, 1925), and the *Speculum humanae salvationis,* ed. J. Lutz and P. Perdrizet (2 vols.; Mulhouse, 1907, 1909), along with M. R. James, "Pictor in Carmine," *Archaeologia,* XCIV (1951), 141–66.

24. *Speculum sacerdotale,* pp. 95 (39) to 96 (5).

25. *Ludus Coventriae,* p. 31 (73–78).

26. *Miroure of Mans Saluacionne,* p. 69.

27. *Meditations on the Life and Passion of Christ,* ed. Charlotte D'Evelyn, 1921, EETS o.s. 158, pp. 33–34 (1259–64).

28. *York,* p. 54 (297–302).

29. *Ibid.,* pp. 40–41 (14–29).

30. *Ibid.,* pp. 497 (7–8), 499 (57–61).

31. In the Chester *Antichrist,* the *Expositor* carefully narrates the Days before Doom; see pp. 397 ff.

32. The full correspondence is set out in St. Augustine, *The City of God,* XV, 26; see the Healey translation (London, 1945), II, 93–97. See also John Lydgate, *The Minor Poems,* ed. Henry N. MacCracken, 1911, 1934, EETS e.s. 107, 192, pp. 32–33 (43–77).

33. *Meditations on the Life and Passion of Christ,* p. 19 (715–16).

34. *Glossa ordinaria,* in *Patrologia Latina,* Vol. 113, col. 105.

35. *Holkham Bible Picture Book,* fol. 8, and p. 74 n. In Lydgate's translation of Guillaume de Deguileville, *The Pilgrimage of the Life of Man* (ed. F. J. Furnivall and Katharine B. Locock, 1899–1904, EETS e.s. 77, 83, 92, pp. 644–45), Apostasy compares herself to Noah's raven.

36. *Cornish Drama,* I, 89 (1177–80).

37. *Cornish Drama,* I, 88. The stage directions are in a later hand, but the reviser was simply finding further means of emphasizing the intention of his original.

38. *Meditations on the Life and Passion of Christ,* p. 6 (193–96).

39. *Miroure of Mans Saluacionne,* p. 62.

40. *Chester,* pp. 68–69 (113–40). See also John Capgrave, *The Chronicle of England,* ed. Francis C. Hingeston, Rolls Series 1 (London, 1858), pp. 27–28.

41. Craig, *English Religious Drama,* p. 185, judges that the drama concentrates on the sacrifice of Isaac merely because it is a good story.

42. *Missale ad usum . . . Sarum,* I, col. 458.

43. *Ibid.,* col. 618.

44. Daniélou, *From Shadows to Reality,* p. 123.

45. *Non-Cycle Plays,* p. 48 (295–96).

46. *York,* p. 62 (191–92).

47. *Towneley,* p. 47 (219). Rosemary Woolf, "The Effect of Typology on the English Mediaeval Plays of Abraham and Isaac," *Speculum,* XXXII (1957), 813–14, brought this to my notice. This excellent article should be consulted for a fuller study of the history of this particular figure. I repeat little of Miss Woolf's material, although my conclusions are largely the same.

48. *Chester,* p. 81 (415–16).

49. *Ibid.,* pp. 83 (465–68) ff.

50. Mirk, *Festial,* pp. 77 (31) to 78 (8).

51. Daniélou, *From Shadows to Reality,* pp. 124–25.

52. *Towneley,* p. 41 (41–50).

53. Quoted in Daniélou, *From Shadows to Reality,* p. 123.

54. The episode will be discussed further in Chapter 10.

55. See Jeffrey Truby, *The Glories of Salisbury Cathedral* (London, 1948), p. 31.

56. These may be studied in more detail in Daniélou, *From Shadows to Reality,* pp. 158 ff.

57. *The Writings of Tertullian,* ed. Alexander Roberts and James Donaldson, Ante-Nicene Christian Library No. 11 (Edinburgh, 1869), I, 241.

58. Quoted in Daniélou, *From Shadows to Reality,* p. 181.

59. Mirk, *Festial,* pp. 103 (16–22), 127 (23–27).

60. Cornell, *Biblia pauperum,* Pl. 32.

61. *Speculum humanae salvationis,* I, 148–49, 172. The *Biblia pauperum* (see Pl. 40) concentrates on the defeat of Satan, and its types are therefore David and Goliath, Samson and the lion.

62. *Miroure of Mans Saluacionne,* pp. 109–10.

63. *York,* p. 119 (29–32).

64. *Towneley,* p. 68 (136–37).

65. *Towneley,* p. 299 (205–6). E. Catherine Dunn, "The Medieval 'Cycle' as History Play: An Approach to the Wakefield Plays," *Studies in the Renaissance,* VII (1960), 84–86, noticed this echo.

66. Young, II, 105.

67. *York,* p. 142 (135–46).

68. *Digby,* p. 174 (68–69).

69. *Two Coventry Plays,* p. 29 (833–34).

70. *Digby,* p. 87 (856).

71. *Ibid.,* pp. 90–92. The only intervening matter serves to introduce the King of Marcylle, who is a leading character in the second part, and to have a devil report the Harrowing of Hell.

72. *Ludus Coventriae,* p. 341 (145–52).

73. *Chester,* pp. 244–45 (385–88).

74. *Digby,* p. 88 (877–80); *York,* p. 459 (103–9).

75. *Ludus Coventriae,* p. 254 (682–85).

76. Printed as Appendix IV to *The Lay Folks Mass Book,* ed. Thomas F. Simmons, 1879, EETS o.s. 71, p. 130 (71–76).

77. *Digby,* pp. 201–2 (882–99).

78. *Chester,* p. 268 (69–84). *York,* p. 236, has lost its equivalent leaf.

79. *Breviarium ad usum . . . Sarum,* I, col. mlxvii.

80. *Golden Legend,* I, 143.

81. Lydgate, *The Minor Poems,* I, 35–36 (1–8).

82. *Golden Legend,* I, 145.

83. From "Letabundus," Lydgate, *The Minor Poems,* I, 56 (217–20).

84. A synoptic list may be found in Réau, *Iconographie,* I, 201–7; it is studied in detail in Vol. II (1, 2) of the same work.

85. The theory was advanced by Marius Sepet, *Les Prophètes du Christ* (Paris, 1878). The relevant portion of the *sermo,* and various Latin dramatic texts deriving from it, can be found in Young, II, 125 ff.

86. Clark, "Liturgical Influences in the Towneley Plays," p. 71.

87. *Breviarium ad usum . . . Sarum,* I, col. ccccxciii.

88. Clark, "Liturgical Influences," p. 71.

89. The *Heidelberger Passionspiel* played types and antitypes together in pairs in just this way. For example, play XXXIII consists of Abraham and Isaac, followed by Christ carrying the cross. See Woolf, "The Effect of Typology on the English Mediaeval Plays of Abraham and Isaac," p. 809.

90. Ranulph Higden, *Polychronicon,* ed. Churchill Babington, Rolls Series 41, I (London, 1865), 27.

91. St. Augustine, *The City of God,* XXII, 30 (Healey trans., II, 407–8). This is Augustine's most important statement of the idea. He had some thirty-five years earlier expressed it for the first time in *De Genesi contra Manichaeos* I, 23, as a straightforward seven-age system, and including the seven ages of man in his set of correspondences. For this, see *Patrologia Latina,* Vol. 34, cols. 190–94.

92. Bernard Rackham, *The Ancient Glass of Canterbury Cathedral* (London, 1949), Monochrome Pl. 19e, and p. 63.

93. Bede, *Opera de temporibus,* ed. Charles W. Jones (Cambridge, Mass., 1943), p. 303.

94. Bede, *De temporum ratione,* ed. Theodore Mommsen, in *Chronica minora,* Vol. III (*Monumenta Germaniae historica*: Berlin, 1898), pp. 247–48, 325–26.

95. Matthew Paris, *Chronica majora,* ed. Henry R. Luard, Rolls Series 57, I, (London, 1872), 1–53.

96. *Flores historiarum,* ed. Henry R. Luard, Rolls Series 95, I (London, 1890), 1–56.

97. Higden, *Polychronicon,* I, 27.

98. George Boas, *Essays on Primitivism and Related Ideas in the Middle Ages* (Baltimore, 1948), pp. 180–81, includes detailed citations. This work contains some helpful pages, especially pp. 177–85.

99. *A Stanzaic Life of Christ,* ed. Frances A. Foster, 1926, EETS o.s. 166, pp. 3–4 (77–100), 127–28 (3799–804).

100. St. Augustine, *Sermons for Christmas and Epiphany,* trans. Thomas C. Lawler (London, 1952), pp. 39–42.

101. *Cursor Mundi.* See the table of contents provided by the editor, VII, 265–68.

102. *Ibid.,* II, 530 (9197–222).

103. Capgrave, *Chronicle of England,* p. 49.

104. Bede, *Opera historica,* ed. C. Plummer (Oxford, 1896), I, xli–ii, n. 6.

105. Edited by A. Napier, "Altenglische Kleinigkeiten," *Anglia,* XI (1888),

6–7. Another piece following this same pattern, from an eleventh-century manuscript, is edited in this same volume by H. Logeman, "Anglo-Saxonica minora," pp. 105–6.

106. *Golden Legend*, I, 37. This is not an addition of Caxton's but part of the original work: see Jacobus de Voragine, *Legenda aurea*, ed. Th. Graesse (Leipzig, 1850), pp. 84–85.

107. See *Medieval Stage*, II, 425–26.

108. William S. Clark, *The Early Irish Stage* (Oxford, 1955), pp. 10–12.

109. *Hymns to the Virgin & Christ, The Parliament of Devils, and Other Religious Poems*, ed. Frederick J. Furnivall, 1867, EETS o.s. 24, pp. 52–53 (361–78).

110. John Bale, *The Dramatic Writings*, ed. John S. Farmer (London, 1907), pp. 84 ff.

111. Christopher Woodforde, *Stained Glass in Somerset 1250–1830* (London, 1946), p. 173. The sixth figure may have been another prophet, or Christ Himself.

112. Capgrave, *Chronicle of England*, p. 39.

113. *Golden Legend*, II, 40.

114. M. D. Anderson, *The Imagery of British Churches* (London, 1955), p. 99. Rare examples of the fight with Goliath and the battle with the lion (both are types of the Descent into Limbo) are noted.

115. St. Augustine, *The City of God*, XVII, 1 (Healey trans., II, 144).

116. *Ludus Coventriae*, pp. 57 ff. On Lincoln as the probable home of the *Ludus Coventriae*, and on the special dedication both of that city's cathedral and of this drama text to the Virgin and St. Anne, see Craig, *English Religious Drama*, Chap. 7, and especially pp. 276–80. M. D. Anderson in *Drama and Imagery* (pp. 36–37) discusses certain Jesse windows that furnish interesting equivalents to this play, but her insistence that it should be called a Jesse play rather than a Prophets' play perhaps overstresses the novel element in it. It is clearly both. Although the MS ends with an "Explicit Jesse," and the stanza describing it in the Banns begins "Off þe gentyl Jesse rote," its other emphasis is equally (or more clearly) marked in lines like "Kyngys and prophetys . . . Schull prophesye" and "they xal prophecye of a mayde" (*Ludus Coventriae*, p. 4, ll. 105–17).

117. He appears in *Chester*, pp. 99–100; in *Towneley*, pp. 59–60. In the York cycle there is only the recited Prologue to the *Annunciation*, but even here, deriving from Luke 1:32, Christ is related to "dauid sege," pp. 95 (67), 99 (163–64).

118. *Ludus Coventriae*, p. 35 (14–17).

119. *Chester*, pp. 70–71.

120. *York*, pp. 56–57 (17–20).

121. Higden, *Polychronicon*, I, 31.

122. *Speculum sacerdotale*, p. 7 (16–21).

123. That he does not develop from the *Prophetae* has been conclusively proved by P. E. Dustoor, "The Origin of the Play of 'Moses and the Tables of the Law,'" *MLR*, XIX (1924), 459–63.

124. The full list of sixty scenes may be found in Truby, *The Glories of Salisbury Cathedral*, p. 31.

125. Quoted in Craig, *English Religious Drama*, p. 148.

126. One of the Masons' complaints against their assigned play of Fergus (48th out of 51 pageants) was that it often had to be played after darkness fell. G. G. Coulton, *Art and the Reformation* (2d ed.; Cambridge, 1953), p. 394.

127. *Wakefield Pageants*, p. xxv (quoting E. O. James, *Christian Myth and Ritual*, 1933).

128. Craig, *English Religious Drama*, p. 134.

129. *Ibid.*, p. 134; Woolf, "Typology," furnishes a definitive study of the Abraham and Isaac plays; and since my first writing this, Anderson, *Drama and Imagery*, pp. 22–26 and Appendix A, has provided a brief but helpful study of some of this same material.

130. They establish, too, the important differences between these cycles and the much earlier cycle in Cividale, performed in 1298 and 1303. This cycle was played on Pentecost, and had in the first instance no Old Testament plays at all, in the second only a play of Adam and Eve. *Contra* Craig, *English Religious Drama*, pp. 100–101, it was not of the Corpus Christi pattern.

CHAPTER FIVE

Medieval Time and English Place

1. Frank, *Medieval French Drama*, pp. 125–31, 176–89. She writes (p. 134) of *Le Jour du Jugement*, a separate play of the fourteenth century, nearly 2,500 lines long: "Plays about Antichrist and the Last Judgment seem not to have been as common in France as in Germany. No other complete text has survived from France and there are records of only two late performances of plays concerned with the Last Judgment, one at Orleans in 1550, the other at Modane in 1580."

2. George Poulet, *Studies in Human Time*, trans. Elliott Coleman (Baltimore, 1956), p. 10.

3. See, for instance, *Middle English Sermons*, pp. 251 (32) to 252 (9), and p. 255 (8–12).

4. *Ibid.*, pp. 112 (29) to 113 (4).

5. *Chester*, p. 449 (608). In *York*, p. 501 (125), before Judgment begins, the damned souls say, "To aske mercy vs is no nede," which is less a statement of despair than the recognition of a fact about Redemptive time.

6. *Chester*, p. 452 (693–700).

7. Quoted by Wilhelm Levinson, "Bede as Historian," in *Bede: His Life, Times, and Writings,* ed. A. Hamilton Thompson (Oxford, 1935), p. 116.

8. *Chester*, pp. 52 (103, 112), 56 (201–8), for example.

9. *York*, p. 54 (286); *Towneley*, p. 121 (180).

10. Nelson, " 'Sacred' and 'Secular' Currents in The Towneley Play of Noah," p. 399.

11. Arnold Williams, *The Characterization of Pilate in the Towneley Plays* (East Lansing, 1950), pp. 37–51.

12. *Towneley,* pp. 376 (287–91) ff. See also Owst, *Literature and Pulpit in Medieval England,* on satire and sermon technique.

13. Marital relationships, too, are presented in lively, contemporary terms; see *Towneley,* p. 119 (102–8).

14. *Holkham Bible Picture Book,* fol. 34 and p. 139 n.

15. Wickham, *Early English Stages* I, 103. Qualifications to this view are expressed on pp. 108–9, where he suggests that by "contemporary" we need to allow that costumes may have been slightly out of date—i.e., not absolutely the latest fashion—but not out of "time." The qualification is simply in the *degree* of contemporaneity; there is no question of historical verisimilitude. The same qualifications are made by W. L. Hildburgh in *English Alabaster Carvings as Records of the Medieval Religious Drama* (Oxford, 1949), p. 55.

16. Higden completed the original version in 1327 and a longer version in 1342. Trevisa finished his English translation of it in 1387; it was printed (with modifications) by Caxton in 1482, by Wynkyn de Worde in 1495, and by Peter Treveris in 1527. Another English version (in a Harleian MS) *c.* 1432–50, is also extant. Higden, *Polychronicon,* I, xlii, lviii, lxix.

17. Higden, *Polychronicon* (Trevisa trans.), pp. 3, 5.

18. See James W. Thompson and Bernard J. Holm, *A History of Historical Writing* (New York, 1942), I, 277–78, 396–97.

19. Roger of Wendover, *Flowers of History,* trans. J. A. Giles (London, 1849), I, 1, 2. The original work is published in the Rolls Series, No. 95. It is to be noted that such a view of the uses of history was still powerful in the Renaissance.

20. Capgrave, *Chronicle of England,* pp. 2, 60.

21. Higden, *Polychronicon,* I, 19.

22. St. Thomas Aquinas, *Summa theologica,* III–II, Q.lv,4, trans. Fathers of the English Dominican Province (London, 1911–25), XIV, 408–9.

23. Beryl Smalley, *English Friars and Antiquity in the Early Fourteenth Century* (Oxford, 1960), pp. 294–98. Morton W. Bloomfield, "Chaucer's Sense of History," *JEGP,* II (1952), 301–13, argues that Chaucer had achieved a stronger feeling for accurate chronology and cultural diversity than any other English writer of his day, with the possible and more obvious exceptions of Mandeville and Wycliffe. Chaucer's travels in Italy may have put him in touch with the new ideas of history that were being developed there.

24. John Gower, *The English Works,* ed. G. C. Macaulay, 1900, 1901, EETS c.s. 81, 82, I, 4 (52–60).

25. *Chester,* p. 119 (398); *York,* p. 308 (33).

26. Rose, *The Wakefield Mystery Plays,* p. 145, brought this to my notice.

27. *The Pepysian Gospel Harmony,* ed. Margery Goates, 1922, EETS o.s. 157, xlvii.

28. *Chester,* pp. 115–16 (287–96).

29. Salter, *Mediaeval Drama in Chester,* p. 96.

30. *Chester,* p. 132 (5–8).

31. *Ibid.,* p. 143 (259–60).

32. *Ibid.,* p. 159 (651–52).

33. *Ibid.*, p. 194 (217–20).

34. *Towneley*, p. 29 (200). See also *Wakefield Pageants*, p. 96 n.

35. *Towneley*, p. 19 (366–67). See also *Wakefield Pageants*, p. 93 n.

36. *Towneley*, p. 130 (454–57). "At the crokyd thorne," p. 129 (403), is also a Horbury reference.

37. *Wakefield Pageants*, p. 110 n.

38. *Towneley*, p. 127 (350–53).

39. *Ludus Coventriae*, p. 123 (13–32).

40. *Chester*, p. 293 (325–28).

41. *Cornish Drama*, I, 197 (2585–94), II, 9 (91–94), 31 (377). See notes on these place names, II, 473–514, contributed by E. Hoblyn Pedler.

42. *Chester*, pp. 121–22 (441–60).

43. *The Apocryphal New Testament*, ed. M. R. James (corr. ed.; Oxford, 1953), p. 45 (XVII, 2).

44. *Towneley*, p. 371 (125–28).

45. Quoted by Auerbach, "Figura," p. 43. Tertullian also had written that in God there is no *differentia temporis* (ibid., p. 42).

46. St. Augustine, *The City of God*, XXII, 30 (Healey trans., II, 408); *Golden Legend*, I, 8–9.

47. See William Caxton, *Mirrour of the World*, ed. Oliver H. Prior, 1913, EETS e.s. 110, p. 10, for an eloquent statement of this idea.

48. St. Augustine, *The Confessions*, XI, 11, trans. Sir Tobie Matthew, rev. Dom Roger Hudleston (London, 1954), p. 338.

49. *Golden Legend*, III, 100. The fact that Good Friday is a movable date varying from year to year is ignored. Perhaps the assumption is that the historical crucifixion happened on this day. The same congruence is versified in *The South English Legendary*, ed. Charlotte D'Evelyn and Anna J. Mill, 1956, 1959, EETS o.s. 235, 236, 244, I, 127–28 (1–24). Cf. Donne's poem "Upon the Annunciation and Passion Falling Upon One Day. 1608," where an actual occurrence brings the paradox to mind.

50. Hans Meyerhoff, *Time in Literature* (Berkeley, 1955), pp. 20–21. This book is concerned with post-Renaissance literature only, but the first chapter has a broader relevance.

51. Auerbach, "Figura," p. 72. Craig, *English Religious Drama*, p. 16, also has a brief but perceptive discussion.

52. *Chester*, p. 81 (415–16).

53. *Cornish Drama*, I, 201 (2641–43), 207 (2727–29, 2723).

54. Quoted by Smalley in *The Study of the Bible in the Middle Ages*, p. 90.

55. *Chester*, p. 117 (337–44).

CHAPTER SIX

Religious Laughter

1. The single study that offers any real help on the problem is to be found in Ernst R. Curtius, *European Literature and the Latin Middle Ages*, trans. Wil-

lard R. Trask (London, 1953), Excursus IV, "Jest and Earnest in Medieval Literature," pp. 417–35. Of this, Section 2, "The Church and Laughter," pp. 420–22, is particularly relevant. Curtius sets down the evidence he has gathered, chiefly from Latin writings of Continental origin to the thirteenth century, and suggests possible conclusions. I do not duplicate his material, and recommend his few masterly pages as a supplement to the English material I present here. Frederik T. Wood, "The Comic Elements in the English Mystery Plays," *Neophilologus,* XXV (1939–40), 39–48, 194–206, is without value. Louis Cazamian, *The Development of English Humor* (Durham, N.C., 1952), and J. S. P. Tatlock, "Mediaeval Laughter," *Speculum,* XXI (1946), 289–94, are concerned entirely with secular laughter and wit.

2. *Jacob's Well,* ed. Arthur Brandeis, 1900, EETS o.s. 115, p. 221 (18–28). Another version may be found in Mirk, *Festial,* pp. 64–65.

3. *An Alphabet of Tales,* ed. Mary M. Banks, 1904, 1905, EETS o.s. 126, 127, p. 458 (21–25). This tale is headed, "Ridere non debent habentes oculum ad iudicium vltimum"; another says, "Ridere non debent aduertentes pericula mundi" (p. 459).

4. Mirk, *Festial,* pp. 63 (36) to 64 (4). See also *Religious Lyrics of the XIVth Century,* ed. Carleton Brown, rev. G. V. Smithers (Oxford, 1952), lyric No. 27, p. 33 (57–64).

5. *Cursor Mundi,* p. 1080 (18855–56). [Cotton MS.]

6. *Wycliffite Sermon,* p. 226 (19–20). Susie I. Tucker, "Laughter in Old English Literature," *Neophilologus,* XLIII (1959), 225–26, identifies the source of this tradition in a thirteenth-century forgery known as the *Letter of Lentulus,* which claimed to furnish an eye-witness description of Christ, and included this detail. The silence of the Gospels about this matter made such a conclusion possible.

7. See, for instance, *Wycliffite Sermon,* p. 238 (12–13), pp. 241 (25) to 242 (2).

8. Bartholomeus Anglicus, *De proprietatibus rerum,* V, xli (fol. 61). Beatrice White, "Mediaeval Mirth," *Anglia,* LXXVIII (1960), 285, uses this same example.

9. From Notker Labeo's *De partibus logicae* and *De definitione,* quoted in Helen Adolph, "On Mediaeval Laughter," *Speculum,* XXII (1947), 251.

10. *Ibid.,* p. 252.

11. St. Hildegard of Bingen, in the twelfth century, developed this notion in a most remarkable way; see Boas, *Essays on Primitivism,* p. 77.

12. *Ratis Raving and Other Moral and Religious Pieces,* ed. J. Rawson Lumby, 1870, EETS o.s. 43, p. 80 (103–6). See also the advice given by Solicitudo to Mankind in *The Castell of Perseverance* (*Macro Plays,* p. 126, ll. 1653–56), and *Minor Poems of the Vernon MS.,* p. 534 (177–80).

13. *The Rule of St. Benet,* ed. Ernst A. Kock, 1902, EETS o.s. 120, p. 77 (1063–70).

14. Pecock, *The Reule of Crysten Religioun,* p. 394.

15. *Chartularium Universitatis Parisiensis,* ed. Henri Denifle, IV (Paris, 1897), 653.

16. *Alphabet of Tales,* pp. 5–6.

17. Robert Henryson, *The Poems and Fables,* ed. H. Harvey Wood (2d ed.; Edinburgh, 1958), p. 3 (19–28).

18. *A Hundred Mery Talys,* pp. 93–103.

19. *Ibid.,* p. 103.

20. Cited by G. R. Owst, *Preaching in Medieval England* (Cambridge, 1926), p. 185.

21. *York Memorandum Book,* II, 124. The Masons also complained that this play often had to be performed after nightfall.

22. *York,* p. xxvii. See also the note to this entry: it seems that *Fergus* was later revived from time to time, possibly in an altered form. The editor apparently did not know of the Masons' 1431 request to be released from the play.

23. Mirk, *Festial,* p. 223 (23–32). The source is probably "The Discourse of St. John the Divine," printed in the *Apocryphal New Testament,* p. 208; the Jew is there called Jephonias.

24. Chambers, OHEL, p. 14, Owst, *Literature and Pulpit,* pp. 483, 485, and G. G. Coulton, *Medieval Panorama* (Cambridge, 1938), p. 96, have all mentioned it briefly. It survives in six manuscripts and several printed editions (Pynson in 1493, Wynkyn de Worde in 1496, and Berthelet in 1536). Bibliographical information may be found in articles by H. G. Pfander, "Dives et Pauper," in *The Library,* Fourth Ser., XIV (1934), 299–312; and H. G. Richardson, "Dives and Pauper" in the same periodical, XV (1935), 31–37. Pfander's belief that the author was a Franciscan friar seems to me to survive Richardson's doubts.

25. *Diues et Pauper,* Precept 3, chap. 17. I have expanded the usual printer's contractions.

26. *Ibid.,* Precept 3, chap. 18. The Wycliffite preacher also closes with this example of David and Michol as an example of proper play, but his description of the incident emphasizes only David's humility in submitting to scorn for God's sake; there is no sense of pleasure involved. *Wycliffite Sermon,* p. 242 (6–22).

27. Adam, after 900-odd wearisome years of life, learns that at last he can die, and then laughs for the first time, in *Cursor Mundi,* p. 88 (1399–1402) [Cotton MS]: "Quen he herd he suld liue namare, / þan he logh, bot neuer are."

28. Rossiter, *English Drama,* pp. 38, 74.

29. *Mediaeval Stage,* I, 274–371; II, 279–87.

30. *Wakefield Pageants,* p. xxiv.

31. *Mediaeval Stage,* I, 287–88.

32. *Ibid.,* p. 294.

33. *Ibid.,* p. 305.

34. *Ibid.,* pp. 321–23.

35. *Ibid.,* I, 340–70, and II, 282–87 (where the Sarum Office for the feast is printed). See also Enid Welsford, *The Fool* (London, 1935), p. 201, where much the same conclusion is reached.

36. *Mediaeval Stage,* I, 342–43.

37. *Meditations on the Life and Passion of Christ,* p. 38 (1447–48).

38. *Chester,* p. 7 (138–41).

39. The Towneley Cain's mocking of God's voice may offer an exception; it is difficult to estimate how a medieval audience would have responded to it.

40. The York *Nativity* has no midwife in the text as it stands, though an "obstetrix" was included in the Burton 1415 description of the play. *York*, p. xxi.

41. *Apocryphal New Testament*, pp. 45, 74. For English social background to this trial, see George C. Homans, *English Villagers of the Thirteenth Century* (Cambridge, Mass., 1942), p. 169.

42. Rossiter, *English Drama*, p. 71.

43. *The Book of the Knight of La Tour-Landry*, ed. Thomas Wright, rev. 1906, EETS o.s. 33, p. 42 (4–11). For other versions see *Handlyng Synne*, pp. 290–92, and (with St. Augustine substituted for St. Brice) those in *The Lay Folks Mass Book*, pp. 136–38, and in *Minor Poems of the Vernon MS.*, pp. 501–2. A misericord in Ely Cathedral illustrates the story; see M. D. Anderson, *Drama and Imagery*, pp. 173–74.

44. Dante, *Inferno*, XXXIII (148–50). I quote the translation by Dorothy L. Sayers published by Penguin Books (Harmondsworth, 1949), p. 282.

45. *The Ancrene Riwle*, trans. M. B. Salu (London, 1955), p. 82. For other statements, equally interesting, expressing this general idea, see Pecock, *Reule of Chrysten Religioun*, pp. 148–49, and *Miroure of Mans Saluacionne*, p. 138.

46. *The Pricke of Conscience*, ed. Richard Morris (Berlin, 1863), p. 78 (2844–47). See also *Speculum Christiani*, ed. Gustaf Holmstedt, 1933, EETS o.s. 182, p. 120 (24–26); *Minor Poems of the Vernon MS.*, p. 500 (265–76); *Cursor Mundi*, p. 1334 (23333–50). R. M. Lumiansky has studied the function of the damned alewife in "Comedy and Theme in the Chester *Harrowing of Hell*," *Tulane Studies in English*, X (1960), 5–12.

47. Young, II, 243–44.

48. *Ibid.*, p. 175.

49. *Chester*, p. 95 (233–36).

50. *Ludus Coventriae*, pp. 19 (79–82), 27 (349–56).

CHAPTER SEVEN

The Invention of Comic Action

1. Since I first wrote this chapter, two essays concerning the Towneley *Noah* have appeared, which reach conclusions similar to those offered here. Because my analysis of the play is part of a larger argument and because it differs in certain particulars from these others, I have let my pages stand. See Alan H. Nelson, " 'Sacred' and 'Secular' Currents in the Towneley Play of Noah," *Drama Survey*, III (1964), 393–401, and Howard H. Schless, "The Comic Element in the Wakefield Noah," in *Studies in Medieval Literature*, ed. MacEdward Leach (Philadelphia, 1961), pp. 229–43.

2. Woolf, "Typology," p. 805.

3. Geoffrey Chaucer, *Works*, ed. F. N. Robinson (2d ed.; London, 1957), pp. 51–52 (3538–43).

4. Domestic brawling, in which the wife is shown beating the husband, was a common subject of misericord carving in English churches. For illustrations, see M. D. Anderson, *The Choir Stalls of Lincoln Minster* (London, 1951), Fig. 20, and the same author's *Misericords* (Penguin Books, 1954), Pl. 43.

5. *Purity,* ed. Robert J. Menner (New Haven, 1920), p. 12 (251–52).

6. See *Towneley,* pp. 23 (15–23), 3 (77–81), 4 (94–98), 25 (76–77, 91–92), 26 (110, 120–21).

7. *York,* pp. 41 (33–34), 43 (104).

8. Chapter 10 will examine this in greater detail, with learned evidence.

9. In *Sammlung Altenglischer Legenden,* ed. C. Horstmann (Heilbronn, 1878), p. 222 (25).

10. *Chester,* p. 33 (317–20). See also *York,* pp. 33–34 (135–54).

11. See also *Miroure of Mans Saluacionne,* p. 13, and *Altenglische Legenden, Neue Folge,* ed. C. Horstmann (Heilbronn, 1881), p. 351 (150–53).

12. *The Early English Carols,* ed. Richard L. Greene (Oxford, 1935), No. 407, pp. 272–73.

13. *Chester,* p. 52 (109–12). See also Lydgate, *The Minor Poems,* II, 457–60 (29–119), for a full-scale satire.

14. *Non-Cycle Plays,* p. 22 (100–102).

15. *Ibid.,* p. 23 (121–23). This use of the devil is unique in the dramatic versions and makes the Newcastle Play inferior in suggestiveness to the others. Anna Jean Mill, "Noah's Wife Again," *PMLA,* LVI (1941), 613–26, lists a great many analogues from foreign folktales and other religions, none really relevant to the English drama except perhaps the illuminations in *Queen Mary's Psalter,* discussed on pp. 620–21. See, too, Marvin A. Owings, *The Arts in the Middle English Romances* (New York, 1952), plate facing p. 128.

16. *Towneley,* p. 33 (354–60).

17. *Ibid.,* p. 35 (409).

18. *Ibid.,* p. 33 (343–47).

19. *Ibid.,* p. 35 (415–23). That the Wakefield Master was capable of using an easy repetition of words to carry a weight of meaning is clear also in the *Secunda Pastorum,* where the mock-adoration of the sheep is related to the true adoration of the Infant Christ by having a shepherd address both sheep and Christ as "lytyll day starne." *Towneley,* pp. 134 (577), 139 (727).

20. St. Augustine, *De Genesi contra Manichaeos,* in Migne, *Patrologia Latina,* vol. 34, col. 190.

21. *Stanzaic Life of Christ,* pp. 37–38 (1105–16).

22. The Mak episode of Towneley II will not be discussed in detail here. The reader is referred to Homer A. Watt, "The Dramatic Unity of the 'Secunda Pastorum,' " in *Essays and Studies in Honor of Carleton Brown* (New York, 1940), pp. 158–66, and the notes to lines 442 and 577 of the play in *Wakefield Pageants,* pp. 110–11. Alan H. Nelson's study of the Mak episode, now in progress, promises to throw much new light on its meaning. Neither the Mak episode nor that of the Fools of Gotham is "invented," merely used. Both probably derive from folktales.

23. *Chester,* pp. 133 (11–16), 135 (77–82).

24. *Mirrour of the Blessed Lyf of Jesu Christ,* p. 7. Augustine is credited as source.

25. *Stanzaic Life of Christ,* p. 208 (6133–36).

26. *Golden Legend,* I, 32.

27. See also Mirk, *Festial,* p. 23 (27–30); *Religious Lyrics of the XVth Century,* ed. Carleton Brown (Oxford, 1939), pp. 215 (13–14), 275 (61–69); *Golden Legend,* I, 9, 12; a Kentish sermon in *Selections from Early Middle English, 1130–1250,* ed. Joseph Hall (Oxford, 1920), I, 219–20; William Langland, *Piers the Plowman. in Three Parallel Texts,* ed. Walter W. Skeat (Oxford, repr. with Bibliographical additions, 1954), I, 487 (C-text, XIX, 138 ff.); *Cursor Mundi,* p. 862 (15063–64); *Meditations on the Life and Passion of Christ,* p. 33 (1241–44); and Lydgate, *The Minor Poems,* I, 241 (97–104). For a supremely beautiful modern use of the metaphor, see T. S. Eliot's *Four Quartets,* East Coker IV: "The wounded surgeon plies the steel," etc.

28. *Cornish Drama,* II, 125 (1632, 1648, 1651–52).

29. *Ludus Coventriae,* pp. 238–39 (222–51).

30. *Chester,* pp. 210–11 (158–72).

31. *Ibid.,* p. 214 (253–54).

32. *Ibid.,* p. 230 (18–28).

33. *Ibid.,* p. 150 (441–42).

34. Stephen Manning, *Wisdom and Number* (Lincoln, Neb., 1962), p. 156.

35. *Lay Folks Mass Book,* Appendix III, p. 125 (18–22). See also Lydgate, *The Minor Poems,* I, 41 (182–84).

36. In the York cycle, after the death of Mary, Thomas describes the work he and the other disciples perform; among their activities is this: "For þat laboure is lufsome, ilke lede for to leche" (p. 490, l. 302).

37. *Chester,* p. 158 (619–26).

38. *Ibid.,* pp. 158–59 (627–44).

39. *Ludus Coventriae,* p. 150 (119–34) also has Joseph charge them to testify, an idea that had found earlier expression in the Latin drama of the Church as well. The Towneley play clearly trades upon the notion that the shepherds were types or figures of the later exegetes who would find Christ in Holy Scripture, thereby allowing them (in Towneley I) long learned prophecies of the Messiah, more suitable to the exegete-shepherd (clerk) than to plain herdsmen. See *Wakefield Pageants,* note to line 332, pp. 102–3. The incongruity is made the subject of comedy, *Towneley,* p. 112 (386–92).

40. *Old English Homilies of the Twelfth Century, Second Series,* p. 41.

41. *The Southern Passion,* ed. Beatrice D. Brown, 1927, EETS o.s. 169, p. 82 (2250–54).

42. *Chester,* pp. 140 (189–96), 141 (213–16).

43. *Ibid.,* pp. 142–45 (239–310).

44. For more on this custom, see J. M. J. Fletcher, *The Boy Bishop at Salisbury and Elsewhere* (Salisbury, 1921).

45. In *Altenglische Legenden,* ed. C. Horstmann (Paderborn, 1875), pp. 84–85 (399–403).

46. *Chester,* p. 108 (97–100); *Ludus Coventriae,* p. 119 (92–93); *Towneley,* p. 99 (67–69); *York,* p. 101 (sung at the end of the play).

47. *Ludus Coventriae,* p. 158 (219–22).

48. *Towneley,* p. 155 (475–78).

49. *Chester,* p. 168 (193–96); see also p. 174 (350–57).

50. *Chester,* p. 144 (299–300).

51. *Ibid.,* p. 142 (237–40).

52. *Ibid.,* p. 143 (257).

53. *Towneley,* pp. 103–6 (101–90). The Mak subplot, essentially a parallel adoration, may be related to this theme as well: there is a quarrel over the deception, culminating in a merciful judgment (the strict justice for sheep stealing was death).

54. *Ibid.,* p. 106 (180). See also Millicent Carey, *The Wakefield Group in the Towneley Cycle* (Göttingen, 1930), pp. 171–73.

55. The "pagan" and "ritual" critics alone make something of it, grasping at the fact that the shepherds quarrel over a flock of imaginary sheep after the First Shepherd has stated that all his sheep are dead, and that he is going to the fair to buy a new flock. Making this the central point of the episode, they say winter dearth is here seen turning to spring plenty, etc. A close reading of the text suggests to me that the quarrel is simply a mock-quarrel among friends amusing themselves, even though it later leads to blows. The crucial point is the First Shepherd's speech, p. 106 (188 ff.) in which he asks the boy "How are *our* sheep" and the boy says they are well and in richly grassed pasture. Now this is very surprising (no one seems ever to have noticed it): the shepherd apparently *has* sheep—they have been in the boy's keeping all along. In Towneley II, the flocks are also kept by the boy, and the pasture is as good (pp. 121–22, ll. 177–81). These facts suggest that the "Fools of Gotham" action is included for the sake of its "play" quarrel, just as the wrestling is done in a "play" sequence of discord, struggle, and deposition.

56. *Speculum sacerdotale,* p. 5 (27–30). See also *Ancrene Riwle,* p. 110.

57. Mirk, *Festial,* p. 21 (22–24).

58. *Early English Carols,* No. 21 (C), p. 15; see also No. 42, p. 28, and No. 66, p. 41.

59. *Chester,* p. 145 (305–10).

60. *Ibid.,* p. 159 (648–50).

61. *Towneley,* p. 137 (641).

62. *Two Coventry Plays,* p. 9.

63. Carey, *Wakefield Group,* p. 134.

64. *Chester,* pp. 137 (133), 138 (141).

65. Carey, *Wakefield Group,* p. 163.

66. A. C. Cawley, "The 'Grotesque' Feast in the *Prima Pastorum*," *Speculum,* XXX (1955), 213–17.

67. Cawley, (*ibid.,* p. 215), plays with the idea that the Towneley feast may be imaginary, because one of the shepherds says they won't need spoons for eating it. But this is surely far-fetched: as Cawley himself admits, the obvious

interpretation is that they will use their fingers; Chester shows that such pasture feasts were in fact staged.

68. See the article on "Advent" in *Lexikon für Theologie und Kirche,* ed. Joseph Höfer and Karl Rahner (2d ed.; Freiburg, 1957——), cols. 160–61.

69. See John T. McNeill and Helena M. Gamer, *Medieval Handbooks of Penance* (New York, 1938), pp. 212 (and n. 164), 227; *Stanzaic Life of Christ,* p. 171 (5073–104); *Golden Legend,* I, 7.

70. *Speculum sacerdotale,* pp. 74 (23–31), 62 (18–19), 76 (2–6); also p. 75 (17–22 and 30–34).

71. *Ibid.,* pp. 90 (19–24), 91 (6–11), 7 (8–10). For a similar statement of the seasons, see *Golden Legend,* I, 64.

72. *Speculum sacerdotale,* p. 53 (3–18).

73. *Early English Carols,* No. 3, pp. 4–5. The manuscript credits this carol to James Ryman, a Franciscan, and author of many other known pieces. The editor queries this attribution in his notes, and I concur in his judgment that Ryman's talents, which ran to dogged, banal works of piety, could never have produced this carol. It is difficult to tell precisely what audience it has in mind: stanza 14 (not quoted above) seems to indicate it is spoken on behalf of the laity, but the matter is not clear. Its provenance is apparently Kentish. See also No. 4, p. 5, for a fragment of a similar carol, also comparing Advent to Lent.

74. Ben Jonson, *Complete Works,* ed. C. H. Herford and Percy Simpson (Oxford, 1925–52), VII, 440.

75. *Speculum sacerdotale,* p. 62 (25–27).

76. Francis Bond, *Wood Carvings in English Churches. Misericords* (London, 1910), p. 127, mentions carvings of December feasting scenes in Burnham and York, and Christopher Woodforde, *The Norwich School of Glass-Painting in the Fifteenth Century* (London, 1950), gives examples of feasting in both December and January, in Books of Hours and in glass, pp. 149–50 (n. 3), and pp. 150, 155–57. January is usually represented as the month of feasting, rather than December, no doubt because December is mostly a time of fasting, whereas the Christmas feasting goes on until the Epiphany, with the meat stocks lasting well beyond. See also James Fowler, "On Mediaeval Representations of the Months and Seasons," *Archaeologia,* XLIV (1873), 137–224, especially the summary tables printed on pp. 190–92.

77. Homans, *English Villagers of the Thirteenth Century,* p. 357. For the belief that in the East, the home of the Magi, men set out on Christmas Day enough food to last until Twelfth Night, see *The Three Kings of Cologne,* ed. C. Horstmann, 1886, EETS o.s. 85, p. 140 (10–18).

78. Homans, *English Villagers,* p. 357. The character of "Christmas" in Thomas Nashe's *Summer's Last Will and Testament* (1600) is a mean, modern sort who defends his refusal to hold a Christmas feast for common men thus: "To feede the poore twelue dayes, & let them starue all the yeare after, would but stretch out the guts wider then they should be, & so make famine a bigger den in their bellies than he had before." Thomas Nashe, *Works,* ed. Ronald B. McKerrow (Oxford, repr. 1958), III, 285 (1641–44).

79. *Early English Carols,* No. 135, p. 93.

80. Quoted by Homans, *English Villagers,* p. 358.

81. Quoted by Rupert H. Morris, *Chester in the Plantagenet and Tudor Reigns* (Chester [1895]), item no. 88a, pp. 336–37. He does not date the document precisely.

82. *Missale ad usum ... Sarum,* col. 48.

83. In *Legends of the Holy Rood,* ed. Richard Morris, 1871, EETS o.s. 46, p. 211 (33–45). See also Lydgate, *The Minor Poems,* I, 41 (185–92).

84. *Golden Legend,* I, 141–42.

85. See *Chester,* p. 142 (233–36).

86. *Towneley,* pp. 100 (1–9), 120 (127–30).

87. *Old English Homilies of the Twelfth Century, Second Series,* p. 33.

88. In *Religious Pieces in Prose and Verse (Thornton MS),* p. 42 (13–14).

89. *Mirrour of the Blessed Lyf of Jesu Christ,* p. 48.

90. *Towneley,* p. 138 (685–87). See also *Ludus Coventriae,* p. 148 (64–65).

91. *York,* pp. 112–13 (15–53).

92. *Towneley,* pp. 112–13 (398–403). The EETS edition reads "Samyne," erroneously. I have followed Cawley's reading of the manuscript as "Saturne" (translating Virgil's *Saturnia regna*), in his edition of *The Wakefield Pageants.*

93. Lydgate, *The Minor Poems,* II, p. 674 (57–58, 74–75). Nevill Coghill called my attention to this mumming. Wickham, *Early English Stages* I, 199–200, discusses other aspects of it.

94. Carey, *Wakefield Group,* pp. 114–15.

95. *Non-Cycle Plays,* p. 2 (29–32).

96. *Holkham Bible Picture Book,* notes, p. 90, and fol. 13. Shepherds from the south of Italy, called *zampognari,* still come north at Christmas to play bagpipes in the streets of such cities as Milan, Florence, and Rome.

97. *Towneley,* pp. 113, 137. See Nan C. Carpenter, "Music in the *Secunda Pastorum,*" *Speculum,* XXVI (1951), 696–700, for a detailed technical study of the terms and types of music involved.

98. *Chester,* p. 149 (411–18).

99. *Towneley,* p. 137 (659–64).

100. Richard Rolle de Hampole, *English Prose Treatises,* ed. George G. Perry, 1866, 1921, EETS o.s. 20, p. 17 (4–7); cited in notes to the *Holkham Bible Picture Book,* p. 90. The *Holkham* shepherds also sing "glum glo" and their song is described in English, though the work is otherwise in Anglo-Norman.

101. *Towneley,* p. 113 (424–25).

102. *Chester,* p. 158 (617–22).

103. *Two Coventry Plays,* pp. 15–16 (446–51). One of the Norwich Cathedral roof bosses shows the shepherds leaving the stable, a curious subject for the visual arts; it may indicate a close relationship to drama traditions. See Anderson, *Drama and Imagery,* p. 95.

104. *Religious Lyrics of the XVth Century,* pp. 115–16 (17–24). See also "The Mirror of St. Edmund" in *Religious Pieces in Prose and Verse (Thornton MS),* p. 42 (20–23).

105. Samuel B. Hemingway, *English Nativity Plays* (New York, 1909), p. xv.
106. G. K. Chesterton, "The Architect of Spears," in *Selected Essays,* ed. Dorothy Collins (London, 1949), pp. 178–79.

CHAPTER EIGHT

The Passion and Resurrection in Play and Game

1. Walter Oakeshott, *The Sequence of English Medieval Art* (London, 1950), p. 20; see also Rosemary Woolf, "Doctrinal Influences on *The Dream of the Rood*," *Med. Aev.*, XXVII (1958), 145; and for a good eleventh-century example, see *Early Medieval Illumination,* intro. Hans Swarenzenski (New York, 1951), Pl. XV.
2. Young, I, 492.
3. *Ibid.,* p. 502. This is from one of the poems printed by Young as most closely approaching dramatic form.
4. *Ibid.,* pp. 514–16, 518–33. The Italian fragment is described on p. 537.
5. *Ibid.,* p. 532.
6. *The Northern Passion (Supplement)*, ed. Wilhelm Heuser and Frances A. Foster, 1930, EETS o.s. 183, p. 77 (1029–32).
7. *Cursor Mundi,* pp. 948 (16629–30), 954 (16715–16). [Cotton MS.]
8. *Towneley,* p. 249 (179–87). See the entire section, pp. 248–50.
9. *Ibid.,* pp. 245 (74), 248 (150–51).
10. *Stanzaic Life of Christ,* p. 186 (5541–48).
11. *Towneley,* p. 267 (284–86).
12. *Ibid.,* p. 233 (166).
13. *York,* p. 261 (184–85).
14. *Ibid.,* p. 280 (235, 237).
15. *Ibid.,* p. 261 (192).
16. *Ibid.,* pp. 295 (82–83), 296 (120–21, 112–13).
17. *Ibid.,* p. 265 (290–91).
18. *Ibid.,* p. 263 (245).
19. *Ibid.,* p. 266 (310–29). See also *Ludus Coventriae,* p. 275 (118–21).
20. *York,* pp. 297 (148), 298 (164–65); see also p. 300 (230).
21. *Ibid.,* pp. 298 (186), 301 (245). Jesus' silence before Herod is termed "a false sotylte" in *Ludus Coventriae,* p. 285 (421).
22. *York,* p. 301 (263).
23. The *Miroure of Mans Saluacionne,* p. 73, also describes this as done by Herod "in his japes." See, too, *Ludus Coventriae,* p. 287 (475).
24. *York,* p. 308 (43).
25. *Ibid.,* p. 224 (117).
26. *Ibid.,* p. 286 (387).
27. *Cornish Drama,* I, 301 (999–1001).
28. *York,* p. 267 (332–33).
29. In *Towneley,* Christ's sabbath healing is called a "bowrdyng" (p. 207,

l. 117); it is said He must stop His "gawdys" (p. 209, l. 153); and Judas describes Christ's acceptance of the precious ointment as "his bowrdyng" (p. 211, ll. 228 ff.).

30. *York*, p. 267 (358); *Ludus Coventriae*, p. 277 (170); *Towneley*, p. 239 (344). See also *Wakefield Pageants*, p. 121.

31. This illumination is reproduced in *Medieval England*, ed. Austin L. Poole (Oxford, 1958), II, Pl. 134a, facing p. 615.

32. W. L. Hildburgh, *English Alabaster Carvings*, Pl. XVIIa.

33. Quoted in Owst, *Literature and Pulpit in Medieval England*, p. 510. The manuscript corrects "biliried" to "byrlyryhode" in the margin.

34. See, for instance, *Religious Lyrics of the XVth Century*, p. 19 (33–36).

35. *Ludus Coventriae*, p. 277 (168–72).

36. *York*, p. 268 (372).

37. *Ibid.*, p. 269 (383–86). In *Ludus Coventriae*, p. 286 (450), Herod stops the scourging because he thinks Jesus is finding it "good game."

38. *York*, p. 338 (27–28).

39. Hildburgh, *English Alabaster Carvings*, p. 81 and Pl. XVIIb. He argues for a very close relationship between alabaster carvings and the cycle-drama.

40. *Cornish Drama*, I, 433–39. *The Northern Passion (Supplement)*, pp. 116–17 (2547–604), includes this action in a straightforward way, without the joking, playful quality of the drama.

41. *Towneley*, p. 240 (370–88).

42. See Émile Mâle, *L'Art Religieux de la Fin du Moyen Age en France* (5th ed.; Paris, 1949), p. 90. It is worth noting that this detail had passed into a gospel harmony edited as "The Middle English *Evangelie*" by Gertrude H. Campbell, *PMLA*, XXX (1915), 601 (1482–89).

43. *Digby*, p. 216 (1341–47).

44. *Chester*, p. 304 (561–64, 569–72).

45. *Ibid.*, p. 305 (585–88). *The Southern Passion*, following a tradition deriving from the *Meditationes* attributed to Bonaventura, describes Christ crucified by use of ladders on a cross previously erected (p. 53, ll. 1459–61). The drama never follows this tradition.

46. *York*, p. 355 (188–204).

47. *Ibid.*, p. 356 (213).

48. *Towneley*, p. 263 (167–68).

49. *Chester*, p. 303 (533–36). See also the York *Christ Led up to Calvary*, in which the executioners temporarily forget their assigned task in order to engage in a contest of abuse with the lamenting Marys. *York*, p. 344 (211–20).

50. *Southern Passion*, p. 55 (1499–1502).

51. *Towneley*, p. 242 (427–32). Cawley, *Wakefield Pageants*, pp. 122–23, would emend "crate" to "trate," meaning "old woman." See also p. 228 (1–2). On p. 257 (416) the carrying of the cross to Calvary is called a "chace."

52. *Towneley*, pp. 260 (83–85), 261 (89–92).

53. *Ibid.*, pp. 261 (101–18), 264 (200–202). *Ludus Coventriae*, pp. 302–3

(887–90) includes a brief verbal joke: the *tortores* pretend they have set up a scarecrow to frighten ravens from cornfields.

54. *Towneley*, p. 293 (9–10). Williams, *The Drama of Medieval England*, p. 129, has also noticed the serious meaning involved in this joke-figure.

55. In *Legends of the Holy Rood*, p. 148 (518–20).

56. First printed by Rosemary Woolf, "The Theme of Christ the Lover-Knight in Medieval English Literature," *RES*, XIII (1962), 12. She thinks the vernacular phrases in the sermon suggest an English version known to the author. Christ explains his "armoure" to Mary Magdalene in *York*, p. 424 (94–105).

57. *Towneley*, p. 300 (225–32).

58. See *Chester*, p. 184 (197–200), for example.

59. Woolf, "The Theme of Christ the Lover-Knight," pp. 1–3, possibly understates its currency and importance in her interest in an associated theme.

60. See Wilbur Gaffney, "The Allegory of the Christ-Knight in *Piers Plowman*," *PMLA*, XLVI (1931), 158–60.

61. Langland, *Piers the Plowman*, I, 520–22 (B-text, XVIII, 10–35); see also p. 490 (160–66), p. 524 (78–87), which has Longinus "joust" against Jesus, and p. 530 (179).

62. *Death and Liffe*, ed. James H. Hanford and John M. Steadman, Jr., *SP*, XV (1918), 273 (367–72) and ff. The date of the poem is discussed on pp. 231–32; for evidence that the author knew *Piers the Plowman*, see pp. 246–48.

63. *York*, p. 244 (89–90). Miss Toulmin Smith glosses "turnement" as "? *for* torment." She may be right, but it is possible, as I have shown, that the MS reading is intended.

64. See, for example, *Religious Lyrics of the XIVth Century*, p. 28 (5–6), p. 67 (11–14), and p. 82, No. 63; *Religious Lyrics of the XVth Century*, p. 141 (35–40); *Middle English Sermons*, pp. 37 (32) to 38 (36); Lydgate, *The Minor Poems*, I, 219 (57–64), 251 (41–48); the Anglo-Norman *Livre de Seyntz Medicines*, quoted in Pantin, *The English Church in the Fourteenth Century*, p. 232; *Meditations on the Life and Passion of Christ*, p. 42 (1573–1604); William Dunbar, *The Poems*, ed. W. Mackay Mackenzie (London, 1932), pp. 159–60 (1–40).

65. See *The Middle English Harrowing of Hell and Gospel of Nicodemus*, ed. William H. Hulme, 1908, EETS e.s. 100, p. 3 (1–8); and *York*, p. 498 (33–36). The *Judgment* is also defined as a contest or fight, *ibid.*, p. 505 (217–18).

66. *Cornish Drama*, I, 465 (3067–69).

67. *Ludus Coventriae*, p. 306 (1010–14); see also l. 997.

68. *York*, pp. 380 (139–44), 382 (178–80).

69. Satan is bound and cast into hell pit, pp. 391–92 (335–48).

70. Hildburgh, *English Alabaster Carvings*, Pls. XXIa and XXId offer useful examples; see also C. J. P. Cave, *Roof Bosses in Medieval Churches* (Cambridge, 1948), Fig. 193. Adolf Katzenellenbogen, *Allegories of the Virtues and Vices in Mediaeval Art* (London, 1939), Pls. X and XI, shows the same device applied to moral allegory: the Virtues stand triumphant with the Vices under their

feet. The resurrected Christ stands so on Herod himself in an altarpiece by Giovanni del Biondo, reproduced in Millard Meiss, *Painting in Florence and Siena after the Black Death* (Princeton, 1951), Pl. 68; see also Pls. 69 and 71 for Vices again prostrate in defeat.

71. *York*, p. 406.

72. *Chester*, pp. 341 (274–77), 339 (228–29).

73. *Ludus Coventriae*, p. 267 (1035–36).

74. *Ibid.*, p. 265.

75. *Ibid.*, p. 297.

76. "The Middle English *Evangelie*," pp. 598 (1328–32), 601–2 (1506–10).

77. Richard Rolle de Hampole, *The Psalter or Psalms of David and Certain Canticles. With a Translation and Exposition in English,* ed. H. R. Bramley (Oxford, 1884), p. 57 (16:12).

78. *Meditations on the Life and Passion of Christ,* p. 37 (1393–94).

79. *Towneley*, p. 197 (77–84). John goes on to draw a contemporary moral: children should be brought to church for baptism. But chiefly this serves to prevent the Baptist from seeking Christ before Christ is ready to come to him.

80. *Chester*, p. 232 (56–59). This is based on John 9: 1–3.

81. *Chester*, p. 351 (520–25).

82. *Southern Passion*, p. 3 (68).

83. *Chester*, p. 277 (305–12). The longer of the two Passion plays in the Benediktbeuern manuscript also uses the John version. See Young, I, 526.

84. *Ludus Coventriae*, p. 265 (973–96).

85. Young, I, 514. He writes, p. 517, "The playwright's reason for altering this sequence of events is not obvious." The explanation I propose above seems to me most likely.

86. *Northern Passion (Supplement)*, pp. 68–69 (688–704).

87. *York*, p. 251 ff., and pp. 325–29. The incident of the banners dipping in reverence is based on the Gospel of Nichodemus; see *Apocryphal New Testament*, pp. 97–98. Williams, *The Drama of Medieval England*, p. 81, writes of this whole event, "Dramatically, this is waste motion—it makes no point, and the outcome of the trial is unaffected by the incident." (See also p. 124.) My reading makes another judgment possible.

88. *York*, p. 351 (75–76).

89. *Religious Lyrics of the XIVth Century,* p. 85 (17–20). Printed also in *Early English Carols* as No. 157, in four versions.

90. *Chester*, pp. 98–100, summarized by *Expositor*, pp. 101–2; and *ibid.*, pp. 182–83, especially ll. 169–80.

91. Discussed by Réau, *Iconographie,* I, 260.

92. *Ludus Coventriae*, p. 288 (507–10). See also *Stanzaic Life of Christ,* p. 323 (9561–64).

93. *Religious Lyrics of the XVth Century,* p. 133 (49–52). For an alternate critical account of these plays, sensitive and interesting, see Waldo F. McNeir, "The Corpus Christi Passion Plays as Dramatic Art," *SP*, XLVIII (1951), 601–28.

CHAPTER NINE

Natural Man and Evil

1. *Chester,* p. 444 (489–92).
2. The exceptions are few: some cycles allow brief councils in hell, and *Ludus Coventriae* stages a Parliament of Heaven; all cycles present a Harrowing of Hell, the sole point of which is Christ's victory—hell's torments are not displayed. In this drama, heaven and hell are chiefly places where strategy on earth is planned.
3. Wickham, *Early English Stages,* I, 315.
4. Young, II, 117. Rachel is important as a figure of Mary, just as the Innocents figure Christ. See *Religious Lyrics of the XIVth Century,* p. 48 (53–54).
5. Young, II, 106.
6. *Ibid.,* p. 111.
7. *Ibid.,* p. 113. The Compiègne text is printed on pp. 53–56. In the late Christmas play from Benediktbeuern, Rachel does not appear, and the natural mothers are given a long formal lament, but there is no realism as such: see p. 189. See also Anderson, *Drama and Imagery,* p. 97.
8. *Chester,* p. 117 (325–44). See also Capgrave, *Chronicle of England,* p. 58.
9. Quoted in *O.E.D.,* "natural" (sense 4a). In earlier translations, *animalis ... homo* was usually rendered as "beestely man"; see *The Pauline Epistles,* ed. Margaret J. Powell, 1916, EETS e.s. 116, p. 56; and *A Fourteenth Century English Biblical Version,* ed. Anna C. Paues (Cambridge, 1904), p. 58 (which reads "bestych man"). See *York,* p. 15 (22) as well. The chapter on "Nature" in C. S. Lewis, *Studies in Words* (Cambridge, 1960), is of great interest.
10. Quoted in Boas, *Primitivism,* p. 84.
11. *York,* p. 293 (17).
12. *Cornish Drama,* II, 169 (2249–52).
13. *Towneley,* p. 20 (393).
14. *Cornish Drama,* I, 421 (2507–12).
15. *Ibid.,* pp. 407–9 (2319–24).
16. *Northern Passion* (Supplement), p. 67 (635–36).
17. *Ludus Coventriae,* p. 267.
18. *York,* p. 292 (1–6).
19. *Towneley,* p. 258 (1–13).
20. *Ibid.,* p. 285 (193).
21. *Digby,* p. 120 (1734–39).
22. *Towneley,* p. 283 (145–52); see also p. 282 (117–20).
23. *Ludus Coventriae,* p. 14 (444–45).
24. *York,* p. 49 (113–26).
25. *Chester,* p. 283 (85–88). See also *York,* pp. 279 (219–22), 333 (401).
26. *York,* p. 350 (35–36).
27. *Ludus Coventriae,* p. 317 (1316–25).
28. *Digby,* p. 108 (1421–22).

29. *York,* p. 252 (273).

30. Satan, in a fine phrase, describes Christ as "borne of a deadlish woman" and draws the wrong conclusion therefrom, in *Chester,* p. 218 (27).

31. *Cornish Drama,* II, 49 (598–600).

32. *Towneley,* p. 320 (478–81).

33. *Ludus Coventriae,* p. 32 (111–15).

34. *Chester,* p. 85 (25–32). Based on Exodus 20:19.

35. *Digby,* p. 20 (501–2).

36. *Cursor Mundi,* p. 852 (14880–81). [Cotton MS.] T. S. Eliot uses a Chorus of the Women of Canterbury to state these "natural" attitudes in *Murder in the Cathedral.*

37. *Southern Passion,* p. 45 (1235–37).

38. *Speculum Gy de Warewyke,* ed. Georgiana Lea Morrill, 1898, EETS e.s. 75, p. 22 (447–50). See also *Religious Lyrics of the XIVth Century,* p. 226 (32–36) where the same judgment seems implied. Satan in *Ludus Coventriae* says he has marked for hell the "membrys" of those who are playing with Jesus (p. 287, ll. 474–77), but these are very specifically forgiven by Christ later (p. 299, ll. 778–81).

39. *Cornish Drama,* I, 441 (2773–78), 443 (2779).

40. *Ibid.,* I, 453 (2920–21).

41. *Ibid.,* I, 463 (3019–25). The Latin stage direction is on p. 462.

42. *Meditations on the Supper of Our Lord, and the Hours of the Passion,* trans. Robert Manning of Brunne, ed. J. Meadows Cowper, 1875, EETS o.s. 60, p. 27 (855–58).

43. *Mirrour of the Blessed Lyf of Jesu Christ,* p. 246.

44. *Ludus Coventriae,* p. 299 (779).

45. *York,* p. 368 (291–312).

46. See *Towneley,* pp. 267 (290–96), 276 (597–600).

47. *Chester,* p. 309 (699).

48. *Ibid.,* p. 313 (783–84).

49. See especially *Ludus Coventriae,* pp. 290–93, for a brilliant handling of the crowd's role.

50. Richard Lavynham, *A Litil Tretys on the Seven Deadly Sins,* ed. J. P. W. M. van Zutphen (Rome, 1956), p. 11 (19–25).

51. *Ibid.,* pp. 13–15; also, William of Shoreham, *Poems,* ed. M. Konrath, 1902, EETS e.s. 86, pp. 109–10 (309–24); and *Mirrour of the Blessed Lyf of Jesu Christ,* p. 182. Morton W. Bloomfield, *The Seven Deadly Sins* (East Lansing, 1952), offers a learned study of the tradition.

52. *Ludus Coventriae,* p. 251 (589).

53. *York,* p. 324 (141–44).

54. *Chester,* p. 354 (49–52).

55. *Cornish Drama,* I, 467 (3091–94).

56. *Towneley,* p. 169 (114–21). Herod as an angry man is based on Matthew 2:16.

57. *Ibid.,* pp. 169 (100), 170 (139–40).

58. Mirk, *Instructions for Parish Priests*, pp. 30–32. See also *Speculum Christiani*, p. 58 (13–17).

59. *York*, p. 308 (17–28). The introductory soliloquy, so useful for getting a new episode under way, is often put to this secondary use.

60. *Non-Cycle Plays*, p. 95 (211–12).

61. *Ludus Coventriae* furnishes two unique exceptions: in *The Parliament of Heaven*, Pax, Veritas, Justicia, and Misericordia debate; and in *The Trial of Joseph and Mary*, Raise Slander and Backbiter voice the charges against Mary.

62. *Jacob's Well*, pp. 44 (26) to 45 (5).

63. *Towneley*, pp. 211–13 (240–81); *Chester*, pp. 259–60 (265–96); *York*, pp. 225–26 (127–54).

64. *Ludus Coventriae*, pp. 249–51 (534–85), gives the other apostles effective speeches commenting on the betrayal.

65. *Southern Passion*, p. 51 (1405–6).

66. *Towneley*, p. 303 (328–30).

67. See Lavynham, *A Litil Tretys on the Seven Deadly Sins*, pp. 18 (37) to 19 (4); and "The Middle English *Evangelie*," pp. 596–97 (1271–78). Compare also Mankind shouting "A roppe! a rope! a rope! I am not worthy!" when he hears Mercy is searching for him, in the morality play *Mankind*, in *Chief Pre-Shakespearean Dramas*, p. 321 (793).

68. *York*, p. 226 (157–71).

69. *Queen Mary's Psalter*, ed. George Warner (London, 1912), Pl. 5.

70. *Ratis Raving*, p. 5 (143–45). See also *Ancrene Riwle*, p. 135.

71. *Towneley*, p. 298 (166–71).

72. *Chester*, p. 323 (121–28).

73. *Apocryphal New Testament*, p. 98.

74. *Handlyng Synne*, p. 15 (393–98). He includes three other possible causes: overindulgence in food and drink, too much fasting, and too much study.

75. Allardyce Nicoll, *Masks, Mimes, and Miracles* (London, 1931), pp. 187–88.

76. *Miroure of Mans Saluacionne*, pp. 79–80. See also *Middle English Harrowing of Hell*, p. 34 (two MSS only). *The Northern Passion (Supplement)* has Satan appear in the dream in the guise of an angel, p. 87 (1419–38); Langland, *Piers the Plowman*, I, 540 (B-text, XVIII, 292–303) also attributes the dream to the devil. See also *Hymns to the Virgin & Christ*, pp. 47–48 (209–20). For general background to this question of Satan's role, see the editor's introduction to *The Southern Passion*, pp. lxxii–iv.

77. *Southern Passion*, p. 54 (1484–86). The speech recalls the devil's words when he tempted Christ in the wilderness, on the pinnacle of the temple.

78. *York*, p. 277 (159–76).

79. *Cornish Drama*, I, 445 (2811–16).

80. *Ludus Coventriae*, p. 288 (487–91).

81. *Ibid.*, p. 289 (stage direction and ll. 531–34).

82. *Ibid.*, p. 291 (587–90).

83. Aquinas, *Summa theologica*, III–II, Q. 47, Art. 1, p. 298.

84. For the patristic background, see Williams, *The Characterization of Pilate in the Towneley Plays*, pp. 1–7.

85. *Ibid.*, p. 9, and *Apocryphal New Testament,* p. 157; *The South English Legendary,* pp. 697–706, includes a representative life. Mirk, *Festial,* narrates the whole in a Good Friday sermon, pp. 120–21. *Jacob's Well,* p. 22 (4–5), and *The Northern Passion (Supplement),* p. 90 (1531–32), judge him to be in hell.

86. *Cornish Drama,* II, 133 (1752–54).

87. *Towneley,* p. 244 (31–34).

88. In a Passion shaped into *play* actions, it is good that at least one character other than Jesus be serious, be outside the *game.*

89. Williams, *Characterization of Pilate,* p. 16.

90. *Ibid.,* p. 19.

91. *Ibid.,* p. 23.

92. *Ibid.,* p. 77. This view of the Towneley Pilate is incorporated into Williams' more recent book on the drama, as well: see *The Drama of Medieval England,* pp. 81–82.

93. Aquinas, *Summa theologica,* III–II, Q. 31, Art. 1, p. 53; Q. 1, Art. 4, p. 13.

94. *Ludus Coventriae,* p. 300 (826–27).

95. *Towneley,* p. 266 (279). Earlier, in the Garden of Gethsemane, Trinitas has re-explained the whole redemptive mission to Christ, referring it to Adam's sin (p. 221, ll. 528–55).

96. *York,* pp. 350–51 (49–64).

CHAPTER TEN

Goodness and Natural Man

1. John Fisher, *The English Works,* ed. John E. B. Mayor, 1876, EETS e.s. 27, p. 201 (5–17).

2. See, for instance, the poem "De principio creationis mundi" in *Altenglische Legenden, Neue Folge,* p. 351 (123–24). It is translated from an original by Grosseteste.

3. Quoted in Boas, *Primitivism,* p. 179. See also *York,* p. 469 (129–32).

4. *York,* p. 175 (101–5). See also Deguileville, *Pilgrimage of the Life of Man,* pp. 26–27 (985–92), and *Minor Poems of the Vernon MS.,* p. 180 (263–64).

5. *York,* p. 498 (37–40).

6. *Macro Plays,* e.g., pp. 141 (2135–38), 142 (2174–79), 145 (2277–82).

7. *York,* p. 440 (221). In the *Castell of Perseverance,* Mary is described as a "lessun" to lead a chaste life; see *Macro Plays,* p. 146 (2314–17).

8. It is most often used simply to mean "the favor of God"; after the Annunciation it sometimes occurs in its full theological meaning. It can be used anachronistically, as when the Chester Cain says, "I am damned without grace" (p. 46, l. 666). And the Old Testament "figures" are sometimes so described. About Abraham, for example, is said: "And present hym with bread and wyne / for grace of God is him withine" (*Chester,* p. 65, ll. 61–62). On this matter, see also the pilgrim's conversation with Lady Hagiography, in Deguileville, *Pilgrimage of the Life of Man,* pp. 595–96 (22289–326).

9. *York,* pp. 121 (102–7), 122 (113–19).

10. *Chester,* pp. 90–91 (141–44, 155–60).

11. *York,* p. 345 (246–60).

12. *Chester,* pp. 297–98 (401–24).

13. *Towneley,* pp. 97–98 (13–33).

14. *Ibid.,* pp. 32–33 (328–31).

15. *York,* pp. 143 (173–82), 144 (205–6).

16. *Two Coventry Plays,* p. 45 (363–66).

17. *Chester,* p. 237 (198–99).

18. *York,* p. 62 (209–13).

19. *York,* p. 76 (129–34).

20. *Cornish Drama,* I, 316.

21. *York,* p. 244 (104–7). See also Mirk, *Festial,* p. 45 (29–32), and Woolf, "Typology," p. 815.

22. *Towneley,* pp. 337–38 (7–12).

23. Petrus Comestor, *Historia scholastica,* in Migne, *Patrologia Latina,* Vol. 198, col. 1082.

24. Rabanus Maurus, *Commentariorum in Genesim,* in *ibid.,* Vol. 107, col. 513.

25. Jacques Dupont and Cesare Gnudi, *Gothic Painting* (New York, 1954), p. 148.

26. Paul Biver, "Some Examples of English Alabaster Tables in France," *Archaeological Journal,* LXVII (1910), Pl. XIX. An illumination in British Museum Add. MS. 18192, f. 52, uses the same motif; it has been published as British Museum postcard B2.

27. From a Book of Hours executed for Engelbert of Nassau, MS Douce 219, fol. 133ʳ, published as Bodleian postcard C32.

28. *Chester,* p. 153 (507–16). Joseph's old age is stressed in no less than four of the apocrypha; see C. Philip Deasy, F.S.C., *St. Joseph in the English Mystery Plays* (Washington, D.C., 1937), p. 14.

29. *York,* p. 110 (247–58).

30. The Chester shepherds who hear the announcement of Christ's birth at first think the angel was either a sheep stealer, or (because it was "semelie" and "wondrous defte") a shepherd like themselves; see p. 149 (405–8).

31. Deasy, *St. Joseph,* pp. 17–19.

32. *Ibid.,* pp. 53, 104. I think Father Deasy's study to be otherwise exemplary.

33. *Two Coventry Plays,* pp. 46–48 (423–62).

34. *Ibid.,* p. 48 (463–70, 479–80).

35. Brother Cornelius Luke, *The Rôle of the Virgin Mary in the Coventry, York, Chester and Towneley Cycles* (Washington, D.C., 1933), p. 49, notes in connection with Joseph's doubts that it is his own wretchedness, his lament at having married, and his wrath at the true father of the child that become the focus of his speech and action, never the apparent "guilt" of Mary. So, here, his complaints amount to an extravagant statement of his age and infirmity, made, as it were, for the record.

36. *Two Coventry Plays,* p. 48 (487–94).

37. *Ibid.*, p. 49 (518–21).

38. *Ibid.*, p. 50 (538–45).

39. *Ibid.* (558–60).

40. *Ludus Coventriae*, pp. 136–37 (31–46). This incident, based on the Gospel of Pseudo-Matthew (see *Apocryphal New Testament*, p. 75) is most familiar to modern readers in a harsher form as "The Cherry-Tree Carol." See also *Altenglische Legenden* (1875), pp. 5–7 (89–144).

41. *Two Coventry Plays*, p. 56 (736–37). See also the comment of a doctor in *York*, p. 170 (271–76).

42. *Chester*, p. 61 (317–20).

43. *Ibid.*, p. 53 (149–52). This may be influenced by 2 Peter 3:4–9, where God is credited with a similar slowness in bringing forward the day of Doom (to which the Flood is related as figure). In Mirk, *Festial*, p. 72 (15–20) the motive is transferred to God. But it is significant that in this Flood play the idea is Noah's, and forms no part of his divine instructions.

44. *Chester*, p. 62 (365–68).

45. A resumé and discussion may be found in James G. Frazer, *Folk-lore in the Old Testament* (abridged ed.; London, 1923), pp. 48–66. The latest translation is by N. K. Sandars, *The Epic of Gilgamesh* (Penguin Books, 1960), pp. 105–10.

46. *Cursor Mundi*, p. 100 (1599–1624), finds a devious way out of this embarrassment by saying that when God "rued" that He made man, He intended this as a prophecy of the "ruth" He would have *for* man in His incarnation. The word play is less interesting than the fact that some explanation of God's conduct seemed necessary to the poet.

47. *Purity*, p. 10 (203–4).

48. *Ibid.*, p. 13 (281–85). See the editor's note on this, p. 80.

49. *Ibid.*, p. 14 (302).

50. *Ibid.*, p. 21 (513–20).

51. *Ibid.*, p. 23 (561–62).

52. *Cornish Drama*, I, 73 (967–72), 81 (1077–78), 93 (1209, 1223–28), 93–95 (1231–38).

53. Discussed in the editor's Introduction: *Non-Cycle Plays*, pp. xliv–liv. The Dublin version may well be from Northampton.

54. *Non-Cycle Plays*, p. 31 (170–85).

55. *Ibid.*, pp. 32 (216–19), 33 (240–41).

56. *Ibid.*, p. 32 (220).

57. *Ibid.*, p. 34 (275–80).

58. *Ibid.*, p. 26 (18–21).

59. The tradition of Isaac as a young child is also followed by the *Ludus Coventriae* and by Chester, which may in fact be a corrupt version of an earlier Brome text. On this possible relationship, see J. Burke Severs, "The Relationship between the Brome and Chester Plays of *Abraham and Isaac*," *MP*, XLII (1945), 137–51. On the question of Isaac's age, see Woolf, "Typology," p. 813. The Brome tradition was stated in the Middle Ages by Nicholas de Lyra; the alter-

native tradition (as in York) has Isaac about thirty years old, which allows a closer figural relationship with Christ. This is represented in the influential *Historia scholastica* of Petrus Comestor. The versions that use a child-Isaac pay so much attention to this fact that in the Dublin version, which does not specify his age, we should perhaps understand an older Isaac to be implied. Certainly that is the choice I would recommend to a producer of that play.

60. *Non-Cycle Plays*, p. 43 (190–93).

61. *Ibid.*, p. 44 (205–6).

62. *Ibid.*, p. 50 (358–66). These lines display a certain sympathy for the sheep, which Miss Woolf, "Typology," p. 824, relates to medieval sentimentality about animals. It seems to me slightly tougher and more joyous; Isaac certainly blows up the fire for its sacrifice with alacrity (p. 51, ll. 375–76).

63. *Ibid.*, p. 51 (377–82). See also *Towneley*, p. 49 (281–84).

64. Isaac neither hears nor sees the angel's message to Abraham; both the command and the release remain for him a human event attributed to God. See *Non-Cycle Plays*, pp. 49 (337) ff. Later, when God speaks the blessing, Isaac hears and sees the divine actor for the first time. See p. 51 (389) ff.

65. *Ibid.*, p. 52 (414–18).

66. *Towneley*, pp. 48–49 (271–74).

67. *Non-Cycle Plays*, p. 38 (43–46).

68. Any collection of medieval sermon *exempla* will illustrate this abundantly.

69. Pecock, *Reule*, pp. 456–57.

70. From "On Funeral Customs," G. K. Chesterton, *Selected Essays*, p. 48.

71. *Chester*, pp. 56 (201–8), 57 (225–32, and n. to l. 232). For a carol depicting the pleasures of "good gossips" drinking together at the ale house, too long to quote in full and too good to quote in brief, see *Early English Carols*, No. 419, pp. 280–84. It is entirely good-humored, meant to please both husbands and wives.

72. *York*, pp. 49 (143–44), 50 (151–52), 53 (269–70).

73. Thomas à Kempis, *De imitatione Christi*, ed. John K. Ingram, 1893, EETS e.s. 63, p. 141 (24–27). Chapters 59 and 60 of Book III develop this distinction with great eloquence and interest.

74. *Ludus Coventriae*, p. 106 (277–78).

CHAPTER ELEVEN

Conclusion

1. From a sermon preached on Candlemas day, probably in 1626/27; in *The Sermons of John Donne*, ed. Evelyn M. Simpson and George R. Potter (Berkeley, 1954), VII, 328–29.

2. Craig, *English Religious Drama*, p. 15.

3. J. Huizinga, *The Waning of the Middle Ages* (London, 1924), pp. 229–30.

4. *Cornish Drama*, II, 199 (2643–46). The Digby *Killing of the Children*, a play for Candlemas day, also ends in a command to dance, though it is not clear whether the audience is meant to join in. *Digby*, p. 23 (563–66).

Bibliography

The following list does not constitute a complete bibliography of medieval drama but simply a list of books and articles actually referred to in the body of this work. It is divided into four parts: I. Reference Works; II. Drama Texts; III. Other Primary Sources; IV. Scholarly Studies. The arrangement of titles is alphabetical within each part. All primary works are arranged according to the name of their author, or if anonymous (as in the case of most of the medieval sources) by the title of the work. No text is ever entered under the name of its editor or of its translator. A complete bibliography was attempted by Father Stratman in the volume listed under his name in Part I; this may be supplemented by the book lists included in the works of Hardin Craig and Glynne Wickham listed in Part IV, by volumes of *The Year's Work in English Studies,* and by the annual *PMLA* bibliographies.

I. REFERENCE WORKS

The Catholic Encyclopedia. Ed. Charles G. Herbermann and others. 15 vols. and Index. New York, 1907–14.
Duff, E. Gordon. *Fifteenth Century English Books.* (Bibliographical Society Illustrated Monographs, No. XVIII.) Oxford, 1917.
Lexikon für Theologie und Kirche. Ed. Joseph Höfer and Karl Rahner. 2d ed.; Freiburg, 1957——.
Middle English Dictionary. Ed. Hans Kurath, Sherman M. Kuhn, and John Reidy. Ann Arbor, 1954——.
The Oxford Dictionary of the Christian Church. Ed. F. L. Cross. London, 1957.
The Oxford English Dictionary. Ed. James A. H. Murray, Henry Bradley, W. A. Craigie, C. T. Onions. 12 vols. and Supplement. Corr. ed.; Oxford, 1933.
Stratman, Carl J., C.S.V. *Bibliography of Medieval Drama.* Berkeley, 1954.
Wells, John Edwin. *A Manual of the Writings in Middle English 1050–1400.* New Haven, 1916; with nine Supplements, 1919–51.

II. DRAMA TEXTS

The Ancient Cornish Drama. Ed. and trans. Edwin Norris. 2 vols. Oxford, 1859.
The Chester Plays. Ed. Hermann Deimling and J. Matthews. 1892, 1916, EETS e.s. 62, 115.

Chief Pre-Shakespearean Dramas. Ed. Joseph Quincy Adams. Cambridge, Mass., 1924.

The Digby Plays. Ed. F. J. Furnivall. 1896, EETS e.s. 70.

"Dux Moraud." Ed. W. Heuser. *Anglia,* XXX (1907), 180–208.

"An English Mystery Play Fragment Ante 1300." Ed. Rossell Hope Robbins. *MLN,* LXV (1950), 30–35.

Everyman. Ed. A. C. Cawley. Manchester, 1961.

Everyman and Medieval Miracle Plays. Ed. A. C. Cawley. London, 1956.

Greban, Arnoul. *Le Mystère de la Passion.* Ed. Gaston Paris and Gaston Raynaud. Paris, 1878.

Ludus Coventriae or The Plaie Called Corpus Christi. Ed. K. S. Block. 1922, EETS e.s. 120.

The Macro Plays. Ed. F. J. Furnivall and Alfred W. Pollard. 1904, EETS e.s. 91.

Le Mystère d'Adam. Ed. Henri Chamard. Paris, 1925.

The Non-Cycle Mystery Plays. Ed. Osborn Waterhouse. 1909, EETS e.s. 104.

"A Sixteenth Century English Mystery Fragment." Ed. Rossell Hope Robbins. *English Studies,* XXX (1949), 134–36.

Skelton, John. *Magnyfycence.* Ed. Robert Lee Ramsay. 1908, EETS e.s. 98.

The Towneley Plays. Ed. George England and Alfred W. Pollard. 1897, EETS e.s. 71.

Two Coventry Corpus Christi Plays. Ed. Hardin Craig. 2d ed.; 1957, EETS e.s. 87.

The Wakefield Pageants in the Towneley Cycle. Ed. A. C. Cawley. Manchester, 1958.

York Plays. Ed. Lucy Toulmin Smith. Oxford, 1885.

Young, Karl. *The Drama of the Medieval Church.* 2 vols. Oxford, 1933.

III. OTHER PRIMARY SOURCES

An Alphabet of Tales. Ed. Mary Macleod Banks. 1904, 1905, EETS o.s. 126, 127.

"Altenglische Kleinigkeiten." Ed. A. Napier. *Anglia,* XI (1888), 1–10.

Altenglische Legenden. Ed. C. Horstmann. Paderborn, 1875.

Altenglische Legenden, Neue Folge. Ed. C. Horstmann. Heilbronn, 1881.

The Ancrene Riwle. Trans. M. B. Salu. London, 1955.

"Anglo-Saxonica minora." Ed. H. Logeman. *Anglia,* XI (1888), 105–6.

The Apocryphal New Testament. Ed. Montague Rhodes James. Corr. ed.; Oxford, 1953.

Aquinas, St. Thomas. *Summa theologica.* Trans. Fathers of the English Dominican Province. 20 vols. London, 1911–25.

St. Augustine. *The City of God.* Trans. John Healey. 2 vols. London: Everyman's Library, 1945.

———. *The Confessions.* Trans. Sir Tobie Matthew; rev. Dom Roger Hudleston. London, 1954.

———. *De Genesi contra Manichaeos.* Ed. in Migne, *Patrologia Latina,* Vol. 34.

———. *Sermons for Christmas and Epiphany.* Trans. Thomas Comerford Lawler. (Ancient Christian Writers, No. 15.) London, 1952.

Bale, John. *The Dramatic Writings of John Bale.* Ed. John S. Farmer. London, 1907.

Bartholomeus Anglicus. *De proprietatibus rerum.* Trans. John Trevisa. Printed by Wynkyn de Worde, 1495.

Bede. *De temporum ratione.* Ed. Theodore Mommsen, in *Chronica minora,* Vol. III (*Monumenta Germaniae historica*). Berlin, 1898.

———. *Opera de temporibus.* Ed. Charles W. Jones. Cambridge, Mass., 1943.

———. *Opera historica.* Ed. C. Plummer. 2 vols. Oxford, 1896.

Biblia Sacra vulgatae editionis. London: Bagster, n.d.

The Book of the Knight of La Tour-Landry. Ed. Thomas Wright. Rev. 1906, EETS o.s. 33.

Breviarium ad usum insignis ecclesiae Sarum. Ed. Francis Procter and Christopher Wordsworth. 3 vols. Cambridge, 1879–86.

Capgrave, John. *The Chronicle of England.* Ed. Francis Charles Hingeston. (Rolls Series, No. 1.) London, 1858.

Caxton, William. *Mirrour of the World.* Ed. Oliver H. Prior. 1913, EETS e.s. 110.

Chartularium Universitatis Parisiensis, Vol. IV. Ed. Henri Denifle. Paris, 1897.

Chaucer, Geoffrey. *The Works of Geoffrey Chaucer.* Ed. F. N. Robinson. 2d ed.; London, 1957.

Chesterton, G. K. *Selected Essays.* Ed. Dorothy Collins. London, 1949.

Comestor, Petrus. *Historia scholastica.* Ed. in Migne, *Patrologia Latina,* Vol. 198.

Cursor Mundi. Ed. Richard Morris. 1874–92, EETS o.s. 57, 59, 62, 66, 68, 99.

Dante. *Inferno.* Trans. Dorothy L. Sayers. Harmondsworth: Penguin Books, 1949.

Death and Liffe. Ed. James Holly Hanford and John Marcellus Steadman, Jr. *SP,* XV (1918), 221–94.

Deguileville, Guillaume de. *The Pilgrimage of the Life of Man.* Trans. John Lydgate, ed. F. J. Furnivall and Katharine B. Locock. 1899–1904, EETS e.s. 77, 83, 92.

Diues et Pauper. Printed by Pynson, 1493.

Donne, John. *The Sermons of John Donne,* Vol. VII. Ed. Evelyn M. Simpson and George R. Potter. Berkeley, 1954.

Dunbar, William. *The Poems of William Dunbar.* Ed. W. Mackay Mackenzie. London, 1932.

Early Medieval Illumination. Introduction by Hans Swarenzenski. New York: Iris Books, 1951.

The Early English Carols. Ed. Richard Leighton Greene. Oxford, 1935.

EETS e.s.: Publications of the Early English Text Society, Extra Series, London.

EETS o.s.: Publications of the Early English Text Society, Original Series, London.

The Epic of Gilgamesh. Trans. N. K. Sandars. Harmondsworth: Penguin Books, 1960.

Fisher, John. *The English Works.* Ed. John E. B. Mayor. 1876, EETS e.s. 27.

Flores historiarum. Ed. Henry Richards Luard. (Rolls Series, No. 95.) Vol. I; London, 1890.

A Fourteenth Century English Biblical Version. Ed. Anna C. Paues. Cambridge, 1904.

Glossa ordinaria. Ed. in Migne, *Patrologia Latina,* Vols. 113–14.

The Golden Legend: or Lives of the Saints as Englished by William Caxton. Ed. F. S. Ellis. 7 vols. London: Temple Classics, 1900.

Gower, John. *The English Works.* Ed. G. C. Macaulay. 1900, 1901, EETS e.s. 81, 82.

Handlyng Synne. [See Wadington, William of.]

Henryson, Robert. *The Poems and Fables.* Ed. H. Harvey Wood. 2d ed.; Edinburgh, 1958.

Higden, Ranulph. *Polychronicon.* Ed. Churchill Babington. (Rolls Series, No. 41.) Vol. I; London, 1865.

Historical Poems of the XIVth and XVth Centuries. Ed. Rossell Hope Robbins. New York, 1959.

The Holkham Bible Picture Book. Ed. W. O. Hassall. London, 1954.

A Hundred Mery Talys. Ed. Herman Oesterley. London, 1866.

Hymns to the Virgin & Christ, The Parliament of Devils, and Other Religious Poems. Ed. Frederick J. Furnivall. 1867, EETS o.s. 24.

Illustrations of the Book of Genesis. Ed. M. R. James. London: Roxburghe Club, 1921.

Jacob's Well. Ed. Arthur Brandeis. 1900, EETS o.s. 115.

Jonson, Ben. *The Complete Works of Ben Jonson.* Ed. C. H. Herford and Percy Simpson. 11 vols. Oxford, 1925–52.

Kempis, Thomas à. *De imitatione Christi.* Ed. John K. Ingram. 1893, EETS e.s. 63.

Langland, William. *Piers the Plowman. In Three Parallel Texts.* Ed. Walter W. Skeat. 2 vols. Oxford, 1886; reprint with bibliographical additions, 1954.

Lavynham, Richard. *A Litil Tretys on the Seven Deadly Sins.* Ed. J. P. W. M. van Zutphen. Rome, 1956.

The Lay Folks' Catechism. Ed. Thomas Frederick Simmons and Henry Edward Nolloth. 1901, EETS o.s. 118.

The Lay Folks Mass Book. Ed. Thomas Frederick Simmons. 1879, EETS o.s. 71.

Legends of the Holy Rood. Ed. Richard Morris. 1871, EETS o.s. 46.

The Life of Saint Anne. Ed. Roscoe E. Parker. 1928, EETS o.s. 174.

Lydgate, John. *The Assembly of Gods.* Ed. Oscar Lovell Triggs. 1896, EETS e.s. 69.

————. *The Minor Poems.* Ed. Henry Noble MacCracken. 1911, 1934, EETS e.s. 107, 192.

Maurus, Rabanus. *Commentariorum in Genesim.* Ed. in Migne, *Patrologia Latina,* Vol. 107.

Meditations on the Life and Passion of Christ. Ed. Charlotte D'Evelyn. 1921, EETS o.s. 158.

Meditations on the Supper of Our Lord, and the Hours of the Passion. Trans. Robert Manning of Brunne, ed. J. Meadows Cowper. 1875, EETS o.s. 60.

"The Middle English *Evangelie.*" Ed. Gertrude H. Campbell. *PMLA,* XXX (1915), 529–613.

The Middle English Harrowing of Hell and Gospel of Nicodemus. Ed. William Henry Hulme. 1908, EETS e.s. 100.

Middle English Sermons. Ed. Woodburn O. Ross. 1940, EETS o.s. 209.

The Minor Poems of the Vernon MS. Ed. Carl Horstmann and F. J. Furnivall. 1892, 1901, EETS o.s. 98, 117.

Mirk, John. *Festial: A Collection of Homilies.* Ed. Theodor Erbe. 1905, EETS e.s. 96.

———. *Instructions for Parish Priests.* Ed. Edward Peacock, rev. F. J. Furnivall. 1902, EETS o.s. 31.

The Miroure of Mans Saluacionne. Ed. Alfred H. Huth. London: Roxburghe Club, 1888.

The Mirrour of the Blessed Lyf of Jesu Christ. Trans. Nicholas Love, ed. Lawrence F. Powell. Oxford, 1908.

Missale ad usum insignis et praeclarae ecclesiae Sarum. Ed. Francis Henry Dickinson. 4 vols. Burnt Island, 1861–83.

Nashe, Thomas. *The Works of Thomas Nashe.* Ed. Ronald B. McKerrow. 5 vols. Oxford, reprint 1958.

The Northern Passion. Ed. Frances A. Foster. 1913, 1916, EETS o.s. 145, 147.

The Northern Passion (Supplement). Ed. Wilhelm Heuser and Frances A. Foster. 1930, EETS o.s. 183.

Old English Homilies of the Twelfth Century, Second Series. Ed. R. Morris. 1873, EETS o.s. 53.

Paris, Matthew. *Chronica majora.* Ed. Henry Richards Luard. (Rolls Series, No. 57.) Vol. I; London, 1872.

Patrologiae cursus completus: Patrologia Latina. Ed. J. P. Migne. 221 vols. Paris, 1844–64.

The Pauline Epistles. Ed. Margaret Joyce Powell. 1916, EETS e.s. 116.

Pecock, Reginald. *The Reule of Crysten Religioun.* Ed. William Cabell Greet. 1927, EETS o.s. 171.

The Pepysian Gospel Harmony. Ed. Margery Goates. 1922, EETS o.s. 157.

The Pricke of Conscience. Ed. Richard Morris. Berlin, 1863.

Purity. Ed. Robert J. Menner. New Haven, 1920.

Queen Mary's Psalter. Ed. George Warner. London, 1912.

Ratis Raving and Other Moral and Religious Pieces. Ed. J. Rawson Lumby. 1870, EETS o.s. 43.

Religious Lyrics of the XIVth Century. Ed. Carleton Brown (1924), rev. G. V. Smithers. Oxford, 1952.

Religious Lyrics of the XVth Century. Ed. Carleton Brown. Oxford, 1939.

Religious Pieces in Prose and Verse (Thornton MS). Ed. George G. Perry. 1867, rev. 1914, EETS o.s. 26.

Rolle, Richard, de Hampole. *English Prose Treatises.* Ed. George G. Perry. 1866, 1921, EETS o.s. 20.

——. *The Psalter or Psalms of David and Certain Canticles, with a Translation and Exposition in English.* Ed. H. R. Bramley. Oxford, 1884.

The Rule of St. Benet. Ed. Ernst A. Kock. 1902, EETS o.s. 120.

Sammlung Altenglischer Legenden. Ed. C. Horstmann. Heilbronn, 1878.

Selections from Early Middle English 1130–1250. Ed. Joseph Hall. 2 vols. Oxford, 1920.

"A Sermon against Miracle-plays." Ed. Eduard Mätzner. *Altenglische Sprachproben,* I, Part II (Berlin, 1869), 222–42.

Shoreham, William of. *Poems.* Ed. M. Konrath. 1902, EETS e.s. 86.

Sir Gawain & the Green Knight. Ed. J. R. R. Tolkien and E. V. Gordon. Corr. ed.; Oxford, 1930.

The South English Legendary. Ed. Charlotte D'Evelyn and Anna J. Mill. 1956, 1959, EETS o.s. 235, 236, 244.

The Southern Passion. Ed. Beatrice Daw Brown. 1927, EETS o.s. 169.

Specimens of Old Christmas Carols. Ed. Thomas Wright. (Percy Society, No. 4.) London, 1841.

Speculum Christiani. Ed. Gustaf Holmstedt. 1933, EETS o.s. 182.

Speculum Gy de Warewyke. Ed. Georgiana Lea Morrill. 1898, EETS e.s. 75.

Speculum humanae salvationis. Ed. J. Lutz and P. Perdrizet. 2 vols. Mulhouse, 1907, 1909.

Speculum sacerdotale. Ed. Edward H. Weatherly. 1936, EETS o.s. 200.

A Stanzaic Life of Christ. Ed. Frances A. Foster. 1926, EETS o.s. 166.

The Tale of Beryn. Ed. F. J. Furnivall and W. G. Stone. 1909, EETS e.s. 105.

Tertullian. *The Writings of Tertullian,* Vol. I. Ed. Alexander Roberts and James Donaldson. (Ante-Nicene Christian Library, No. 11.) Edinburgh, 1869.

Textus antiqui de festo Corporis Christi. Ed. Petrus Browe, S.J. Fasc. IV of *Opuscula et textus.* Monasterii Typis Aschendorff. Münster, 1934.

The Three Kings of Cologne. Ed. C. Horstmann. 1886, EETS o.s. 85.

Voragine, Jacobus de. *Legenda aurea.* Ed. Th. Graesse. Leipzig, 1850.

Wadington, William of. *Handlyng Synne.* Trans. Robert of Brunne, re-ed. F. J. Furnivall. 1901, 1903, EETS o.s. 119, 123.

Wendover, Roger of. *Flowers of History.* Trans. J. A. Giles. 2 vols. London: Bohn Library, 1849.

York Memorandum Book, Vol. II. Ed. Maud Sellers. (Surtees Society, No. 125.) York, 1915.

IV. SCHOLARLY STUDIES

Adolph, Helen. "On Mediaeval Laughter," *Speculum,* XXII (1947), 251–53.

The Age of Chaucer. Ed. Boris Ford. Harmondsworth: Penguin Books, 1954.

Anderson, M. D. *The Choir Stalls of Lincoln Minster.* London, 1951.

——. *Drama and Imagery in English Medieval Churches.* Cambridge, 1963.

——. *The Imagery of British Churches.* London, 1955.

————. *Misericords*. Harmondsworth: Penguin Books, 1954.

Auerbach, Erich. "Figura." Trans. Ralph Manheim, in *Scenes from the Drama of European Literature* (New York: Meridian Books, 1959).

Biver, Paul. "Some Examples of English Alabaster Tables in France," *Archaeological Journal*, LXVII (1910), 66–87.

Blair, Lawrence. "A Note on the Relation of the Corpus Christi Procession to the Corpus Christi Play in England," *MLN*, LV (1940), 83–95.

Bloomfield, Morton W. "Chaucer's Sense of History," *JEGP*, LI (1952), 301–13.

————. *The Seven Deadly Sins*. East Lansing, 1952.

Boas, George. *Essays on Primitivism and Related Ideas in the Middle Ages*. Baltimore, 1948.

Bond, Francis. *Wood Carvings in English Churches. Misericords*. London, 1910.

Brown, Carleton. "Caiaphas as a Palm Sunday Prophet," in *Anniversary Papers by Colleagues and Pupils of George Lyman Kittredge*. Boston, 1913.

————. "Sermons and Miracle Plays," *MLN*, XLIX (1934), 394–96.

————. "The Towneley *Play of the Doctors* and the *Speculum Christiani*," *MLN*, XXXI (1916), 223–26.

Campbell, Lily B. *Divine Poetry and Drama in Sixteenth Century England*. Berkeley, 1959.

Carey, Millicent. *The Wakefield Group in the Towneley Cycle*. Göttingen, 1930.

Carpenter, Nan Cooke. "Music in the *Secunda Pastorum*," *Speculum*, XXVI (1951), 696–700.

Cave, C. J. P. *Roof Bosses in Medieval Churches*. Cambridge, 1948.

Cawley, A. C. "The 'Grotesque' Feast in the *Prima Pastorum*," *Speculum*, XXX (1955), 213–17.

Cazamian, Louis. *The Development of English Humor*. Durham, N.C., 1952.

Chambers, E. K. *English Literature at the Close of the Middle Ages*. (Oxford History of English Literature.) Corr. ed.; Oxford, 1947.

————. *The Mediaeval Stage*. 2 vols. Oxford, 1903.

Clark, Edward Murray. "Liturgical Influences in the Towneley Plays," *Orate Fratres*, XVI (1941), 69–79.

Clark, Eleanor Grace. "The York Plays and the *Gospel of Nichodemus*," *PMLA*, XLIII (1928), 153–61.

Clark, William Smith. *The Early Irish Stage*. Oxford, 1955.

Coffman, George R. "The Miracle Play in England—Nomenclature," *PMLA*, XXXI (1916), 448–65.

Cohen, Gustave. *Le Théâtre en France au Moyen Age*. 2 vols. Paris, 1928, 1931.

Cornell, Henrik. *Biblia pauperum*. Stockholm, 1925.

Coulton, G. G. *Art and the Reformation*. 2d ed.; Cambridge, 1953.

————. *Medieval Panorama*. Cambridge, 1938.

Craddock, Lawrence G., O.F.M. "Franciscan Influences on Early English Drama," *Franciscan Studies*, X (1950), 383–417.

Craig, Hardin. "The Corpus Christi Procession and the Corpus Christi Play," *JEGP*, XIII (1914), 589–602.

————. *English Religious Drama*. Oxford, 1955.

————. "The Origin of the Passion Play: Matters of Theory as Well as Fact," in *Studies in Honor of A. H. R. Fairchild,* ed. Charles T. Prouty (Columbia, Mo., 1946).

Curtius, Ernst Robert. *European Literature and the Latin Middle Ages.* Trans. Willard R. Trask. London, 1953.

Cutts, Cecilia. "The Croxton Play: An Anti-Lollard Piece," *MLQ,* V (1944), 45–60.

Daniélou, Jean, S.J. *From Shadows to Reality. Studies in the Biblical Typology of the Fathers.* Trans. Dom Wulstan Hibberd. London, 1960. [Original title: *Sacramentum futuri.*]

Deasy, C. Philip, F.S.C. *St. Joseph in the English Mystery Plays.* Washington, D.C., 1937.

Dunn, E. Catherine. "The Medieval 'Cycle' as History Play: An Approach to the Wakefield Plays," *Studies in the Renaissance,* VII (1960), 76–89.

Dupont, Jacques, and Cesare Gnudi. *Gothic Painting.* New York: Skira, 1954.

Dustoor, P. E. "The Origin of the Play of 'Moses and the Tables of the Law,'" *MLR,* XIX (1924), 459–63.

Fletcher, J. M. J. *The Boy Bishop at Salisbury and Elsewhere.* Salisbury, 1921.

Fowler, James. "On Mediaeval Representations of the Months and Seasons," *Archaeologia,* XLIV (1873), 137–224.

Frank, Grace. *The Medieval French Drama.* Oxford, 1954.

Frazer, James G. *Folk-lore in the Old Testament.* Abridged ed.; London, 1923.

Frye, Northrop. *Anatomy of Criticism.* Princeton, 1957.

Gaffney, Wilbur. "The Allegory of the Christ-Knight in *Piers Plowman,*" *PMLA,* XLVI (1931), 155–68.

Gardiner, Harold C., S.J. *Mysteries' End.* New Haven, 1946.

Gilson, Etienne. *Painting and Reality.* London, 1958.

Greg, W. W. *Bibliographical and Textual Problems of the English Miracle Cycles.* London, 1914. [Reprinted from *The Library,* 1914.]

————. *The Trial & Flagellation With Other Studies in the Chester Cycle.* Oxford: Malone Society, 1935.

Hemingway, Samuel B. *English Nativity Plays.* New York, 1909.

Hildburgh, W. L. *English Alabaster Carvings as Records of the Medieval Religious Drama.* Oxford, 1949. [Reprinted from *Archaeologia,* XCIII.]

Homans, George Caspar. *English Villagers of the Thirteenth Century.* Cambridge, Mass., 1942.

Huizinga, J. *Homo ludens.* London, 1949.

————. *The Waning of the Middle Ages.* London, 1924.

Hunningher, Benjamin. *The Origin of Theatre.* Amsterdam, 1955.

James, M. R. "Pictor in Carmine," *Archaeologia,* XCIV (1951), 141–66.

Joseph, Bertram. "The Elizabethan Stage and Acting," in *The Age of Shakespeare,* ed. Boris Ford (Harmondsworth: Penguin Books, 1955).

Katzenellenbogen, Adolf. *Allegories of the Virtues and Vices in Mediaeval Art.* London, 1939.

Kretzmann, Paul Edward. *The Liturgical Element in the Earliest Forms of the Medieval Drama.* Minneapolis, 1916.

Leach, A. F. "Some English Plays and Players, 1220–1548," in *An English Miscellany Presented to Dr. Furnivall* (Oxford, 1901).

Levinson, Wilhelm. "Bede as Historian," in *Bede: His Life, Times, and Writings,* ed. A. Hamilton Thompson (Oxford, 1935).

Lewis, C. S. *Studies in Words.* Cambridge, 1960.

Lukc, Brother Cornelius. *The Rôle of the Virgin Mary in the Coventry, York, Chester and Towneley Cycles.* Washington, D.C., 1933.

Lumiansky, R. M. "Comedy and Theme in the Chester *Harrowing of Hell,*" *Tulane Studies in English,* X (1960), 5–12.

Lyle, Marie C. *The Original Identity of the York and Towneley Cycles.* Minneapolis, 1919.

McKisack, May. *The Fourteenth Century.* (Oxford History of England.) Oxford, 1959.

McNeill, John T., and Helena M. Gamer. *Medieval Handbooks of Penance.* New York, 1938.

McNeir, Waldo F. "The Corpus Christi Passion Plays as Dramatic Art," *SP,* XLVIII (1951), 601–28.

Mâle, Emile. *L'Art Religieux de la Fin du Moyen Age en France.* 5th ed.; Paris, 1949.

Manning, Stephen. *Wisdom and Number.* Lincoln, Nebr., 1962.

Marshall, Mary Hatch. "Boethius' Definition of *Persona* and Mediacval Understanding of the Roman Theatre," *Speculum,* XXV (1950), 471–82.

———. "The Dramatic Tradition Established by the Liturgical Plays," *PMLA,* LVI (1941), 962–91.

———. "*Theatre* in the Middle Ages: Evidence from Dictionaries and Glosses," *Symposium,* IV (1950), 1–39, 366–89.

Medieval England. Ed. Austin Lane Poole. 2 vols. Oxford, 1958.

Meiss, Millard. *Painting in Florence and Siena after the Black Death.* Princeton, 1951.

Meyerhoff, Hans. *Time in Literature.* Berkeley, 1955.

Mill, Anna Jean. "Noah's Wife Again," *PMLA,* LVI (1941), 613–26.

Morris, Rupert H. *Chester in the Plantagenet and Tudor Reigns.* Chester [1895].

Nelson, Alan H. " 'Sacred' and 'Secular' Currents in The Towneley Play of Noah," *Drama Survey,* III (1964), 393–401.

Nicoll, Allardyce. *Masks, Mimes, and Miracles.* London, 1931.

Oakeshott, Walter. *The Sequence of English Medieval Art.* London, 1950.

Owings, Marvin Alpheus. *The Arts in the Middle English Romances.* New York, 1952.

Owst, G. R. *Literature and Pulpit in Medieval England.* 2d ed.; Oxford, 1961.

———. *Preaching in Medieval England.* Cambridge, 1926.

Pantin, W. A. *The English Church in the Fourteenth Century.* Cambridge, 1955.

Pfander, H. G. "Dives et Pauper," *The Library,* Fourth Series, XIV (1934), 299–312.

Pierson, Merle. "The Relation of the Corpus Christi Procession to the Corpus Christi Play in England," *Transactions of the Wisconsin Academy of Sciences, Arts, and Letters,* XVIII (1915), 110–65.

Poulet, Georges. *Studies in Human Time*. Trans. Elliott Coleman. Baltimore, 1956.

Prosser, Eleanor. *Drama and Religion in the English Mystery Plays*. Stanford, 1961.

Rackham, Bernard. *The Ancient Glass of Canterbury Cathedral*. London, 1949.

Réau, Louis. *Iconographie de l'Art Chrétien*. 3 parts. Paris, 1955–59.

Richardson, H. G. "Dives and Pauper," *The Library,* Fourth Series, XV (1935), 31–37.

Rickert, Margaret. *Painting in Britain: The Middle Ages*. London, 1954.

Rose, Martial. *The Wakefield Mystery Plays*. London, 1961.

Rossiter, A. P. *English Drama from Early Times to the Elizabethans*. London, 1950.

Salmon, P. B. "The 'Three Voices' of Poetry in Mediaeval Literary Theory," *Med. Aev.,* XXX (1961), 1–18.

Salter, F. M. *Mediaeval Drama in Chester*. Toronto, 1955.

Schless, Howard H. "The Comic Element in the Wakefield Noah," in *Studies in Medieval Literature,* ed. MacEdward Leach (Philadelphia, 1961).

Sepet, Marius. *Les Prophètes du Christ*. Paris, 1878.

Severs, J. Burke. "The Relationship between the Brome and Chester Plays of *Abraham and Isaac*," *MP, XLII* (1945), 137–51.

Shull, Virginia. "Clerical Drama in Lincoln Cathedral, 1318 to 1561," *PMLA, LII* (1937), 946–66.

Smalley, Beryl. *English Friars and Antiquity in the Early Fourteenth Century*. Oxford, 1960.

———. *The Study of the Bible in the Middle Ages*. 2d ed.; Oxford, 1952.

Southern, Richard. *The Medieval Theatre in the Round*. London, 1957.

Stevens, John. "Music in Mediaeval Drama," *Proceedings of the Royal Musical Association,* LXXXIV (1958), 81–95.

Swenson, Esther L. *An Inquiry into the Composition and Structure of Ludus Coventriae*. Minneapolis, 1914.

Tatlock, J. S. P. "Mediaeval Laughter," *Speculum,* XXI (1946), 289–94.

Taylor, George C. "The Relation of the English Corpus Christi Play to the Middle English Religious Lyric," *MP,* V (1907), 1–38.

Thompson, James Westfall, and Bernard J. Holm. *A History of Historical Writing*. 2 vols. New York, 1942.

Truby, Jeffrey. *The Glories of Salisbury Cathedral*. London, 1948.

Tucker, Susie I. "Laughter in Old English Literature," *Neophilologus,* XLIII (1959), 222–26.

Vriend, Joannes, S.J. *The Blessed Virgin Mary in the Medieval Drama of England*. Purmerend, 1928.

Watt, Homer A. "The Dramatic Unity of the 'Secunda Pastorum,' " in *Essays and Studies in Honor of Carleton Brown* (New York, 1940).

Weir, Evangeline G. *The Vernacular Sources of the Middle English Plays of the Blessed Virgin Mary*. Unpublished Ph.D. dissertation, Stanford University, 1941.

Welsford, Enid. *The Fool*. London, 1935.

White, Beatrice. "Medieval Mirth," *Anglia*, LXXVIII (1960), 284–301.

Wickham, Glynne. *Early English Stages 1300 to 1660*. Vols. I and II (Part I). London, 1959, 1963.

Williams, Arnold. *The Characterization of Pilate in the Towneley Plays*. East Lansing, 1950.

———. *The Drama of Medieval England*. East Lansing, 1961.

Wilson, Robert H. "The Stanzaic Life of Christ and the Chester Plays," *SP*, XXVIII (1931), 413–32.

Wolff, Erwin. "Die Terminologie des Mittelalterlichen Dramas in Bedeutungs-geschichtlicher Sicht," *Anglia*, LXXVIII (1960), 1–27.

Wood, Frederik T. "The Comic Elements in the English Mystery Plays," *Neophilologus*, XXV (1939–40), 39–48, 194–206.

Woodforde, Christopher. *The Norwich School of Glass-Painting in the Fifteenth Century*. London, 1950.

———. *Stained Glass in Somerset 1250–1830*. London, 1946.

Woolf, Rosemary. "Doctrinal Influences on *The Dream of the Rood*," *Med. Aev.*, XXVII (1958), 137–53.

———. "The Effect of Typology on the English Mediaeval Plays of Abraham and Isaac," *Speculum*, XXXII (1957), 805–25.

———. "The Theme of Christ the Lover-Knight in Medieval English Literature," *RES*, XIII (1962), 1–16.

Young, Karl. "An *Interludium* for a Gild of Corpus Christi," *MLN*, XLVIII (1933), 84–86.

Index

Index